SPEECH AND LANGUAGE
IMPAIRMENTS IN CHILDREN

Speech and language impairments in children:
Causes, characteristics, intervention and outcome

edited by

Dorothy V.M. Bishop
University of Oxford, UK

Laurence B. Leonard
Purdue University, Indiana, USA

Ψ Psychology Press
Taylor & Francis Group

HOVE AND NEW YORK

First published 2000 by Psychology Press Ltd
27 Church Road, Hove, East Sussex BN3 2FA

http://www.psypress.com

Simultaneously published in the USA and Canada
by Taylor & Francis Inc
270 Madison Avenue, New York NY 10016

Reprinted 2001, 2004, 2007

Psychology Press is part of the Taylor & Francis Group, an Informa business

British Library cataloguing in Publication Data
A catalogue record for this book is available from the British Library

Cover design by Jim Wilkie
Typeset by Graphicraft Limited, Hong Kong
Printed and bound in England by Antony Rowe Ltd, Chippenham, Wiltshire

This publication has been produced with paper manufactured to strict
environmental standards and with pulp derived from sustainable forests.

ISBN 978-0-86377-569-7

Contents

List of Contributors

Dorothy V.M. Bishop, Department of Experimental Psychology, University of Oxford, South Parks Road, Oxford OX1 3UD, UK

Nicola Botting, Centre for the Study of Language Impairments, School of Education, University of Manchester, Manchester M13 9PL, UK

Gina Conti-Ramsden, Centre for the Study of Language Impairments, School of Education, University of Manchester, Manchester M13 9PL, UK

Philip Dale, Department of Communication Science and Disorders, University of Missouri, Columbia MO 65211, USA

Thierry Deonna, Neuropaediatric Unit, Univ. Children's Hospital, C.H.U.V., Rue de Bugnon, Lausanne CH 1011, Switzerland

Marc Fey, Intercampus Program in Communicative Disorders, Department of Hearing and Speech, University of Kansas Medical Center, Kansas City KS 66160–7605, USA

Janet E. Fischel, Department of Pediatrics and Psychology, State University of New York at Stony Brook, Stony Brook, New York 11794–8111, USA

Ian Goodyer, Developmental Psychiatry Section, University of Cambridge, Douglas House, 18b Trumpington Road, Cambridge CB2 4AH, UK

Laurence B. Leonard, Audiology and Speech Sciences, Heavilon Hall, Purdue University, West Lafayette Indiana 47907, USA

Rhea Paul, Department of Communication Disorders and Yale Child Study Center, Davis Hall, Southern Connecticut State University, 501 Crescent Street, New Haven CT 06515–1355, USA

Robert Plomin, Social, Genetic and Developmental Psychiatry Research Centre, Institute of Psychiatry, De Crespigny Park, London SE5 8AF, UK

Kerry Proctor-Williams, Intercampus Program in Communicative Disorders, Department of Hearing and Speech, University of Kansas Medical Center, Kansas City KS 6610–7605, USA

Mabel Rice, Child Language Program, 1082 Dole Center, University of Kansas, Lawrence KS 66045, USA

Michael Rutter, Social, Genetic and Developmental Psychiatry Research Centre, Institute of Psychiatry, De Crespigny Park, London SE5 8AF, UK

Margaret Snowling, Department of Psychology, University of York, York YO10 5DD, UK

Joy Stackhouse, Department of Human Communication Science, University College London, Chandler House, 2 Wakefield Street, London WC1N 1PG, UK

Paula Tallal, Center for Molecular and Behavioral Neuroscience, Rutgers University, 197 University Avenue, Newark NJ 07102, USA

Michael Tomasello, Max Planck Institute for Evolutionary Anthropology, Inselstrasse 22, D-04103 Leipzig, Germany

Susan Ellis Weismer, Department of Communicative Disorders, University of Wisconsin-Madison, 1975 Willow Drive, Madison WI 53706, USA

Grover J. Whitehurst, Department of Psychology, State University of New York at Stony Brook, Stony Brook, New York 11794–2500, USA

Foreword

Linguists have long been intrigued by children's astonishing language-learning facility. A typical child can, by four years of age, produce long and complex sentences, speak clearly and intelligibly, and understand a vocabulary of tens of thousands of words. Perhaps even more astonishing is the resilience of language learning in the face of wide environmental and biological variation. The quantity and quality of language that the child hears may have some effect on the rate of language learning, but, except in extreme circumstances of neglect, the final level of grammatical competence appears similar for most children. And brain damage affecting the left cerebral hemisphere may have little impact on language abilities, provided it is incurred in the first few years of life.

This view of language acquisition as a rapid and robust process does, however, disguise wide individual variation. There are many children, estimated as around 5–10% in a recent US survey, whose communicative development does not proceed in such a straightforward fashion. Delayed development of speech and/or language is one of the commonest reasons for parents of preschool children to seek the advice of a paediatrician. Although some children do appear to grow out of their problems, others have persistent difficulties. Studies following the progress of children with more severe early language delays paint a fairly bleak picture of a high risk of later literacy problems, lack of friendships, and increased rates of psychiatric disorder. Quite simply, speech and

language disorders in childhood constitute a major problem for society, in terms both of the human misery that they cause, and the economic costs inevitably incurred when a subset of the population cannot participate fully as members of the community.

In 1968, Margaret Green, a speech and language therapist, decided that more needed to be done to address the problems of these children. She founded what was then known as the Association for All Speech Impaired Children, a charity whose goals were to provide support and information for parents of affected children, and to raise public awareness of these disorders. The charity has grown and has developed a network of parent support groups, a telephone helpline, and information sheets. It plays an active role in lobbying government, runs activity holidays for children, and organises training and conferences for parents and professionals. Over time, as the charity found itself increasingly addressing the needs of young adults with developmental speech and language problems, it no longer seemed appropriate to restrict interest to children, or to speech, and so the acronym AFASIC has been superseded by the name Afasic.

Those working for Afasic have increasingly recognised the importance of research on speech and language disorders. When one considers how common these disorders are, the amount of research focusing on this clinical group is remarkably small. This is emphasised by contrasting the amount of research focusing on autistic disorder with that concerned with speech and language disorders, which are approximately 100 times as common. A computerised literature search revealed 71 journal articles published in Britain on the topic of language disorder/language impairment in children in the period 1991–1997, compared with 127 studies on autistic disorder in children. For the US, the figures were 343 papers on childhood language disorder/impairment, compared with 523 papers on autism. We have to consider why relatively few researchers decide to focus on speech and language disorders, and ask what can be done to stimulate more academic interest in this topic.

Afasic has played an important role in addressing these issues. In 1987, they organised the First International Symposium on children's speech and language disorders in Reading, followed by the Second International Symposium in Harrogate in 1991, and the Third International Symposium in York in 1999. The plenary papers from the Third International Symposium are the basis for this book.

The levels of attendance at the York meeting testify to the wide interest in children's speech and language impairments. Also impressive was the diversity of professional disciplines represented, including speech and language therapy, special education, psychology, genetics, paediatrics, psychiatry, neurology, and audiology. In contrast to many scientific meetings, parents of language-impaired children are encouraged to attend Afasic symposia, and were well represented and gave valuable input. As well as more academically-oriented plenary sessions, there was a good selection of workshops run by practitioners, as well as poster sessions that encouraged cross-disciplinary discussion. Such a diverse range of participants does not make for an easy mix: those who live or work with language-impaired children on a day-to-day basis tend to have very different concerns from the theoretical questions that preoccupy academics. However, Afasic is committed to the notion that there is value in bringing together the whole range of people interested in discovering more about children's speech and language impairments. To be maximally effective, research and practice must inform one another.

There are many controversies in the field of specific language impairment, and no expert would agree with all the opinions expressed in this volume. As editors, we regarded our job as assisting each author in saying what they have to say as clearly as possible, rather than dictating the content. We have aimed to produce a book that will appeal to a wide readership, including academics, professionals and parents. The primary task given to each author was to provide a snapshot of state-of-the-art research in a particular area. Although many of the authors use their own research to illustrate the points they make, they have been encouraged to place this in a broader context, avoiding the kind of highly technical research paper that appeals only to specialists.

Although the conference papers were grouped in terms of broad areas of causes, characteristics, intervention, and outcome, a number of themes emerged that cut across these boundaries. One is the importance of understanding the process of normal language learning if we are to gain insights into language disorders. For many years, theorising about language acquisition has been dominated by linguists working in the tradition of Noam Chomsky, who argued that grammar is quite distinct from other aspects of language, and required specialised, innate, language-learning mechanisms in order to be acquired. These theoreticians mount a powerful body of arguments to support their case, and many experts believe that speech and language impairment (SLI) can be characterised as a disorder in which part of this specialised grammar-learning mechanism fails to develop, or matures late. The extended optional infinitive theory, described in the chapter by Mabel Rice, illustrates this approach, and the author demonstrates how a well-articulated theory of grammatical deficits in SLI can give precise predictions about the kinds of grammatical constructions that these children find difficult. In the past decade, we have moved a long way from simply talking about "omission of grammatical inflections' to gain understanding of why different grammatical endings might be more or less vulnerable. Rice emphasises that a clearer theory of the underlying deficit is not just of academic interest; it helps us develop better language assessments that ultimately may prove useful in defining homogeneous subgroups of children, and can also help focus intervention.

The Chomskyan approach has been around a long time and has undoubtedly provided a useful theoretical framework for the study of SLI, but in recent years it has increasingly been challenged by those working on language development. Michael Tomasello's opening chapter provides an invaluable introduction to an alternative "construction" approach to language acquisition. He uses both observational and experimental evidence from typically-developing young children to question whether it makes sense to describe children's first utterances in terms of abstract grammatical categories. Young children appear to imitate whole chunks of language, and only become aware of the more abstract regularities in underlying structure gradually, as language is acquired. This view of language learning provides food for thought for those working with SLI, because it suggests that the grammatical problems of these children might be at least in part due to a failure to generalise from one construction to another, to recognise common underlying patterns. In fact, the approach from construction grammar meshes well with what many practitioners actually do when attempting to help children overcome their grammatical limitations. Fey and Proctor-Williams discuss the different methods that have been adopted when attempting to help children master specific grammatical forms: it is not so difficult to persuade a child to imitate, for instance, an inflected form. However, the real problem is in finding a way to make the child generalise that knowledge to other inflected forms.

Laurence Leonard's chapter illustrates how useful it can be to broaden one's perspective from a narrow focus on English. By contrasting language acquisition and language impairment in different languages, one can start to identify which linguistic characteristics are important. One factor that seems important in both typical and atypical language development is the stress patterning of words in a sentence. Practitioners have been quick to see the potential value of this information, and Susan Ellis Weismer describes a series of experimental intervention studies in which the role of

factors such as stress and rate of presentation can be examined.

Another therapeutic approach that has come to the forefront in the past few years is the FastForword intervention programme developed in the USA by Paula Tallal and her collaborators. Although the theoretical origins of this work are quite distinct, it does have some broad similarities with the other therapeutic approaches discussed in the book. As with Ellis Weismer's work, the focus is not on trying to train specific grammatical structures, but rather on modifying the speech signal to make it easier to process. And, as with more traditional behavioural approaches exemplified by Fey and Proctor-Williams, the goal is to achieve learning by intensive practice. What makes this intervention distinctive is that it uses computerised games to train children's auditory and phonological skills, making it possible to administer thousands of training trials in a relatively short space of time.

Another field in which we have seen exciting progress is that of genetics of language disorders. Robert Plomin and Philip Dale show how one can use genetic research to go beyond demonstrating that a disorder is heritable. Behaviour genetic methods allow us to look at underlying relationships between different cognitive processes, and to consider questions such as whether language impairment is part of normal variation, or a distinct disorder.

Issues of classification of speech and language disorders have never been more critical than they are now. In order to discover which children will benefit most from a specific intervention, or which disorders have a genetic basis, we must develop some coherent way of subgrouping the heterogeneous category of childhood speech-language disorders. This topic is still very much in its infancy: many of us working in the field remain unclear whether the way forward is to identify smaller, finer categories, or rather to broaden our viewpoint to recognise similarities between conditions that are currently regarded as distinct. This is well exemplified in Thierry Deonna's chapter on acquired epileptic aphasia (AEA). AEA, also known as Landau-Kleffner syndrome, has traditionally been regarded as quite distinct from other forms of developmental language disorder. Deonna, however, raises the question of whether there might be continuities with SLI on the one hand, and regressive kinds of autistic disorder on the other. The notion that some hidden epileptic process might underlie at least some cases of SLI is currently much under debate, and the evidence is controversial. Another traditional viewpoint that is currently under attack is the idea that SLI is truly "specific". Dorothy Bishop suggests that a clear-cut division between specific and pervasive developmental disorders may be unrealistic, and that there are many intermediate cases of children who may be thought of as having "pragmatic language impairment". In a thought-provoking chapter, Ian Goodyer looks at SLI from the perspective of a child psychiatrist, noting that there is substantial comorbidity between communication impairments and psychiatric disorders. He suggests that we might obtain a more coherent subclassification of language disorders if we took into account behavioural as well as linguistic characteristics of the children.

Another point of convergence is between language disorders and literacy problems. It is increasingly recognised that many children who have obvious difficulties with oral speech and language in the preschool years go on to have major difficulties with literacy once they move into school. Three chapters in this book focus on links between language and literacy. Joy Stackhouse looks specifically at aspects of speech processing in relation to later reading and spelling skills. She makes the point that it is not always the most obvious problems with speech production that put the child at risk for later literacy problems. Some young children with immature articulation catch up with their peers and go on to do well in reading and spelling. For other children, the speech problems appear to have been resolved, but detailed testing reveals underlying weaknesses in the processing of phonological information, which are linked to poor literacy. Margaret Snowling also notes the vulnerability of phonological processing in children with early language impairments, but argues that this is not the only reason for later literacy problems. Many of these children also lack the semantic and syntactic skills that are important for understanding written text, and for inferring meaning of written words on the basis of partial information. She concludes that different aspects of language processing assume importance at different stages in learning to read. There are striking resonances between these conclusions and those reached by Grover Whitehurst and Janet Fischel in their study of a very different population, namely children growing up in conditions of economic poverty. All too often, these children are ignored by researchers, because it is assumed that their problems are in some way "caused" by their poor social circumstances, and are very different in kind from those of more affluent children with SLI or specific reading disability. The data presented by Whitehurst and Fischel challenge this view, and suggest that there is a subset of children in their economically-deprived sample who are qualitatively distinct and might reasonably be regarded as "dyslexic".

One factor that makes it difficult to classify speech and language impairments in children is that they change over time. Which children should we focus our therapeutic efforts on, and which can be expected to improve spontaneously? In a provocative chapter, Rhea Paul questions the common assumption that intervention efforts should be focused primarily on young, preschool children. Her own longitudinal study found that many children who had marked expressive language delays at 2 years of age went on to catch up with their peers by the time they were in school. She cautions against generalising from this study to other populations who might have additional risk factors, or where receptive language is impaired. Nevertheless, her message is an important one to take into consideration when considering how to allocate scarce speech and language therapy resources. We need to balance the benefits of starting intervention early before secondary impairments develop, against the risk of wasting intervention resources on children whose difficulties are likely to resolve spontaneously.

The question of just who does get intervention is likely to vary hugely from one country to another. Even within the UK context, for many years we have known little about the characteristics of those children who attend "language units", i.e. special classes within regular schools where the children receive additional support for developing language skills. Gina Conti-Ramsden and Nicola Botting describe a survey of 7-year-old children attending language units in England and Wales. According to their calculations, these pupils are a tiny minority of all children with SLI. Most children in language units do have very specific difficulties with speech and language, but these are quite varied in nature, and the ones with the poorest prognosis are not necessarily those with the lowest scores on conventional tests. Conti-Ramsden and Botting endorse Goodyer's claim that behavioural difficulties are a common correlate of SLI: in the language unit sample, 40% of children had additional behavioural problems.

Michael Rutter concludes the book with an overview of the nature of research in specific language impairment. We anticipate that this chapter will be helpful both to those who have little experience of conducting research, and to seasoned researchers. For the former group, it outlines the kinds of questions that researchers ask, and the kinds of methods that are appropriate for

addressing them. It should help those reading about research findings to look at them with an appropriately critical stance, and to form an impression of which findings should be taken most seriously. For the latter, it lays out clearly the kinds of questions one should ask oneself when planning a research study, and what are the pitfalls to avoid.

We would like to end this foreword by thanking Norma Corkish, whose term as chief executive of Afasic came to an end just after the York meeting in March 1999. Norma's enthusiasm and hard work were a vital factor in making all three International Symposia such a great success, and she successfully steered a balance between academics and practitioners with tact and good humour. We hope that her insistence that speakers talk in plain English rather than abstruse academic jargon has filtered through to good effect in this collection of chapters, and that the book will advance the integration of theory with practice.

Dorothy Bishop and Laurence Leonard
October 1999

1

Acquiring syntax is not what you think

Michael Tomasello

Many developmental psycholinguists assume that young children operate with adult syntactic categories. This assumption has never had strong empirical support, but recently a number of new findings have emerged — both from systematic analyses of children's spontaneous speech and from controlled experiments — that contradict it directly. In general, the key finding is that most of children's early language is item based, and therefore their language development proceeds in a piecemeal fashion with no indication of any system-wide syntactic categories, schemas, or parameters. Since nativist theories of language acquisition rely explicitly on adult linguistic categories as their major analytic tools (i.e. as these are embodied in formal grammars), the implications of these new findings for nativist theories are discussed. Also discussed are the outlines of an alternative, constructivist theory of child language acquisition.

INTRODUCTION

Most approaches to the study of first language acquisition use adult-like grammatical categories and rules to describe children's language. This is especially true of the dominant approach to the study of children's syntactic development, namely, the theoretical paradigm based on Chomsky's universal grammar (see Pinker, 1994). In this paradigm, it is hypothesised that children innately possess the abstract syntactic competence of adults, and all they must do in development is discover how that applies to the particular language they are learning. So, for example, all children are born with a "head-direction parameter"; that is, they know innately that their language is either head-first (as in the Spanish *casa grande*, where the noun is the head of the phrase and comes first) or head-last (as in the English *big house*, where the noun/head is last). Hearing a particular language simply sets the head-direction parameter in one way or the other. Once the requisite parameters are set, children have essentially adult-like syntactic competence. This has come to be known as the nativist view of language acquisition, because the child's innate knowledge is seen as all-important, and processes of social learning and imitation are not thought to play any important role in acquisition.

My colleagues and I are currently developing a theoretical approach to child language acquisition that conflicts with this Chomskyan approach in a number of important ways. My goal in this chapter is to sketch out the broad outlines of that approach. It has at least four elements that are surprising from the point of view of nativist (i.e. Chomskyan) theorising about language development, especially with regard to the syntactic dimensions of the process.

- Imitative learning is a necessary and crucially important part of language acquisition — albeit imitative learning of a very special type described more broadly as "cultural learning" (Tomasello, Kruger, & Ratner, 1993).
- The language that children acquire initially is almost totally concrete, that is, it is based not on abstract linguistic entities such as noun phrases, verb phrases and transitivity, but rather on the particular words and phrases of a particular language. Children construct more abstract linguistic categories and schemas only gradually, and they do this in an unsystematic, piecemeal fashion — so that at any given developmental moment there may also be great variety in the abstractness of the linguistic units with which a child can operate.
- The linguistic units that children acquire via imitative learning are not only small things like words but also larger things like phrases, clauses and, indeed, whole speech acts. Thus, at any given developmental moment there may be great variety in the complexity of the linguistic units that a child can use.
- This more pluralistic way of looking at linguistic units implies that in many cases chil-

dren's creative linguistic combinations are a pastiche of linguistic units varying from one another in both complexity and abstractness.

We have been led to this new view of language acquisition first and foremost by some new observations of children's early language that appear to be quite consistent and robust across languages — and across methodologies (naturalistic observation and experimentation) as well. In addition, this view both benefits from and is supported by some new approaches in theoretical linguistics, known broadly as cognitive and functional linguistics (e.g. Langacker, 1987, 1991; Lakoff, 1987; see papers in Tomasello, 1998a). These approaches provide a rigorous foundation for identifying the kinds of linguistic units (referred to as "linguistic constructions") that children experience in the adult language around them. I shall first present the new data and then provide some theoretical reflections on their implications for the study of child language acquisition.

SOME RECENT DATA

The central issue of current concern is whether children are operating from the outset of development with adult-like linguistic categories and schemas (as espoused in one form or another by the different varieties of linguistic nativism) or, alternatively, whether children begin the acquisition process with only highly specific and concrete linguistic items and structures. To make the distinction as clearly as I can, the question is whether children's earliest utterances are underlain by such things as noun phrases, verb phrases, prepositional phrases, head direction parameters, functional categories, and so forth, or whether, alternatively, they are underlain by less abstract units of varying sizes. As always, there are two basic methodological approaches to this question: (1) the observation and analysis of children's spontaneous speech, and (2) experiments with children's linguistic comprehension and production.

Observational studies

Following in the footsteps of pioneers such as Braine (1976), in my 1992 diary study I documented virtually all of my English-speaking daughter's earliest verbs and linguistic constructions from 15–24 months of age (Tomasello, 1992). The major findings of that study may be summarised as follows:

- Of the 162 verbs used, almost half were used in one and only one construction type, and over two-thirds were used in one or two construction types — where construction type means verb-participant configuration (e.g. *Draw car* and *Draw tree* are the same construction type, whereas *Draw on paper* (locative), *Mommy draw* (agent), and *Draw with pencil* (instrument) are three additional construction types).

- At any given developmental period, there was great unevenness in how different verbs, even those that were very close in meaning, were used. For example, at 23 months of age the verb *cut* was used in only one simple construction type (*Cut + X*) whereas the somewhat similar verb *draw* was used in many different construction types, some with much complexity (e.g. *I draw on the man, Draw it by Santa Claus*). Where information on adult usage was available for a given verb, there was a very good match with child usage.

- There was also great unevenness in the syntactic marking of the "same" participant across verbs such that, for example, at a given developmental period, one verb would have its instrument marked with *with* or *by* but another verb, even when used in utterances of the same length and complexity, would not have this marker. Some verbs were used with lexically expressed subjects whereas others at the same time were not, even though they were used in comparable construction types and in comparable pragmatic contexts. For instance, there were subjects for *take* and *get* (I take and you get it) but not for *put* (put it there).

- Morphological marking (e.g. past tense -ed) on verbs was also very uneven. Roughly two-thirds of all verbs were never marked morphologically for tense or aspect, one-sixth were marked for past tense only, one-sixth marked for present progressive only, and only four verbs (2%) marked for both of these functions at any time during the second year of life.

- On the other hand, within any given verb's development, there was great continuity such that new uses of a given verb almost always replicated previous uses and then made one small addition or modification (e.g. the marking of tense or the adding of one new participant). By far the best predictor of the use of a given verb on a given day was not the child's use of other verbs on that same day, but rather her use of that same verb on immediately preceding days.

The resulting hypothesis, the Verb Island Hypothesis, was that children's early language is organised and structured totally around individual verbs and other predicative terms, that is, the 2-year-old child's syntactic competence is comprised totally of verb-specific constructions with open participant slots. Other than the categorisation of participants, nascent language learners possess no linguistic abstractions or forms of syntactic organisation. This means that the syntactic categories with which children are working are not such verb-general things as "subject" and "object", or even "agent" and "patient", but rather such verb-specific things as "hitter", "hittee", and "thing hit with".

Using a combination of periodic sampling and maternal diaries, Lieven, Pine, and Baldwin (1997; see also Pine & Lieven, 1993; Pine, Lieven, & Rowland, 1998) have found similar results in a sample of 12 English-speaking children from 1–3 years of age. In particular, they found that virtually all children used most of their verbs and predicative terms in only one construction type early in language development. In addition, they examined the children's subject-verb-object (SVO) utterances for evidence that they knew how to syntactically mark subjects and objects. Looking at those SVO sentences that used personal pronouns, they found basically no evidence that children knew that such forms as *I* and *me*, *we* and *us*, and *they* and *them* contrasted in their participant roles (nor was there any evidence of verb-general participant marking from SVO utterances using full noun phrases). Following along these same lines, Pine and Lieven (1997) found that when young English-speaking children begin to use the determiners *a* and *the* they do so with almost completely different sets of nouns (i.e. there is almost no overlap in the sets of nouns used with the two determiners), suggesting that children at this age do not have any kind of abstract category of determiner that includes both of these lexical items.

A number of systematic studies of children learning languages other than English have found very similar results. For example, Pizzuto and Caselli (1992, 1994) investigated the grammatical morphology used by three Italian-speaking children on their simple, finite, main verbs, from approximately 1.5–3 years of age. Although there are six forms possible for each verb root (first-person singular, second-person singular, etc.), 47% of all verbs used by these children were used in one form only, and an additional 40% were used with two or three forms. Of the 13% of verbs that appeared in four or more forms, approximately half of these were highly frequent, highly irregular forms that could be learned only by rote. The clear implication is that children do not master the whole verb paradigm (i.e. all six persons and numbers) for all their verbs at once, but rather they master some endings with some verbs — and often different ones with different verbs. Rubino and Pine (1998), Berman (1982), and Berman and Armon-Lotem (1995), have found very similar patterns for Brazilian Portuguese and Hebrew-speaking children, respectively.

Of special note are so-called overgeneralisation errors in spontaneous speech because, presumably, children have not heard such forms used in adult speech. In the context of a focus on syntax, the overgeneralisations of most interest are those involving sentence-level constructions (for example, *She falled me down* or *Don't giggle me*), in which the child uses verbs in syntactic constructions in an "incorrect" way that seems to indicate that she has some abstract, verb-general schema for such things as a transitive SVO construction. Bowerman (1982, 1988) in particular

has documented a number of such overgeneralisations in the speech of her two English-speaking children, and Pinker (1989) has compiled examples from other sources as well. The main result of interest in the current context is that Bowerman's children and the other children produced very few sentence-level overgeneralisations before about 3 years of age and virtually none before 2.5 years of age — suggesting that very young children do not have verb-general syntactic constructions.

These data-intensive studies from a number of different languages together show a very clear pattern. Young children's earliest linguistic productions revolve around concrete items and structures — particular verbs such as *push, pull, cut,* and *draw,* and the basic sentence-level constructions in which they participate. There is absolutely no evidence that young children are using abstract categories and schemas in their spontaneous linguistic productions, other than the participant slots in these verb island constructions. Rather, each of these items and structures undergoes its own development — presumably based on the child's linguistic experience and other factors affecting learning — in relative independence of other items and structures. This pattern persists in most cases until around the third birthday. Those who argue that young children *do* possess abstract, adult-like categories such as "subject", "object", "agent", or "patient", must maintain that their naturally occurring language for some reason does not reflect their underlying syntactic competence.

Experimental studies

There is no question that young children comprehend and produce adult-like linguistic items and structures from early in development, even if this is only with some items and structures (Braine, 1971; Brown, 1973; Bloom, 1992; DeVilliers & DeVilliers, 1973). But, as noted earlier, the adult-like production and comprehension of language by children is not diagnostic of the underlying processes involved. Adult-like comprehension and production may emanate either from abstract, adult-like linguistic knowledge or from item- and structure-specific knowledge in which children are simply reproducing the words and sentences they have heard from adults.

The main way to test for underlying process is to introduce children to novel linguistic items that they have never heard before, and then see what they do with them — as in the famous wug-test of Berko (1958). For questions of syntax in particular, the method of choice is to introduce young children to a novel verb in one syntactic construction and then see whether and in what ways they use that verb in other, syntactic constructions — perhaps with some form of discourse encouragement such as involving leading questions. A useful metaphor in this regard is to think of the novel verb as a kind of "tracer" element like those sometimes used in medical diagnosis — that is, experimentally introduced into the system and its fate then followed. If the experimental element is used in novel yet canonical ways, the inference is that it has been taken up by some kind of system, in this case abstract syntactic categories and schemas. If it is not used in any novel and canonical ways, but only in ways the child has experienced, the inference is either that: (i) there is no abstract system present to take up the new element (and the child is learning by imitation); or (ii) for some reason the existing abstract system is unable to take up the new element. This latter possibility in the case of language development means, for the most part, that performance factors (e.g. limited processing skills) might prevent children from demonstrating their syntactic competence in the experiment — a possibility that must always be considered.

Experiments using novel verbs as tracer elements have demonstrated conclusively that children at 3.5 years of age and older can quite readily assimilate novel verbs into abstract syntactic schemas that they bring to the experiment. For example, with special reference to the simple transitive construction, Maratsos et al. (1987) taught children from 4.5–5.5 years of age the novel verb *fud* for a novel transitive action (human operating a machine that transformed the shape of playdough). Children were introduced to the novel verb in a series of intransitive sentence frames such as "It finally fudded", "The dough wouldn't

fud", and "The dough's fudding in the machine". Some children were left to their own devices to use the new word as they saw fit in playing with the novel apparatus, while others were prompted with biasing questions such as "What are you doing?" (which encourages a transitive response such as "I'm fudding the dough"). Pinker, Lebeaux, and Frost (1987) used a similar experimental design except that they introduced children to the novel verb in a passive construction, "The fork is being floosed by the pencil", and then asked them the question "What is the pencil doing?" to pull for an active, transitive response such as "It's floosing the fork". In all of these studies, the general finding was that the vast majority of children from 3.5–8 years of age (two-thirds or more of the sample in most cases) could produce a canonical transitive utterance with the novel verb, even though they had never heard it used in that construction. These results suggest quite strongly that children of this age come to the experiment with some kind of abstract, verb-general, SVO transitive construction to which they readily assimilate the newly learned verb simply on the basis of observing the real world situation to which it refers (and, in some cases, hints from the way adults ask them questions about this situation).

Over the past few years my collaborators and I have pursued a fairly systematic investigation of English-speaking children's ability to produce simple transitive SVO sentences with verbs they have not heard used in this construction, but focusing mainly on children below the ages represented in these previous studies. The focus on younger children is important because most theories of the acquisition of syntactic competence single out the age range from 2–4 years as especially important, and indeed by virtually all theoretical accounts, both nativist and constructivist, children of 3.5 years and older should possess much syntactic competence. Reviewing these studies with children beginning at 2 years thus provides an opportunity to look for some kind of developmental trajectory in children's earliest syntactic competence with novel verbs. In all studies the basic methodology was to teach children a made-up verb in just one syntactic construction and then see what novel things they could do with it. Two exemplars of these studies should suffice.

- First, Brooks and Tomasello (1999) exposed 20 children (average age = 2;10) to one novel verb in the context of a passive model, such as *The cup got tammed by Ernie*, and another novel verb in the context of an active transitive model, such as *Big Bird meeked the ball* — each for a highly transitive and novel action in which an agent is doing something to a patient. They then asked them agent questions of the type *What is X doing?*, where X was acting out the role of agent. This agent question pulls for a transitive utterance such as *He's tamming the cup* or *He's meeking the ball*, which would be novel for *tam* since it was heard only as a passive, but not novel for *meek* because it was heard only as an active transitive. Overall in two studies, only 28% of the children who heard exclusively passive models with the novel verb were able to use that verb in a transitive utterance. On the other hand, 93% of the children in the control condition, who heard exclusively active-voice transitive models with the novel verb, were able to use that verb in exactly that way.

- Second, Tomasello and Brooks (1998) exposed 16 children at 2;0 and 16 children at 2;6 (note younger age) to one novel verb in the context of an intransitive model such as *The sock is tamming*, and another novel verb in the context of a transitive model such as *Big Bird is meeking the ball* — each for a highly transitive and novel action in which an agent is doing something to a patient. They then asked agent questions of the type *What is X doing?* Again this question prompts for a transitive utterance such as *He's tamming the sock* or *He's meeking the ball*, which would be novel for *tam* since it was heard only as an intransitive, but not novel for *meek* because it was heard only as a transitive. With the intransitively introduced verb, only one of 16 children at 2;0 (7%) and only 3 of 16 children at 2;6 (19%) produced a novel transitive utterance. With the transitively introduced verb

in the control condition, however, 11 of the 16 younger children and all 16 of the older children produced a novel transitive utterance — demonstrating again that they can use novel verbs in the transitive construction when they have heard them used in that way.

We have done similar studies exposing children to made up verbs in a presentational construction such as "This is called gorping" (Olguin & Tomasello, 1993; Akhtar & Tomasello, 1997; Dodson & Tomasello, 1998), and in an imperative construction such as "Tam, Anna!" (Lewis & Tomasello, submitted) — and then tried to elicit transitive utterances with these verbs. In all of these studies the overall finding is that — despite our most diligent efforts — children below 3 years of age are very poor at using their newly learned verbs in the transitive construction, with the vast majority of children below this age never producing a single transitive utterance. This is despite the fact that we have also taught them novel nouns, and they use these quite freely in novel syntactic constructions (Tomasello & Olguin, 1993; Tomasello, Akhtar, Dodson, & Rekau, 1997), suggesting that we are not dealing with a general reluctance on the part of young children to use newly learned words in novel linguistic constructions. And we have also given them comprehension studies in which, after we have taught them a novel verb in a presentational construction ("Tamming! This is called tamming!"), we then ask them to act out a transitive construction with that verb: "Show me: The dog's tamming the cat". Surprisingly, children younger than 3 years of age do no better in comprehension than they do in production (Akhtar & Tomasello, 1997). Using experimental procedures with made up verbs (although slightly different syntactic constructions), very similar findings have also been reported by Berman (1993) for Hebrew, and Childers and Tomasello (submitted) for Chilean Spanish.

All of these studies involve children producing or failing to produce canonical utterances that go beyond what they have heard from adults. Their general failure to do so at early ages suggests that they do not possess the abstract structures that would enable this generativity, but there are many reasons why children do not do things. However, one recent study may be of special importance because it succeeded in inducing children to produce noncanonical ("incorrect") English utterances (which should not be possible if certain innate parameters, such as linguistic head direction, were already set). Akhtar (1999) modelled novel verbs for novel events with young children at 2;8, 3;6, and 4;4 years old. One verb was modelled in canonical English SVO order, as in *Ernie meeking the car*, whereas two others were in non-canonical orders, either SOV (*Ernie the cow tamming*) or VSO (*Gopping Ernie the cow*). Children were then encouraged to use the novel verbs with neutral questions such as *What's happening?* Almost all of the children at all three ages produced exclusively SVO utterances with the novel verb when that is what they heard. However, when they heard one of the non-canonical SOV or VSO forms, children behaved differently at different ages. In general, the older children used their verb-general knowledge of English transitivity to "correct" the non-canonical uses of the novel verbs (they match the peculiar word orders less); the younger children, however, much more often matched the ordering patterns they had heard with the novel verb, no matter how bizarre that pattern sounded to adult ears.

The main point is that children come to their understanding of the English transitive construction as a verb-general construction only gradually. Indeed, when all of the findings just reviewed are compiled and quantitatively compared, we see a very gradual and continuous developmental progression (see Fig. 1.1). Figure 1.1 was constructed by computing a single number for the productivity of children at each age group in each of the experimental studies reported above. In the vast majority of cases this number was simply the proportion of children who produced at least one novel and canonical transitive utterance (regardless of the number of imitative utterances they produced, which in some cases was quite high). Despite variations in experimental design and procedure, virtually all of the studies fall on a curve that slopes steadily upward from age 2–4, at which point the slope becomes more shallow, reaching close to 100% by 8 years of age. In my view, this overall pattern is not consistent with the nativist hypothesis, but rather with the constructivist hypothesis in which young children begin language acquisition conservatively by imitatively learning linguistic items and structures directly from adult language, only later discerning the kinds of patterns that enable them to construct adult-like linguistic categories and schemas.

Summary

Together, the naturalistic and experimental studies of children's productivity with the basic SVO configuration of English transitive utterances are clear and consistent. Before 3 years of age only a few children manage to produce canonical transitive utterances with verbs they have not heard used in this way. We see this pattern when we look at their naturalistic utterances carefully and systematically, including the various ways in which particular verbs are and are not used. We also see this pattern when we look at their performance in experimental situations in which they must "get to" the transitive utterance from a variety of different constructions (presentational, intransitive, passive, imperative, non-canonical), using different tasks in a variety of types of discourse interactions with adults. Explanations in terms of children's problems in producing language and other syntactically extraneous factors are not a likely explanation for these findings because young children:

- are very productive with novel nouns (ruling out a general reluctance to use newly learned forms in novel ways);
- perform at similar levels in tests of their comprehension and production of novel transitive utterances (ruling out many production factors since comprehension tasks pose fewer performance demands); and
- produce transitive utterances with novel verbs if they first hear adults use those verbs in transitive utterances (ruling out many other performance factors since this control condition has most of the same performance demands as the experimental condition).

FIGURE 1.1

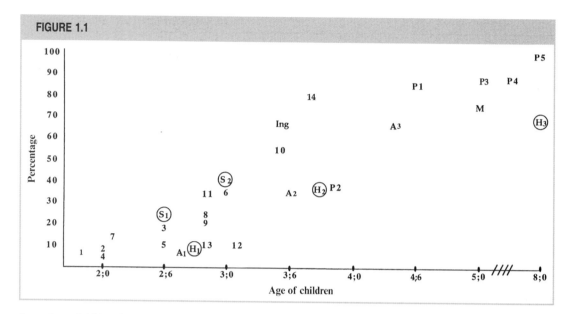

Percentage of children (or in some cases responses) who produced productive transitive utterances using novel verbs in different studies (see key to identify studies and some of their characteristics).

KEY to Fig. 1.1   1. Studies used; 2. How they are designated in figure; 3. Age of children; 4. What percentage of children (or responses) were productive; 5. The type of linguistic model used; 6. The type of elicitation question used; 7. Some notes on how the productivity score was calculated.

1	2	3	4	5	6	7
Tomasello et al. (1997)	1	1;10	0.07	Presentational	Neutral	% children
Tomasello & Brooks (1999)	2	2;0	0.06	Intransitive	Agent	% children
	3	2;6	0.19			
Lewis & Tomasello (in prep)	4	2;0	0.06	Imperative	Neutral	% children
	5	2;6	0.13			
	6	3;0	0.38			
Olguin & Tomasello (1993)	7	2;1	0.13	Presentational	Neutral	% children
Dodson & Tomasello (1998)	8	2;10	0.25	Presentational	Neutral	% children
Brooks & Tomasello (1999), Studies 1 & 2	9	2;10	0.20	Passive	Agent	% children
	10	3;5	0.55			
	11	2;10	0.35			
Akhtar & Tomasello (1997), Studies 1 & 2	12	3;1	0.20	Presentational	Neutral	% children
	13	2;9	0.10			
	14	3;8	0.80			
Ingham (1993)	Ing	3;5	0.67	Intransitive (low freq English verbs)	Agent	% responses
Pinker et al. (1987), Studies 1, 2, & 3	P1	4;6	0.86	Passive	Agent	% responses (action verbs)
	P2	3;10	0.38			
	P3	5;1	0.88			
	P4	6;1	0.88			
	P5	7;11	1.00			
Maratsos et al. (1987)	M	5;0	0.75	Intransitive	Agent	% children, (3 of 10 in 0–7% group)
Akhtar (1999)	A1	2;8	0.08	SOV & VSO	Neutral	% children (consistently correct)
	A2	3;6	0.33			
	A3	4;4	0.67			
Berman (1993)	H1	2;9	0.09	Intransitive (Hebrew)	Sentence completion	% responses (fully correct)
	H2	3;9	0.38			
	H3	8;0	0.69			
Childers & Tomasello (submitted)	S1	2;6	0.25	1st or 3rd person verb (Spanish)	Neutral	% children
	S2	3;0	0.38			

The general finding for children under 3 years of age is thus always the same no matter the method: they use some of their verbs in the transitive construction — namely, the ones they have heard used in that construction — but they do not use other of their verbs in the transitive construction — namely, the ones they have not heard in that construction. When applied across the board, the finding is that children's language development is gradual and piecemeal in the extreme, with individual items and structures being learned on a one-by-one basis, and generalisations and abstractions coming only some time later.

THEORETICAL DISCUSSION

As clearly demonstrated in the data just reviewed, the gradual and piecemeal nature of child language acquisition is difficult to reconcile with the nativist view. In its strongest and most straightforward form, the nativist view maintains that children have full linguistic competence from birth and only fail to express this competence because of extraneous factors.

In response to these data, nativists can make one of three basic theoretical moves. First, they can claim that performance limitations inhibit the full expression of children's innate linguistic competence. But I believe that our many control procedures as just outlined have effectively ruled out this option. Second, nativists may posit that children are not born with adult-like syntactic categories; their earliest language learning might be item-based or in other ways messy and piecemeal, but the genes that make adult-like categories and schemas available to the child begin to mature and make themselves manifest some time between 2 and 3 years of age (e.g. Boerer & Wexler, 1992; Rizzi, 1994). The problem in this case is that, in the data reviewed, the gradual and piecemeal developmental process was all within the same syntactic structure, namely, the English transitive construction. Different genes maturing at different rates cannot account for gradual and piecemeal acquisition within a single syntactic structure. Third, nativists may argue that at early

stages of development children may not have experienced enough of the right kind of language to trigger some of their innate syntactic structures (e.g. Hyams, 1994). In the case of the current experiments the claim would be that to assimilate a newly learned verb to the innate structures involved in the transitive construction (presumably involving head-direction and the like), children would have to hear that specific verb used in that specific construction. This amendment to the nativist proposal works to explain the data, but at the cost of the whole point of linguistic nativism which classically posits that human beings possess and use linguistic abstractions early, independent of specific linguistic experiences other than a minimal triggering event.

The alternative I am proposing derives from the classic accounts such as those of Braine, Bowerman, Maratsos, Slobin, Bates and MacWhinney, and others, but some theoretical advances in modern linguistics give us fresh insights into the process so we can begin to work out some crucial details. Most importantly, linguists — especially those who do cross-linguistic work — are creating models of language use that are more psychologically realistic than formal Chomsky-type models, in the sense that they rely explicitly and exclusively on theoretical constructs that psychologists employ such as symbols, categories, schemas, attention, perspective, communicative strategies, and so on. As I have argued in numerous places previously, these approaches — known collectively as Cognitive and Functional Linguistics — are much better suited to the needs of developmentalists than are the more mathematically based approaches of formal (i.e. Chomskyan) linguistics (Tomasello, 1992, 1995, 1998a, 1998b).

In cognitive and functional linguistics, natural languages are seen as consisting exclusively and exhaustively of linguistic constructions; there are no subjacency constraints, empty categories, projection principles, or other entities lying beneath the surface (Langacker's, 1987, "content requirement"). Linguistic constructions may be either simple or complex, e.g. a word, a phrase, or a clause. Totally independent of complexity, they may be either concrete (based on particular linguistic items or structures) or abstract (based on categories or schemas). Thus, many idioms are complex but totally concrete in that they are based on particular words (*Nothing ventured, nothing gained*), while some quite simple constructions, such as the English possessive *'s*, are highly abstract. And, indeed, many constructions are made up of some abstract and some concrete elements all in one. Most famous is Fillmore, Kaye, and O'Conner's (1988) study of the *let alone*-construction, as in "I wouldn't live in America, let alone New York". This construction revolves around the lexical item *let alone*, but it is also quite productive in the sense that many different things may be put into comparison in this way. Cognitive linguists have also studied some totally abstract constructions, e.g. Goldberg's (1995) analysis of the ditransitive construction as in "X verbed Y the Z". My own personal favourite is Langacker's (1991) analysis of the so-called incredulity construction, as in "Him be a doctor!" What is interesting is that this is a very productive construction — it forms a very neat little pattern from which all of us can proceed to produce novel exemplars: "My mother ride a motorcycle!", "Her come to the party!" — but at the same time it does not fit, to say the least, with other English constructions. No other English sentence-level construction has a subject in the accusative (objective) case and the main verb in non-finite form. This highly productive construction thus falls outside of Chomskyan "core grammar", as do the *let alone* construction, all idioms, all metaphorical uses of language and, indeed, the majority of language in everyday use. One other example is the "normal extraposition" construction, as in "It's amazing the people you see here", which does not follow typical English sentence patterns. In the cognitive–functional view there is no distinction between core and periphery; all natural language use is of interest and all varieties are explained in terms of the same basic theoretical principles. I repeat: a natural language is composed exclusively and exhaustively of linguistic constructions of different shapes and sizes and degrees of abstraction.

With this theoretical background (that is, assuming that what children are learning is linguistic constructions such as words, phrases, and clauses), let me specify the three language acquisition processes that I believe are most crucial:

- imitative learning
- abstraction
- structure combination

Given the data I have presented, the first and most important process is cultural (i.e. imitative) learning (Tomasello et al., 1993). Imitative learning in this context does not mean children repeating adult utterances immediately or simply mimicking the surface form of utterances only. Rather, it means children trying to reproduce the language that adults produce and for the same communicative function: they are imitatively learning to say "It's flying", for instance, in situations in which they wish to indicate to someone else (as someone is now indicating for them) that something is flying. At one level of analysis, this absolutely must be true as all children learn the language they are raised in. Furthermore, for all non-core aspects of language structure — all idioms, lexical items, quirky constructions, and the like — no one has ever proposed any mechanism other than some form of imitative learning. My proposal is simply that, initially, imitative learning is *all* that children do for all constructions, regular and irregular alike. Indeed, this is by far the most natural explanation for the data I have presented: children reproduce what they hear and form their own abstractions later and only very gradually. This approach, of course, highlights the role of the language that children hear around them, since that is all they have to learn from and imitate. It also takes seriously the possibility of individual differences based both on variations in children's perceptual and learning skills and on their different language learning environments.

There are at last a couple of phenomena of child language acquisition that are often taken to be evidence against an imitative learning hypothesis, but which I think are actually evidence for it: if we look at exactly what children do and do not hear. For example, many young children say things like "Her open it", an accusative subject which they supposedly have not heard from adults. There are a number of possible explanations for this phenomenon, but one is fairly simple. Children hear things like "Let her open it" or "Help her open it", and so they produce just the end part of the sentence "Her open it". Very telling is the fact that children almost never make the complementary error "Mary hit I" or "He kissed she". The reason they do not make this mistake is they never hear anything like this anywhere in the language around them. A similar account can be given for some of the findings going under the general rubric of optional infinitives (Rice, 1998, chapter 2, this volume). In this case there are probably other factors at work as well because small and unstressed elements are often vulnerable in language processing (see Leonard et al., 1997; Leonard, chapter 7, this volume). But I also think that a major part of the explanation is the large number of nonfinite verbs that children hear in various constructions in the language addressed to them, especially in questions such as "Should he open it?" and "Does Anna eat grapes?" The child might then later say, in partially imitative fashion: "He open it" and "Anna eat grapes". And so, first and foremost, if we want to explain children's early language development, we must pay attention to the language children actually hear and the processes by which they imitatively (i.e. culturally) learn it.

The second important process — and one to which I have given insufficient attention here — is abstraction. I have noted that children abstract something like a category of concrete noun quite early (Tomasello & Olguin, 1993). But they abstract across more complex relational structures as well, for example, whole constructions such as the simple transitive construction after 3–3.5 years of age. No one knows exactly how they do this. Some of the work that I think is most relevant is the work of Gentner on children's analogies and what she calls "structure mapping", that is, finding a common relational structure (abstracting across objects or participants) in two events or situations (Gentner & Markman, 1997). The idea is that children must engage in this kind of process to see the similarity in utterances such as "I draw tree", "I do it", "I hit Jeffrey", "You kiss Mommy", "Jamie kicks the ball", and so on. In the same

way we must all do this to see the commonality in "Him be a doctor!", "My mother drive a motorcycle!", etc. I assume that there must be some "critical mass" of exemplars of particular utterance types necessary for the human cognitive apparatus to be able to make the requisite analogies and subsequent categories and schemas. One guess might be that the critical factor is the number of different verbs heard in the construction, since verbs are the central organising element in utterance-level constructions (and since many exemplars with only one or a few verbs would seem to be a very inadequate basis for generalising the construction).

Third and finally, children also combine various kinds of linguistic constructions creatively, involving both concrete and abstract constructions of varying levels of complexity, and this is also a process about which we know very little. For example, I can point to some of my daughter's earliest utterances with three or more words. At around 20–22 months of age she began saying things like "See Daddy's car". But previously she had said things like "See ball" and "See Mommy", on the one hand, and also things like "Daddy's shirt" and "Daddy's pen", on the other. So, my supposition is that she creatively combined something like a See X construction with a Daddy's X construction (or perhaps even a more general possessive NP construction). Unfortunately, we do not know what this child actually heard or did not hear along the lines of "See Daddy's car", so we do not know the extent to which this was a truly creative combining of constructions.

A somewhat more complex example of structure combining comes from the work of Diessel and Tomasello (1999) on children's earliest complex sentences. We looked at six children in the CHILDES database (MacWhinney & Snow, 1990), and examined, among other things, their complex utterances with sentential complements. We found that virtually all early complement sentences were composed of a simple sentence schema the child had already mastered combined with one of a handful of main verbs (see also Bloom, 1992). These matrix verbs were of two types: so-called epistemic verbs which refer to mental states such as *think* and *know*, and

TABLE 1.1

Some examples of complex sentences from two children, with an epistemic marker for Sarah and with an attention-getter for Nina (Diessel & Tomasello, 1999).

w/Epistemic Marker (Sarah):	w/Attention-Getter (Nina):
I think he's gone	*See* that monkey crying
I think it's in here	*See* Becca sleeping
I think my daddy took it	*See* that go
I think I saw one	*See* my hands are washed
it's a crazy bone, *I think*	*See* he bite me
I think dis is de bowl	*See* him lie down

NB: (1) Almost all epistemics in first person only; almost all attention-getters as imperatives only.
(2) There are almost never complementisers (e.g. *that*).
(3) There are virtually no past or future tenses.
(4) There are virtually no negatives.

attention-getters such as *look* and *see*. As illustrated in Table 1.1, each child typically used any given matrix verb in only one or two ways, as dictated by the pragmatics of their use. Thus Sarah used *I think* to indicate her own uncertainty about something — and she never used the verb in anything but the first-person form. Nina used *see* as an attention-getter in imperative form, and virtually never in any other way. Although there was some variety among children, within a given child each matrix verb was used in only one or two ways throughout its early use (sometimes lasting for 1–2 years). It is also important that across children virtually all of the epistemic matrix verbs were used almost exclusively in first-person as in *I think . . .*, *I know . . .*, *I bet . . .*, etc. (or sometimes in second-person as in *Do you know . . . ?* or *Do you mean . . . ?*) but almost never in third person. In contrast, all the verbs functioning as attention-getters were used almost exclusively as imperatives as in *See . . .*, *Look . . .*, *Watch . . .*, etc., and virtually never in first or third person. Also, these complex sentences:

- almost never had complementisers (i.e., not *I think that I saw one*, but rather *I think I saw one*)
- were almost always in the present tense (98–99% of the time)
- virtually never contained negatives

Together, all these facts point to the proposition that these early complex sentences are not abstract sentence embeddings, as they are treated by many formal theories, but rather they are pastiches of well-learned linguistic patterns — specifically, a simple sentence-level structure (perhaps item-based, perhaps more general) juxtaposed with a specific epistemic or attention-getting expression such as *I think*, *You mean*, or *See*.

CONCLUSION

In some ways, we may formulate the theoretical choice in front of us as a methodological choice between using formal grammars and the phenomena they generate or using more richly psychological approaches to children's language that attempt to describe it in its own terms. There is no question that child language may be described in the abstract syntactic categories of a formal grammar; many things can be. For example, generative grammars have been applied not just to language but also to music (Jackendoff, 1983), to genetics (Collado-Vides, 1991), and to dreaming (Foulkes, 1978). But the question is whether formal grammars are psychologically real for young children. The most straightforward reading of the evidence of child language acquisition is that abstract, formal, adult-like, syntactic analyses may be useful heuristics for some researchers, but they are not psychologically real entities that generate children's language (see Slobin, 1985, 1997).

Instead, I believe that children's early language acquisition is an integral part of their cognitive and social-communicative development in general, and that we may therefore account for the largest part of language acquisition via three main processes (see Tomasello & Brooks, 1999, for elaboration):

- *Cultural (Imitative) Learning.* Quite simply, children hear individual pieces of language (concrete items and structures) and imitate them. These concrete pieces of language are not just words, as in most traditional accounts, but also linguistic constructions with differing types and amounts of linguistic complexity.
- *Analogy and Abstraction.* After some critical mass of linguistic items and structures of a particular type have been learned, children begin to use their own cognitive skills to construct for themselves, from patterns in the language they hear around them, linguistic categories, schemas and, in general, the kinds of abstract linguistic constructions on which mature linguistic competence is based. The children do this in a piecemeal fashion for different linguistic items and structures. Our research is beginning to discover some of the specifics in how this is done. For example, for English-speaking children an abstract category of noun is constructed quite early, but sentence-level argument structure constructions are found only much later.
- *Structure Combining.* At all points along the way children combine linguistic items and structures in creative ways. This does not just mean combining words, but many different kinds of linguistic items and structures of different levels complexity and abstraction as children attempt to communicate with others.

Thanks to the theoretical advances made by functional and cognitive linguistics, especially construction grammar, we now know that adults' language, like children's language, is also made up of a motley collection of linguistic constructions of all shapes and sizes and degrees of abstractness. The process of language acquisition is thus best seen as continuous throughout the lifespan: it is the process by which human beings acquire the productive use of the linguistic constructions used by those around them, generalise the use of these constructions in novel ways, and combine these constructions creatively in discourse interactions with others.

REFERENCES

Akhtar, N. (1999). Acquiring basic word order: Evidence for data-driven learning of syntactic structure. *Journal of Child Language, 26,* 339–356.

Akhtar, N., & Tomasello, M. (1997). Young children's productivity with word order and verb morphology. *Developmental Psychology, 33,* 952–965.

Berko, J. (1958). The child's learning of English morphology. *Word, 14,* 150–77.

Berman, R. (1982). Verb-pattern alternation: the interface of morphology, syntax, and semantics in Hebrew child language. *Journal of Child Language, 9,* 169–91.

Berman, R. (1993). Marking verb transitivity in Hebrew-speaking children. *Journal of Child Language, 20,* 641–670.

Berman, R.A., & Armon-Lotem, S. (1995). How grammatical are early verbs? Paper presented at the *Colloque International de Besançon sur l'Acquisition de la Syntaxe.* Besançon, France: November, 1995.

Bloom, L. (1992). *Language development from two to three.* Cambridge: Cambridge University Press.

Borer, H., & Wexler, K. (1992). Bi-unique relations and the maturation of grammatical principles. *Natural language and linguistic theory, 10,* 147–87.

Bowerman, M. (1982). Reorganizational processes in lexical and syntactic development. In L. Gleitman & E. Wanner (Eds), *Language acquisition: The state of the art* (pp. 231–259). Cambridge: Cambridge University Press.

Bowerman, M. (1988). The "no negative evidence" problem: How do children avoid constructing an overgeneral grammar? In J.A. Hawkins (Ed.), *Explaining language universals* (pp. 73–101). Oxford: Basil Blackwell.

Braine, M.D.S. (1971). On two types of models of the internalization of grammars. In D.I. Slobin (Ed.), *The ontogenesis of grammar* (pp. 153–186). New York: Academic Press.

Braine, M. (1976). Children's first word combinations. *Monographs of the Society for Research in Child Development, 41*, no. 1.

Brooks, P., & Tomasello, M. (1999). Young children learn to produce passives with nonce verbs. *Developmental Psychology, 35*, 29–44.

Brown, R. (1973). *A first language: The early stages.* Cambridge, MA: Harvard University Press.

Childers, J., & Tomasello, M. (submitted). Spanish-speaking children's syntactic productivity with novel verbs.

Collado-Vides, J. (1991). A syntactic representation of the units of genetic information. *Journal of Theoretical Biology, 148*, 401–429.

DeVilliers, J., & DeVilliers, P. (1973). Development of the use of word order in comprehension. *Journal of Psycholinguistic Research, 2*, 331–341.

Diessel, H., & Tomasello, M. (1999). *Why complement clauses do not include a* that-*complementizer in early child language.* Paper presented to the Berkeley Linguistics Society.

Dodson, K., & Tomasello, M. (1998). Acquiring the transitive construction in English: The role of animacy and pronouns. *Journal of Child Language, 25*, 555–574.

Fillmore, C., Kaye, P., & O'Conner, M. (1988). Regularity and idiomaticity in grammatical constructions: The case of let alone. *Language, 64*, 501–38.

Foulkes, D. (1978). *A grammar of dreams.* New York: Basic Books.

Gentner, D., & Markman, A. (1997). Structure mapping in analogy and similarity. *American Psychologist, 52*, 45–56.

Goldberg, A. (1995). *Constructions: A construction grammar approach to argument structure.* Chicago: University of Chicago Press.

Hyams, N. (1994). Non-discreteness and variation in child language: Implications for principle and parameter models of language acquisition. In Y. Levy (Ed.), *Other children, other languages* (pp. 11–40). Hillsdale, NJ: Lawrence Erlbaum Associates Inc.

Ingham, R. (1993). Critical influences on the acquisition of verb transitivity. In D. Messer (Ed.), *Critical influences on child language acquisition and development* (pp. 45–81). London: Macmillan.

Jackendoff, R. (1983). *A generative theory of tonal music.* Cambridge, MA: MIT Press.

Lakoff, G. (1987). *Women, fire, and dangerous things: What categories reveal about the mind.* Chicago: University of Chicago Press.

Langacker, R. (1987). *Foundations of cognitive grammar, Volume 1.* Stanford, CA: Stanford University Press.

Langacker, R. (1991). *Foundations of cognitive grammar, Volume 2.* Stanford, CA: Stanford University Press.

Leonard, L., Eyer, J., Bedore, C., & Grela, B. (1997). Three accounts of the grammatical morpheme difficulties of English-speaking children with SLI. *Journal of Speech, Language, and Hearing Research, 40*, 741–753.

Lewis, L., & Tomasello, M. (in preparation). Young children's productivity with imperative and indicative constructions.

Lieven, E., Pine, J., & Baldwin, G. (1997). Lexically-based learning and early grammatical development. *Journal of Child Language, 24*, 187–220.

MacWhinney, B., & Snow, C. (1990). The child language data exchange system: An update. *Journal of Child Language, 17*, 457–472.

Maratsos, M., Gudeman, R., Gerard-Ngo, P., & DeHart, G. (1987). A study in novel word learning: The productivity of the causative. In B. MacWhinney (Ed.), *Mechanisms of language acquisition* (pp. 89–114). Hillsdale, NJ: Lawrence Erlbaum Associates Inc.

Olguin, R., & Tomasello, M. (1993). Twenty-five month old children do not have a grammatical category of verb. *Cognitive Development, 8*, 245–272.

Pine, J., & Lieven, E. (1993). Reanalysing rote-learned phrases: Individual differences in the transition to multi-word speech. *Journal of Child Language, 20*, 551–571.

Pine, J., & Lieven, E. (1997). Slot and frame patterns in the development of the determiner category. *Applied Psycholinguistics, 18*, 123–138.

Pine, J., Lieven, E., & Rowland, G. (1998). Comparing different models of the development of the English verb category. *Linguistics, 36*, 4–40.

Pinker, S. (1989). *Learnability and cognition: The acquisition of verb-argument structure.* Cambridge, MA: Harvard University Press.

Pinker, S. (1994). *The language instinct: How the mind creates language.* New York: Morrow.

Pinker, S., Lebeaux, D.S., & Frost, L.A. (1987). Productivity and constraints in the acquisition of the passive. *Cognition, 26*, 195–267.

Pizutto, E., & Caselli, C. (1992). The acquisition of Italian morphology. *Journal of Child Language, 19*, 491–557.

Pizutto, E., & Caselli, C. (1994). The acquisition of Italian verb morphology in a cross-linguistic perspective. In Y. Levy (Ed.), *Other children, other languages* (pp. 137–188). Hillsdale, NJ: Lawrence Erlbaum Associates Inc.

Rice, M. (1998). (Ed.) *Toward a genetics of language.* Mahwah, NJ: Lawrence Erlbaum Associates Inc.

Rizzi, L. (1994). Early null subjects and root null subjects. In T. Hoekstra & B. Schwartz (Eds.), *Language acquisition studies in generative grammar* (pp. 151–176). Amsterdam: John Benjamins.

Rubino, R., & Pine, J. (1998). Subject-verb agrement in Brazilian Portuguese: What low error rates hide. *Journal of Child Language, 25*, 35–60.

Slobin, D. (1985). Crosslinguistic evidence for the language-making capacity. In D.I. Slobin (Ed.), *The crosslinguistic study of language acquisition, Volume 2: Theoretical issues* (pp. 1157–1256). Hillsdale, NJ: Lawrence Erlbaum Associates Inc.

Slobin, D. (1997). Why are grammaticizable notions special? — A reanalysis and a challenge to learning theory. In D.I. Slobin (Ed.), *The crosslinguistic study of language acquisition, Volume 5* (pp. 265–323). Hillsdale, NJ: Lawrence Erlbaum Associates Inc.

Tomasello, M. (1992). *First verbs: A case study in early grammatical development.* Cambridge: Cambridge University Press.

Tomasello, M. (1995). Language is not an instinct. *Cognitive Development, 10*, 131–156.

Tomasello, M. (1998a). (Ed.) *The new psychology of language: Cognitive and functional approaches.* Mahwah, NJ: Lawrence Erlbaum Associates Inc.

Tomasello, M. (1998b). The return of constructions. *Journal of Child Language, 25*, 431–488.

Tomasello, M., Akhtar, N., Dodson, K., & Rekau, L. (1997). Differential productivity in young children's use of nouns and verbs. *Journal of Child Language, 24*, 373–87.

Tomasello, M., & Brooks, P. (1998). Young children's earliest transitive and intransitive constructions. *Cognitive Linguistics, 9*, 375–395.

Tomasello, M., & Brooks, P. (1999). Early syntactic development. In M. Barrett (Ed.), *The development of language.* Hove, UK: Psychology Press.

Tomasello, M., Kruger, A., & Ratner, H. (1993). Cultural learning. *Behavioral and Brain Sciences, 16*, 495–511.

Tomasello, M., & Olguin, R. (1993). Twenty-three-month-old children have a grammatical category of noun. *Cognitive Development, 8*, 451–464.

2

Grammatical symptoms of specific language impairment

Mabel L. Rice

This chapter lays out a programme of investigation aimed at the identification of a clinical grammatical marker for the condition of Specific Language Impairment (SLI) in children (and adults), beginning with a description of the theoretical framework and predictions, followed by an overview of available evidence from longitudinal studies of affected and control children and from family history data that indicate a pattern of familiality (as would be expected for an inherited condition). It is argued that a primary benefit from this line of inquiry is that it helps further our understanding of "immature" language that may or may not be "outgrown" and possible causes of grammatical limitations. The chapter concludes with a discussion of the clinical implications of the grammatical marker and the promise of the marker for investigations of the etiology of SLI.

INTRODUCTION

A long-standing issue for researchers and clinicians is the question of how to identify young children with language impairments. Children with Specific Language Impairment (SLI) pose particular challenges because they do not show other developmental delays, and their immature language could be attributed to a simple delay in onset which they will subsequently "outgrow".

At the same time, it has long been observed that children with SLI are very late in acquiring grammatical morphemes, a characteristic symptom thought to be a hallmark of the condition (cf. Bishop, 1997; Leonard, 1998). Although this observation has powerful clinical implications, only recently have we come to appreciate the full import of the grammatical symptoms of SLI for identification purposes.

In addition to the obvious clinical implications, there is strong interest among researchers in the development of a clinical marker of the condition of SLI that will accurately identify affected children, for the purpose of studying possible inherited contributions to the condition. Accurate and precise specification of the clinical symptoms of language impairment is essential for investigations of genetic factors, as well as for increasing our understanding of the nature of the language impairment and its relationship to other domains of competence, such as nonverbal intelligence.

This chapter provides an overview of the rationale, outcomes, and conclusions of a programme of research in which the grammatical symptoms of SLI are investigated as a clinical marker of the condition in young children. The content is laid out in the following sequence. The chapter begins with a discussion of what constitutes a clinical marker and how it differs from conventional standardised test assessment. It is argued that the two approaches are complementary and both are essential for advancing our knowledge of language impairments in children. At the same time, grammatical symptoms offer a uniquely informative domain in which to focus our attention, for reasons of interpretive power as well as empirical advantages not available with conventional psychometric measurements. The basis for the interest in grammatical morphology is laid out, with a description of the Optional Infinitive stage of normative development of English-speaking children, and a discussion of the predictions to be evaluated with children with SLI. In the following section, a summary of recent empirical evidence is provided, including the long-term outcomes of preschool children with SLI in the domain of morphology, with illustrative growth curves and comparison to control children. Evidence of change over time for both production and grammaticality judgement tasks, it is argued, strongly points toward a problem in highly specified underlying grammatical representations. Etiological information is then reported in the form of positive evidence of familiality, showing that the children with grammatical symptomology are more likely than control children to have family members with positive histories of speech/language impairment. The concluding section argues that the evidence

is very promising for the existence of a clinical grammatical marker which differentiates affected from unaffected children. Furthermore, it is a marker that can be interpreted in terms of the development of language in unaffected children and progress toward an adult grammar. In effect, it helps further our understanding of "immature" language that may or may not be "outgrown", and possible causes of grammatical limitations. The final section discusses the clinical implications for the identification of affected children, possible treatment options, and the promise of a clinical grammatical marker for investigations of the etiology of SLI.

THE PSYCHOMETRIC APPROACH OF OMNIBUS LANGUAGE TESTS

Let us begin with an examination of the conventional means of assessment via traditional standardised omnibus tests, an approach referred to here as "psychometric" because of the underlying assumptions. A fundamental construct is the idea of variation across children in their language abilities. Virtually all of the currently available standardised language tests assume, for a given age, an underlying normal distribution of children on a general language dimension. This is based on the well-known bell-shaped curve (see Fig. 2.1). In this distribution, individuals are scattered along a range of performance levels such that a few people display very high values (along the right-hand side of the scale), and a few people exhibit very low values (along the left-hand side), and most (about 66%) score in the middle. Furthermore, the bell-shaped curve has well-known distributional properties, such that 16% of the people will score 1 SD or more below the mean; 2% will score 2 or more SD below the mean. For example, if we were to examine the size of children's vocabularies, say all 6-year-olds, we could expect that a few children would have a large number of words in their vocabularies, a few would have very few words, and most children would have a moderate number of words.

FIGURE 2.1

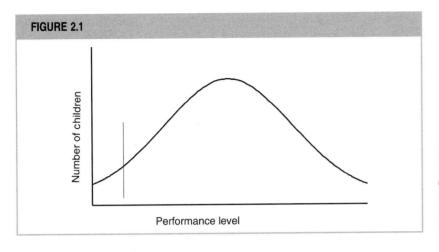

Bell shaped curve.
(Rice, 1998). Copyright
© 1998 American
Speech–Language–
Hearing Association.
Reprinted with permission.

A related, and very important, notion is that children with SLI are those who fall at the bottom end of the normal distribution of language competence. This is a pervasive assumption, articulated most cogently by Leonard (1991, 1998). In essential ways, the low-normal interpretation views the problem as one of quantity rather than quality, as one where the affected child has less of a general language aptitude than that of unaffected children of the same development level (indexed by chronological age).

Positive uses of the psychometric approach

The psychometric approach has been, and will continue to be, a vitally important means of assessing and identifying children with language impairments. Let me provide two examples of recent, highly significant applications. One example is the utilisation of standardised tests for recent epidemiological investigations that report updated prevalence figures for the condition of SLI. Tomblin et al. (1997) carried out a state-of-the-art study establishing that about 7% of kindergarten children show this condition. This estimate is based on a psychometric definition of two or more of five composite language scores from the Test of Language Development–2 Primary (TOLD–2:P, Newcomer & Hammill, 1988; supplemented by a spontaneous sample narrative task) at least 1.25 SD below the mean expected

for a child's age group (i.e. the 10th percentile or lower). The cut-off level was previously found to be compatible with clinical practices (Tomblin, Records, & Zhang, 1996). For the SLI diagnosis, the children also met conventional exclusionary criteria (i.e. performed within normal range on a nonverbal intelligence assessment and did not show other signs of neurological impairments, hearing loss, or clinical sociobehavioural impairments). A follow-up study by Shriberg, Tomblin, and McSweeny (1999) reported that in the overall population of 5-year-old children sampled, the co-occurrence of speech and language impairments was estimated as less than 2%; for the children with SLI, speech disorders were evident in approximately 5–8% of the children. So the psychometric method reveals that the prevalence of SLI in a 5-year-old sample of children is 7% and only about 5–8% of the children with language impairments showed clinically significant speech disorders.

A second example of the usefulness of psychometric methods is an investigation of the outcomes of childhood speech/language impairments for young adults. A recent study by Johnson et al. (1999) used a clinical criterion of performance below 1 SD on two language tests, the Peabody Picture Vocabulary Test–Revised (Dunn & Dunn, 1981) and the Test of Adolescent Language–3 (TOAL–3; Hammill, Brown, Larsen, & Wiederhold, 1994). Children were identified as language impaired if they scored below the criterion level on both tests, or if they scored more than 2 SD below the local mean on any TOAL–3 subtest. As with Tomblin et al. (1996), Johnson et al. (1999) compared their psychometric criteria to practitioner ratings, which led to a somewhat more conservative criterion. The prevalence estimate of SLI for their sample at age 5 years was 10.5% using the experimental criteria; when adjusted by practitioner ratings, it dropped to 6.7%, very similar to that of Tomblin et al. (1997). A second major finding was that the scores for the children with language impairment at age 5, relative to age expectations, were very similar to their age-referenced scores at age 18–20 years. In other words, the existence of a language impairment in a young child is highly prognostic of a relatively low level of language performance when that child grows to become a young adult. This is modulated by the finding that outcomes were somewhat more favourable for individuals with SLI than for individuals with concomitant sensory, structural, neurological or cognitive deficits.

These examples show that the use of psychometric methods, referenced to a normative distribution, allows us to determine such important facts as the prevalence of SLI (about 7% in 5-year-old children), the likelihood of concomitant speech and language impairment (less than 2% in the general population of 5-year-olds), and the long-term prognosis (individuals are likely to retain their relatively poor performance on language assessment compared to unaffected individuals).

Limitations of the omnibus test/psychometric approach

These advantages notwithstanding, there are important limitations of the assumption of a normal distribution. Let me enumerate the limitations most relevant to this discussion. First, there is no intrinsic criterion for where to draw the line between "normal" and "affected", shown on the left in Fig. 2.1. Instead, a certain arbitrariness is inevitable. Although investigators take care to determine the cut-off points as judiciously as possible, there remains considerable uncertainty as to the "best" place to draw the boundary

between "affected" and "unaffected" (cf. Johnson et al., 1999; Tomblin et al., 1997). To return to the vocabulary example: how can we know who does not know enough words? Who is "impaired" in vocabulary development? Without an obvious way to separate "normal" and "affected", we may falsely identify as affected those children who are not affected, or we may falsely identify children as unaffected who really have an underlying language deficit. If the line is drawn at the 10th percentile, or at 1 SD below the age mean, a child may fall a point or two on either side of the line, with a few points determining "affectedness".

A second limitation is that there is no obvious way to interpret the actual test score in terms of particular linguistic content. Because the tests are constructed according to a general description of language (e.g. "expressive" vs. "receptive" modes, or "vocabulary" vs. "grammatical morphemes"), usually there are no clear indications of how to translate a child's score into particular linguistic competencies that may or may not be affected. In other words, one cannot know what to teach by knowing a child's standardised test score.

A third limitation is that it is not possible to interpret a child's performance relative to the expected adult model of language, or a child's level of progress toward that level. There is no way to determine if a child with a standard score of 85 is mostly in line with an adult grammar or mostly far away. With regard to marking age-related progress toward a full language competence, "language age" scores are sometimes reported. These are the mean scores for a particular age group. Therefore, a 5-year-old child whose score is the same as the average for children of 3 years of age is said to have a "language age" of 3 years. But the meaning of this is unclear. There is no way to know if the 5-year-old missed the same items as the 3-year-olds. One must look very closely to determine whether or not a gain of a few items would raise a child's "language age" from 3 to 4 years. The point here is that, although the notion of a normal distribution is a vitally important one for the identification of young children with language impairments, it has important limitations as it is implemented in omnibus language tests.

A GRAMMATICAL MARKER APPROACH

Distributional properties

By their very nature, fundamental grammatical rules do not follow a normal distribution across individuals. For example, consider the rule for plurals: regular nouns that refer to more than one must be marked with -s to denote plurality. Under this rule, a phrase like (1) *these ball is ungrammatical (here I will follow the convention that utterances marked with an * are ungrammatical). It is not something that speakers can choose to ignore, or show only partial knowledge of. It is obligatory. In like fashion, speakers must insert a form of "be" in a sentence where a copula is required (e.g. (2) She is walking, vs. (3) *she walking). Likewise, the third person singular -s morpheme is required in contexts such as (4) she walks outside; (5) *she walk outside is ungrammatical in Standard English. Other examples are: (6) yesterday she walked outside; (7) *yesterday she walk outside; (8) Does she like to walk? (9) *She like to walk? Grammatical properties such as these are understood by people who know English. In order to work as a conventional language, the community of users know these properties

and follow them. Grammar-users are not distributed as in a bell curve; instead they are all bunched at the top end of the distribution, because they know these grammatical principles.

Now let us consider children. It is well known that by the time they go to kindergarten, children can be expected to know the properties of grammar illustrated above (i.e. rules for plurals, the use of "be" forms, regular third person singular -s, regular past tense -ed, auxiliary "do"). But children do not show this knowledge at the outset of their language, in their first simple sentences. So we know children differ from adults, and over time they come to be like adults in their use of these grammatical properties. In order to identify children with language impairments, we must find those children who are not on their way to the adult grammar in the expected time line.

In the areas of grammatical morphology illustrated above, most 5-year-old children are very much like adults. Figure 2.2 illustrates an hypothesised distribution of 5-year-old children, showing that most of them are at the upper levels of adult-like performance. Consider the possibility that children with language impairments do not know this part of the grammar by 5 years of age. If so, they would cluster at the bottom of the distribution, as shown by the cluster at the left of Fig. 2.2, in the broken line. With these

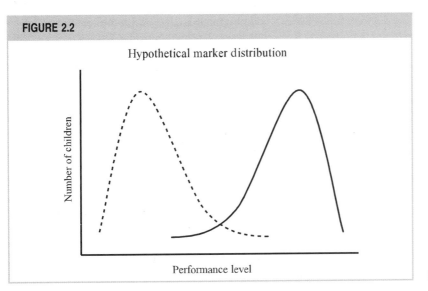

FIGURE 2.2

Hypothetical marker distribution

Number of children

Performance level

Bimodal distribution.

distributional properties, grammatical limitations would offer distinct advantages for the identification of affected individuals, because individuals are expected to know the grammatical rules and to use them as an obligatory feature of a clause. If individuals apply the rules only some of the time, as if they were optional, those individuals would clearly differ from the expected levels of performance.

Clinical characteristics of a grammatical marker

A grammatical marker that followed the distributional properties of Fig. 2.2 (a bimodal distribution) instead of Fig. 2.1 (a normal, bell-shaped distribution), could have the following properties:

1. *By a certain age, grammatical markers would show little variation across unaffected children.* That is, children would show the adult grammar, or a close approximation of the adult grammar. They would know that certain grammatical morphemes are obligatory. They would cluster at the upper ends of the distribution.[1]

2. *Affected children would perform below the unaffected children.* They would cluster at the lower ends of the distribution.

3. Because of this bimodal distribution of children, *grammatical markers would have high levels of sensitivity and specificity.* Sensitivity is the rate of identifying true cases of affectedness. Specificity is the rate of identifying true cases of unaffectedness. Just as we would want to have cancer testing with methods of high specificity and selectivity, we would prefer clinical methods with high accuracy for identifying true cases of language impairment that do not falsely identify unaffected children as having a language impairment.

4. *The content of assessment would be meaningful for interpretation of a child's language deficits.* It would be possible to see which grammatical knowledge was affected, which could in turn be used to

plan intervention, to know what language competencies to teach.

5. The *child's performance would be interpretable in terms of the adult grammar.* It would be possible to see which gaps persisted as a child moved toward full grammatical competence.

6. *Grammatical markers could persist over time.* Long-standing grammatical differences would increase the likelihood that children would be identified, because they could be detected at different age levels.

A search for grammatical markers of SLI: An extended optional infinitive

In the programme of research summarised here, investigation has targeted this question: *Can we identify children with SLI because they are extremely slow in acquiring a part of the grammar that unaffected children are also slow in acquiring?* Wexler (1994, 1996) identified tense-marking as a part of the grammar that is relatively slow to emerge in unaffected young English-speaking children. This period is known as an *Optional Infinitive* stage. This stage is interesting because new models of the adult grammar, such as Chomsky (1995), focus on how this part of the grammatical system is crucial for the formulation of grammatical sentences, across many languages. So there is a direct link between models of the adult grammar and children's grammar, which shows us which grammatical morphemes are likely to be affected and which ones are likely to be unaffected. One consequence is that we do not expect a pervasive grammatical limitation, but instead a constrained deficit. The verbal morphemes of interest are those illustrated above, in examples 2–9 (i.e. past tense, 3rd person singular -*s*, "be", and "do"). For this set of morphemes, our prediction is that, as shown above, the children can be expected to sometimes use them and sometimes omit them. We expect younger unaffected children to do this, but to move out of this immature grammar faster than the children with SLI, who seem to get stuck with an immature grammar for an extended time. Therefore, we call it an *Extended Optional Infinitive (EOI)* stage.

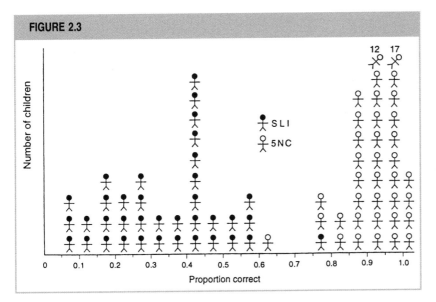

FIGURE 2.3

Distribution of individual children's performance on a composite TNS marking score: SLI and age controls. (Rice, 1998). Copyright © 1998 American Speech–Language–Hearing Association. Reprinted with permission.

Findings

An important initial finding is that children with SLI have much lower levels of performance on tense-marking morphemes than do control children. Figure 2.3 shows the performance of two groups of 5-year-old children, one group of 37 children identified as expressive/receptive SLI, and a control group of 45 children of the same age (cf. Rice & Wexler, 1996a). The measure is the percentage correct for the obligatory use of the tense-marking morphemes (indexed here by a composite measure, summed across the different morphemes). Clearly, the SLI group falls below the 60% accuracy level, whereas the control children are at 80% or better. Only one child in each of the two groups moved across the border area. If the cut-off is set for 80%, 97% of the true cases are identified (sensitivity) and 98% of the true non-cases are identified (specificity). These are very encouraging findings, suggesting that it may be possible to identify young children with language impairments on the basis of certain grammatical morphemes.

We just completed the first longitudinal study of young children with SLI and control children, for the age range of 3–8 years, in this area of the grammar. Longitudinal evidence shows that the

children with SLI remain behind their control groups throughout the period sampled, when they were 5 to 8 years of age. Figure 2.4 shows this pattern (cf. Rice, Wexler, & Hershberger, 1998). In this figure, the line on the lower left, beginning at 3 years and going to 8 years shows the growth in tense-marking for young unaffected children (N = 20), at the same mean length of utterance (MLU) as the SLI group (N = 21) at the beginning of the study. We can see that the younger control group reaches adult-like levels somewhere between 4 and 4.5 years. The consistency of performance levels across age levels is shown in the top line on the right, which is the unaffected age peers (N = 23) of the SLI group. These children maintain adult-like performance once they get to that level. On the other hand, the SLI group, the lower right curve, is lower than the control children throughout the time of the study, and they continue to be lower at age 8 years. Although the unaffected children have been at adult levels for years, the children with SLI continue to fall behind even in elementary school. There is no evidence that they "outgrow" their problem in this domain. Formal statistical analyses show that the pattern of growth is similar for the SLI group and the younger unaffected children, but the SLI group does not "catch up" with their peers

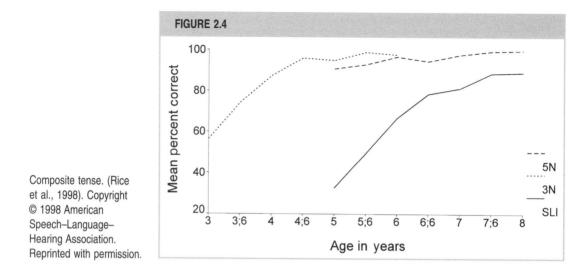

FIGURE 2.4

Composite tense. (Rice et al., 1998). Copyright © 1998 American Speech–Language–Hearing Association. Reprinted with permission.

in the age range studied (cf. Rice, Wexler, & Hershberger, 1998).

Further analyses addressed the question of what factors may predict the growth curves in the tense-marking morphemes. Four predictors, which were measured at the first round of data collection, were evaluated. A child's mother's education was of interest because mother's education is known to be associated with the amount of talking to children (cf. Hart & Risley, 1995; Hoff-Ginsberg, 1998; Wells, 1985), which in turn is predictive of children's vocabulary development (cf. Hoff-Ginsberg, 1998; Huttenlocher, Haight, Bryk, Seltzer, & Lyons, 1991). Although there was reason to expect that maternal education levels would positively predict grammatical development, there was also reason to question this expectation. In a separate sample of children who were followed from birth and assessed at age 4 years on their past-tense morphology, Rice, Spitz, and O'Brien (1999) found that maternal education did not predict performance on the tense measure although it was associated with vocabulary performance on the Peabody Picture Vocabulary Test-Revised (PPVT-R; Dunn & Dunn, 1981). The PPVT-R was also evaluated as a predictor of grammatical growth in Rice, Wexler, and Hershberger (1998), along with an estimate of the children's nonverbal intelligence (scores from the Columbia Mental Maturity

Scales; Burgemeister, Blum, & Lorge, 1972) and the child's mean length of utterance (MLU).

The result of the predictor analyses showed that growth in this linguistic domain is not predicted by a child's mother's education, a child's initial receptive vocabulary, or performance on nonverbal intelligence tests. In other words, a child's grammatical growth did not depend on initial vocabulary scores or nonverbal intelligence score, or the education levels of his or her mother. A weak predictor (1% of the variance) was a child's initial MLU. Mostly, however, grammatical growth was not related to these predictors. These conclusions held for the children with SLI as well as the control children.

It is important to know that not all grammatical morphemes are affected in this way. For example, the acquisition of regular plural -s (as in "cats") is relatively unaffected, even though it is phonetically very similar to the third person -s verbal morpheme. Figure 2.5 shows the same age period for performance on plurals, where it is clear that this morpheme is quite stable during this time, and very near adult-like levels of performance, even for the SLI group. Thus, we can see that the problem is not a general one of being unable to acquire grammatical rules, nor is it likely that the children cannot perceive the difference in morphemes.

FIGURE 2.5

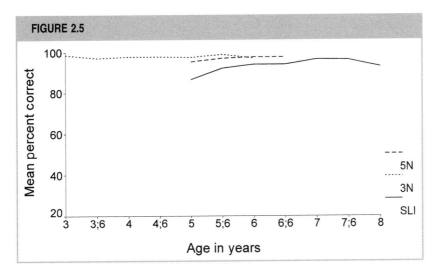

Regular -s plurals. (Rice et al., 1998). Copyright © 1998 American Speech–Language–Hearing Association. Reprinted with permission.

In the outcomes summarised so far, all the measures have required children to produce the target morphemes. Measures drawn from spontaneous samples and from experimental production probes show the same effect (cf. Rice, Wexler, & Cleave, 1995; Rice, Wexler, & Hershberger, 1998). If the limited production performance is attributable to underlying grammatical representations, it should be evident in children's understanding of the forms as well as their productions. In order to evaluate this corollary of the EOI theory, a set of grammaticality judgement tasks was developed, which evaluated children's judgements of sentences such as items 2–7 above.[2] Essentially, we expected that the children with SLI who showed an EOI grammar would accept both the grammatical and the ungrammatical items. That is to say that children's judgements would parallel their productions, such that they would accept as grammatical the kinds of sentences they were likely to produce. A further implication addresses grammatical errors that children are unlikely to produce, such as "*He am hurt". If children's judgements are guided by their underlying grammatical representations, and their representations, as predicted by the EOI model, do not allow such grammatical formulations, then they should regard these errors as ungrammatical, even though the grammatical errors are embedded in the middle of the sentence, in an unstressed position.

In order to evaluate their grammaticality judgements, the same children who participated in the longitudinal study were assessed, beginning at the third round of data collection, when the younger control group was 4 years of age and the SLI group and age control group were 6 years of age, and continuing for five subsequent rounds of testing, for a full two years of assessment. The study is reported in Rice, Wexler, and Redmond (1999). Figure 2.6 shows the outcomes for the children's judgements of the utterances depicted in items 2–7 above, as indexed by an A′ value which can be roughly interpreted as a percent correct in detecting grammatical versus ungrammatical sentences in which tense-marking is dropped, adjusted for children's bias to say that a response is "good". Note that this figure looks much like Fig. 2.4, showing the outcomes of composite tense-marking. The children with SLI perform at lower levels than the control groups throughout. At the same time that they are likely to accept utterances such as "*she walking", they are less likely to accept other grammatical violations, such as "*he is cough", or "*he am hurt". This is shown in Fig. 2.7, for the SLI group, where the continuous line on the bottom is for utterances such as 2–7 above, the small dotted line is for utterances with subject-verb agreement errors such as "*he am hurt", and the large dotted line is for utterances with dropped progressive -ing, such as "*he

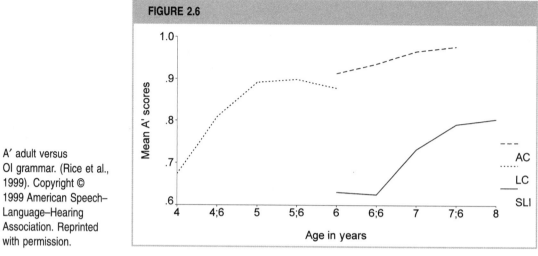

FIGURE 2.6

A′ adult versus OI grammar. (Rice et al., 1999). Copyright © 1999 American Speech–Language–Hearing Association. Reprinted with permission.

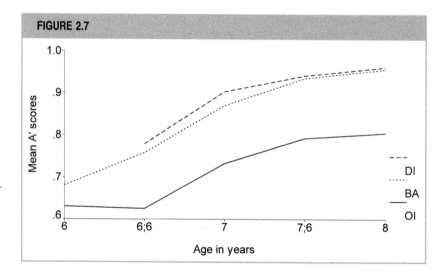

FIGURE 2.7

A′ for grammar types OI, BA, and DI for the SLI group. (Rice et al., 1999). Copyright © 1999 American Speech–Language–Hearing Association. Reprinted with permission.

is cough". The conclusion is that the protracted period of limited tense-marking for children with SLI is evident in grammaticality judgements as well as their productions. Further, just as their productions do not show affectedness for all morphology, their grammaticality judgements do not show uniform limitations across all kinds of grammatical violations.

As with the production data for the growth of tense-markers, there is reason to wonder about which factors predict change in grammaticality judgements over time. To investigate the predic-

tors of the observed grammaticality judgement growth curves, Rice, Wexler, and Redmond (1999) replicated the analyses of Rice, Wexler, and Hershberger (1998), in which the predictors were maternal education, nonverbal intelligence, receptive vocabulary, and MLU. The outcomes showed strong replication of the modelling for the tense-marker growth curves: maternal education was not a predictor, nor were any of the other variables.

To summarise the outcomes of the programme of investigation described here, let us return to the clinical characteristics of a grammatical marker. As is shown by the findings, in a particular area of the grammar with known properties in the adult grammar (i.e. that of tense-marking and tense-related syntactic knowledge), early school-age children affected with SLI perform below unaffected peers, even below children two years younger. In effect, the findings show that the unaffected children cluster at the top levels of performance, as expected, whereas the affected children cluster at the low levels of performance. This leads to high levels of sensitivity and specificity, and the ability to identify affected children while being unlikely to falsely identify unaffected children. In this domain, we can see rather directly the exact nature of the children's grammatical deficits and how their performance relates to the target adult grammar, and their progress toward that level of performance. Furthermore, it is readily apparent that this narrowly defined deficit in their grammar can persist for a long time. A further property of a grammatical marker of SLI is that children's performance is not predicted by maternal education, nonverbal intelligence, or receptive vocabulary development. This fact points toward a relatively discrete linguistic marker of SLI, that grows independently of the environmental benefits attributed to maternal education, or the child's level of nonverbal intelligence, or the number of words understood.

It would be wrong to leave the impression that only tense-marking is to be expected as a grammatical consequence of an OI/EOI period. The general theory underlying this programme of investigation also assigns a strong role to tense and agreement marking in the assignment of case. In English this shows up as case-marking on personal pronouns. Wexler, Schütze, and Rice (1998) carried out a detailed analysis of case-marking in the same samples of children studied in the tense-marking studies reported above. The main finding is that case marking is linked with subject-verb agreement marking, which is apparently also vulnerable in the children with SLI and the younger controls. For example, the adult grammar expects nominative case marking on subjects, as in "he cries". Children sometimes say "him" instead of "he", and children with SLI are more likely to

make such case errors than are unaffected peers (Loeb & Leonard, 1991). Wexler et al. (1998), show that the likelihood of "him" as a subject is closely associated with whether or not the verb shows tense/agreement marking, such that "him cry" is much more likely than "him cries" or "he cry". Although the details of the interpretation further clarify the mechanisms for the tense/agreement marking, they go beyond the scope of this chapter. Because the more detailed model does not affect the generalisations laid out above, it will not be discussed further. The major point is that the properties of tense and agreement-marking are just now beginning to be more fully understood in adult languages. The OI/EOI model does not rule out the discovery of additional linked properties, nor does it rule out the subsequent discovery of grammatical markers unrelated to the OI/EOI stage. These matters remain for further inquiry.

ETIOLOGICAL CONSIDERATIONS

There is converging evidence that language impairments are heritable (cf. Rice, 1996). Early on, Rice and Wexler (1996b) argued that deficits in tense-marking, as a grammatical symptom of the condition of SLI, could be manifestations of underlying inherited language capacities that are less fully developed in individuals with SLI. If this is the case, then it would be expected that the families of children with grammatical symptoms of this sort would show a higher-than-expected occurrence of language impairments of this sort. Although there are a number of family studies that report a higher occurrence of affectedness if there is a member of the family known to have language impairments (cf. Rice, Haney, & Wexler, 1998; Tomblin, 1996), none of the previous studies documented that the target affected family member (the proband) had limited tense-marking ability. Rice, Haney, and Wexler (1998) investigated the families of the children studied in the longitudinal studies summarised above. In this sample, about 22% of the immediate family members (i.e. parents and siblings) of the probands reported a positive history of speech/language impairments compared to 7% of the control children's family members (a percentage virtually identical to the population estimate of Tomblin et al., 1997). So it is clear that one condition of a possibly inherited language impairment is met (i.e. that it is more likely to appear in families where someone is known to be language impaired).

Rice, Wexler, and Hershberger (1998) and Rice, Wexler, and Redmond (1999) interpret the grammatical symptoms as evidence of an immature stage of a relatively discrete inherited grammatical ability. Recall that a major index of environmental influence, that of maternal education, does not predict growth in tense-marking, for either the observed production outcomes or for the closely related grammatical judgement tasks, for either the affected children or the controls. This points away from environmental influences and toward nonenvironmental contributions. Recall also that children's vocabulary scores did not predict grammatical growth for the target structures, nor did nonverbal intelligence. Considered together, these outcomes point toward a differential weighting of etiological factors for vocabulary versus grammatical development, and a relative dissociation with nonverbal intelligence.

Studies of twins with SLI can shed some further light on this issue. Twin studies comparing identical (monozygotic) and nonidentical (dizygotic) twins have established that there is a much greater likelihood that both members of the twin pair will be affected if they share their genes (i.e. if they are identical twins; Bishop, North, & Donlan, 1995; Dale et al., 1998; Lewis & Thompson, 1992; Tomblin & Buckwalter, 1998). Dale et al. (1998) report that genetic contributions to early vocabulary development are much stronger for 2-year-old children at the bottom of the developmental distribution than for children in the upper ranges of performance, with a heritability estimate of 73% for the low-level group as compared to 25% for the higher level children. Conversely, the estimated environmental influence is 18% for the low group as compared to 69% for children with faster vocabulary growth. Dale et al. (1998) conclude that the children whose early vocabularies are small, compared to other children,

in effect have a qualitatively different status than the children with more robust vocabularies; they are not just at the low end of the normal distribution. In other words, the emergence of first vocabulary items may function much like a clinical marker in affected children, although whether or not vocabulary status retains this marker function for older children remains to be seen. It may be that first vocabulary acquisition serves as a valuable indicator of the fact that affected children's language emerges late relative to unaffected children. Rice and Wexler (1996b) likened the late emergence of language to a train that leaves the station late. What is not known is how the late emergence relates to the subsequent nature of the language impairment (or, to continue the train metaphor, the configuration of the carriages and linkages of the train). The causes of a late start-up could be linked to the immature emergence of certain grammatical markers, if we assume that what may be slow in unaffected children can be very slow in affected children.

Similar to the findings of Dale et al. (1998) with twins, Rice, Spitz, and O'Brien (1999) found, for their sample of sixty-nine 4-year-old children who were placed in an intensive care unit at birth, that the association of maternal education with the children's vocabulary scores was strong for children in the upper range of performance, but not in the lower levels of performance. Rice, Spitz, and O'Brien (1999) suggested that the more intensive levels of language stimulation provided by more educated mothers can be helpful for children with relatively intact language learning mechanisms but may not be sufficient to facilitate language growth in children at biological risk. At the same time, neither maternal education or the families' social economic status was associated with children's performance on a measure of past tense, regardless of the relative level of performance by the children. Interestingly, there was no evidence of familiality of speech/language or reading/learning impairments in the biological risk sample of Rice, Spitz, and O'Brien (1999). This is the first explicit evidence of the very reasonable assumption that biological risk and inherited risk can lead to similar symptoms from diverse etiologies.

Another twin study yielded findings congruent with the findings of Dale et al. (1998). Ganger, Pinker, Baker, and Chawla (1998) studied 76 pairs of twins, beginning at age 15 months. They reported that, in the range of normal development, vocabulary growth showed very small heritability whereas the appearance of first word combinations showed high heritability. They conclude that the sources of grammatical competencies required for first word combinations is more likely to be genetically influenced than is early vocabulary development.

What these findings suggest to me is the following. Although the picture is just beginning to come into focus, what seems to be emerging is the strong possibility that when we look carefully at different dimensions of language competency and patterns of growth, we will see etiological contributions that work differently according to the language domains investigated, and according to the relative levels of competency assessed. For both affected and unaffected children, the grammatical symptoms of tense-marking (i.e. the grammatical features of an OI/EOI stage), are not closely tied to environmental indices such as maternal education, even though environmental factors are implicated in vocabulary growth for unaffected children. At the same time, environmental enrichment may not be sufficient to accelerate limited vocabulary abilities in children with language impairments. This suggests that underlying inherited limitations may operate to depress the rate of language growth regardless of a child's environmental resources.

IMPLICATIONS FOR CLINICAL ASSESSMENT

As noted in the earlier section describing the psychometric approach of omnibus language tests, conventional language assessments — assuming an underlying normal distribution among the individuals who are assessed — yield vitally important information. Most simply put, there is no reason to discard these instruments. At the same time, there is high potential clinical value in the utilisation of relatively constrained clinical markers in the domain of morphosyntax. These advantages can be seen in the identification of affected children, possible treatment options, and the promise of a clinical grammatical marker for investigations of the etiology of SLI.

Identification of affected children

In the current omnibus language tests, the selection of grammatical morphemes to be investigated is atheoretical, seeming to follow a descriptive/structural approach. In the OI/EOI model, the focus is on a small set of grammatical markers that have a common linguistic function, that of marking tense and subject-verb agreement. It is in this domain, for this linguistic function, that we can see sharp delineation of affected from unaffected individuals. Note that the picture looks very different for the regular plural -s morpheme, which does not differentiate affected from unaffected individuals in the ages studied in the investigations reported here. For this reason, if a test of morphology intermingled items designed to test plurals with items to test tense marking, the ability to identify affected children would be greatly affected.

Instead of trying to capture all dimensions of language competency in an identification instrument, there would be great value in targeting those dimensions that accurately identify affected children (i.e. show high levels of sensitivity), as well as unaffected children (i.e. show high levels of specificity). This could greatly improve the "hit" rate in determining who to regard as exhibiting SLI and who to regard as developing in a typical manner.

Of equal importance is the fact that a grammatical marker can be interpreted rather directly in terms of the adult grammar, expected levels of progress toward the adult grammar, and slowed growth curves. In testing terminology, a grammatical marker has high content validity, because the content of the testing can be readily seen and interpreted. To return to Figs 2.4 and 2.6, it is clear that in the area of tense-marking there is an expected progression toward the adult grammar for children speaking English, and children with SLI can fall far behind in this progression. In fact, there is now reason to wonder if some of the affected children ever do make it to a fully adult-like grammatical system.

Although the findings reported here are highly coherent and encouraging, it is necessary to obtain further empirical evidence in order to know how pervasive the grammatical markers are for children with language impairments, and how these grammatical markers of the EOI stage do or do not appear in variants of English and in other languages. Studies relevant to this need are under way in a number of labs, with differing samples of children and differing varieties of English and other languages.

Of most importance, perhaps, is that field testing is under way for a new generation of assessment instruments designed to evaluate grammatical markers as a way of identifying children during the late preschool/early school-age period of time. Such instruments could prove to be a very useful part of a practitioner's clinical methods for the identification of affected youngsters. It will surely be helpful to know how a child stands relative to other children in the acquisition of a grammatical feature that is essential for the formulation of well-formed clauses.

Treatment options

Just as it is helpful to know how a child is progressing toward the adult grammar for the purpose of identification, it is helpful to know this for the purpose of planning for intervention. Incomplete knowledge of fundamental grammatical properties is an appropriate target for language intervention. This does not imply that a child should be immediately placed in an intervention programme consisting of rote grammar drills. In fact, there is probably good reason not to do that. Instead, a child's progress in this domain could be monitored for signs of an increased frequency of use of the target morphemes, which could be used as a guide for when to start intervention focused on the obligatory use of tense-marking morphemes.

Another vitally important implication for intervention is that there is strong reason to think in terms of the underlying linguistic function, that of tense-marking, that unifies a set of surface morphemes that have different surface properties and diverse grammatical properties. For example, a very important insight to be derived from the OI/EOI model is that the function of the finite forms of "be" and "do" in English is to mark tense and subject-verb agreement (where the forms of "be" vary according to person and number marking on the subject, i.e. "am", "is" and "are"). These forms have unique properties as copulas or auxiliaries, and at the same time share properties with the third person singular present-tense marker, -s, and past-tense morphology as well. These underlying similarities are important to recognise in the planning of intervention, given that the set of morphemes seems to cohere as children progress toward the adult grammar. The findings show that as children make gains in one of the target morphemes, they are likely to make gains in others as well. For this reason, it suggests that a practitioner would want to track development across the set of morphemes, and to train them as a related set.

Note that the morphemes do not share surface properties: "be" and "do" appear as individual syllable forms whereas past tense and third person singular present-tense forms appear as affixes on lexical verbs. This suggests that treatment approaches that are heavily dependent on manipulations of prosodic information or perceptual salience probably will not be a complete answer.

Further, notice that the marking of grammatical tense applies to present tense as well as to the more familiar past-tense affixation. In English, present-tense marking appears with forms of "be" copula and auxiliary and "do" auxiliary (in questions) and the third person singular -s. Although there is often a tendency in intervention materials to think only of past-tense marking when tense is discussed, it is important to recognise the need to mark present tense as well, even though it does not add much semantic information to the utterance because the present-tense marking is generally assumed.

A crucial element of the OI/EOI model is the notion of "finiteness" (cf. Rice & Wexler, 1996b, Wexler, 1996). "Finite" refers to verbs that show tense/agreement marking, and to the idea that such marking is restricted to certain sites in a clause. For example, in "she walked home", the verb "to walk" is finite, showing past tense. Note that in "she made the dog walk home", the verb "to walk" is nonfinite, which we can see by the following, "*she made the dog walked home". The reason this is crucial is that children with SLI may omit tense-marking forms, but they are very unlikely to mark finiteness in an unlicensed site (cf. Rice & Wexler, 1996a; Rice, Wexler, & Hershberger, 1998; Rice, Wexler, & Redmond, 1999). Practitioners can observe whether children follow the underlying licensing constraints for finiteness-marking. If such errors do not occur, it would be appropriate to note this as part of a child's knowledge base; if such errors do occur, it would be important to follow up with further examination to see if explicit instruction is needed in where finiteness is allowed in a clause.

The investigations of grammaticality judgements (Rice, Wexler, & Redmond, 1999) suggest that even if children with SLI are able to increase their consistency of use of tense-marking forms, they may still regard omitted forms as an allowable option. This suggests that language intervention could benefit from a final phase of instruction in which children are given practice in making grammaticality judgements, with an emphasis on learning about the obligatory properties of tense-marking morphology. This could well prove to be an important transition phase for working with written forms of English, to look for omitted markers in text as well as spoken utterances.

A final implication for intervention is that, just as the set of tense-marking morphemes show an association at a given time during the period of 3–8 years of age, and an association over time, they are also likely to be linked to other properties of the grammar. The current evidence points most directly at the assignment of case to personal pronouns. According to the findings of Wexler, Schütze, and Rice (1998), there would be good reason to teach case assignment in tandem with tense/agreement marking. The choice of "he" versus "him" is tightly linked with the choice of whether or not to omit third person singular -s, or the forms of "be" or "do". It may well enhance a child's use of each system (i.e. case-marking and tense/agreement marking), if those two systems are taught simultaneously.

It is perhaps somewhat ironic that although the grammatical limitations of children with SLI have been known for some time, we are now taking another look at this limitation and finding it to be both more subtle and more pervasive than perhaps we had realised. The contribution of the OI/EOI model, and the notion of grammatical markers, is the recognition that it is crucial to define carefully the grammatical markers that are involved and their underlying grammatical functions, and to recognise that other forms such as plurals are not likely to be affected whereas case-marking may well be. The positive news is that the grammatical marker may be relatively constrained. The not positive news is that the limitation can persist for a very long time, and the full extent of grammatical linkages is relatively unexplored.

Etiological information

In recent years, the advances in human genetics have brought a major shift in our thinking about the causes of language impairments in children. The likelihood of genetic contributions to language impairments is now widely accepted. The announcement of Fisher et al. (1998) of the identification of a particular gene locus for a family with speech and language impairments is a major breakthrough. At the rate of current inquiry, it is very likely that converging findings will be appearing from other investigators and other laboratories.

A grammatical marker is relevant in two ways for furthering our understanding of genetic contributions. First, it provides an interpretive window into the nature of the language impairment. The OI/EOI hypothesis is that there is an inherited contribution to grammatical acquisition, and children who show a grammatical marker may well be children who have inherited a faulty mechanism for grammatical growth, that leaves children in an immature grammatical phase for an extended period of time. Because the grammatical symptoms seem to be relatively unlinked to other domains of language development, it may be that the grammatical marker arises from different etiological sources than other symptoms of language impairment. Although this can seem to be a rather radical claim, let me note that until just recently it was assumed that speech impairments and language impairments were tightly linked, although that assumption is heavily challenged by new epidemiological findings of Shriberg, Tomblin, and McSweeney (1999). The clinical implication of a possible differential etiology is that some dimensions of language may be more resistant to intervention procedures than others. As noted above, there is reason to believe that general environmental input may be more facilitative for the development of vocabulary than for tense marking, although other findings suggest that the vocabulary effect may be lessened at the lower end of performance. This implies that practitioners should plan for a prolonged period of intervention for grammatical markers. It does not imply that grammatical deficits should be written off as hopelessly locked into an individual's deficit structure. Instead it means that the difficulty of learning in this area should be recognised and planned for, including the use of convergent methods to prevent burn-out on the part of the person receiving intervention services.

The second reason that a grammatical marker is relevant for etiological studies is that the identification of affected genes, assuming that certain genes differ in individuals with language impairment, will be enhanced by a behavioural symptom that shows high sensitivity and specificity (cf. Rice, 1996). Because the grammatical marker described here shows the highest levels of sensitivity and specificity that I know of at present for the condition of SLI in young children, it is a very promising candidate for a clinical symptom that can be linked to inherited limitations. A number of investigations are under way to evaluate this prediction. Whether or not definitive answers can be found remains to be seen.

ACKNOWLEDGEMENTS

This discussion of language assessment is based on the findings from a current programme of research carried out in my lab in collaboration with Ken Wexler of MIT and a group of talented student research assistants and staff personnel, supported by funding from the National Institute of Deafness and Communicative Disorders.

NOTES

1. The notion of "little variation" of an obligatory grammatical rule must, of course, be referenced to possible dialectal variations that allow usage different from the standard rules. If a rule allows optional application in some contexts but not others, then the obligatory context for use would be the appropriate one to target for assessment. For example, in American Black English, it can be allowable to say "he happy" or "he be happy" where the inflected form of the verb "to be" can be dropped, or an infinitival form of "be" can be used. At the same time, the "be" forms are less likely to be dropped in questions, such as "Is he going home?" or in elliptical contexts, such as "He is?"

2. The use of "do" and "be" verb forms in questions is evaluated in separate experimental tasks not reported here. Briefly, the outcomes for tense marking in questions also shows that, as expected, omission of these forms is likely to be acceptable for children with SLI.

REFERENCES

Bishop, D.V.M. (1997). *Uncommon understanding: Development and disorders of language comprehension in children.* Hove, UK: Psychology Press.

Bishop, D.V.M., North, T., & Donlan, C. (1995). Genetic basis of specific language impairment: Evidence from a twin study. *Developmental Medicine and Child Neurology, 37,* 56–71.

Burgemeister, B.B., Blum, L.H., & Lorge, I. (1972). *Columbia Mental Maturity Scale.* San Antonio, TX: Psychological Corporation.

Chomsky, N. (1995). *The minimalist program.* Cambridge, MA: MIT Press.

Dale, P.S., Simonoff, E., Bishop, D.V.M., Eley, T.C., Oliver, B., Price, T.S., Purcell, S., Stevenson, J., & Plomin, R. (1998). Genetic influence on language delay in two-year-old children. *Nature Neuroscience, 1,* 324–328.

Dunn, A., & Dunn, A. (1981). *Peabody Picture Vocabulary Test–Revised*. Circle Pines, MN: American Guidance Service.

Fisher, S.E., Vargha-Khadem, F., Watkins, K.E., Monaco, A.P., & Pembrey, M.E. (1998). Localization of a gene implicated in a severe speech and language disorder. *Nature Genetics, 18*, 168–170.

Ganger, J., Pinker, S., Baker, A., & Chawla, S. (1998). *The contribution of heredity to early vocabulary and grammatical development: A twin study.* Paper presented at the 23rd Annual Boston University Conference on Language Development, November.

Hammill, D., Brown, V., Larsen, S., & Wiederhold, J. (1994). *Test of Adolescent/Adult Language–3*. Austin, TX: Pro-Ed.

Hart, B., & Risley, T.R. (1995). *Meaningful differences in the everyday experience of young American children*. Baltimore, MD: Paul H. Brookes.

Hoff-Ginsberg, E. (1998). *What explains the SES-related difference in children's vocabularies and what does that reveal about the process of word learning?* Paper presented at the 23rd Annual Boston University conference on Language Development, Boston, MA, November.

Huttenlocher, J., Haight, W., Bryk, A., Seltzer, M., & Lyons, T. (1991). Early vocabulary growth: Relation to language input and gender. *Developmental Psychology, 27*, 236–248.

Johnson, C.J., Beitchman, J.H., Young, A., Escobar, M., Atkinson, L., Wilson, B., Brownlie, E.B., Douglas, L., Taback, N., Lam, I., & Wang, M. (1999). Fourteen-year follow-up of children with and without speech/language impairments: Speech/language stability and outcomes. *Journal of Speech, Language, and Hearing Research, 42*, 744–760.

Leonard, L.B. (1991). Specific language impairment as a clinical category. *Language, Speech, and Hearing Services in Schools, 22*, 66–68.

Leonard, L.B. (1998). *Children with specific language impairment.* Cambridge, MA: MIT Press.

Lewis, B.A., & Thompson, L.A. (1992). A study of developmental speech and language disorders in twins. *Journal of Speech and Hearing Research, 35*, 1086–1094.

Loeb, D., & Leonard, L.B. (1991). Subject case marking and verb morphology in normallydeveloping and specifically language-impaired children. *Journal of Speech and Hearing Research, 34*, 340–346.

Newcomer, P.L., & Hammill, D.D. (1988). *Test of Language Development 2–Primary.* Austin, TX: Pro-Ed.

Rice, M.L. (Ed.) (1996). *Toward a genetics of language.* Mahwah, NJ: Lawrence Erlbaum Associates Inc.

Rice, M.L., Haney, K.R., & Wexler, K. (1998). Family histories of children with SLI who show extended optional infinitives. *Journal of Speech, Language, and Hearing Research, 41*, 419–432.

Rice, M.L., Spitz, R.V., & O'Brien, M. (1999). Semantic and morphosyntactic language outcomes in biologically at-risk children. *Journal of Neurolinguistics, 12*, 213–234.

Rice, M.L., & Wexler, K. (1996a). Toward tense as a clinical marker of specific language impairment in English-speaking children. *Journal of Speech and Hearing Research, 39*, 1239–1257.

Rice, M.L., & Wexler, K. (1996b). A phenotype of specific language impairment: Extended optional infinitives. In M.L. Rice (Ed.), *Toward a genetics of language* (pp. 215–237). Mahwah, NJ: Lawrence Erlbaum Associates Inc.

Rice, M.L., Wexler, K., & Cleave, P.L. (1995). Specific language impairment as a period of extended optional infinitive. *Journal of Speech and Hearing Research, 38*, 850–863.

Rice, M.L., Wexler, K., & Hershberger, S. (1998). Tense over time: The longitudinal course of tense acquisition in children with specific language impairment. *Journal of Speech, Language, and Hearing Research, 41*, 1412–1431.

Rice, M.L., Wexler, K., & Redmond, S.M. (1999). Grammaticality judgments of an extended optional infinitive grammar: Evidence from English-speaking children with specific language impairment. *Journal of Speech, Language, and Hearing Research, 42*, 943–961.

Shriberg, L.D., Tomblin, J.B., & McSweeny, J.L. (1999). Prevalence of speech delay in 6-year-old children and comorbidity with language impairment. *Journal of Speech, Language, and Hearing Research, 42*, 1461–1481.

Tomblin, J.B. (1996). Genetic and environmental contributions to the risk for specific language impairment. In M.L. Rice (Ed.), *Toward a genetics of language* (pp. 191–210). Mahwah, NJ: Lawrence Erlbaum Associates Inc.

Tomblin, J.B., & Buckwalter, P.R. (1998). Heritability of poor language achievement among twins. *Journal of Speech, Language, and Hearing Research, 41*, 188–199.

Tomblin, J.B., Records, N.L., & Zhang, X. (1996) A system for diagnosing specific language impairment in kindergarten children. *Journal of Speech, Language, and Hearing Research, 40*, 1245–1260.

Tomblin, J.B., Records, N.L., Buckwalter, P., Zhang, X., Smith, E., & O'Brien, M. (1997). Prevalence of specific language impairment in kindergarten children. *Journal of Speech, Language, and Hearing Research, 40,* 1245–1260.

Wells, G. (1985). *Language development in the pre-school years.* Cambridge: Cambridge University Press.

Wexler, K. (1994). Optional infinitives, head movement and the economy of derivations. In N. Hornstein & D. Lightfoot (Eds.), *Verb movement* (pp. 305–350). New York: Cambridge University Press.

Wexler, K. (1996). The development of inflection in a biologically-based theory of language acquisition. In M.L. Rice (Ed.), *Toward a genetics of language* (pp. 113–144). Mahwah, NJ: Lawrence Erlbaum Associates Inc.

Wexler, K., Schütze, C.T., & Rice, M.L. (1998). Subject case in children with SLI and unaffected controls: Evidence for the Agr/Tns omission model. *Language Acquisition, 7,* 317–344.

3

Genetics and early language development: A UK study of twins

Robert Plomin and Philip S. Dale

New developments in behavioural genetics and in molecular genetics have great potential for characterising speech and language impairments and for understanding their aetiology and developmental course. In this chapter, we illustrate some of this potential in the context of a uniquely large-sample study of early language delay, the Twins' Early Development Study (TEDS), which will eventually include measures of language development at ages 2, 3, and 4. The results at age 2 for 3000 twin pairs born in 1994 in England and Wales demonstrate substantial differences in the aetiology of individual differences within the normal range and the aetiology of low performance. Multivariate analyses clarify the role of genetic and environmental factors in explaining the correlation between language and nonverbal measures, and the correlation among language components such as vocabulary and grammar. Similar analyses can address the aetiology of longitudinal patterns of change and continuity as well. These behavioural genetic findings will help to chart a course for molecular genetic research in order to identify specific genes in multiple-gene systems responsible for genetic influence on language abilities and disabilities.

INTRODUCTION

In the 1960s and 1970s, the overwhelming emphasis on the role of the environment as a determinant of behaviour and development that had dominated the behavioural sciences for most of this century began to give way to a more balanced view that recognised the importance of genetics as well as environment. This shift came first in psychiatry when twin and adoption studies showed a substantial genetic component to schizophrenia. Although much more evidence of strong genetic factors had already been amassed for cognitive abilities than for psychiatric disorders (e.g. Erlenmeyer-Kimling & Jarvik, 1963), more data and more time were needed before these results began to be widely accepted (Plomin & McClearn, 1993). The role of genetics has only relatively recently begun to be considered in the study of language (Rice, 1996), despite the strong trend of much linguistic theorising to invoke an innate basis for language (Pinker, 1994). As discussed in this chapter, twin and adoption studies suggest that language abilities and disabilities may be among the most heritable cognitive traits. Moreover, some success has already been achieved towards identifying specific genes responsible for this heritable influence.

Why study genetic influences when we cannot change genes? Although causes are not necessarily related to cures, increased understanding of the genetic and environmental aetiologies of language abilities and disabilities, the aetiological links between abilities and disabilities, and the developmental interplay between nature and nurture are likely to improve description, prediction, intervention and prevention (e.g. Gilger, 1997). New analysis techniques allow us to go far beyond merely asking whether and how much genetic factors influence development. For example, as described in the first part of this chapter, genetic analyses can explore the extent to which disorders are aetiologically distinct from normal variation rather than simply being the low end of the same genetic and environmental continuum

responsible for the normal range of variation. Also mentioned in this chapter is multivariate genetic analysis that can investigate the extent to which genetic and environmental factors that affect one area of language overlap with genetic and environmental effects on another area of language or cognition. Research of this type for language and cognitive impairments may lead to diagnoses based on aetiology rather than symptomatology. As discussed in the last section of this chapter, identification of specific genes will provide much greater precision in description and diagnoses, developmental predictions, and individually tailored educational programmes and therapies. Most importantly, gene-based early prediction of children at risk offers the hope of prevention rather than waiting to intervene when language problems are full blown and cast a long and wide shadow over children's cognitive and social development. Finally, recognition of the importance of nature as well as nurture fosters a growing recognition of the need to understand their developmental interplay, that is, the interactions between genes and environment by which genotypes (the genetic information in each individual's DNA) become phenotypes (the observable physical and behavioural outcomes of development).

In the first two parts of this chapter, we provide an overview of genetic research on language abilities (individual differences throughout the range) and disabilities (extremes). We focus on recent results from an exceptionally large population-based UK twin study at 2, 3 and 4 years of age called the Twins Early Development Study (TEDS). Two years is a particularly appropriate age to begin to study individual differences in language development because it follows a period of rapid acceleration in the acquisition of words in the second half of the second year of life, and the emergence of word combinations by most children before this age. The transition from infancy to early childhood is a time of dramatic change, and a major goal of TEDS is to chart genetic and environmental sources of change and continuity as we turn to data at 3 and 4 years.

INDIVIDUAL DIFFERENCES IN LANGUAGE ABILITIES

Human behavioural genetics focuses on behavioural differences within the human species and the extent to which genetic and environmental differences can account for these observed differences in behaviour. The human genome contains about 3 billion steps, each a base pair of amino acids, in the spiral staircase of DNA, and some 3 million of these DNA base pairs differ from one person to the next. Thus 99.9% of DNA base pairs are identical for all human beings; this includes the DNA that makes us in turn, by virtue of shared genetic information, mammals, primates, and human. The 0.1% of DNA that differs is what makes each of us unique biologically, and this DNA is the source of genetic influence on behavioural as well as biological differences among individuals. Note that, in contrast, most language theory and research has focused on universals of our species rather than variations on these universal themes (Hardy-Brown, 1983). For example, man is a natural language user in the sense that nearly all members of our species readily use language given a normal environment. At this level of analysis, language is so important that natural selection tolerates no genetic variation. However, with greater magnification, individuals can be seen to differ in rates of language acquisition during development and in their ultimate facility with language. Even if our species' natural use of language is deeply rooted in genes which have been selected in evolution, individual differences in language are not necessarily due to genetic differences because the causes of universals (i.e. the species' mean for traits) are not necessarily related to the causes of individual differences (i.e. variance within the species on those traits). That people have arms is a species universal under genetic control, with no genetic variation, but arm length varies from person to person, and there is good evidence that bone length, including arm length, has a substantial genetic influence. The study of universals and differences represents different levels of analysis. One level of analysis is not more important than another, but it is important to keep in mind that human genetic methods address individual differences whereas language theorists have largely focused on universals.

To what extent are individual differences in rates of language development due to children's environmental differences and to genetic differences? It is perfectly reasonable to think that the environment is the source of language differences between children. For decades, psychology was dominated by an environmentalism that assumed that we are what we learn. It is self-evident that we are not born with vocabulary words; we have to learn them. Since vocabulary is the product of learning from experience, it is a plausible next step to assume that differences in experience must therefore be responsible for language differences among individuals. Specific environmental hypotheses leap to mind to explain, for example, differences in vocabulary production. For instance, parents differ both in the words they use with their children and in their communicative style. Many studies have demonstrated that the quantity and quality of parental language is correlated with children's rate of language development (e.g. Gallaway & Richards, 1994; Hampson & Nelson, 1993; Hart & Risley, 1995; Huttenlocher, Haight, Bryk, Seltzer, & Lyons, 1991). Similarly, schools differ in the quality of educational experiences that they provide. Indeed, we can decide just to pick up a dictionary and memorise words.

What about genetics? Given the reasonableness of these environmental hypotheses, we might expect to find that genetic differences have no impact whatsoever on variation in vocabulary. However, as we shall see, genetic research during the past century — and bigger and better studies in the past few years — consistently points to a substantial role for nature (genetics) in addition to nurture (environment) for individual differences in cognitive, especially verbal, abilities and disabilities. Finding genetic influence on individual differences in vocabulary does not contradict the assumption that words are learned. It means that DNA differences between people affect how easily they learn, remember, and use words. Genetic

influence is more like an appetite than an aptitude. A more subtle point is that finding genetic
influence on individual differences in language
development offers a different interpretation of
research showing correlations between the quantity and quality of parental language and children's language development. Such correlations
are equally consistent with explanations based
on child-driven influence, that is, more rapidly
developing children might elicit different language
from caregivers than more slowly developing
children (Lytton, 1980). Another possibility is
that parents and children resemble each other in
language proficiency because they share genes
(Plomin, 1994).

Twin and adoption studies of verbal ability and language

Twin and adoption studies are quasi-experimental
designs that broach the fundamental issue of
nature and nurture, that is, estimating the relative
influence of genetic and environmental factors
(Plomin et al., in press). The twin method capitalises on an experiment of nature: humans, like
many other species, produce two types of multiple
births that differ in their genetic relatedness. Identical twins are genetically identical because they
derive from the same fertilised egg or zygote that
divides into two during the first two weeks after
conception. These are called monozygotic (MZ)
twins in contrast to the other type of twin, called
dizygotic (DZ, non-identical, fraternal), which are
derived from two separately fertilised eggs. DZ
twins, like other siblings, are 50 per cent similar
genetically. Because sex is determined genetically,
half of DZ twin pairs are the same sex and half
are opposite sex, whereas MZ twins are always
the same sex. If MZ twins are no more similar
for a trait than are DZ twins despite the twofold
greater genetic similarity of MZ twins, we conclude that genetic factors are of no importance.
Genetic influence is thus implied to the extent
that MZ twins correlate more highly for a trait
than do DZ twins. Heritability, a statistic that
indexes the size of the genetic effect, refers to the
proportion of phenotypic (observed) variance that
can be attributed to genetic variation. Doubling

the difference between the correlations for MZ
and DZ twins provides a good first approximation
to heritability.

The remainder of phenotypic variance can be
attributed to two types of environmental influence.
The first would be illustrated by the (hypothetical)
case that children's vocabulary scores were totally dependent on the vocabulary heard by the
child. In the normal case where twins grow up in
the same household hearing much of the same
language, we would expect them to resemble each
other because they are exposed to the same environmental influence. This is an example of "shared
environmental influence", and it would be manifested in similar, substantial correlations between
members of a twin pair regardless of whether
they are MZ or DZ twins. A second type of
environmental influence involves random factors
uncorrelated with either genetics or family variables. Such "nonshared environmental" influences,
which include both external influences and measurement error, are manifested in low correlations
for both MZ and DZ twins. In practice, structural
equation model-fitting analyses rather than simple
comparisons of correlations are typically used to
estimate genetic and environmental parameters and
to provide confidence intervals for these estimates
(Plomin et al., in press).

The twin method has been robustly defended
as a reasonable device to screen for genetic influence (e.g. Martin, Boomsma, & Machin, 1997),
although there are concerns, for example, that
MZ twins may be treated more similarly than DZ
twins. Fortunately, there is another very different
design, the adoption method, that can be used to
check the results of the twin method. The adoption design uses the social experiment of adoption which produces first-degree relatives who
share genetics but not family environment (e.g.
birth parents and their adopted-away offspring)
and those who share family environment but not
genetics (e.g. adoptive parents and their adopted
children). On the whole, and especially for cognitive abilities, twin and adoption studies yield
similar results.

Genetic studies on cognitive abilities in adults
have frequently included measures of verbal
ability such as vocabulary and word fluency.

Results from twin and adoption studies across the life span and in several countries indicate that the heritability of verbal ability is about 50 percent (Plomin & DeFries, 1998). That is, about half of the variance in tests of verbal ability can be ascribed to genetic differences among individuals.

Genetic studies of verbal ability in childhood also show genetic influence. A recent summary and meta-analysis of twin studies of verbal IQ in childhood yielded weighted mean correlations (based on aggregating the data from the separate studies) of .82 for MZ and .49 for DZ, suggesting heritability greater than 60 percent (Stromswold, in press). The longitudinal Colorado Adoption Project, which includes over 200 adopted children studied from infancy through adolescence, their birth and adoptive parents, and over 200 matched control (nonadopted) children and their parents, shows increasing genetic influence on verbal ability from childhood through adolescence (Plomin et al., 1997). These and other findings concerning increasing heritability for many cognitive and personality measures with development (that is, increasing discrepancy between the MZ and DZ correlations) constitute some of the most important results of modern behavioural genetic research, as they illustrate the extent to which genetics and environment may be interdependent (Gilger, 1997; Plomin et al., in press). Although it is possible that new genes turn on during development, it is more likely that the explanation for this finding is that experience (that is, environment), is affected by the child's own characteristics, which are in turn influenced by the child's genotype, and this phenomenon becomes increasingly important with development.

Other language measures also show genetic influence in childhood. A meta-analysis of twin studies covering a wide age range in childhood yielded estimates of substantial genetic influence for spoken vocabulary, reading, and other measures of language (Stromswold, in press). The Colorado Adoption Project also included measures of language development. At 2 and 3 years of age, a comparison of nonadoptive and adoptive sibling correlations indicated substantial genetic influence for the Sequenced Inventory of Com-

munication Development (SICD), a standardised clinical measure of pronunciation, vocabulary, and grammar (Thompson & Plomin, 1988). Substantial genetic influence was also suggested in analyses of transcripts of naturalistic verbal interactions between infants and their mothers at 1 and 2 years of age (Hardy-Brown & Plomin, 1985).

In summary, twin and adoption studies consistently suggest substantial genetic influence on measures of verbal ability as do measures of specific language structures and processes. Indeed, a case could be made that verbal measures are among the most heritable behavioural traits. Some evidence suggests that verbal measures are heritable even early in life, although the magnitude of genetic effects appears to increase during childhood.

TEDS language results for individual differences at 2 years

The TEDS sample was recruited from birth records of twins born in England and Wales in 1994, 1995 and 1996. The analyses reported in this chapter are based on measures at 2 years of age for the first (1994) cohort, with complete data for nearly half of the entire population of English and Welsh twins. The sample is representative of 1994 UK census data in terms of maternal education and ethnicity. The twins were diagnosed for zygosity using a parental rating instrument, which yielded a 96% accuracy rate compared to DNA testing in a TEDS analysis of a subset of same-sex twins. Twins were excluded for medical problems, extreme perinatal problems, hearing problems, and when English was not the primary language spoken at home. The current analyses are based on approximately 3000 pairs of twins, divided nearly equally between MZ, same-sex DZ and opposite-sex DZ.

At 2, 3 and 4 years of age, parents were sent booklets for each twin that included measures of language and nonverbal cognitive development. The 2-year booklet included an adaptation of the MacArthur Communicative Development Inventory (MCDI; Fenson et al., 1994) from which three scores were derived: production of root words, a vocabulary measure; the extent to which words are combined into sentences, a grammar measure; and use of language for displaced reference, i.e. talking about nonpresent objects, or past or future events. The MCDI has been widely used in studies of early language development and has been demonstrated to show excellent internal consistency and test-retest reliability as well as concurrent validity as measured by correlations with tester-administered measures (Fenson et al., 1994).

The 2-year booklet also included a newly devised measure of nonverbal (performance) cognitive abilities, the Parent Report of Children's Abilities (PARCA; Saudino et al., 1998). The PARCA consists of both parent-report questions (e.g. "Does your child recognise himself/herself when looking in a mirror?") and parent-adminis-

tered items (e.g. copying a design, building with blocks). Using PARCA and MCDI scores with a sample of 107 2-year-olds, these parent-based assessments predicted the Mental Development Index (MDI) of the Bayley Scales of Infant Development-II as accurately as the MDI is typically predicted by tester-administered tests (Saudino et al., 1998).

Similar booklets were developed and used to assess language development and nonverbal cognitive development at 3 and 4 years. Details of the TEDS sample and measures are available elsewhere (Dale et al., 1998; Eley et al., 1999; Price et al., in press).

As shown in Fig. 3.1, moderate genetic influence and substantial shared environmental influence were found in TEDS at 2 years for vocabulary (Dale et al., 1998), grammar and displaced refer-

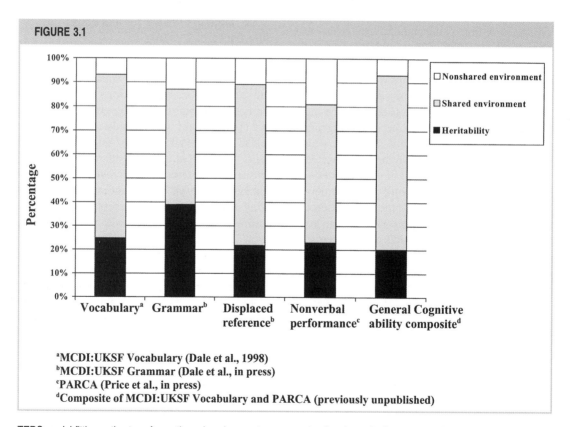

FIGURE 3.1

[a]MCDI:UKSF Vocabulary (Dale et al., 1998)
[b]MCDI:UKSF Grammar (Dale et al., in press)
[c]PARCA (Price et al., in press)
[d]Composite of MCDI:UKSF Vocabulary and PARCA (previously unpublished)

TEDS model-fitting estimates of genetic and environment components of variance for language and cognitive measures at 2 years of age.

ence (Dale, Dionne, Eley, & Plomin, in press), and PARCA nonverbal performance (Price et al., in press). Similar results emerged when verbal (vocabulary) and nonverbal (PARCA) performance were combined to assess general cognitive development (previously unpublished). Heritability estimates, with 95% confidence intervals in brackets, are .25 (.21–.28) for vocabulary, .39 (.33–.46) for grammar, .22 (.17–.26) for displaced reference, .25 (.21–.28) for PARCA nonverbal performance, and .20 (.13–.25) for the composite measure of general cognitive ability. The significantly greater heritability for grammar than for the other measures is noteworthy and will be a focus of replication analyses using the 1995 cohort. The small confidence intervals for these estimates reflect the large sample size.

Examples of additional genetic analyses of individual differences in TEDS include interactions with sex (Galsworthy, Dionne, Dale, & Plomin, in press) and with prematurity (Koeppen-Schomerus, Gringras, Wolke, & Plomin, in press). Research on sex differences is usually limited to describing mean differences between males and females. As expected, girls have significantly higher vocabulary scores than boys at 2 years of age, although gender accounts for only 3% of the variance in these scores. Although the main behavioural genetic analyses focus on MZ and same-sex DZ twins, opposite-sex DZ twins provide an additional, within-family comparison, for gender differences. Girls and boys in opposite-sex DZ pairs differ almost as much as girls and boys in same-sex DZ pairs, suggesting that mean differences between the sexes are caused by biological or social factors that operate within families rather than between families. Twin analyses can also provide a deeper insight into the aetiology of sex differences by comparing the influence of genetic and environmental factors separately for boys and girls. In TEDS, the heritability of vocabulary is slightly but significantly greater for boys (26%) than for girls (19%). The use of more complex statistical models (sex-limitation models) also makes it possible to assess the extent to which the same genetic factors affect boys and girls. These analyses for vocabulary suggest that genetic influences may differ for boys and girls.

Heritability of vocabulary also interacts with prematurity which is usually conceptualised as an environmental influence. Although very preterm infants (<32 weeks gestational age) were excluded from the main TEDS analyses, an analysis focused on this group showed significantly lower heritability (9%) than for the rest of the sample, one of the few reports of a significant genotype-environment interaction. A possible explanation is that the normal influence of genetic factors on individual differences in vocabulary development is overwhelmed by the shock of very premature birth. We predict that this genotype-environment interaction will disappear by early childhood as the impact of prematurity loosens its grip on cognitive development.

In summary, TEDS analyses of individual differences support the conclusion emerging from research on older children that genetic factors play a significant role in normal language development in infancy. These TEDS results for early vocabulary are similar to those of another twin study in which a parent-report measure of vocabulary was used (Reznick, Corley, & Robinson, 1997). Although another, recent study of infant twins reported near zero heritability for vocabulary, its small sample (43 MZ, 33 DZ) limits the reliability of this estimate (Ganger, Pinker, Baker, & Chawla, 1998). At least 200 MZ twin pairs and 200 DZ twin pairs are needed to detect a heritability of 25% with 80% power (Cohen, 1988). For nonverbal performance also (the PARCA measure), the TEDS heritability estimates are similar to other studies in infancy that used a tester-administered measure (Reznick et al., 1997; Wilson, 1983).

These TEDS 2-year-old results for the 1994 birth cohort will be tested for replication using the 1995 birth cohort. In addition, these analyses will be extended longitudinally to 3 and 4 years when similar measures are assessed. Our hypothesis, based on developmental research on general cognitive ability (e.g. Fulker, DeFries, & Plomin, 1988; Plomin et al., 1997), is that the heritability of these language measures will increase during childhood.

EXTREMES (LANGUAGE DISABILITIES)

The previous section considered the normal range of variation in language development. What about abnormal development? It is possible that the genetic and environmental aetiologies of disabilities differ from those responsible for the normal range of ability. For example, a gene associated with normal variation in language development might not be responsible for language impairment and vice versa. Genetic influence on language impairment will be reflected in greater twin concordance for MZ than for DZ twin pairs, where concordance is the proportion of pairs in which both members of the pair meet some cut-off criterion, typically a diagnosis. The first twin studies of language impairment were conducted only recently and they indicate much greater concordance for MZ than DZ twins for children and adolescents of a wide age range, pointing to substantial genetic influence (Bishop, North, & Donlan, 1995; Lewis & Thompson, 1992; Tomblin & Buckwalter, 1998). These twin data, together with results from an adoption study (Felsenfeld & Plomin, 1997), suggest that genetic influence on language disability might be greater than genetic influence on the normal range of variation.

Twin concordance can provide only a rough index of genetic influence. Information is lost because concordance assumes a dichotomous diagnosis and thus does not take into account cases in which one member of the pair just misses the cut-off. Moreover, concordance assumes the reality of a dichotomous (qualitative) diagnosis rather than considering a dimensional (quantitative) distribution. A genetic method called DF extremes analysis (DeFries & Fulker, 1985, 1988) addresses the aetiology of the links between the normal and abnormal. Rather than assigning dichotomous diagnoses and assessing concordance for the disorder, it compares the quantitative trait scores of the twin partners (co-twins) of affected individuals who do meet the diagnostic category (probands). The essence of DF extremes analysis is that if the mean difference between the probands and the population is due to genetic factors, the language scores of co-twins of MZ probands will be more impaired than co-twins of DZ probands. This is not just a statistical nicety: DF extremes analysis broaches the aetiological links between the normal and abnormal. DF extremes analysis can yield evidence for genetic influence only to the extent that the quantitative trait is genetically linked to the disorder, that is, to the extent that the same genes affect the disorder and the dimension.

It is also possible to compare heritabilities of disability and ability. DF extremes analysis estimates the heritability of disability. This is called *group heritability* to distinguish it from the more commonly used heritability estimate discussed above. That measure could be called *individual differences heritability*, because it is an estimate of the role of genetic factors in producing variance in the entire population. In contrast, group heritability assesses the extent to which genetic factors are responsible for the mean difference between children with language impairment and the rest of the population. It does not refer to genetic influences on individual differences among children with language impairment. That is, the question is not why in a group of 2-year-olds with language impairment some children have no recognisable words and other children have one or two words. The issue is why as a group these children are very slow in language development as compared to most 2-year-old children who speak dozens of words.

TEDS DF extremes analyses at 2 years

The large, representative sample of TEDS makes it possible to test directly for differences in heritability at the low end of language learning (group heritability) versus heritability of individual differences in the normal range (individual differences heritability). In TEDS, DF extremes analyses focused on children in the lowest 5% of the distribution of MCDI vocabulary (Dale et al., 1998). These children were reported by their parents at 2 years of age to have used 0–8 of the 100 words on the MCDI vocabulary list as compared to the average of 48 words for the entire sample. For twin pairs in which at least one member of the pair was in the lowest 5% of MCDI vocabulary scores, concordances were 81% for MZ twins (75 pairs), 42% for same-sex DZ twins (60 pairs), and 42% for opposite-sex DZ twins (79 pairs). These results suggest substantial genetic influence and little influence of shared environment. Figure 3.2 illustrates DF extremes analysis of these data using quantitative scores on MCDI vocabulary. For the entire sample of nearly 6000 individuals, one twin's vocabulary score is plotted against the co-twin's score. The tight scatterplot reflects the high average twin correlation (.83) for MZ and DZ twins. On the vertical axis, twins are selected who are in the lowest 5% of the normal distribution. On the horizontal axis, it can be seen that the quantitative scores of the MZ co-twins of the probands are tightly clustered and hardly regress at all to the population mean. In contrast, the quantitative scores of the DZ co-twins are spread out and regress much farther back towards the population mean. Application of DF extremes model-fitting analysis to these data yielded a group

heritability estimate of .73 (.38–1.0 CI), indicating that most of the mean difference between the probands and the population can be ascribed to genetic factors.

The group heritability estimate (73%) is significantly greater than the individual heritability estimate (25%). This is the first time that a significant difference has been reported between the two types of heritability for any trait. These findings suggest that genetic factors have far stronger effects for the lowest 5% of the distribution as compared to the rest of the distribution. DF extremes analyses conducted using cut-offs less extreme than 5% indicated that the high group heritability for the 5% cut-off diminished with more lenient cut-offs. Group heritability was 73% for the 5% cut-off, 42% for the 10% cut-off, and about 30% for cut-offs of 15%, 20% and 25%. Individual heritability for the entire sample (i.e. no cut-off) was 25%. This suggests that the greater genetic influence on low vocabulary at 2 years is

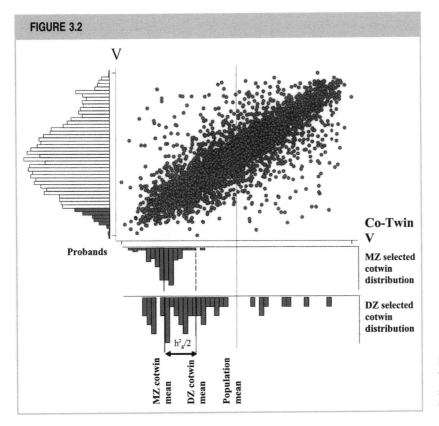

FIGURE 3.2

DF extremes analysis for TEDS MCDI Vocabulary scores at 2 years. (See text for explanation.)

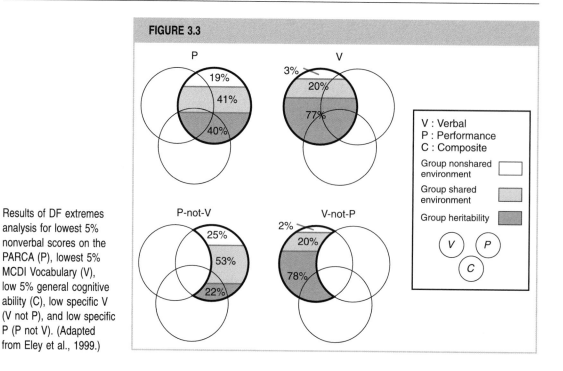

FIGURE 3.3

Results of DF extremes analysis for lowest 5% nonverbal scores on the PARCA (P), lowest 5% MCDI Vocabulary (V), low 5% general cognitive ability (C), low specific V (V not P), and low specific P (P not V). (Adapted from Eley et al., 1999.)

largely limited to scores in the lowest 5% of the distribution.

This example of DF extremes analysis was based on children selected from the lowest 5% of the distribution of vocabulary (V) regardless of their scores on nonverbal (performance, P) cognitive development as assessed by the PARCA. What happens if we examine specific language impairment by selecting those children who are low in V but not low in P? Deleting 43 (24%) of the V probands who were also low in P yielded a group heritability estimate of 78% (.48–1.0 CI), which is similar to the estimate of 73% when co-morbid cases were included (Eley et al., 1999). The results are quite different when the focus is on low P. The group heritability estimate for P is 40%, which is lower than for low V, and it is reduced still further to 22% (.00–.52 CI) when co-morbid cases were excluded. Finally, for the small group of 43 probands comorbid for V and P, group heritability was 94% (.49–1.0 CI), which is consistent with the hypothesis that genetic influence on cognitive disability is strong as long as V is low.

These differing results for low V and low P suggest that they are better considered separately rather than combined into a composite measure of general cognitive impairment as is typically done in research on mental handicap, as the group heritability is much stronger for low V than for low P. This conclusion suggests that general mental retardation at 2 years might be a less promising target for molecular genetic studies, the search for specific genes to be discussed below, than V delay.

These results at 2 years for the 1994 cohort of TEDS are summarised in Fig. 3.3. Again, the results will be replicated with the 1995 birth cohort and extended longitudinally at 3 and 4 years.

MULTIVARIATE GENETIC ANALYSIS

In the previous sections of this chapter, the analyses have been univariate, focusing on the variance of a single variable. Even the analysis of specific language impairment (V-not-P) just discussed was univariate based on a single composite variable. Multivariate genetic analysis represents a major methodological advance that assesses genetic and environmental influences on the *relation* between two variables (Martin & Eaves, 1977; Plomin & DeFries, 1979). In other words, multivariate genetic analysis assesses the extent to which the two (or more) variables of interest are influenced by the same genetic factors. Like univariate analyses, multivariate analyses contrast correlations for MZ and DZ twins, and the magnitude of the discrepancy indexes a genetic effect. But in multivariate analyses, the relevant correlations are cross-correlations, that is, measure A for twin 1 with measure B for twin 2. Using these correlations, the analysis estimates the genetic correlation, which is literally a correlation between the genetic effects on the two variables. A genetic correlation of 1.0 indicates that the genetic effects on X are the same as genetic effects on Y, and a genetic correlation of .00 means that genetic effects on X have no effect at all on Y. Note that the genetic correlation is independent of heritability. That is, the heritabilities of X and Y could be modest but the genetic correlation could be 1.0 if the genes that only modestly affect both X and Y are identical; conversely, heritabilities of X and Y could be high but the genetic correlation could be .00 if entirely different sets of genes affect X and Y.

As an example, consider an important multivariate genetic result from psychiatry. Anxiety and depression, thought to represent major diagnostic categories of mood disorders, show a genetic correlation near 1.0 (Kendler, Neale, Kessler, Heath, & Eaves, 1992). This means that these different disorders are the same thing genetically — what makes them different is environment. In other words, if a gene were found to be associated with anxiety the same gene would be associated with depression. The issue of genetic correlation is crucial in cognitive neuroscience in general (e.g. Pinker, 1994) and language in particular (e.g. Bishop, 1997) because cognitive processes are assumed to be modular, that is, domain specific and independent. Although the issue of modularity is not usually considered in relation to individual differences, from a genetic perspective on indi-

vidual differences, modularity would predict low genetic correlations among cognitive processes. In contrast, multivariate genetic analyses from childhood to adulthood comparing verbal ability to other specific cognitive abilities such as spatial ability indicate that the genetic correlation is near 1.0 (Petrill, 1997). This finding predicts that genes associated with verbal ability will also be associated with other cognitive processes.

What about early cognitive development? Multivariate genetic analysis of TEDS verbal (MCDI vocabulary) and non-verbal abilities (PARCA) at 2 years found only a modest genetic correlation between them (Price et al., in press). The genetic correlation was estimated at .30 (.17–.42 CI). The modest genetic correlation in TEDS has been replicated in one twin study in infancy (Robinson, Mervis, & Matheny, 1999), but another twin study using different measures of verbal and non-verbal abilities reported a genetic correlation of .00 at 20 months and .61 at 24 months (Reznick, Corley, & Robinson, 1997). The dramatically different results at 20 and 24 months are inexplicable other than by fluctuations due to the relatively small sample size, but it is noteworthy that the average of these genetic correlations is similar to the estimate from TEDS.

When this TEDS finding is considered in the context of multivariate genetic results from childhood showing high genetic correlations between verbal and non-verbal abilities, the modest genetic correlation at 2 years of age suggests that genetic correlations will reverse during the next four years. This hypothesis, which is contrary to a theory that posits that cognition differentiates during development (Karmiloff-Smith, 1992), can be tested in TEDS using data from 3- and 4-year-olds. This hypothesis is supported by a recent multivariate genetic study of 6- and 7-year-olds (66 MZ and 60 same-sex DZ pairs) (Hohnen & Stevenson, 1999). Vocabulary and phonological awareness yielded very high genetic correlations with performance IQ.

TEDS data at 2 years were also used to conduct a multivariate genetic analysis within language, comparing vocabulary to grammar and to the use of language with displaced reference (Dale et al., in press). Genetic correlations were .61

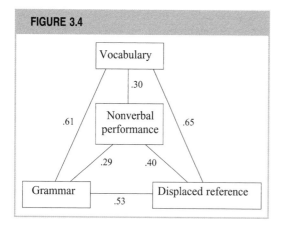

FIGURE 3.4

Multivariate genetic correlations among language measures (vocabulary, grammar, displaced reference) and between language measures and nonverbal performance. (Adapted from Dale et al., in press).

between vocabulary and grammar, .65 between vocabulary and displaced reference, and .53 between grammar and displaced reference. In other words, genetic effects on these aspects of language development largely overlap. In contrast, the genetic correlations between these language measures and non-verbal cognitive development are much smaller, indicating some genetic specificity for language. The genetic correlations with the PARCA measure of non-verbal development were .30 for vocabulary as noted above, .29 for grammar, and .40 for displaced reference (Dale et al., in press). These genetic correlations are summarised in Fig. 3.4. The twin study mentioned above (Hohnen & Stevenson, 1999) also found very high genetic correlations between vocabulary and phonological awareness, even when performance IQ was controlled.

These multivariate genetic analyses between verbal and non-verbal ability and between aspects of language development involve individual differences throughout the range of ability. What about disability rather than ability? As discussed above, DF extremes analysis permits an estimate of the role of genetic factors in extremely low performance on a single measure. Recently an extension of DF extremes analysis appropriate for the bivariate case has been developed. It estimates the role of genetic factors in producing overlap

between low performance on two measures, in contrast to the multivariate analyses discussed earlier in this section which are addressed to variation across the entire distribution. This new method was first used to show that genetic effects on hyperactivity and on spelling disability largely overlap (Stevenson, Pennington, Gilger, DeFries, & Gillis, 1993). A similar bivariate DF extremes analysis was applied to TEDS data for the lowest 5% of the sample on vocabulary (V) at 2 years as compared to their co-twin's non-verbal (PARCA) performance (P) scores (Purcell et al., submitted). The results indicated a genetic correlation of 1.0 between low V and P. This finding suggests that genetic effects responsible for low V are also responsible for decrements in P. That is, if specific genes were found to be associated with low V at 2 years, the same genes would also be associated with lower P in these low V children.

These multivariate genetic analyses of V and P in TEDS indicate again that results can differ for ability and disability. The genetic correlation between V and P is modest (.30) for the normal range of variability but high (1.0) when probands are selected for low V. Again, these TEDS analyses will be replicated with the 1995 cohort and extended longitudinally to 3 and 4 years.

MOLECULAR GENETICS: IDENTIFYING SPECIFIC GENES

One of the most exciting directions for future research on language abilities and disabilities is to identify specific genes responsible for their substantial heritability. For complex traits and common disorders, the goal is not to find the gene for a particular trait but rather to find some of the many genes that contribute to the variance of the trait. In order to emphasise this distinction, genes in multiple-gene systems have been given a special name, quantitative trait loci (QTLs). The name indicates that complex traits influenced by multiple genes are distributed as continuous, quantitative dimensions rather than as discontinuous, qualitative disorders (Plomin, Owen, & McGuffin, 1994).

In the case of single-gene effects like phenyl-ketonuria, which causes severe mental retardation, the gene is necessary and sufficient for the development of the disorder. About 5000 single-gene disorders are known but most are very rare, typically affecting from 1 in 5000 to 1 in 50,000 people. Many single-gene disorders such as phenylketonuria (1 in 10,000) and fragile X (1 in 5000 males) have broad effects that include language. Recently, a single-gene disorder with its primary effect on language has been reported for the first time, albeit for a single family (Fisher et al., 1998). This family included 15 linguistically-impaired relatives whose speech has low intelligibility and who have deficits in nearly all aspects of language but especially grammar. The family showed a simple dominant mode of inheritance that could be traced to one grandmother. A region on the long arm of chromosome 7 (7q31) was found that is linked to the disorder in this family. The same region has also been linked with autism (International Molecular Genetic Study of Autism Consortium, 1998).

Language disorders in childhood are much more common than typical single-gene disorders, about 1 in 20. (It is unclear whether the family studied by Fisher et al. have a condition which is rare and different from more common SLI, or simply a much more severe version of it.) Although inherited according to the same Mendelian laws as any other gene, QTLs contribute interchangeably and additively like probabilistic risk factors. A revolutionary implication of the QTL perspective is that there may be no disorders from a genetic perspective. Disorders may be merely the quantitative extreme of the same genetic factors that contribute to heritability throughout the dimension. That is, there may be no genes specific to a disorder — genes associated with a disorder might have the same effect throughout the distribution. This is the thrust of DF extremes analyses described earlier.

Methodologically, traditional methods for identifying single-gene effects are unlikely to succeed in identifying QTLs because the effect size of individual QTLs — the individual genes in a system which is influenced by multiple genes — will be relatively small. This may be the reason why

during the past decade reports of specific genes linked to the major psychiatric disorders failed to replicate and current research has not yet had much success, whereas recent research in the cognitive domain has enjoyed some quick successes. The earliest attempts to find genes for behavioural disorders focused on schizophrenia and manic-depressive psychosis at a time when gene-hunting techniques were limited to identifying a single gene necessary and sufficient to cause the disorder. These techniques involved the use of large family pedigrees in which the co-segregation of DNA markers and a disorder can be traced across several generations in order to identify the chromosomal location of the gene linked to the disorder. Although there has never been any solid evidence that these disorders are caused by a single gene, this single-gene approach was all that was available at that time for finding genes. It was like the adage about losing your wallet in a dark alley but looking for it under the street lamp because the light is better.

Molecular genetic studies in the cognitive domain were begun recently, after the QTL revolution, and thus leap-frogged single-gene approaches by using QTL approaches from the start (e.g. Smith, Pennington, & DeFries, 1996). Two other little-known genetic facts may also be relevant to the greater success in finding QTLs for cognitive abilities and disabilities: assortative mating and additive genetic variance. Assortative mating, the tendency for like to mate with like, is much greater for cognitive abilities, especially verbal abilities, than for any other physical or behavioural traits. For example, couples obviously sort themselves by height but the spousal correlation for height is only .25. In contrast, the spousal correlation for general cognitive ability is .45 and is even higher for verbal ability, perhaps because verbal ability is more readily apparent and relevant upon first meeting people than are other cognitive abilities such as spatial ability. Assortative mating increases genetic variance cumulatively generation after generation. If one parent is high in ability, the other parent is also likely to be high in ability, which means that the offspring are likely to be higher in ability than if they just had one parent high in ability (see Plomin et al., in press, for details).

Can it be coincidence that both assortative mating and heritability are so high for verbal ability?

Second, assortative mating increases a particular type of genetic variance called additive genetic variance, which is caused by the independent effects of alleles that "add up" to affect the trait. Nonadditive genetic variance is created by alleles that interact in their effect. The hallmark of non-additive genetic variance is an MZ correlation which is more than twice as large as the DZ correlation, or MZ concordances which are similarly higher than DZ concordances. Because MZ twins have exactly the same alleles at all loci, they are identical for all genetic effects even when many genes interact. For many psychiatric disorders, MZ twins are much more than twice as similar as DZ twins, thus suggesting nonadditive genetic variance. For example, for schizophrenia, MZ concordance is 45% and the DZ concordance is only 15%; for autism, MZ concordance is 60% and DZ concordance is less than 5%. In contrast, for cognitive disabilities and abilities, the pattern of MZ and DZ resemblance indicates the presence of additive genetic influence: MZ and DZ concordances are 66% and 43%, respectively, for reading disability and MZ and DZ correlations are about .80 and .60 for verbal ability. Nonadditive genetic variance greatly increases the difficulty of finding genes because genes will only be identified as they interact with other genes. Thus, the presence of assortative mating, which increases genetic variance, and additive genetic variance, which means we are looking for "main effects" rather than interactions, may make it easier to find QTLs in the cognitive domain, and especially language, than in other behavioural domains.

The first behavioural QTL (a gene on chromosome 19 that codes for apolipoprotein-E) was found for late-onset dementia (Alzheimer's disease) in 1993 (Corder et al., 1993), an association that has been replicated in scores of studies and remains the only known predictor of this common disorder in later life. Although a particular allele in this gene leads to a fivefold increased risk for Alzheimer's disease, it is a QTL in the sense that many people with this allele do not have Alzheimer's disease and most people with Alzheimer's disease do not have this genetic risk

factor. In 1994, a QTL for reading disability was detected and replicated on chromosome 6 (Cardon et al., 1994), a finding that also has been consistently replicated in follow-up studies (Fisher et al., 1999; Gayán et al., 1999; Grigorenko et al., 1997). The linkage to chromosome 6 appears for both phonological and orthographic reading measures. When the specific gene is identified (so far, the QTL linkage has only been tracked to its neighbourhood of several million base pairs of DNA rather than to a specific location), it will of great interest to investigate the extent to which the gene's effects are specific to reading or affect language more broadly or even reach out to affect other cognitive processes. Conversely, it will be interesting to follow up on reports of QTLs associated with general cognitive ability (Chorney et al., 1998; Fisher et al., 1999) in order to assess their potential role in language abilities and disabilities.

Although the emphasis now is on finding genes, we predict that in the next few years many genes associated with language abilities and disabilities will be discovered and the focus will turn to how these genes produce their effect. Such so-called functional genomics is usually phrased in terms of the molecular biological level of analysis. The agenda of molecular biology is clear: identify the gene product and understand how the gene is expressed and how its product works at a cellular level. However, higher levels of analysis are equally valid, such as understanding the gene's effects at the level of brain function or at the behavioural level of cognitive processes. Identifying replicable QTLs associated with language will make it possible to use measured genotypes to address questions about development, differential diagnosis, the neurocognitive pathways between genes and behaviour, and gene-environment interplay (Plomin & Rutter, 1998).

DNA analysis is coming to an area near you. Language researchers need to be prepared to take advantage of the power offered by the identification of specific genes to incorporate DNA markers in their research as risk factors. Although it is difficult and expensive to find genes, it is relatively easy and inexpensive to use genes once they have been identified as relevant in a particular area. For example, it is no longer necessary to obtain DNA through blood — cheek swabs can be used to obtain enough DNA to genotype thousands of DNA markers and cost less than £10 per subject. Indeed, we suggest that DNA ought to be obtained now for any valuable sample, not to find genes but rather to be in a position to use genes as they are found. Looking a bit further into the future, we suggest that clinicians will routinely use DNA in order to identify children at risk for language disorders, to diagnose children, and to design interventions to ameliorate language problems and its cascade of cognitive, social, and emotional sequelae of language problems.

As is the case with most important advances, identifying genes for language abilities and disabilities will also raise new ethical issues. These concerns must be taken seriously, but they are largely based on misconceptions about genetic research, and on a lack of appreciation of the way complex traits and common disorders are influenced by multiple genes as well as multiple environmental factors (Rutter & Plomin, 1997). As an antidote to such concerns, we propose a toast to celebrate these major scientific advances that will not only revolutionise research on language development but will also, we hope, substantially improve our chances of intervening early in development to ameliorate or even prevent language problems.

ACKNOWLEDGEMENTS

We thank the parents of the twins in the Twins Early Development Study (TEDS) for making the study possible. TEDS is supported by a programme grant from the UK Medical Research Council.

REFERENCES

Bishop, D.V.M. (1997). *Uncommon understanding: Development and disorders of language comprehension in children*. Hove, UK: Psychology Press.

Bishop, D.V.M., North, T., & Donlan, C. (1995). Genetic basis of specific language impairment: Evidence from a twin study. *Developmental Medicine and Child Neurology, 37*, 56–71.

Cardon, L.R., Smith, S.D., Fulker, D.W., Kimberling, W.J., Pennington, B.F., & DeFries, J.C. (1994). Quantitative trait locus for reading disability on chromosome 6. *Science, 266*, 276–279.

Chorney, M.J., Chorney, K., Seese, N., Owen, M.J., Daniels, J., McGuffin, P., Thompson, L.A., Detterman, D.K., Benbow, C.P., Lubinski, D., Eley, T.C., & Plomin, R. (1998). A quantitative trait locus (QTL) associated with cognitive ability in children. *Psychological Science, 9*, 159–166.

Cohen, J. (1988). *Statistical power analysis for the behavioral sciences (2nd ed.)*. Hillsdale, NJ: Lawrence Erlbaum Associates Inc.

Corder, E.H., Saunders, A.M., Strittmatter, W.J., Shmechel, D.E., Gaskell, P.C., Small, G.W., Roses, A.D., Haines, J.L., & Pericak-Vance, M.A. (1993). Gene dose of apolipoprotein E type 4 allele and the risk of Alzheimer's disease in late onset families. *Science, 261*, 921–923.

Dale, P.S., Dionne, G., Eley, T., & Plomin, R. (in press). Lexical and grammatical development: A behavioral genetic perspective. *Journal of Child Language*.

Dale, P.S., Simonoff, E., Bishop, D.V.M., Eley, T.C., Oliver, B., Price, T.S., Purcell, S., Stevenson, J., & Plomin, R. (1998). Genetic influence on language delay in two-year-old children. *Nature Neuroscience, 1*, 324–328.

DeFries, J.C., & Fulker, D.W. (1985). Multiple regression analysis of twin data. *Behavior Genetics, 5*, 467–473.

DeFries, J.C., & Fulker, D.W. (1988). Multiple regression analysis of twin data: Etiology of deviant scores versus individual differences. *Acta Geneticae Medicae et Gemellologiae, 37*, 205–216.

Eley, T.C., Bishop, D.V.M., Dale, P.S., Oliver, B., Petrill, S.A., Price, T.S., Purcell, S., Saudino, K.J., Simonoff, E., Stevenson, J., & Plomin, R. (1999). Genetic and environmental origins of verbal and performance components of cognitive delay in two-year-olds. *Developmental Psychology, 35*, 1122–1131.

Erlenmeyer-Kimling, L., & Jarvik, L.F. (1963). Genetics and intelligence: A review. *Science, 142*, 1477–1479.

Felsenfeld, S., & Plomin, R. (1997). Epidemiological and offspring analyses of developmental speech disorders using data from the Colorado Adoption Project. *Journal of Speech and Hearing Research, 40*, 778–791.

Fenson, L., Dale, P.S., Reznick, J.S., Bates, E., Thal, D., & Pethick, S.J. (1994). *The MacArthur Communicative Development Inventories: Short Form Versions* (unpublished).

Fisher, S.E., Marlow, A.J., Lamb, J., Maestrini, E., Williams, D.F., Richardson, A.J., Weeks, D.E., Stein, J.F., & Monaco, A.P. (1999). A quantitative-trait locus on chromosome 6p influences different aspects of developmental dyslexia. *American Journal of Human Genetics*, 64, 146–156.

Fisher, P.J., Turic, D., McGuffin, P., Asherson, P., Ball, D., Craig, I., Eley, T., Hill, L., Chorney, K., Chorney, M.J., Benbow, C.P., Lubinski, D., Plomin, R., & Owen, M.J. (1999). DNA pooling identifies QTLs for general cognitive ability in children on chromosome 4. *Human Molecular Genetics*, 8, 915–922.

Fisher, S.E., Vargha-Khadem, F., Watkins, K.E., Monaco, A.P., & Pembrey, M.E. (1998). Localisation of a gene implicated in a severe speech and language disorder. *Nature Genetics*, 18, 168–170.

Fulker, D.W., DeFries, J.C., & Plomin, R. (1988). Genetic influence on general mental ability increases between infancy and middle childhood. *Nature*, 336, 767–769.

Gallaway, C., & Richards, B.J. (1994). *Input and interaction in language acquisition*. Cambridge: Cambridge University Press.

Galsworthy, M., Dionne, G., Dale, P., & Plomin, R. (in press). Sex differences in the aetiology of verbal and non-verbal development. *Developmental Science*.

Ganger, J., Pinker, S., Baker, A., & Chawla, S. (1998, October). *The contribution of heredity to early vocabulary and grammatical development: A twin study*. Paper presented at the Boston University Conference on Language Development, Boston, MA.

Gayán, J., Smith, S.D., Cherny, S.S., Cardon, L.R., Fulker, D.W., Brower, A.W., Olson, R.K., Pennington, B.F., & DeFries, J.C. (1999). Quantitative-trait locus for specific language and reading deficits on chromosome 6p. *American Journal of Human Genetics*, 64, 157–164.

Gilger, J.W. (1997). How can behavioral genetic research help us understand language development and disorders? In M.L. Rice (Ed.), *Towards a genetics of language* (pp. 77–110). Hillsdale, NJ: Lawrence Erlbaum Associates Inc.

Grigorenko, E.L., Wood, F.B., Meyer, M.S., Hart, L.A., Speed, W.C., Shuster, A., & Pauls, D.L. (1997). Susceptibility loci for distinct components of dyslexia on chromosomes 6 and 15. *American Journal of Human Genetics*, 60, 27–39.

Hampson, J., & Nelson, K. (1993). The relation of maternal language to variation in rate and style of language acquisition. *Journal of Child Language*, 20, 313–342.

Hardy-Brown, K. (1983). Universals and individual differences: Disentangling two approaches to the study of language acquisition. *Developmental Psychology*, 19, 610–624.

Hardy-Brown, K., & Plomin, R. (1985). Infant communicative development: Evidence from adoptive and biological families for genetic and environmental influences on rate differences. *Developmental Psychology*, 22, 378–385.

Hart, B., & Risley, T.R. (1995). *Meaningful differences in the everyday experience of young American children*. Baltimore: P.H. Brookes.

Hohnen, B., & Stevenson, J. (1999). The structure of genetic influences on general cognitive, language, phonological, and reading abilities. *Developmental Psychology*, 35, 590–603.

Huttenlocher, J., Haight, W., Bryk, A., Seltzer, M., & Lyons, T. (1991). Early vocabulary growth: Relation to language input and gender. *Developmental Psychology*, 27, 236–248.

The International Molecular Genetic Study of Autism Consortium. (1998). A full genome screen for autism with evidence for linkage to a region on chromosome 7q. *Human Molecular Genetics*, 7, 571–578.

Karmiloff-Smith, A. (1992). *Beyond modularity: A developmental perspective on cognitive science*. Cambridge, MA: MIT Press.

Kendler, K.S., Neale, M.C., Kessler, R.C., Heath, A.C., & Eaves, L.J. (1992). Major depression and generalized anxiety disorder: Same genes (partly) different environments? *Archives of General Psychiatry*, 49, 716–722.

Koeppen-Schomerus, G., Gringras, P., Wolke, D., & Plomin, R. (in press). Genotype-environment interaction for prematurity and cognitive development in infancy. *Paediatrics*.

Lewis, B.A., & Thompson, L.A. (1992). A study of developmental speech and language disorders in twins. *Journal of Speech and Hearing Research*, 35, 1086–1094.

Lytton, H. (1980). *Parent-child interaction: The socialization process observed in twin and singleton families*. New York: Plenum.

Martin, N., Boomsma, D., & Machin, G. (1997). A twin-pronged attack on complex trait. *Nature Genetics*, 17, 387–392.

Martin, N.G., & Eaves, L.J. (1977). The genetical analysis of covariance structure. *Heredity, 38,* 79–95.

Petrill, S.A. (1997). Molarity versus modularity of cognitive functioning? A behavioral genetic perspective. *Current Directions in Psychological Science, 6,* 96–99.

Petrill, S.A., Saudino, K.J., Cherny, S.S., Emde, R.N., Hewitt, J.K., Kagan, J., & Plomin, R. (1997). Exploring the genetic etiology of low general cognitive ability from 14 to 36 months. *Developmental Psychology, 33,* 544–548.

Pinker, S. (1994). *The language instinct: The new science of language and mind.* London: Penguin Books.

Plomin, R. (1994). *Genetics and experience: The interplay between nature and nurture.* Newbury Park, CA: Sage Publications.

Plomin, R., & DeFries, J.C. (1979). Multivariate behavioral genetic analysis of twin data on scholastic abilities. *Behavior Genetics, 9,* 505–517.

Plomin, R., & DeFries, J.C. (1998). The genetics of cognitive abilities and disabilities. *Scientific American, May,* 62–69.

Plomin, R., DeFries, J.C., McClearn, G.E., & McGuffin, P. (in press). *Behavioral genetics (4th ed.).* New York: Worth.

Plomin, R., Fulker, D.W., Corley, R., & DeFries, J.C. (1997). Nature, nurture and cognitive development from 1 to 16 years: A parent-offspring adoption study. *Psychological Science, 8,* 442–447.

Plomin, R., & McClearn, G.E. (Eds.) (1993). *Nature, nurture, and psychology.* Washington, DC: American Psychological Association.

Plomin, R., Owen, M.J., & McGuffin, P. (1994). The genetic basis of complex human behaviors. *Science, 264,* 1733–1739.

Plomin, R., & Rutter, M. (1998). Child development, molecular genetics, and what to do with genes once they are found. *Child Development, 69,* 1221–1240.

Price, T.S., Eley, T.C., Dale, P.S., Stevenson, J., & Plomin, R. (in press). Genetic and environmental covariation between verbal and non-verbal cognitive development in infancy. *Child Development.*

Purcell, S., Eley, T.C., Dale, P.S., Oliver, B., Petrill, S.A., Price, T.S., Saudino, K.J., Simonoff, E., Stevenson, J., Taylor, E., & Plomin, R. (submitted). Comorbidity between verbal and non-verbal cognitive delays in 2-year-olds: A bivariate twin analysis.

Reznick, J.S., Corley, R., & Robinson, J. (1997). A longitudinal twin study of intelligence in the second year. *Monographs of the Society for Research in Child Development, 62*(1), 1–160.

Rice, M.L. (Ed.) (1996). *Toward a genetics of language.* Hillsdale, NJ: Lawrence Erlbaum Associates Inc.

Robinson, B.F., Mervis, C.B., & Matheny, A.P. (1999). *Specific and common genetic environmental influences on language and nonverbal ability of toddlers.* Biennial Meeting of the Society for Research in Child Development, April 15–18, Albuquerque, NM.

Rutter, M., & Plomin, R. (1997). Opportunities for psychiatry from genetic findings. *British Journal of Psychiatry, 171,* 209–219.

Saudino, K.J., Dale, P.S., Oliver, B., Petrill, S.A., Richardson, V., Rutter, M., Simonoff, E., Stevenson, J., & Plomin, R. (1998). The validity of parent-based assessment of the cognitive abilities of two-year-olds. *British Journal of Developmental Psychology, 16,* 349–363.

Smith, S.D., Pennington, B.F., & DeFries, J.C. (1996). Linkage analysis with complex behavioral traits. In M.L. Rice (Ed.), *Towards a genetics of language* Hillsdale, NJ: Lawrence Erlbaum Associates Inc., 29–44.

Stevenson, J., Pennington, B.F., Gilger, J.W., DeFries, J.C., & Gillis, J.J. (1993). Hyperactivity and spelling disability: Testing for shared genetic aetiology. *Journal of Child Psychology and Psychiatry, 34,* 1137–1152.

Stromswold, K. (in press). The heritability of language: A review of twin and adoption studies. *Journal of Child Language.*

Thompson, L.A., & Plomin, R. (1988). The sequenced inventory of communication development: An adoption study of 2- and 3-year-olds. *International Journal of Behavioral Development, 11,* 219–231.

Tomblin, J.B., & Buckwalter, P.R. (1998). Heritability of poor language achievement among twins. *Journal of Speech, Language, and Hearing Research, 41,* 188–199.

Wilson, R.S. (1983). The Louisville Twin Study: Developmental synchronies in behavior. *Child Development, 54,* 298–316.

4

Reading and language impairments in conditions of poverty

Grover J. Whitehurst and Janet E. Fischel

Children raised in economic poverty have below average development of language and are over represented among children with reading difficulties. What is the relation between language and literacy development for this population? Do children from low-income families fail at reading for the same reasons as children from middle-class families? Are there subgroups of children among readers from low-income backgrounds whose reading is impaired because of unique disabilities? Results from longitudinal research with a large sample of children in poverty support the conclusions that a) the connection between language and literacy skills is present strongly during the pre-kindergarten period but language and literacy develop independently during the first years of formally learning to read; b) the same skills factors predict reading success and failure in a low-income sample as have been identified for middle-income samples; c) a subgroup of 20–25% of children in a low-income sample may suffer from dyslexia and be distinguishable from their peers.

INTRODUCTION

Children reared in poverty are an important challenge to our understanding of language acquisition and literacy. As a group, their profile of language skills is typically closer to that of children with mild mental retardation than to that of middle class children (Whitehurst, 1997). Likewise, reading achievement is much below normal in this population. For instance, among African-American and Hispanic students in the US (two groups who experience disproportionate rates of poverty) the percentages of fourth graders reading below the basic level are 64% and 60% (National Center for Educational Statistics, 1999). Socio-economic status (SES) is also one of the strongest predictors of performance differences in children at the beginning of first grade (Alexander & Entwisle, 1988). SES differences exist prior to school entry in important developmental antecedents of reading such as letter knowledge and phonological processing skills (Bowey, 1995; Lonigan, Burgess, Anthony, & Barker, 1998; MacLean, Bryant, & Bradley, 1987; Raz & Bryant, 1990).

Clearly language and literacy skills are both impaired in this population, but questions remain:

1. Are differences in language skills causally related to differences in reading achievement and, if so, through what developmental pathways?
2. Do children from low-income families fail at reading for the same reasons as children from middle-class families?
3. Are there subgroups of children among readers from low-income backgrounds whose reading is impaired because of unique disabilities, or are individual differences in reading performance best conceptualised as existing on a continuum or normal curve?

We will address these questions after reviewing research on emergent literacy, which provides a framework for addressing issues of language, literacy, and poverty.

LITERATURE REVIEW

A definition

As defined by Whitehurst and Lonigan (1998), emergent literacy consists of the skills, knowledge and attitudes that are presumed to be developmental precursors to conventional forms of reading and writing (Sulzby, 1989; Sulzby & Teale, 1991; Teale & Sulzby, 1986) and the environments that support these developments (e.g. shared book reading; Whitehurst et al., 1988, 1994, 1999). Note that while most research on literacy problems concentrates solely on individual variation in children's language and phonological skills, and neglects individual differences in children's experiences, this definition of emergent literacy explicitly incorporates experiential differences into the conceptual framework.

Components of emergent literacy

The skill and knowledge base of emergent literacy includes: the domains of language (e.g. vocabulary); conventions of print (e.g. knowing that writing goes from left to right across a page); beginning forms of printing (e.g. writing one's name); knowledge of graphemes (e.g. naming letters of the alphabet); grapheme-phoneme correspondence (e.g. that the letter "b" makes the sound /b/); and phonological awareness (e.g. that the word "bat" begins with the sound /b/) (Whitehurst & Lonigan, 1998). The attitude component of emergent literacy concerns the preliterate child's interest in and motivation to interact with picture books and other printed materials (e.g. the frequency with which the child asks to be read to). The environmental component of emergent literacy includes such activities as shared picture book reading in the home and teaching the alphabet in kindergarten classrooms, among many others.

A substantial body of research has demonstrated positive correlations and longitudinal continuity between individual differences in emergent literacy and later differences in reading. Within the language domain, for example, a longitudinal relation between the extent of oral language and later reading proficiency has been demonstrated with three broadly defined types of children, typically-developing, reading-delayed, and language-delayed (e.g. Bishop & Adams, 1990; Butler, Marsh, Sheppard, & Sheppard, 1985; Pikulski & Tobin, 1989; Scarborough, 1989; Share, Jorm, MacLean, & Matthews, 1984). This relationship is much stronger for reading comprehension (reading for meaning) than for reading accuracy (sounding out individual words), and much stronger for older children than for children who are just beginning to read (Gillon & Dodd, 1994; Vellutino, Scanlon, & Tanzman, 1991; Whitehurst & Lonigan, 1998).

Another domain in which there is substantial evidence of developmental continuity is phonological awareness, which is the ability to detect that spoken words are composed of individual sound units. Individual differences in phonological sensitivity are related to the rate of acquisition of reading skills (Bradley & Bryant, 1983; 1985; Mann, 1984; Share et al., 1984; Stanovich, Cunningham, & Cramer, 1984; Wagner & Torgesen, 1987). Children who are better at detecting syllables, rhymes or phonemes are quicker to learn to read (i.e. decode words), and this relation is present even after variability in reading skill as a result of intelligence, receptive vocabulary, memory skills, and social class is removed statistically (Bryant, MacLean, Bradley, & Crossland, 1990; MacLean et al., 1987; Wagner, Torgesen, & Rashotte, 1994).

The interpretation that is typically applied to findings such as these is that individual differences in emergent literacy are causally and powerfully connected to individual differences in reading achievement. We will call this the emergent literacy model (Whitehurst et al., 1994). The implication of the emergent literacy model for social and educational policy is that reading achievement in children could be enhanced substantially by investing resources to improve emergent literacy, and that it is too late to wait until children begin formal reading instruction to help those who are at risk of reading delays.

Emergent literacy and literacy

Specification of a complete model of how different components of emergent literacy develop, influence each other, and influence the development of conventional forms of reading and writing in the context of other skills is not possible given current research. However, a broad division is possible. The model proposed in Whitehurst and Lonigan (1998) is that emergent and conventional literacy consists of two interdependent sets of skills, processes and sources of information: outside-in and inside-out, as represented in Fig. 4.1 below.

The outside-in units in the figure represent children's understanding of the context in which the writing they are trying to read (or write) occurs. The inside-out units represent children's knowledge of the rules for translating the particular writing they are trying to read into sounds (or sounds into print for writing). Imagine a child trying to read the sentence, "She sent off to the very best seed house for five bushels of lupine seed" (p. 21 from *Miss Rumphius* by Barbara Cooney, New York: Puffin Books, 1982). The ability to decode the letters in this sentence into correct phonological representations (i.e. being able to say the sentence) depends on knowing letters, sounds, links between letters and sounds, punctuation, sentence grammar, and cognitive processes, such as being able to remember and organise these elements into a production sequence. These are inside-out processes, which is to say that they are based on and keyed to the elements of the sentence itself. However, a child could have the requisite inside-out skills to read the sentence aloud and still not read it successfully. What does the sentence mean? Comprehension of all but the simplest of writing depends on knowledge that cannot be found in the word or sentence itself. Who is the "she" referred to in the sentence above? Why is she sending away for seed? Why does she need five bushels? What is lupine? In short what is the narrative, conceptual, and semantic context in which this sentence is found, and how does the sentence make sense within that context? Answering these questions depends on outside-in processes, which is to say that the child must bring to bear knowledge of the world, semantic knowledge,

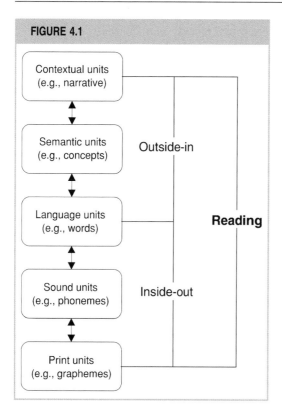

FIGURE 4.1

Fluent reading involves a number of component skills and processes. A reader must decode units of print into units of sound and units of sound into units of language. This is an inside-out process. However, being able to say a written word or series of written words is only a part of reading. The fluent reader must understand those auditory derivations, which involves placing them in the correct conceptual and contextual framework. This is an outside-in process. The bidirectional arrows in the figure illustrate that there is cross talk between different components of reading. For example, the sentence context affects the phonological rendering of the italicised letters in these two phases: "a *lead* balloon," "*lead* me there".

and knowledge of the written context in which this particular sentence occurred. Outside-in and inside-out processes are both essential to reading, and work simultaneously in readers who are reading well (see also Snowling, Chapter 14, this volume).

Emergent literacy and poverty

There is strong continuity between the skills with which children enter school and their later academic performance. Those children who experience early difficulties in learning to read are unlikely to catch up with their peers (Baydar, Brooks-Gunn, & Furstenberg, 1993; Stevenson & Newman, 1986; Tramontana, Hooper, & Selzer, 1988). For instance, Juel (1988) reported that the probability that children would remain poor readers at the end of the fourth grade if they were poor readers at the end of the first grade was .88. Children who enter school with limited reading-related skills are at high risk of qualifying for special education services. In fact, the majority of school-age children who are evaluated for special education services are referred because of unsatisfactory progress in reading (Lentz, 1988). This problem is strongly linked to family income. When schools are ranked by the median socio-economic status of their students, SES correlates .68 with academic achievement (White, 1982). Family income is also one of the strongest predictors of performance differences in children at the beginning of first grade (Alexander & Entwisle, 1988).

Despite the clear relationship between family income, early literacy success in children, and later academic outcomes, very little is known about the predictors of literacy success among children from low-income backgrounds. In particular, knowledge about this topic is scarce in the context of the last decade's explosion of research on the development of reading (Snow, Burns, & Griffin, 1998). This research has provided fundamental insights into the cognitive and neurological foundations of literacy. However, most literacy research explicitly excludes children from impoverished backgrounds, with the implicit rationale that poor reading in such children is complicated by environmental factors, whereas most of the researchers' interest in individual differences focuses on apparently intrinsic, biological variation in literacy. So the very children who are at particular risk for poor literacy are those who are left out of research studies on the grounds that their reading failure is either uninteresting, and/or the causes are just too complex to be analysed. Without longitudinal research that links basic research on the nature of literacy to the individual, family, neighbourhood, and school contexts in which children function, it will be difficult to prevent the vast majority of reading difficulties.

Subtypes of reading performance

There is a long-standing historic interest in identifying subtypes of reading ability. This area has been plagued by theoretical controversies and methodological problems. The dominant approach has been based on the assumption that there are two types of readers, normal and dyslexic. Identification of dyslexia has been based on a gap between a measure of intelligence and a measure of reading. For instance, a child with an IQ at the 50th percentile and reading scores at the 20th percentile would typically be classified as dyslexic, while a child with IQ and reading both at the 20th percentile would not. Stanovich has published numerous studies critical of this approach, based on the finding that there is a common weakness in processing phonological information both in garden variety poor readers (those whose reading scores are on par with their IQ scores) as well as in readers whose reading scores are lower than their IQ scores (so called dyslexics) (Stanovich, 1988; Stanovich & Siegel, 1994). Stanovich calls his approach the phonological-core variable-difference model to denote that there is a core phonological deficit in all poor readers, but variable differences among poor readers based on the presence of other interfering factors such as low IQ. Research conducted on Stanovich's model is clearly supportive of the phonological core deficit in poor readers (Stanovich & Siegel, 1994). Likewise, recent research using cluster analysis methods to subtype readers supports the view that children with reading disability usually display impairments on phonological awareness measures, with discriminative variability on other measures involving language and cognitive skills (Morris et al., 1998; Fletcher et al., 1997).

None of this research, however, addresses the important question of whether poor readers with phonological weaknesses represent the lower end of a normal, bell shaped distribution of phonological processing ability, or whether these children are a distinct subtype, i.e. different in kind from normal readers. This is not a trivial or semantic distinction. If the phonological processing skills of poor readers reflect the lower end of a normal distribution of phonological processing ability, it follows that:

1. The dividing line between poor readers and normal readers is arbitrary. In other words, if the underlying cognitive/neurological processes in reading are normally distributed, then the only appropriate basis for categorising readers as normal vs. poor would be based on whether their absolute level of reading is above or below some level of performance that is required by the setting in which they are situated. This standard will shift with setting, such that, for example, army recruits would be categorised as poor readers at a much lower level of performance than medical students.

2. Teaching strategies for poor readers would likely be more intensive versions of the same teaching strategies that work for good readers. For instance, if Child A, a good reader, differs from Child B, a poor reader, only in that Child A has somewhat more of the same underlying skills than Child B has, then given more time and practice than Child A, Child B ought to be able to catch up.

3. Diagnosis of poor reading would require nothing more than a reliable and valid score on a standardised test of reading ability because that score would correlate directly with the underlying, continuous distributed abilities that are reflected in reading performance.

On the other hand, if some poor readers are different in kind from normal readers, then a diagnosis of dyslexia would have implications for etiology, diagnosis, and treatment. Children from poverty backgrounds represent a special challenge with respect to this issue because so many low-income children experience reading difficulties. Distinguishing children whose reading problems are due primarily to lack of environmental opportunity from those who also suffer from a core deficit in a fundamental reading process could pay large dividends in directing focus and effectiveness of intervention.

A little known but powerful set of statistical techniques for distinguishing normally distributed from categorical differences among individuals has been developed by Meehl (1995) and extended by Waller and Meehl (1998). Classification is approached as a problem in applied mathematics. The methods developed by Meehl and Waller answer the empirical question of whether the latent structure of a group of correlated variables is taxonic (composed of categories) or nontaxonic (composed of dimensions or factors). Just as there are gophers and chipmunks, but no gophmunks, Meehl argues that the existence of taxonic categories underlying human psychological function is not to be a matter of convention or preference. The taxometric procedure developed by Meehl, MAXCOV-HITMAX, provides independent tests of the taxonic hypothesis and good estimates of the rate of occurrence of the taxon, the means of the taxon and non-taxon groups, and the valid and false-positive rates achievable by various diagnostic cuts that can be made on performance scores among correlated measures, e.g. multiple measures of reading ability. The method requires no gold standard criterion, and confidence in the inference to taxonic structure and numerical accuracy of latent values is provided by multiple consistency tests.

One way to gain an intuition about the essence of the MAXCOV-HITMAX procedure is to consider the correlation between hair length and physical strength. In the general population this correlation is highly significant and negative. In a scatter plot the relationship appears to be normal in its distribution. However, we know that the underlying relationship is actually a result of the taxon of gender: Women have longer hair than men and less physical strength than men, on average. When men and women are mixed together in the same sample, we find a correlation between hair length and strength. However, when men and women are separated into two groups (taxons), the relationship between hair length and strength disappears within each group, e.g. men with shorter hair are not typically stronger than men with longer hair. As a contrastive example of a non-taxonic relationship between variables, consider the relationship between a measure of physical strength and a measure of height. As is the case with physical strength and hair length, physical strength and height are strongly correlated in the general population. However, this is not a relationship that is primarily due to the taxon of gender. In other words, for both men and women, the taller one is, the stronger one tends to be.

Because hair length and strength are correlated owing to the admixture of two separate distributions, one for men and one for women, and because within the separate distributions of men and women hair length and strength are uncorrelated, it follows that the correlation between hair length and strength would tend to be greatest at that section of the combined distributions in which the most men and women are found together. Let us say for sake of the example that this would be a band of hair lengths between 10 and 15 centimetres. In contrast, the correlation between hair length and strength would tend to be low within those bands of hair lengths which include predominantly men or women, e.g. the band of hair lengths from 1–5 centimetres, which would include mostly males, and the band of hair lengths from 20–25 centimetres, which would include mostly females. This phenomenon (that the degree of correlation between variables would differ across successive bands of values of one of those variables if the correlation were caused by mixing together two groups of people with significantly different means on those variables) forms the essence of the empirical technique for searching for taxonicity developed by Waller and Meehl (1998). The researcher sorts through multiple measures that are highly correlated. Using a large sample of subjects, correlations or covariances between variables are examined with successive bands of values (cuts) of each variable. If the investigator finds that the correlational values for these successive cut points form a peak within an inverted U pattern, then there is preliminary evidence of taxonicity, i.e. categorical differences among members of the sample. For instance, Fig. 4.2 displays an inverted U pattern of the type that could be produced by an underlying taxon when the covariance between two measures of

FIGURE 4.2

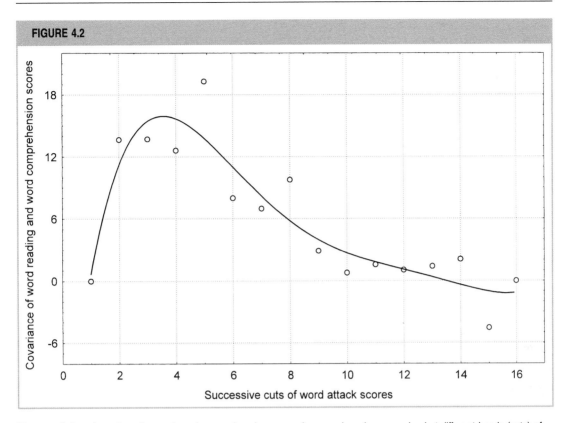

The covariation of word reading and word comprehension scores in second graders, examined at different bands (cuts) of the same children's scores on word attack (a measure of word decoding). The peaked, inverted U pattern indicates that the correlation of word reading and word comprehension is higher within one region of scores than others, suggesting the presence of an admixture of scores from two different taxons.

word comprehension is examined as a function of successive cuts on a measure of word decoding. If multiple measures evidence the same consistent peaked pattern, then there is strong evidence that qualitative differences (taxons) are present in the sample from which the data were collected. On the other hand, if the correlations within each successive cut of the variables are roughly the same or form a U rather than an inverted U function, then the most appropriate conclusion is that the data are non-taxonic, i.e. they reflect normally distributed, quantitative differences among people. For instance, Fig. 4.3 displays the relatively flat or U-shaped pattern that is produced when continuously distributed variables are analysed with the HITMAX-MAXCOV procedure. In this case, the procedure was applied to measures of oral

language and concepts, rather than to measures of reading as in Fig. 4.2.

NEW RESEARCH ON ISSUES OF EMERGENT LITERACY, LITERACY, POVERTY, AND TAXONS

The sample and measures

We have been exploring the relations between language and literacy and the possibility of the presence of a taxon of dyslexia in a sample of 338 children from low-income families (Crone & Whitehurst, 1999; Whitehurst, 1997; Whitehurst et al., 1994; Whitehurst et al., 1999). The children

FIGURE 4.3

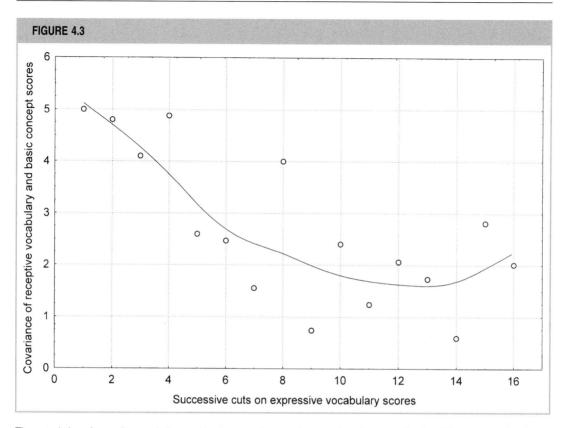

The covariation of receptive vocabulary and basic concept scores in second graders, examined at different bands (cuts) of the same children's scores on expressive vocabulary. The U pattern is characteristic of the joint distribution of normally distributed variables and suggests the absence of taxonicity in the distribution of language scores.

were first encountered when they were 4-year-olds attending Head Start (a federally-funded preschool programme in the US for children whose families live in economic poverty). Demographically, the sample was 43% African–American, 33% European–American, 18% Latino, and 6% other or not identified. Thirty-five percent of children were in single-mother homes, 40% were in two-parent homes, and 25% lived in extended families with more than two adults present. Twenty-nine percent of the participants' mothers had not completed high school, 26% had completed high school but had no further formal education, 40% had some trade school or college experience, and 5% had completed college. As all participants' families qualified for admission into Head Start, all lived below the US federal poverty level (about $14,000

for a family of three). Suffolk County, NY, where this study was conducted, has among the highest housing costs and the highest utility costs in the nation. It is a suburban setting in which jobs and services are dispersed over a wide geographical area, but it has very limited public transport. As a result of these factors, low-income families are particularly stressed economically.

Data presented here were derived from assessments of children in the spring of their Head Start year (when they were 4- and 5-years-old), and from annual follow-up assessments through the end of grade 2 (when the children were 7 and 8 years old). In Head Start and kindergarten, children were administered the Peabody Picture Vocabulary Test–Revised (PPVT) (Dunn & Dunn, 1981), which is a test of receptive vocabulary, the

Expressive One-Word Picture Vocabulary Test–Revised (One Word) (Gardner, 1990), which is a standardised test of expressive vocabulary, and 18 objectives (each consisting of one or more individual questions) from the Developing Skills Checklist (DSC) (CTB, 1990) that measure emergent literacy skills. The DSC objectives are arranged into four subscales:

- Memory (naming pictured letters; identifying sounds and letters; blending C-V-C words)
- Auditory (identifying same/different words; segmenting sentences; segmenting compound words; segmenting words; rhyming)
- Print Concepts (holding a book/turning pages; identifying people engaged in reading; differentiating print from pictures and letters from numerals; identifying functions of print; identifying components of written communication)
- Writing (demonstrating left/right progression; printing first name; drawing a person; writing a message mechanics; writing a message quality).

The DSC consists of multiple questions for each of the 18 objectives that are administered to children individually in the typical style of a standardised test of language or intelligence.

At the time of initial contact during Head Start, each child's principal caregiver filled out the *Stony Brook Family Reading Survey* (Whitehurst, 1993), which uses a multiple-choice format to assess a variety of home demographic and literacy related variables. Items from this instrument have been shown to correlate strongly with children's language and emergent literacy skills (Payne, Whitehurst & Angell, 1994). At the same time, the principal caregiver completed a pencil and paper adaptation of the *Quick Test* (Ammons & Ammons, 1962), a test of adult IQ that correlates highly with scores from individually administered IQ tests such as the Stanford-Binet.

Children were followed up at the end of first grade and second grade on the Word Attack subscale of the Woodcock Reading Mastery Tests–Revised (Word Attack) (Woodcock, 1987), a test of the ability to sound out printed pseudo words, and on various subscales of the Stanford Achievement Test–Eighth Edition (SAT) (Psychological Corporation, 1989) that assess reading for word or passage comprehension, and on the PPVT.

A taxon of dyslexia

We applied Meehl's (1995) HITMAX-MAXCOV procedure, described previously, to four different measures of reading in grade two and examined MAXCOV results from the 12 different ways in which a MAXCOV analysis of 3 variables at a time can be applied to 4 variables. Consistency across multiple tests is a principal criterion for judging taxonicity from the MAXCOV procedure. The average estimate for the baserate of normal readers across the 12 estimates was .77, with the very small standard deviation of .02. In other words, each of 12 attempts using different combinations of reading measures to divide the overall sample into two groups resulted in an estimate that separating the groups between approximately the highest performing 77% ± 2% and the remaining 23% of lowest performing children was the best cut point. Each of these attempts resulted in inverted U-shaped distributions similar to that in Fig. 4.2 relating successive cut points on one measure to covariance of the other measures. These inverted U functions are characteristic of taxonic data (Waller & Meehl, 1998). In other words, the data generate impressively consistent evidence that the overall distribution of reading scores among second graders in the present sample is best characterised as the admixture of two separate distributions, or groups of children. A representation of these two latent group distributions and how they are hidden within the roughly normal distribution of scores for all children is found in Fig. 4.4 for the variable of Word Attack. The cut point for this variable for dividing children into a dyslexic or normal reader group category would be the point of intersect for the two latent distributions. In Fig. 4.4 this cut point is a raw score of 9.5 on Word Attack. Note that some misassignments occur with this cut point, i.e. some children with scores above 9.5 are part of the latent distribution of dyslexic children and some children with scores below 9.5 are part of the latent distribution of normal readers. The

FIGURE 4.4

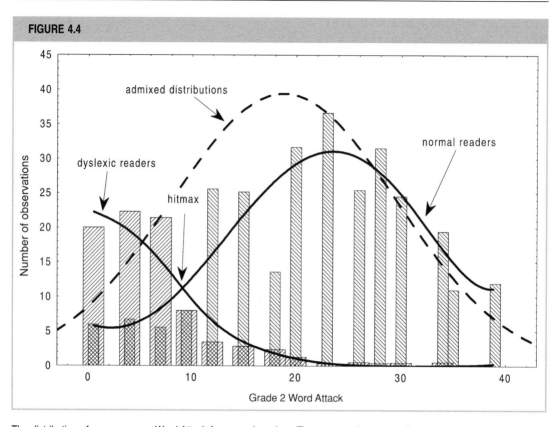

The distribution of raw scores on Word Attack for second graders. Three curves have been fitted to the data: one for the latent distribution of dyslexic readers, a second for the latent distribution of normal readers, and the third for the total distribution which is a result of the admixture of the distributions for dyslexic and normal readers. The hitmax point is that score on Word Attack that most effectively separates dyslexics from normal readers.

average valid positive rate for classification was .95 ($sd = .01$) and the average false positive rate was .36 ($sd = .14$) across the 12 MAXCOV analyses. In other words, very few normal readers are characterised as dyslexic by these procedures, but a moderate proportion of dyslexic children are characterised as normal readers.

For analyses of effects of dyslexia, to be reported subsequently, we needed to make a categorical distinction between children with or without dyslexia. To accomplish this, a Bayesian assignment was made such that children with over a 50% chance of being dyslexic based on the combination of predictions from the 12 MAXCOV analyses previously reported were assigned to the dyslexic group. The remaining children were assigned to the normal group. This resulted in a 20–80% split of children between the dyslexic and normal categories.

Structural equation modelling

We used structural equation modelling (SEM) to examine causal possibilities within the data from the assessments described previously. Although SEM is at the core of modern statistical approaches to correlational data and has become relatively accessible to researchers, it is still sufficiently new that a brief primer on its strengths and limitations may be useful (Byrne, 1994).

Causal modelling

SEM begins with what is a conceptual rather than a statistical component: causal modelling. A causal model is a hypothesis about the field of variables that affect one or more dependent variables of interest, presented formally as a path diagram. The diagram in Fig. 4.5, found later in this chapter, represents causal hypotheses with respect to the links between emergent literacy and literacy skills for the children from low-income backgrounds. A tremendous advantage of causal modelling at the conceptual stage is that it forces researchers to be specific about how they believe the domain they are trying to explain is organised, rather than allowing them to focus on one or two variables at a time. That type of tunnel vision may pay dividends in basic research, but it is doomed to failure in applied field research, which is inherently multivariate and contextually rich.

Measurement

The second step in SEM is to develop a measurement model. One of the principal statistical advances attributable to SEM is a procedure for dealing explicitly with measurement error, which is endemic to social and educational research. Measurement error refers to the fact that when, for example, we give a child a standardised test of reading such as the reading comprehension scale of the Stanford Achievement Test, the child's test score reflects not just reading ability, but also a number of extraneous factors that have nothing to do with reading. Perhaps the child reads well, but does not know how to take a multiple choice test. In this case, the child's test score would contain substantial error with respect to his or her actual reading ability. SEM addresses measurement error by utilising, where possible, multiple indicators of a given ability or construct, and thereby introducing a distinction between latent variables and observed variables. When a particular construct, such as reading ability, is measured with multiple indicators, it is represented in path diagrams as a circle or oval, i.e. as a latent variable. In contrast, when a construct is measured with only one test or instrument, it is represented in path diagrams as a square or rectangle, i.e. as a measured variable. So, for instance, in Fig. 4.5, maternal IQ is represented as a rectangle, a measured variable, because it is indexed with one test,

the Quick Test, whereas reading in Grade 1 is represented as an oval, a latent variable, because it is indexed with two different tests. Relations between variables in SEM, whether the variables are latent or measured, are represented by path diagrams, which are collections of variables connected by lines and arrows. If variables are connected by a line with a single arrowhead, then the variable with the arrowhead pointing into it is being modelled as determined by the variable with the line leading out of it. For example, in Fig. 4.5 reading in grade 1 is modelled as determined (in part) by inside-out emergent literacy skills in kindergarten. Variables that are connected by a line with an arrowhead on each end are being modelled as covarying, i.e. they are correlated without one necessarily being determined by the other, e.g. maternal IQ and race are modelled as correlated but maternal IQ is not modelled as causing race or vice-versa.

Testing fit

The third step in SEM is to collect data with respect to the causal model, using the measurement model that has been defined, and then to assess the model against the data that have been collected. The statistical assessment of a model generates one or more measures of the degree of fit between the model and the covariance matrix of variables to which it has been applied. The Bentler comparative fit index (CFI) is a leading measure of fit (Bentler, 1995). A CFI value above .90 is traditionally viewed as indicating relatively close fit between a model and the underlying data. Along with a measure of fit comes weight estimates for each of the paths in the model. These are like standardised betas in regression or correlation coefficients in simple correlation. They provide a standardised estimate of the strength of influence of a given path. For example, in the model in Fig. 4.5, the path from pre-kindergarten (age 4–5) outside-in reading skills to kindergarten (age 5–6) outside-in reading skills has a weight of .95, which indicates a very large contribution of pre-k skills to kindergarten skills in this domain; in contrast the path from race to inside-out skills during pre-k has a weight of .18, which indicates a relatively small, though still statistically significant, contribution.

A structural equation model

Figure 4.5 is the structural equation model we have applied to the data described above. The data from children in grade 2, which were used to derive the categorical variable of dyslexia that is represented in Fig. 4.5, are not included in the model in Fig. 4.5. To have extended the model through grade 2 or beyond would have introduced circularity because the dyslexia variable would have been predicting to the same variables from which it was derived.

The CFI index for the model is .95. Recall from the previous discussion of SEM that a CFI > .90 is generally taken as suggesting adequate fit between a model and the data to which it has been applied. Thus the fit between this particular model and the data is very good.

The model is arranged in temporal order from the top to the bottom of the figure. With one exception, the dyslexia variable, the temporal ordering of the variables in the model corresponds both to when the data were collected and when the variables in the model are assumed to be operating. Thus the inside-out variable at age 4–5 represents measures of auditory, print, memory, and writing skills taken on children when they were 4 years of age; likewise the inside-out variable at age 5–6 represents those same measures taken on children when they were 5 years of age. The read g1 variable at age 6–7 represents two separate measures of reading (taking when children were at the end of first grade). The outside-in variable at age 4–5 represents measures of expressive and receptive language taken from children when they were 4 and 5 years of age; likewise the outside-in variable at age 5–6 represents the same measures taken a year later when the children were at the end of kindergarten.

The outside-in measure at age 6–7 is represented as a rectangle rather than a circle because it is based on a single measure of language, the PPVT. After kindergarten we dropped the test of expressive language as a second measure of outside-in skills because the correlation between the expressive and receptive tests was very high and we needed to make time in the assessment battery for additional tests of readings.

The measured variables in rectangles at the top of Fig. 4.5 were collected from information provided by each child's principal caretaker based on a survey instrument (Whitehurst, 1993) and an IQ test. The variables are #sibs (the number of siblings in the child's family), race (whether the child was European–American in family background or not), lang (whether the child's principal caretaker's native language was English or not), momIQ (the principal caretaker's IQ), and books (the child's home literacy environment score as derived from measures described in Payne, Whitehurst, & Angell, 1994). We well understand that neither race nor language use in the home are categorical variables. With race, for instance, there were three predominant ethnic categories in our sample, not simply European–American vs. others as represented in Fig. 4.5, and within each of those categories there is substantial variation in important variables such as immigrant status, ethnicity of other family members, and degree of ethnic/racial identity. Likewise within the language variable, which is represented in the model as native English-speaking or not, there is important variability on dimensions such as the caretaker's fluency in English, the language use and English fluency of other family members, and so on. In some cases we do not have sufficient information to represent these differences with the model. In other cases, doing so would raise statistical difficulties in the context of SEM. For these and other reasons, it is likely that the race and lang variables in Fig. 4.5 underestimate the effects of these sources of variation.

The general model

One of the most interesting variables in Fig. 4.5 is labelled "dyslexia". It will be useful to describe the general findings of the model first, leaving dyslexia aside, and then turn to it.

The outside-in inside-out distinction

The path relationships between outside-in and inside-out variables in the model demonstrate

FIGURE 4.5

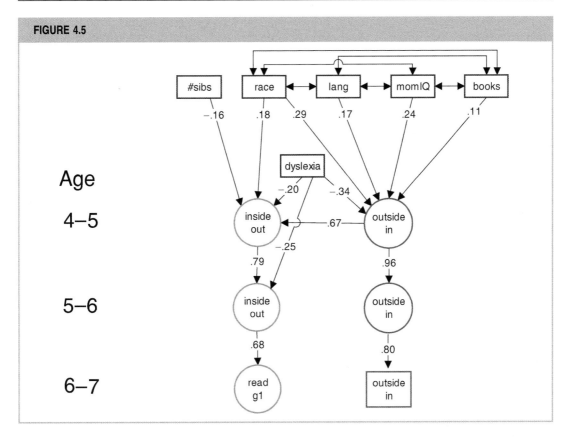

A structural model of literacy outcomes through 1st grade of preschoolers from low-income families. N = 338; CFI = .95. This model is derived from longitudinal data on children who were initially assessed when they began Head Start at age 4 and who were followed until the end of the second grade at age 7–8. Data from second grade are not presented in the model to avoid circularity with the dyslexia variable that was derived from assessments in second grade. To simplify the schematic, neither measurement variables that served as indicators of latent variables (the circles in the figure) nor error variances are represented. The outside-in latent variable was measured using standardised tests of receptive and expressive vocabulary. The inside-out latent variable was indexed with measures of memory for sounds and letters, linguistic awareness, print awareness, and emergent writing. All of the arrows in the figure represent statistically significant paths of influence; the numbers associated with each arrow can be interpreted as standardised regression beta weights.

the utility of this theoretical distinction as drawn by Whitehurst and Lonigan (1998) and illustrated in Fig. 4.1. Notice that inside-out (pre-reading skills such as letter recognition) and outside-in (language and conceptual skills such as receptive vocabulary) are strongly related (.67) at age 4–5. However, the relationship is statistically non-existent at age 5–6 and age 6–7 (kindergarten and first grade): an alternative structural model with paths from outside-in to inside-out skills at ages 5–6 and 6–7 shows these paths to be nonsignificant, and the Wald test for dropping parameters

indicates that they should be removed from the model. In other words, in the preschool period, children's knowledge of language and the extent to which they have acquired specific skills that are preliminaries to reading are related (e.g. children who have larger vocabularies know more letter names). However, during the period in late kindergarten and early elementary school in which children are actually learning to read, their knowledge of language and concepts (outside-in skills) and their reading and pre-reading skills (inside-out) are completely modular, e.g. having a larger vocabulary in first grade does *not* directly help a child learn to read. Any influence of vocabulary size is indirect and mediated by the child's earlier acquisition of inside-out skills.

The determinants of outside-in and inside-out skills

We know more about the sources of origins of individual differences in outside-in skills as reflected in Fig. 4.5 than we know about the origins of differences in inside-out skills. Leaving aside dyslexia, note that only number of siblings and race affect inside-out skills, while race, language status, maternal IQ and literacy environment in the home affect outside-in skills. We need more knowledge of the origins of inside-out skills such as letter recognition and phonological awareness. One source of children's inside-out skills may be experience with alphabet books (Murray, Stahl, & Ivey, 1996; Sénéchal, LeFevre, Thomas, & Daley, 1998), to which low-income children are little exposed (e.g. Heath, 1989; McCormick & Mason, 1986).

All the variables with paths leading into outside-in skills at age 4–5, leaving aside dyslexia, could be broadly conceptualised as constituents of the child's language environment in the home. Race, for instance, reflects in part the likelihood that principal caretakers of European-American background are more likely to use language in interactions with the child that reflects the linguistic style and content that are favoured on tests such as the PPVT. With regard to the lang variable, children whose principal caretakers are native speakers of English are more likely to expose children to English vocabulary, which is the language in which the tests of outside-in skills are administered. Children whose principal caretakers have higher IQs (as measured with an IQ test that primarily assesses adult conceptual vocabulary) will be more frequently exposed to vocabulary that generates higher scores on assessments of inside-out skills. The books variable is the most obvious measure of home language environment because it reflects the child's frequency of exposure to interactions involving picture-books. Of course, the effects of some of these variables, e.g.

momIQ, on children's outside-in skills could also be mediated genetically, but heritability estimates for communicative development during this age range, though significant, leave the majority of variance unaccounted for (Thompson & Plomin, 1988), so it is reasonable to characterise these variables as reflecting, in part, differences in home language environment.

The determinants of reading outcomes

The most important practical issue that can be addressed with the data analyses that are reflected in Fig. 4.5 is the origins of differences in how well children from low-income families learn to read. The picture that emerges from Fig. 4.5 is remarkably clear: Reading success through to the end of first grade is directly and strongly dependent on the inside-out skills that children bring to the task of reading from the preschool and kindergarten period. Note that 46% of the variance in reading outcomes at age 6–7 (grade 1) can be accounted for by the child's inside-out skills at the end of kindergarten (derived by squaring the path weight). In turn, 62% of the variance in inside-out skills at age 5–6 (kindergarten) can be accounted for by inside-out skills from the preschool period (age 4–5). The stability in language trajectories is even higher, with 92% of the variance in outside-in skills at age 5–6 (kindergarten) accounted for by outside-in skills at the end of pre-k, and 64% of the variance in outside-in scores at the end of first grade accounted for by the same variable at the end of kindergarten. Children are behind in these areas at the start of school are likely to stay behind.

The role of dyslexia

Even though the dyslexia variable was a result of a diagnosis obtained when children were seven and eight year olds in grade 2, we placed the variable in the path diagram in Fig. 4.5 as effective prior to age 4. This was done on the rationale that the underlying roots of dyslexia are likely to be in phonological and memory impairments that are chronic and that are already influential during the preschool period, even though they may not be reliably diagnosable until children are in elementary school. The structural model in Fig. 4.5 is an initial test of this hypothesis. The significant negative paths between dyslexia and inside-out as well as outside-in skills at age 4–5 and the significant negative path between dyslexia and inside-out skills at age 5–6 in Fig. 4.5 are consistent with the hypothesis that dyslexic children are different in kind from normal readers, that roots of dyslexia are present during the preschool period, and that the underlying impairments that are reflected in dyslexia in elementary school are also interfering with the acquisition of outside-in and inside-out skills in the preschool period. Other tests using different methods will be needed to confirm the causal implications of Fig. 4.5 with respect to dyslexia.

DISCUSSION

Let us return to the three questions that were raised at the beginning of this chapter.

Are differences in language skills causally related to differences in reading achievement, and if so, through what developmental pathways?

One of the enduring hypotheses among speech and language professionals is that language problems in the preschool years lead to reading problems in school. Many intervention efforts are based on this premise. However, the data related to this question are relatively sparse and open to several interpretations (e.g. Bishop & Adams, 1990; Paul, Chapter 11, this volume; Scarborough & Dobrich, 1994; Whitehurst & Fischel, 1994). The data from the present study should be particularly informative about the relations between language development and later reading because of the large sample size, the relatively low mean level of language skills in this sample during the preschool period (mean performance = 83, sd = 15 on the PPVT at age 4–5), and the use of SEM to model the effects of language in the context of other variables.

Our data and analyses indicate that the effects of language ability on reading outcomes through 6–7 years of age are largely indirect. In particular, the effects of language and the conceptual abilities indexed by language (outside-in skills) on reading are mediated by inside-out skills such as letter recognition, knowledge of letter sounds, print knowledge, and so forth. The connections between language and the developmental pathways that will lead to reading are present in the preschool period, but by age 5, two roads have diverged in the wood. One road is language/conceptual skills (outside-in); the other is the pre-reading skills (inside-out). During the first year of being formally taught to read, substantial individual differences in children's semantic and conceptual knowledge have no effects whatsoever on reading scores.

We believe this disconnect between the outside-in and inside-out developmental pathways is a function of the nature of the reading task during the first years of formal instruction. When children are first learning to read, their task is primarily one of decoding, i.e. translating alphabet symbols into sounds. The words the child is asked to decode are typically simple, high frequency words (e.g. "cat") that are likely to be within the vocabulary and conceptual store of most children, even those from low-income, high risk backgrounds. Having an extensive semantic and conceptual repertoire does not help children with the decoding task any more than such skills would help a sophisticated adult monolingual speaker of English take the first steps in learning to read Russian. It is only after children have acquired sufficient decoding skills to encounter printed material that pushes the envelope of their semantic knowledge that semantic/conceptual abilities and reading should connect up. In data from the present sample collected at later points in their development, we see this connection starting to emerge in grade 3 (age 8–9).

The connection in later grades between outside-in knowledge and reading could take at least two forms. For children with poor vocabulary and conceptual skills, reading for comprehension could be hampered by poor outside-in knowledge; even though the child might be able to sound out words and sentences, some of those words and the narrative/conceptual inferences necessary to understand the meaning of those words might be substantially beyond the child's competence. The second form of connection between reading and semantic development could occur on the other end of the dimension of reading fluency, where for fluent decoders the causal flow is from reading to conceptual knowledge. It is this phenomenon that Stanovich (e.g. 1986) has termed a "Matthew effect" (i.e. the rich get richer while the poor get poorer). Children who read well read more and, as a result, acquire more knowledge in numerous domains (Cunningham & Stanovich, 1998; Echols, West, Stanovich, & Zehr, 1996; Morrison, Smith, & Dow-Ehrensberger, 1995). Nagy and Anderson (1984, p. 328) estimated that the number of words read in a year by a middle-school child who is an avid reader might approach 10,000,000 (about 1200 times the number of words in this chapter), compared to 100,000 for the least motivated middle-school reader. By virtue of the sheer volume read, increased knowledge of the vocabulary and content domains (e.g. science or history) included in the texts would be expected.

The implications for intervention that derive from the data presented in Fig. 4.5 are relatively straightforward: During the preschool period, children from high-risk backgrounds should receive experiences that enrich their vocabulary and conceptual knowledge. These experiences should continue over the course of the child's development. However, by the time children are in the late preschool period, i.e. late 4-year-olds, they also need specific and effective experiences with letters, sounds, and print that will prepare them for the task of decoding when they first encounter formal instruction in reading. Without this preparation, and given the vagaries of much current reading instruction in the schools, chances of reading difficulties are high.

Do children from low-income families fail at reading for the same reasons as children from middle-class families?

It is certainly possible that reading difficulties occur in children reared in poverty for reasons that are different from those that characterise children whose parents are more affluent. One could imagine, for instance, that children from low-income backgrounds might be less socialised to the demands of school and that the resulting inattention to the task of reading might interfere with opportunities to learn. However, we have found that rates of inattention and hyperactivity are not particularly elevated in the present sample of children and that the correlations between hyperactivity and reading outcomes are relatively small (Nania & Whitehurst, 1997). In contrast, the present results are entirely in keeping with data for middle-class and mixed income populations in showing that individual differences in inside-out skills, such as knowing the correspondence between letters and their sounds, are the principal determinants of early reading outcomes (Burgess & Lonigan, 1998; Torgesen & Burgess, 1998; Wagner, Torgesen, & Rashotte, 1994; Wagner et al., 1993, 1997; Whitehurst & Lonigan, 1998). The children who are likely to learn to read quickly and well are the children who know the alphabetic principle, know their letters and some of the sounds those letters make, can print letters, and know a lot about how print works. This is as true for children from low-income backgrounds as it is for children of affluence.

Are there subgroups of children among readers from low-income backgrounds whose reading is impaired because of unique disabilities, or are individual differences in reading performance best conceptualised as existing on a continuum or normal curve?

Our data suggest there is a subgroup of children corresponding to 20–25% of the present sample whose reading performance in second grade is discontinuous with that of their higher performing peers. This is an intriguing group. On what basis do they differ? Is the difference in an underlying ability such as phonological processing or phonological memory and, if so, is this ability impaired and diagnosable before children begin to learn to read? Are these the same children who would be diagnosed as language impaired in the preschool period, and thus might language impairment and dyslexia be related to the same underlying pathology? Alternatively, might the taxon of dyslexia suggested in our analyses be due to environment causes in the same way, for example, that the taxon of French vs. English speakers is determined by a geographical accident of birth? Perhaps the children placed in the dyslexic category have lacked an experience that has been readily available to children in the normal reading group, e.g. access to alphabet books at home, or exposure to effective reading instruction in school.

We believe that the combination of the MAXCOV and SEM statistical procedures employed in the research described here offers an entry portal into the issues raised above that has not been available heretofore with social-behavioural research methods. Everything we have written here about a taxon of dyslexia is preliminary, tentative, and could well be wrong. We have just embarked on the journey and are a long way from our destination.

REFERENCES

Alexander, K.L., & Entwisle, D.R. (1988). Achievement in the first 2 years of school: Patterns and processes. *Monographs of the Society for Research in Child Development, 53* (2, Serial No. 218).

Ammons, R.B., & Ammons, C.H. (1962). *The Quick Test.* Missoula, MT: Psychological Test Specialists.

Baydar, N., Brooks-Gunn, J., & Furstenberg, F.F. (1993). Early warning signs of functional illiteracy: Predictors in childhood and adolescence. *Child Development, 64,* 815–829.

Bentler, P.M. (1995). *EQS: Structural equations program manual.* Encino, CA: Multivariate Software.

Bishop, D.V.M., & Adams, C. (1990). A prospective study of the relationship between specific language impairment, phonological disorders and reading retardation. *Journal of Child Psychology and Psychiatry and Allied Disciplines, 31,* 1027–1050.

Bowey, J.A. (1995). Socioeconomic status differences in preschool phonological sensitivity and first-grade reading achievement. *Journal of Educational Psychology, 87,* 476–487.

Bradley, L., & Bryant, P.E. (1983). Categorizing sounds and learning to read — a causal connection. *Nature, 301,* 419–421.

Bradley, L., & Bryant, P.E. (1985). *Rhyme and reason in reading and spelling.* Ann Arbor: University of Michigan Press.

Bryant, P.E., MacLean, M., Bradley, L.L., & Crossland, J. (1990). Rhyme and alliteration, phoneme detection, and learning to read. *Developmental Psychology, 26,* 429–438.

Burgess, S.R., & Lonigan, C.J. (1998). Bidirectional relations of phonological sensitivity and prereading abilities: Evidence from a preschool sample. *Journal of Experimental Child Psychology, 70,* 117–141.

Butler, S.R., Marsh, H.W., Sheppard, M.J., & Sheppard, J.L. (1985). Seven-year longitudinal study of the early prediction of reading achievement. *Journal of Educational Psychology, 77,* 349–361.

Byrne, B.M. (1994). *Structural equation modeling with EQS and EQS/Windows.* Thousand Oaks, CA: Sage.

Cooney, B. (1982). *Miss Rumphius.* New York: Puffin.

CTB (1990). *Developing skills checklist.* Monterey, CA: CTB/McGraw-Hill.

Crone, D.A., & Whitehurst, G.J. (1999). Schooling effects on emergent literacy and early reading skills. *Journal of Educational Psychology, 91,* 604–614.

Cunningham, A.E., & Stanovich, K.E. (1998). Early reading acquisition and its relation to reading experience and ability 10 years later. *Developmental Psychology, 33,* 934–945.

Dunn, L.M., & Dunn, L.M. (1981). *Peabody Picture Vocabulary Test–Revised.* Circle Pines, NM: American Guidance Service.

Echols, L.D., West, R.F., Stanovich, K.E., & Zehr, K.S. (1996). Using children's literacy activities to predict growth in verbal cognitive skills: A longitudinal investigation. *Journal of Educational Psychology, 88,* 296–304.

Fletcher, J.M., Morris, R., Lyon, G.R., Stuebing, K.K., Shaywitz, S.E., Shankweiler, D.P., Katz, L., & Shaywitz, B.A. (1997). Subtypes of dyslexia: An old problem revisited. In B.A. Blachman (Ed.), *Foundations of reading acquisition and dyslexia: Implications for early intervention* (pp. 95–114). Mahwah, NJ: Lawrence Erlbaum Associates Inc.

Gardner, M.F. (1990). *Expressive One-Word Picture Vocabulary Test–Revised.* Novato, CA: Academic Therapy Publications.

Gillon, G., & Dodd, B.J. (1994). A prospective study of the relationship between phonological, semantic and syntactic skills and specific reading disability.

Reading and Writing: An Interdisciplinary Journal, 6, 321–345.

Heath, S.B. (1989). Oral and literate traditions among Black Americans living in poverty. Special Issue: Children and their development: Knowledge base, research agenda, and social policy application. *American Psychologist, 44*, 367–373.

Juel, C. (1988). Learning to read and write: A longitudinal study of 54 children from first through fourth grades. *Journal of Educational Psychology, 80*, 437–447.

Lentz, F.E. (1988). Effective reading interventions in the regular classroom. In J.L. Graden, J.E. Zins, & M.J. Curtis (Eds.), *Alternative educational delivery systems: Enhancing instructional options for all students.* Washington DC: National Association of School Psychologists.

Lonigan, C.J., Burgess, S.R., Anthony, J.L., & Barker, T.A. (1998). Development of phonological sensitivity in two- to five-year-old children. *Journal of Educational Psychology, 90*, 294–311.

MacLean, M., Bryant, P., & Bradley, L. (1987). Rhymes, nursery rhymes, and reading in early childhood. *Merrill-Palmer Quarterly, 33*, 255–282.

Mann, V.A. (1984). Longitudinal prediction and prevention of early reading difficulty. *Annals of Dyslexia, 34*, 115–136.

McCormick, C.E., & Mason, J.M. (1986). Intervention procedures for increasing preschool children's interest in and knowledge about reading. In W.H. Teale & E. Sulzby (Eds.), *Emergent literacy: writing and reading* (pp. 90–115). Norwood, NJ: Ablex.

Meehl, P.E. (1995). Bootstraps taxometrics: Solving the classification problem in psychopathology. *American Psychologist, 50*, 266–275.

Morris, R.D., Stuebing, K.K., Fletcher, J.M., Shaywitz, S.E., Lyon, G.R., Shankweiler, D.P., Katz, L., Francis, D.J., & Shaywitz, B.A. (1998). Subtypes of reading disability: Variability around a phonological core. *Journal of Education Psychology, 90*, 347–373.

Morrison, F.J., Smith, L., & Dow-Ehrensberger, M. (1995). Education and cognitive development: A natural experiment. *Developmental Psychology, 31*, 789–799.

Murray, B.A., Stahl, S.A., & Ivey, M.G. (1996). Developing phoneme awareness through alphabet books. *Reading and Writing, 8*, 307–322.

Nagy, W.E., & Anderson, R.C. (1984). How many words are there in printed school English? *Reading Research Quarterly, 19*, 304–330.

Nania, O.C., & Whitehurst, G.J. (1997). Inattention-hyperactivity and reading in kindergartners and second graders from low-income families. *Abnormal Child Psychology, 25*, 321–331.

National Center for Educational Statistics (1999). *NAEP 1998 reading report card for the nation and states* (document # 1999–500). Washington, DC: US Department of Education Office of Educational Research and Improvement.

Payne, A.C., Whitehurst, G.J., & Angell, A.L. (1994). The role of literacy environment in the language development of children from low-income families. *Early Childhood Research Quarterly, 9*, 427–440.

Pikulski, J.J., & Tobin, A.W. (1989). Factors associated with long-term reading achievement of early readers. *National Reading Conference Yearbook, 38*, 123–133.

Psychological Corporation (1989). *Stanford achievement test–Eighth edition.* Orlando, FL: Harcourt Brace.

Raz, I.S., & Bryant, P. (1990). Social background, phonological awareness and children's reading. *British Journal of Developmental Psychology, 8*, 209–225.

Scarborough, H. (1989). Prediction of reading dysfunction from familial and individual differences. *Journal of Educational Psychology, 81*, 101–108.

Scarborough, H.S., & Dobrich, W. (1994). On the efficacy of reading to preschoolers. *Developmental Review, 14*, 245–230.

Sénéchal, M., LeFevre, J., Thomas, E.M., & Daley, K.E. (1998). Differential effects of home literacy experiences on the development of oral and written language. *Reading Research Quarterly, 33*, 96–116.

Share, D.L., Jorm, A.F., Maclean, R., & Matthews, R. (1984). Sources of individual differences in reading acquisition. *Journal of Educational Psychology, 76*, 1309–1324.

Snow, C.E., Burns, M.S., & Griffin, P. (Eds.) (1998). *Preventing reading difficulties in young children.* Washington, DC: National Academy Press.

Stanovich, K.E. (1986). Matthew effects in reading: Some consequences of individual differences in the acquisition of literacy. *Reading Research Quarterly, 21*, 360–407.

Stanovich, K.E. (1988). Explaining the differences between the dyslexic and the garden-variety poor reader: The phonological core variable difference model. *Journal of Learning Disabilities, 21*, 590–604.

Stanovich, K.E., Cunningham, A.E., & Cramer, B.B. (1984). Assessing phonological awareness in kindergarten children: Issues of task comparability. *Journal of Experimental Child Psychology, 38*, 175–190.

Stanovich, K.E., & Siegel, L.S. (1994). Phenotypic performance profile of children with reading disabilities: A regression-based test of the phonological-core variable-difference model. *Journal of Educational Psychology, 86,* 24–53.

Stevenson, H.W., & Newman, R.S. (1986). Long-term prediction of achievement and attitudes in mathematics and reading. *Child Development, 57,* 646–659.

Sulzby, E. (1989). Assessment of writing and of children's language while writing. In L. Morrow & J. Smith (Eds.), *The role of assessment and measurement in early literacy instruction* (pp. 83–109). Englewood Cliffs, NJ: Prentice-Hall.

Sulzby, E., & Teale, W. (1991). Emergent literacy. In R. Barr, M. Kamil, P. Mosenthal, & P.D. Pearson (Eds.), *Handbook of Reading Research* (Vol. II) (pp. 727–758). NY: Longman.

Teale, W.H., & Sulzby, E. (Eds.) (1986). *Emergent literacy: Writing and reading.* Norwood, NJ: Ablex.

Thompson, L.A., & Plomin, R. (1988). The sequenced inventory of communication development: An adoption study of two- and three-year olds. *International Journal of Behavioral Development, 11,* 219–231.

Torgesen, J.K., & Burgess, S.R. (1998). Consistency of reading-related phonological processes throughout early childhood: Evidence from longitudinal-correlational and instructional studies. In J.L. Metsala & L.C. Ehri (Eds.), *Word recognition in beginning literacy* (pp. 161–188). Mahwah, NJ: Lawrence Erlbaum Associates Inc.

Tramontana, M.G., Hooper, S., & Selzer, S.C. (1988). Research on preschool prediction of later academic achievement: A review. *Developmental Review, 8,* 89–146.

Vellutino, F.R., Scanlon, D.M., & Tanzman, M.S. (1991). Bridging the gap between cognitive and neuropsychological conceptualizations of reading disability. *Learning and Individual Differences, 3,* 181–203.

Wagner, R.K., & Torgesen, J.K. (1987). The nature of phonological processing and its causal role in the acquisition of reading skills. *Psychological Bulletin, 101,* 192–212.

Wagner, R.K., Torgesen, J.K., & Rashotte, C.A. (1994). Development of reading-related phonological processing abilities: New evidence of bidirectional causality from a latent variable longitudinal study. *Developmental Psychology, 30,* 73–87.

Wagner, R.K., Torgesen, J.K., Laughon, P., Simmons, K., & Rashotte, C.A. (1993). The development of young readers' phonological processing abilities. *Journal of Educational Psychology, 85,* 1–20.

Wagner, R.K., Torgesen, J.K., Rashotte, C.A., Hecht, S.A., Barker, T.A., Burgess, S.R., Donahue, J., & Garon, T. (1997). Changing relations between phonological processing abilities and word-level reading as children develop from beginning to skilled readers: A 5-year longitudinal study. *Developmental Psychology, 33,* 468–479.

Waller, N.G., & Meehl, P.E. (1998). *Multivariate taxometric procedures: Distinguishing types from continua.* Thousand Oaks, CA: Sage.

White, K. (1982). The relation between socioeconomic status and academic achievement. *Psychological Bulletin, 91,* 461–481.

Whitehurst, G.J. (1993). *Stony Brook Family Reading Survey.* Stony Brook, NY: Author.

Whitehurst, G.J. (1997). Language processes in context: Language learning in children reared in poverty. In L.B. Adamson & M.A. Romski (Eds.), *Research on communication and language disorders: Contribution to theories of language development* (pp. 233–266). Baltimore, MD: Brookes.

Whitehurst, G.J., Epstein, J.N., Angel, A., Payne, A.C., Crone, D., & Fischel, J.E. (1994). Outcomes of an emergent literacy intervention in Head Start. *Journal of Educational Psychology, 86,* 542–555.

Whitehurst, G.J., Falco, F.L., Lonigan, C., Fischel, J.E., DeBaryshe, B.D., Valdez-Menchaca, M.C., & Caulfield, M. (1988). Accelerating language development through picture-book reading. *Developmental Psychology, 24,* 552–558.

Whitehurst, G.J., & Fischel, J.E. (1994). Early developmental language delay: What, if anything, should the clinician do about it? *Journal of Child Psychology & Psychiatry & Allied Disciplines, 35,* 613–648.

Whitehurst, G.J., & Lonigan, C.J. (1998). Child development and emergent literacy. *Child Development, 68,* 848–872.

Whitehurst, G.J., Zevenbergen, A.A., Crone, D.A., Schultz, M.D., Velting, O.N, & Fischel, J.E. (1999). Effects of an emergent literacy intervention in Head Start and schools attended on literacy outcomes through second grade. *Journal of Educational Psychology, 91,* 261–272.

Woodcock, R.W. (1987). *Woodcock Reading Mastery Tests–Revised.* Circles Pines, MN: American Guidance Service.

5

Barriers to literacy development in children with speech and language difficulties

Joy Stackhouse

This chapter adopts a psycholinguistic perspective to explore why children with specific speech and language difficulties often have associated literacy problems and examines how and when children at risk for literacy problems might be identified. The findings from a longitudinal study of 47 children with specific speech difficulties and their 47 matched normally developing controls are presented. The performance of the two groups of children on a range of speech, language, auditory discrimination, phonological awareness, letter knowledge, reading, and spelling tasks was compared at three points in time; T1 (CA 4;06), T2 (CA 5;06); and T3 (CA 6;06). At T1, the children who had both speech and language problems performed less well on most of the tasks administered than children with speech problems alone. They had speech input problems as well as more severe speech output problems and appeared at risk of later literacy problems. However, performance at T1 was not predictive of reading and spelling development at T3. At T3, the children were divided into typical vs delayed reader/spellers and their concurrent and past speech processing skills examined. As a result, developmental signs of literacy difficulties at ages 5 and 6 were identified. Case studies of children with persisting vs resolved speech difficulties are used to illustrate speech processing profiles associated with reading and spelling difficulties.

Children with specific speech and language difficulties often have associated literacy problems. In particular their difficulties persist in the areas of phonological awareness and spelling. However, it is not clear what the specific barriers are to their literacy development. This chapter adopts a psycholinguistic framework to explore what speech processing skills are necessary for normal literacy development and how children who are at risk for persisting speech, language and literacy problems might be identified. It will focus on children with hidden as well as children with obvious speech difficulties and examine when a speech difficulty can be said to have resolved.

THE SPEECH PROCESSING SYSTEM

The term "speech processing" is used to refer to "all the skills included in understanding and producing speech, including peripheral skills such as articulatory ability and hearing" (Stackhouse & Wells, 1997, p. 8). Before learning to read and spell, children have already developed a range of speech processing skills to deal with their spoken language. The speech processing system underpinning these skills comprises an input side for receiving spoken information and an output side for selecting and producing spoken words and sentences. In addition, the child needs to store linguistic information about spoken language in a variety of representations within the lexicon (a store of word knowledge). Figure 5.1 illustrates the basic essentials of a psycholinguistic model of speech processing.

On the left of the model in Fig. 5.1 there is a channel for the spoken input of information via the ear, and on the right a channel for the output of information through the mouth. At the top of the model are the lexical representations; a broad term to describe a store of previously processed information about words. For each word there is stored information about its meaning, its grammatical properties, what it sounds like as distinct from other similar sounding words, how to say it, and its orthography so that it can be recognised in print.

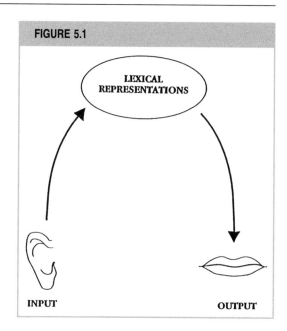

FIGURE 5.1

The basic structure of the speech processing system (from Stackhouse & Wells, 1997, p. 9. Reprinted with permission from Whurr Publishers, London).

Difficulties within this speech processing system can take various forms depending on the locus of the problem within the system. For example, there may be a deficit on the input side evident in problems with auditory discrimination of sounds or sequences of sounds; and/or within the representations because of imprecise storage of the composition of words; and/or on the output side where there may be an inability to assemble, time and coordinate articulatory movements for words and connected speech. There may be an obvious cause for the input speech difficulties such as sensory impairment (e.g. deafness), or for the output speech difficulties such as structural abnormality (e.g. cleft lip and palate) or neurological impairment (e.g. cerebral palsy). However, many speech problems have no obvious causation and are often referred to as phonological impairment or verbal/articulatory dyspraxia. Detailed investigations of children with such difficulties have revealed that they usually have pervasive speech processing problems affecting their input, representation and output systems (Chiat, 1983; Chiat & Hunt, 1993) and that associated literacy problems are common

(Stackhouse & Snowling, 1992; Stackhouse & Wells, 1993, 1997).

A developmentally intact speech processing system is therefore not only necessary for speech to develop normally, but it is also the foundation for written language development (Stackhouse, 1997). Children use this system to develop phonological awareness: their ability to reflect on and manipulate the structure of an utterance (e.g. into words, or syllables, or sounds) as distinct from its meaning. If children cannot learn that words can be broken up into sounds which can be represented by letters, they will not be able to make sense of an alphabetic script such as English.

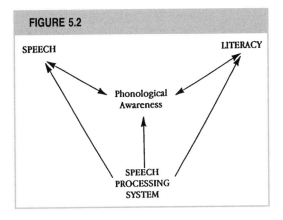

FIGURE 5.2

The connection between speech and literacy development (from Stackhouse & Wells, 1997, p. 58. Reprinted with permission from Whurr Publishers, London).

PHONOLOGICAL AWARENESS: CONNECTING SPEECH AND LITERACY

Lewkowicz (1980) noted that there are at least 10 different phonological awareness tasks (reported in Stackhouse 1997):

1. Recognition of rhyme (e.g. Do these words rhyme: FISH DISH?; Which is the odd one out: FISH DISH BALL?).
2. Isolation of a beginning, medial or final sound (e.g. What is the last sound in FISH?).
3. Sound segmentation (e.g. What are the three sounds in FISH?).
4. Identifying the number of syllables or sounds in a word (e.g. How many beats in POTATO; How many sounds in FISH?).
5. Sound to word matching (e.g. Does FISH start with /f/?).
6. Word to word matching (e.g. Does FISH start with the same sound as FOOT?).
7. Syllable and sound blending (e.g. What does PO-TA-TO say? What does F-I-SH say?).
8. Sound deletion (e.g. Say FISH without /f/; Say FISH without the first sound).
9. Specifying which phoneme has been deleted (e.g. Say MEAT, now say EAT — what sound was left out of the second word?).
10. Sound substitution (e.g. Say MEAT; now say it with /f/ instead of /m/).

This is by no means an exhaustive list. Two other popular phonological awareness tasks involve rhyme production (e.g. Tell me as many words as you can that rhyme with FISH), and sound exchange (e.g. Give me a spoonerism on BIG FISH — answer FIG BISH).

The skills necessary to perform the above tasks are derived from the speech processing system. The skills include: listening, auditory processing, storing and using prior linguistic knowledge, and an ability to output from this store as well as to generate new spoken material. Thus, phonological awareness is not an independent entity as sometimes presented but a product of the speech processing system portrayed in Fig. 5.1. Figure 5.2 illustrates the relationship between speech, literacy and phonological awareness and how all three are dependent on the speech processing system.

Any fault in the speech processing system will have repercussions, not only for a child's spoken language development, but also for their literacy development since the child will be unable to develop phonological awareness and the skills necessary to move language from the spoken to written domain.

It is therefore not surprising that children with speech and language problems often have impaired phonological awareness skills and experience problematic literacy development (Bishop & Adams, 1990; Catts, 1993; Magnusson & Naucler,

1990; Stackhouse, 1997; Stackhouse & Snowling, 1992). Rhyme development in particular has been a focus of attention in studies of young children with speech and language difficulties (Bird & Bishop, 1992; Marion, Sussman, & Marquardt, 1993). However, it is not clear precisely which speech processing skills underpin the successful emergence of phonological awareness skills in normally developing children. For those children with spoken language impairments, attention has more generally concentrated on whether it is the observed "speech" or "language" problem that contributes most to their difficulties with developing phonological awareness skills rather than pinpointing the underlying speech and language processing skills which subsequently affect literacy development.

A number of studies have suggested that early language problems are associated with later literacy problems (Bishop & Adams, 1990; Catts, 1993; Catts, Fey, Zhang, & Tomblin, in press; Magnusson & Naucler, 1990; Scarborough, 1990). However, the relationship between early speech difficulties and literacy development has been less clear. Bird, Bishop, and Freeman (1995) investigated a group of 31 boys in the age range of 5–7 years with expressive phonological impairments (a general term for children's speech difficulties when there is no obvious physical or neurological cause) to see if a) the severity of the speech problem, and b) the presence of additional language impairments were significant prognostic factors for literacy development. The boys' performance on a range of phonological awareness tasks (such as rhyme and word onset matching and segmentation) and reading and spelling tasks (including nonword reading and spelling) was compared to a group of normally developing boys matched on chronological age and nonverbal ability. The boys with phonological disability had particular difficulty with the phonological awareness tasks even when these did not require a spoken response. The majority of them had significant literacy problems when followed up at approximately 7 years 6 months. The presence of language impairments in addition to speech difficulties did not significantly affect children's literacy outcome but the severity and persistence of the speech problem

did. Similarly, speech intelligibility predicted performance on phonological awareness tasks in a study by Webster and Plante (1992). In contrast, Leitao, Hogben and Fletcher (1997) found that it was the children who had both speech and language difficulties who performed the least well on segmentation and blending tasks at 6 years of age compared to normal controls and children with speech but not language difficulties. However, the group of children with speech difficulties alone were not problem-free. As a group, they performed significantly less well than the normal controls on the phonological awareness tasks of segmenting, blending, deletion and invented spelling but the bimodal distribution of results across all of the tasks suggested that approximately half of the children were performing like normal controls while the other half had significant difficulties.

The above studies have contributed much to our understanding of phonological awareness and literacy difficulties in children with speech and language problems, but it is still not clear what underlies poor phonological awareness development in young children or what predicts persisting speech, language and literacy problems. We therefore set up a longitudinal study of children with and without specific speech difficulties in the age range of 4;0–7;0 to examine speech processing and literacy development (Stackhouse, Nathan, Goulandris, & Snowling, 1999).

A LONGITUDINAL STUDY OF CHILDREN'S SPEECH, LANGUAGE AND LITERACY SKILLS

The basic premise of our study was that the skills necessary for successful phonological awareness and literacy development arise from an intact speech processing system. It was predicted that, compared to matched controls, children with specific speech difficulties will have a deficit at one or more points in this speech processing system and that this deficit (or cluster of deficits) will manifest not only in speech difficulty but also affect performance on phonological awareness and later literacy tasks. The children with speech difficulties and their matched controls were assessed at three points in time (T1, T2 and T3) at ages around 4;06 (T1), 5;06 (T2) and 6;06 (T3).

Design and participants

Speech and language therapists in London were requested to refer children on their caseload who met the following criteria:

1. Chronological age 4–5 years.
2. Obvious speech difficulties but no evident physical cause (e.g. not cases with cleft lip and palate, or cerebral palsy).
3. No hearing impairment.
4. No associated medical condition (e.g. epilepsy, a named syndrome).
5. No severe receptive or pragmatic language difficulties.
6. Monolingual English speakers.

Eighty children were referred to the study. Ten of the children were rejected from the study because they had additional complications such as hearing problems. Twenty did not qualify because their performance on the Edinburgh Articulation Test (Anthony, Bogle, Ingram, & McIsaac, 1971) was not significantly impaired (i.e. their standard scores were above 85). However, these children with resolving speech difficulties were followed up as a separate group and will be discussed later in the chapter. Three of the children with specific speech difficulties had above average reading skills from the start and were not included in the main cohort but have been followed separately. This left forty-seven children who met all of the following criteria.

1. Significant speech difficulties (more than one standard deviation below the mean) on the Edinburgh Articulation Test (Anthony et al., 1971).
2. Nonverbal IQ within normal limits, on two subtests of the WPSSI-R; Block Design and Picture Completion (Wechsler, 1992).

TABLE 5.1

The mean and standard deviations of age and nonverbal ability (standard scores) for the group of children with specific speech difficulties (N = 47) and the matched controls (N = 47)

| | Group | | | |
| | Speech difficulties | | Control | |
	Mean	SD	Mean	SD
Age	4.58	0.4	4.64	0.4
Block design	10.28	2.29	10.45	2.83
Picture completion	12.11	2.1	12.13	2.23

3. Nonreaders (raw score of 0) or beginning readers (scoring below 60th centile) on the British Ability Scales (BAS) single word reading test (Elliott, Murray, & Pearson, 1983).

Each child with speech difficulties was matched to a normally developing control child on the basis of chronological age (within a 6 months range), gender, and nonverbal IQ (within 2 points on the averaged standard score of Block Design and Picture Completion, Wechsler, 1992). In 25 of the cases, the control attended the same nursery or school as the matched child with speech difficulties in order to control for teaching environment. Where this was not possible, the control was taken from the same pool of nurseries/schools. All of the children were monolingual English speakers and none of them had a history of speech, language or hearing difficulties. They were nonreaders (i.e. raw score of 0 on the BAS, N = 36) or beginning readers (i.e. scoring below 60th centile on the BAS, N = 11). Means and standard deviations of age and nonverbal ability for the two matched groups are shown in Table 5.1.

The test battery

A range of speech and language tests was selected to investigate: receptive and expressive language, speech input skills, clarity of lexical representations; speech output skills; input and output phonological awareness and letter knowledge. This test battery included both standardised tests and tests devised for the psycholinguistic framework developed by Stackhouse and Wells (1997).

Receptive language tests

Test for the Reception of Grammar — TROG (Bishop, 1989). This assesses a child's understanding of syntactic structures of increasing difficulty. The child is asked to point to one of four pictures in response to a spoken stimulus.

British Picture Vocabulary Scale — BPVS (Dunn, Dunn, Whetton, & Pintilie, 1982). This is a standardised measure of receptive vocabulary. The child is asked to listen to a spoken stimulus and point to the corresponding picture from a choice of four.

Expressive language tests

Renfrew Action Picture Test (Renfrew, 1989). The child is shown 10 pictures and asked a question about each one. Two scores are calculated: an information score and a grammar score.

The Renfrew Bus Story (Renfrew, 1995). The child is told a short story with accompanying pictures about a naughty bus and requested to retell the story to the examiner using the pictures. The test is scored for a) information, and b) mean length of utterance (MLU).

Naming Test (after Snowling, van Wagtendonk, & Stafford, 1988). The child's word-finding abilities are tested by requesting her/him to name a series of 20 pictures. Two scoring systems were adopted: a) accuracy of the production of the name of the item, and b) accuracy of retrieving the lexical item even if speech errors are made.

Auditory processing tasks (speech input)

Auditory Discrimination — Same–Different Task (after Bridgeman & Snowling, 1988). This

auditory discrimination task comprised 10 pairs of words and 10 pairs of nonwords. These were equally divided into two lists (A and B) so that each contained 5 pairs of words and 5 pairs of nonwords; the nonwords were presented first. The pairs of words differed either by a feature change (e.g. /s/–/t/, as in LOSS/LOT or VOS/VOT) or a sequence change (e.g. /st/–/ts/, as in LOST/LOTS or VOST/VOTS). The child was asked to say if a pair of stimuli (words or nonwords) spoken by the tester sounded the same or different. The child does not need to understand the meaning of the real words in order to perform the task and therefore the real and nonword tasks can be performed in a similar way. Thus, this task does not rely on a child's prior knowledge of the test items.

Auditory Discrimination Picture Task (after Locke, 1980). This was an auditory lexical decision task using 24 pictures. The child was asked to look at a picture and decide if a pre-recorded stimulus was the name of that picture (e.g. picture of a PLATE presented and the child hears "PATE", or "PLATE"). A toy monkey was used to explain the task. The child was told that the monkey is sometimes a "clever monkey" and sometimes a "silly monkey". When the stimulus was produced correctly on the tape recording, the child was expected to say that the monkey had been right or clever and when the stimulus was said incorrectly, the child was expected to say that the monkey had been wrong or silly.

Unlike the auditory discrimination same–different task above, the auditory discrimination picture task requires the child to draw on his/her own lexical knowledge. Detecting whether the name of a picture is produced correctly or not involves comparison of stored phonological and semantic representations of that word. The task therefore comprises lexical decision as well as auditory discrimination and it assesses the precision of a child's phonological representations.

ABX Auditory Discrimination. This task consisted of 12 pairs of nonwords. Two toy monkeys were used to illustrate the task: each monkey "said" a different nonword (e.g. monkey 1: [vɛʃ]; monkey 2: [fɛʃ]) and then one of these nonwords is repeated, e.g. [fɛʃ] for the child to decide which monkey had said this nonword. This task does not require access to stored linguistic information since all the test items are nonwords. However, it does have more of a memory load than the other auditory discrimination tasks used.

Repetition tasks (speech output)

Real Word Repetition. Each child was asked to repeat 24 single words. There were eight 1-syllable words (e.g. BRUSH), eight 2-syllable words (e.g. TRACTOR), eight 3/4-syllable words (e.g. ELEPHANT). Stimuli were presented via a tape recording but one live repetition was given if the child failed to respond to a stimulus or requested a repetition. This test examines children's ability to articulate familiar words. They are helped in doing this task if they already have an accurate motor programme stored for the production of the word.

Nonword Repetition. Each child was asked to repeat 24 nonwords which had been derived from the real words in the repetition task above by changing the vowels (the consonants remained the same). There were eight 1-syllable nonwords (e.g. [brɪʃ]), eight 2-syllable nonwords (e.g. [trɛktɪ]), eight 3/4-syllable nonwords (e.g. [ælɪfɒnt]). The task was presented to the child using a toy monkey who said "made up, monkey words". The child was told that s/he would not know these words and was asked to say each word like the monkey had said it.

In contrast to the real word repetition task, the items to be repeated are unfamiliar to the children. This task therefore assesses children's ability to assemble and execute new motor programmes for unfamiliar words.

Speech Rate. Speech rate was measured by asking the children to repeat one real word and one nonword ten times on three different occasions as fast and as well as they could (after Muter, Hulme,

& Snowling, 1997). Rate, accuracy and consistency of responses were scored.

Input and output phonological awareness

Rhyme Production. In this rhyme generation task each child was asked to produce as many rhymes as possible for a stimulus, e.g. DOG. There were 6 items and the child was allowed 20 seconds per item. Both real and nonword rhyme responses were accepted as correct.

This task assesses children's ability to manipulate the onset and rime of words by carrying out a lexical search for rhyming words and/or by filling in the onset slot in a more "mechanical" way via the motor programmer (Wells, Stackhouse, & Vance, 1996).

Rhyme Detection Task — picture presentation. On this task each child had to identify which two pictures out of three rhymed with each other. The third item — the distractor — was either a semantically related item (e.g. for the stimulus DOG, the rhyming word was FROG and the semantic distractor was BONE), or an alliterative distractor, i.e. a word sharing the same initial phoneme (e.g. for the stimulus KITE, the rhyming word was LIGHT and the alliterative distractor was CAKE) or an unrelated item (e.g. for the stimulus PRAM, the rhyming word was JAM and the unrelated item was BRUSH). The task was preceded by a picture-naming task to ensure that all the pictures used were known by the child.

Unlike the rhyme production task, this is a "silent task" as neither the tester nor the child has to produce the words. The task therefore requires a child to access his/her own semantic and phonological representations of the test items. Matching which two out of three words rhyme is dependent on the clarity of the phonological representations.

Phoneme Completion Task (Muter, Hulme, & Snowling, 1997). In this task, each child looked at a picture and heard the examiner name the picture with the final phoneme omitted. The child was then required to supply the final phoneme (e.g. the examiner says [geɪ] for the picture of a GATE and the child should respond /t/). As with the silent rhyme detection task using pictures, phoneme completion is also dependent on the stored lexical representations of a word. Children have to access the name of the picture, identify the relevant segments of the word and then supply the segment they believe to have been omitted by the tester.

Letter Name Knowledge. All the letters of the alphabet were presented randomly on separate cards to each child for naming. This procedure establishes if a child has learned to associate a name with a letter shape.

Additional tests at T2 and T3

Literacy tests

1. British Ability Scales Word Reading (Elliott et al., 1983).
2. Neale Analysis of Reading Ability (Neale, 1989).
3. Graded Nonword Reading Test (Snowling, Stothard, & McLean, 1996).
4. British Ability Scales Spelling (Elliott et al., 1983).
5. Spelling animal names from pictures.
6. Nonword spelling (T3 only).

Phonological awareness

7. Alliterative fluency (e.g. Tell me as many words as you can beginning with "k").
8. Phoneme deletion, (e.g. Say WIND without the "w").
9. Rhyme oddity (T3 only) (e.g. Which is the odd one out in these words: JOB, KNOCK, ROB. From Snowling, Hulme, Smith, & Thomas, 1994).

Language measures

10. Recalling sentences (Semel, Wiig, & Secord, 1987).
11. Semantic fluency (e.g. Tell me as many animals as you can).

Speech measures

12. Low frequency real word and nonword repetition.

The children's speech processing, phonological awareness and language skills were investigated at T1 (Stackhouse, Nathan, & Goulandris, 1997; 1999) and at T2. At T3 the children with speech difficulties were divided into typical and delayed reader/spellers and their concurrent and past speech and language processing skills were examined (Nathan, Stackhouse, & Goulandris, 1999; Nathan, Stackhouse, Goulandris, & Snowling, 1999).

Speech processing and language skills at T1

Following earlier studies (e.g. Bird et al., 1995; Leitao et al., 1997), the speech processing skills of the children with speech only problems were compared to those who had both speech and language problems (Nathan, Stackhouse, & Goulandris, 1998). The 47 children with speech difficulties were subgrouped according to presence/ absence of a language difficulty. The criteria for additional language impairment was set as a score at or below the 10th centile on two or more of the language measures (which could be receptive and/or expressive). Twenty-eight children (59.6% of the sample) were classified as having speech-only difficulties and nineteen children (40.4% of the sample) had additional language impairment. Eleven of the speech/language subgroup had both expressive language and receptive language problems, and eight had expressive language problems alone.

As might be expected, the group of children with specific speech difficulties as a whole had performed less well than their controls on the speech output tasks (e.g. real word and nonword repetition). However, when the group was divided into the two subgroups (presence vs absence of language problem), the speech/language group performed significantly less well than the speech-only group. The children with both speech and language difficulties had more severe speech output problems than children with specific speech problems alone (see Fig. 5.3).

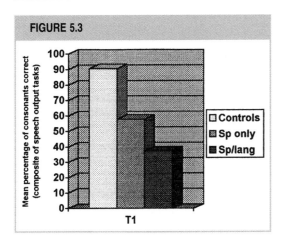

FIGURE 5.3

Mean differences in speech outcome performance of the speech-only subgroup, the speech and language subgroup and the controls at age 4.

A similar finding emerged on the auditory discrimination picture task (which tested the precision of phonological representations). The children in the speech/language subgroup performed less well than both their control group and the speech-only subgroup, suggesting that their input as well as their output processing skills were compromised. This does not bode well for their lexical (Constable, Stackhouse, & Wells, 1997; Stackhouse & Wells, 1997) or literacy development (Elbro, Borstrom, & Peterson, 1998; Snowling & Nation, 1997; Swan & Goswami, 1997). In contrast, there was no significant difference between the speech-only subgroup and their controls on the auditory-lexical task, indicating that their difficulties were more specifically within the output processing domain.

In summary, the children with both speech and language difficulties performed differently from children with specific speech-only problems on tasks investigating both speech output skills and phonological representations. Their speech difficulties were more severe and they demonstrated more pervasive speech processing problems involving both input and output channels. The children in the speech-only subgroup had intact phonological representations, less severe speech difficulties and appropriate language skills. Thus, children with specific speech output difficulties

do not necessarily have input deficits affecting the precision of their phonological representations. However, if language problems co-occur then input processing problems are more likely to be present.

Given that the children with speech and language difficulties had more severe speech input and output problems than the children with speech problems alone, it might be predicted that they were more likely to develop reading and spelling difficulties. We therefore examined the relationship between the children's speech and language skills and their reading and spelling performance at T3 (CA 6;06).

Reading and spelling performance at T3

At T3 the children with speech difficulties were classified as "delayed" reader/spellers if they scored below −1 standard deviation on the BAS Word Reading and/or BAS Spelling Tests and as "typical" reader/spellers if they scored above −1 standard deviation on one of these tests. According to this criterion, 36.2% of the children with speech difficulties had poor literacy skills for their age at T3, and 63.8% of the group had age appropriate or above literacy skills. On the face of it, this would seem a favourable result for children with speech difficulties. However, it would be wrong to assume at this early stage of literacy development that children in the typical reader/speller group will not develop problems later on. Children with a history of specific speech difficulties are particularly at risk for developing spelling problems around the age of 8 years (Dodd, Russell, & Oerlemans, 1993) and follow-up studies have revealed that literacy difficulties can become apparent as late as the teenage years (Stothard, Snowling, Bishop, Chipchase, & Kaplan, 1998).

Examination of the subgroups of speech vs speech and language revealed that not all of the children with speech and language problems did go on to have poor literacy skills at T3. Some children with speech-only problems also had difficulties with their reading and spelling (see Table 5.2). This suggests that the speech vs language dichotomy may not be a useful way of predicting literacy difficulties. An alternative

TABLE 5.2

Numbers of children with typical vs delayed reading/spelling in the speech only vs speech and language subgroups

Reader/spellers	Speech only	Speech & language	Total %
Typical	21	9	63.8
Delayed	7	10	36.2

approach adopted in our longitudinal study was to examine in retrospect a wider range of skills to establish if there are any early developmental signs (e.g. at T1 or T2) that differentiated the typical and delayed readers at T3.

Early developmental signs of reading and spelling problems

The children who had poor literacy skills at T3 were also likely to have more severe speech difficulties, additional language problems and auditory processing problems. However, the developmental signs of potential literacy problems changed over the three ages tested.

Table 5.3 summarises which areas tested at the three ages differentiated between the children in the typical and delayed reader/speller groups at the end of the study. The first observation is that there was no significant difference between children with typical and delayed reading/spelling at T3 on any of the measures taken at T1. Performance on the speech output, grammar, and auditory lexical decision tasks narrowly missed being significant signs of future literacy problems. It was only at T2 and T3 that the typical and delayed reading/spelling groups were differentiated statistically.

The same/different judgement auditory discrimination task (Bridgeman & Snowling, 1988) and the auditory discrimination picture task were successful in identifying which children at T1 were having difficulties with auditory discrimination and with storing precise phonological representations. However, at T2 it was the auditory discrimination (Bridgeman & Snowling, 1988) task and the more challenging ABX task that differentiated the typical and delayed reader/speller groups.

Persisting speech difficulties at T2 (on real and nonword repetition) and T3 (on naming and repetition of low frequency real and nonwords) were an important developmental sign of potential literacy difficulties, as was delayed grammatical skills at T2 (TROG and The Bus Story) and T3 (Renfrew Action Picture Test). This may be because tests such as the Bus Story (Renfrew, 1995) involve both input and output speech and language processing. It is also the case that children with unintelligible speech may perform poorly on such language tests because their responses are difficult to score, e.g. if they are unable to mark morphological endings because of their speech difficulties.

Finally, what about phonological awareness measures? Although the children with speech difficulties in general performed less well than their controls on the rhyme detection and production tasks administered, rhyme does not feature in Table 5.3 because it did not differentiate between the typical vs delayed reader/spellers. In fact, at T2 and T3 the delayed readers performed as well as the typical readers on rhyme tasks. Performance on alliteration fluency at T2 and on phoneme deletion and completion at T3 were more closely associated with reading and spelling development. Letter name knowledge was also a significant sign of reading and spelling skill at both T2 and T3.

IDENTIFYING TYPICAL VS DELAYED READERS

Two children from the longitudinal study will be compared to illustrate how a speech and literacy

TABLE 5.3

The tests that differentiated between the children in the typical and delayed reading/spelling groups at the three different ages (T1, T2 and T3)

Age	Tests
T1 - 4;06	None
T2 - 5;06	Auditory discrimination (Bridgeman & Snowling, 1988 and ABX) Speech output (real word and nonword repetition) Grammar (TROG and Bus Story) Alliteration fluency Letter names
T3 - 6;06	Speech output (naming and low frequency repetition) Grammar (Renfrew Action Picture Test) Phoneme deletion and completion Letter names

difficulty can unfold between 4 and 6 years of age, and what the "at risk" signs may be. The first, Zara, had specific speech difficulties but no additional language problem; the second, Tom, had both speech and language problems. The speech processing profiles presented in Figs 5.4, 5.5, 5.7, and 5.8 are based on the simple psycholinguistic model of Stackhouse and Wells (1997) presented in Fig. 5.1 and summarise the children's input and output speech processing performance. Question A in these figures is at the level of the ear in Fig. 5.1 and includes basic auditory perceptual skills as well as hearing acuity. Questions A–F relate to input processing. Question K is at the level of the mouth in Fig. 5.1. Questions G–K relate to output processing. Tasks used to answer questions nearer the top of the profile require the child to access stored linguistic information (top-down), while those tasks used to answer questions lower down on the profile do not require access to as much stored information. Question L represents the link between output and input skills and taps a child's monitoring of his/her own speech. This format allows a systematic collation of test results and gives a quick visual impression of a child's input vs output as well as top-down vs

bottom-up speech processing skills. Ticks on the speech processing profile show that performance is no different from normal controls, i.e. within 1 SD from the mean. Crosses show where performance is significantly poorer than the controls. The number of crosses marks the degree of severity, i.e. $X = -1$ SD; $XX = -2$ SD; $XXX = -3$ SD.

Zara

Zara presented as a lively and chatty little girl. At 4;03 (T1) she had an obvious speech difficulty but was intelligible most of the time. On a standardised speech assessment (Edinburgh Articulation Test, Anthony et al., 1971) she had a standard score of 80 and an articulation age level of 3 years. However, her language skills were age appropriate on tests of verbal comprehension, receptive and expressive vocabulary and expressive language (both on information and grammar).

Fig. 5.4 presents Zara's speech processing profile at T1 (CA 4;03). This revealed that she had no input processing difficulties. She performed as well as controls on tests of auditory discrimination and input phonological awareness tasks such as rhyme. However, she had specific speech output

FIGURE 5.4

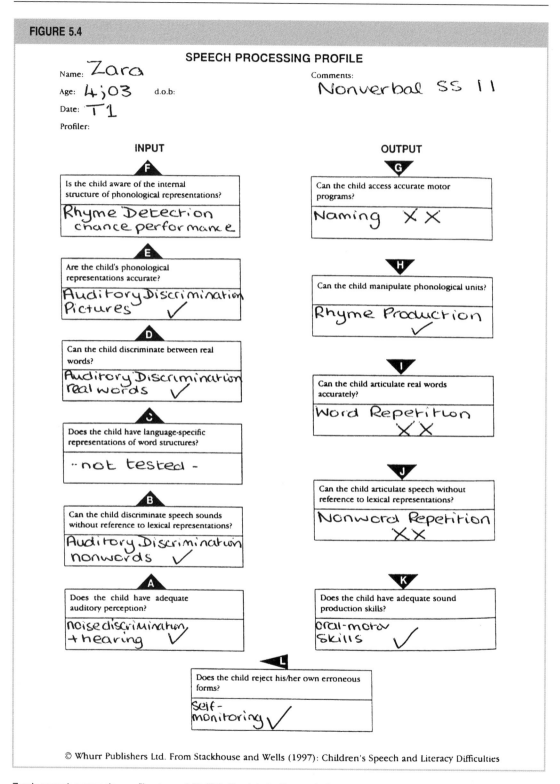

SPEECH PROCESSING PROFILE

Name: Zara

Age: 4;03   d.o.b:

Date: T1

Profiler:

Comments: Nonverbal SS 11

INPUT

F
Is the child aware of the internal structure of phonological representations?

Rhyme Detection
chance performance

E
Are the child's phonological representations accurate?

Auditory Discrimination
Pictures   ✓

D
Can the child discriminate between real words?

Auditory Discrimination
real words   ✓

C
Does the child have language-specific representations of word structures?

·· not tested -

B
Can the child discriminate speech sounds without reference to lexical representations?

Auditory Discrimination
nonwords   ✓

A
Does the child have adequate auditory perception?

noise discrimination
+ hearing   ✓

OUTPUT

G
Can the child access accurate motor programs?

Naming   X X

H
Can the child manipulate phonological units?

Rhyme Production
              ✓

I
Can the child articulate real words accurately?

Word Repetition
         X X

J
Can the child articulate speech without reference to lexical representations?

Nonword Repetition
         X X

K
Does the child have adequate sound production skills?

oral-motor
Skills   ✓

L
Does the child reject his/her own erroneous forms?

Self-
monitoring ✓

© Whurr Publishers Ltd. From Stackhouse and Wells (1997): Children's Speech and Literacy Difficulties

Zara's speech processing profile at age 4;03 (T1). Reprinted with permission.

difficulties on naming, word and nonword repetition. By T2 (CA 5;03) her speech problem had resolved and her speech processing profile was no different from controls on either input or output tasks (see Fig. 5.5).

At age 6;03 she had a BAS Reading Age of 7;11 and a percentile rank of 92. Fig. 5.6 shows her performance on the animal picture spelling test. On this test the children are shown a picture book of animals and they write down the name of each one. The tester does not produce the name for them verbally so the children are dependent on their own lexical representations of the word as a basis for their spelling attempts. She scored 7/12 correct which was above-average performance on this task (control group mean: 4.3) Her errors revealed that she had good sound segmentation skills and can assign letters to sounds even if she does not yet know how to spell the words in a conventional way (e.g. CROCODILE → crocerdiel, GORILLA → gerriler).

Tom

Tom presented as a shy little boy. At 4 years of age, he initiated little language and was very difficult to understand. He seemed unable to use strategies to help himself when not understood; he would simply repeat what he had said with increasing frustration. On the Edinburgh Articulation Test (Anthony et al., 1971), he only achieved a standard score of 60 which gave him an age equivalent below the baseline of the test (less than 3 years). He was also below average on all of the language tests. His speech processing profile at T1 showed difficulties on both the input and output sides of the profile (see Fig. 5.7). Apart from the obvious speech output difficulties, he also performed poorly on the nonword auditory discrimination task and the auditory discrimination picture task. This suggests that he had impaired ability to discriminate between unfamiliar words and that his phonological representations were inaccurately or incompletely stored.

Unlike Zara, Tom's speech difficulties were still apparent at T2 (see Fig. 5.8). Examination of his speech processing profile at T2 (CA 5;02) revealed persisting input (on real and nonword auditory

discrimination and auditory discrimination picture tasks) and speech output processing problems. Although he performed as well as controls on rhyme detection and production, he scored poorly on other phonological awareness tasks focusing on the phoneme (alliteration fluency and phoneme completion). Letter knowledge was also 2 standard deviations below the control group mean.

At T3 (CA 6;02), he scored 0 on the British Ability Scale single word reading test (Elliott et al., 1983), giving him a percentile rank of 7 and age equivalent of less than 5 years. Figure 5.9 shows his performance on the animal picture spelling test. None of his spelling responses are correct. More important, however, is the observation that his errors do not resemble the target words. For example, he has difficulty marking the correct number of syllables (e.g. ELEPHANT → m) and does not transcribe the beginning or end of test items correctly (e.g. SPIDER → olxlm). His choice of letters appears random, showing a difficulty with developing phoneme to grapheme (sound to letter) correspondence.

Tom's speech processing deficits are much more pervasive and persistent than Zara's and a poor foundation on which to build his literacy skills. He is a typical example of a child with obvious and persisting difficulties. At least, his problems could not be ignored. In contrast, Zara's speech difficulties had resolved by T2 and she had no residual underlying speech processing problems. She was progressing well with her literacy without any additional help.

However, there are children who fall between these two examples. These are children who appear to have recovered from their earlier speech difficulties but who still go on to have literacy problems and require specialist help. Unfortunately, a hidden speech processing problem can be missed so these children do not receive the appropriate therapy or specialist teaching they need (Stackhouse & Wells, 1991). A strength of the psycholinguistic approach is that it uncovers hidden problems and provides a basis for appropriate remediation which targets the underlying strengths and weaknesses (Stackhouse & Wells, 1997; in press).

FIGURE 5.5

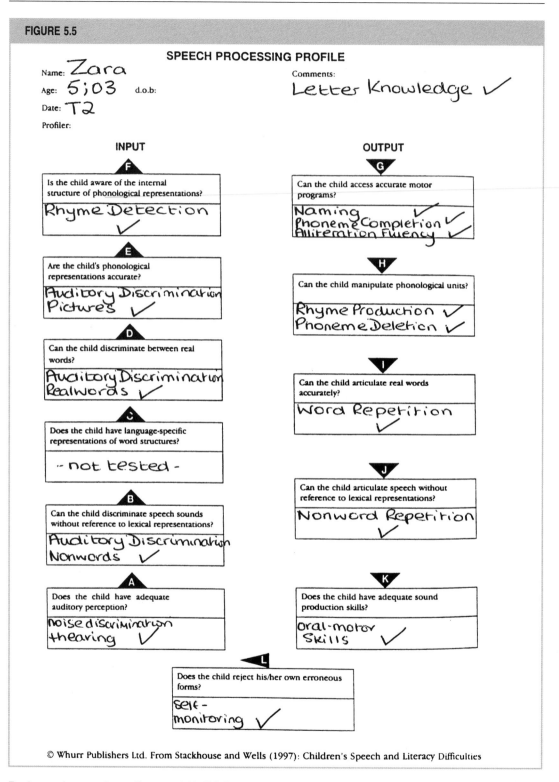

Zara's speech processing profile at age 5;03 (T2). Reprinted with permission.

FIGURE 5.6

P1. rAbbit	7. hen
1. camel	8. Elerefint
2. cat	9. Beterfly
3. tigger	10. Dog
4. crockcerpirel	11. spider
5. pig	12. gererfer
6. gerriler	

Zara's spelling from
pictures at age 6;03 (T3).

WHEN HAS A SPEECH DIFFICULTY RESOLVED?

Many children diagnosed at primary or secondary school age as having specific literacy problems (dyslexia) have attended speech and language therapy in the preschool years but were discharged following improved intelligibility. Even adults with developmental dyslexia who appear to have no speech difficulties show residual problems arising from earlier speech and language difficulties on specific articulatory testing (Lewis & Freebairn, 1992; see also Snowling, Chapter 14 this volume).

Literacy problems are most likely when the earlier speech problem was described as a "phono-

logical disorder' rather than a delay (Dodd et al., 1995). They are less common in cases of articulatory difficulty arising from a structural abnormality (Stackhouse, 1982) or neurological condition such as cerebral palsy (Bishop, 1985). This fits well with the view put forward in this chapter that children who go on to have literacy problems have more than peripheral speech difficulties; their speech processing problems are pervasive and affect both the speech and language domains.

In our longitudinal study described above, all the children in the main cohort had speech difficulties significantly below age level at T1. However, there were 20 other children referred by their speech and language therapists who were not included in the main study because their speech difficulties at T1 were not significantly impaired

FIGURE 5.7

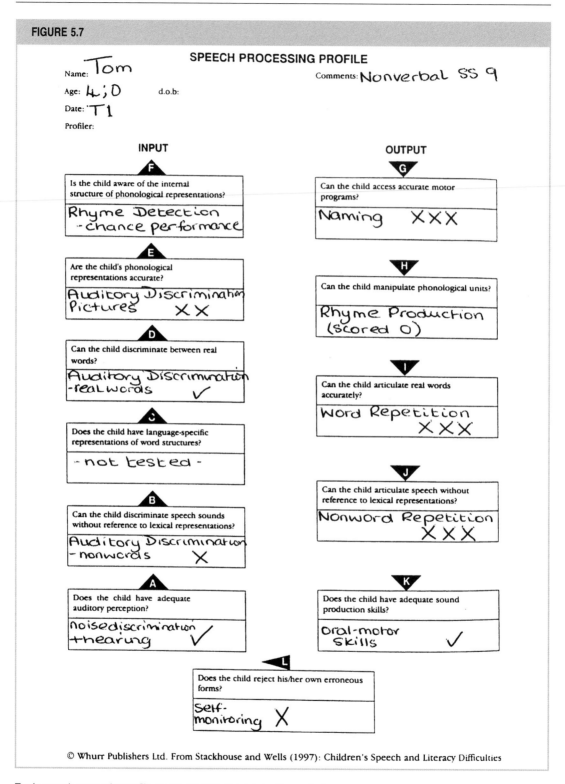

SPEECH PROCESSING PROFILE

Name: Tom

Comments: Nonverbal SS 9

Age: 4;0   d.o.b:

Date: T1

Profiler:

INPUT

F — Is the child aware of the internal structure of phonological representations?
Rhyme Detection - chance performance

E — Are the child's phonological representations accurate?
Auditory Discrimination Pictures   XX

D — Can the child discriminate between real words?
Auditory Discrimination - real words   ✓

C — Does the child have language-specific representations of word structures?
- not tested -

B — Can the child discriminate speech sounds without reference to lexical representations?
Auditory Discrimination - nonwords   X

A — Does the child have adequate auditory perception?
noise discrimination + hearing   ✓

OUTPUT

G — Can the child access accurate motor programs?
Naming   XXX

H — Can the child manipulate phonological units?
Rhyme Production (scored 0)

I — Can the child articulate real words accurately?
Word Repetition   XXX

J — Can the child articulate speech without reference to lexical representations?
Nonword Repetition   XXX

K — Does the child have adequate sound production skills?
Oral-motor Skills   ✓

L — Does the child reject his/her own erroneous forms?
Self-monitoring   X

© Whurr Publishers Ltd. From Stackhouse and Wells (1997): Children's Speech and Literacy Difficulties

Tom's speech processing profile at age 4;0 (T1). Reprinted with permission.

FIGURE 5.8

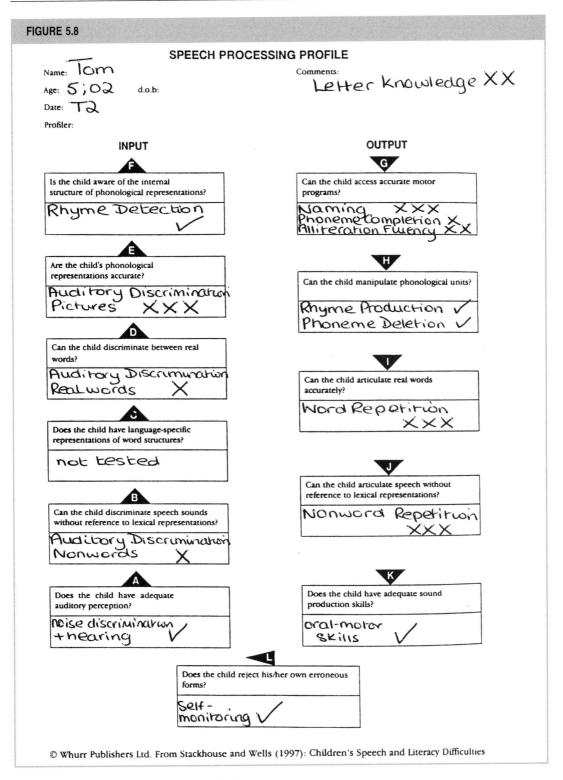

SPEECH PROCESSING PROFILE

Name: Tom

Age: 5;02   d.o.b:

Date: T2

Profiler:

Comments:

Letter knowledge XX

INPUT

F
Is the child aware of the internal structure of phonological representations?

Rhyme Detection ✓

E
Are the child's phonological representations accurate?

Auditory Discrimination Pictures   XXX

D
Can the child discriminate between real words?

Auditory Discrimination Real words   X

C
Does the child have language-specific representations of word structures?

not tested

B
Can the child discriminate speech sounds without reference to lexical representations?

Auditory Discrimination Nonwords   X

A
Does the child have adequate auditory perception?

Noise discrimination + hearing   ✓

OUTPUT

G
Can the child access accurate motor programs?

Naming   XXX
Phoneme Completion X
Alliteration Fluency XX

H
Can the child manipulate phonological units?

Rhyme Production ✓
Phoneme Deletion ✓

I
Can the child articulate real words accurately?

Word Repetition   XXX

J
Can the child articulate speech without reference to lexical representations?

Nonword Repetition   XXX

K
Does the child have adequate sound production skills?

oral-motor Skills   ✓

L
Does the child reject his/her own erroneous forms?

Self-monitoring ✓

© Whurr Publishers Ltd. From Stackhouse and Wells (1997): Children's Speech and Literacy Difficulties

Tom's speech processing profile at age 5;02 (T2). Reprinted with permission.

FIGURE 5.9

Tom's spelling from pictures at age 6;02 (T3).

when measured on the Edinburgh Articulation Test (Anthony et al., 1971). The fact that they had been considered severe enough at some point to warrant a referral to speech and language therapy made them a useful "resolved" group for comparison with other children in the study. Twelve of these "resolved" cases were followed up when they were around 5 years of age, using a similar battery to that used at T2 in the main study (Nimmo, 1998). Table 5.4 shows the close matching on chronological age and nonverbal IQ of the resolved group with the children with significant speech disorders and the normal controls from the main study.

There were no significant differences between the resolved group and the controls on any of the

TABLE 5.4

The chronological age (CA) and nonverbal IQ (NV) of the 12 children with resolved speech difficulties compared to the children with the persisting speech difficulties (Sp Diff.) and the normal controls

	Resolved	Controls	Sp Diff.
CA	5.64	5.63	5.48
SD	0.4	0.53	0.43
NV*	12.83	13.36	12.21
SD	1.48	1.89	2.02

* WISC-R Block Design and Picture Completion

language, auditory or phonological awareness measures. As a group, their nonword reading and spelling was in line with that of the controls and their mean reading performance was slightly above that of the controls. However, the resolved group was significantly poorer than the controls on the speech output tasks (e.g. real and nonword repetition, and speech rate, accuracy and consistency).

Compared to the children with obvious speech difficulties, the resolved group was significantly better on language, auditory discrimination, phonological awareness and reading and spelling measures but not on the speech output measures. In summary, the so-called "resolved" group had residual speech difficulties when tested on specific speech output tasks.

Each child in the residual group was examined individually (see Table 5.5 for summary of results). In only 2 out of the 12 children (numbers 3 and 8) had the speech difficulties completely resolved. These two children were also significantly better than controls on reading and spelling. The remaining ten children all had some difficulty on the

speech repetition and/or speech rate tasks. Only two of the children (numbers 1 and 4) performed significantly less well than the controls on phonological awareness tasks. Two of the children (1 and 2) scored −1 SD below the mean on reading measures and 5 scored −1 SD on spelling measures (1,2,4,5,7). They were therefore hovering around a point at which they may or may not go on to have significant literacy problems.

Let us take one of these children (number 5) to illustrate how less obvious speech and literacy problems can unfold.

Luke

When Luke was followed up one year later at age 6;05, it was clear that he had developed literacy difficulties. Table 5.6 shows his test results at T3. His reading and spelling performance was significantly below his age level (10th and 25th percentile respectively). In contrast, Luke's receptive and expressive language skills were at least age appropriate. In fact his performance on the Action

---

TABLE 5.5

Individual profiles of children in the "resolved" speech difficulties group at 5 years of age

Child	Speech repetition & rate	Phonological awareness	Reading	Spelling
1	***	**	*	*
2	*	=	*	*
3	=	=	=	=
4	***	**	=	*
5	**	=	=	*
6	**	=	=	=
7	**	=	=	*
8	=	=	=	=
9	*	=	=	=
10	***	=	=	=
11	***	=	=	=
12	**	=	=	=

Key for comparison with controls:
*   −1SD to −2.4 SD
**   −2.5 SD to −3.4 SD
***   < −3.4 SD
=   same as or significantly better than controls

TABLE 5.6

Luke's test results when followed up at CA 6;05

Language

British picture vocabulary test	108 (standard score)
Test of reception of grammar	50th percentile
Renfrew action picture test	8 yrs (age equivalent)

Speech (SD = standard deviations)

Edinburgh articulation test	SD 0.14
Real word repetition	SD −0.16
Nonword repetition	SD −1.69

Phonological awareness

Rhyme production:	SD 0.053
Phoneme deletion:	SD −2.56
Phoneme completion:	SD −1.18

Reading and spelling (percentiles)

British ability scale word reading	10th
Snowling graded nonword reading	10th
British ability scale spelling	25th

Letter knowledge (RS = raw score)

Letter names	RS:25, SD −0.33
Letter sounds	RS:1, SD −5.56

Picture Test (Renfrew, 1989) was superior for his age. This made him different from the children with persisting speech difficulties and associated literacy problems in the main study who had grammatical difficulties.

It was understandable that his speech difficulties had been considered "resolved" as there were no obvious problems. On the picture naming and real word repetition tasks he performed no differently from the normal controls. However, on the nonword repetition task his performance was significantly poorer (−1.69), indicating a persisting difficulty assembling motor programmes for unfamiliar words. Similarly, there was a mixed performance on the phonological awareness tasks. Although he could perform rhyme production tasks as well as controls (0.053), tasks targeting

the phoneme level specifically were more difficult (e.g. phoneme completion: −1.8; phoneme deletion: −2.56). This was reflected in his letter knowledge. In spite of learning all but one of the letter names (he substituted "B" for "D"), he had not abstracted the letter sound from these names or learned to link the letter sound with the orthographic form apart from the sound /k/ for the letter "K". On this task he was severely impaired compared to the normal controls (−5.56) and consequently had significant spelling problems. Figures 5.10 and 5.11 show Luke's performance on the animal picture spelling test at T2 and T3.

A first impression is that there is very little difference between the two spellings of the same words even though they were done 12 months apart. At T3, 7 out of the 12 initial sounds are transcribed correctly but only one final sound is represented appropriately. Another important feature to note about Luke's spelling is the voice/voiceless confusion, e.g. /g/→/k/ in TIGER → tk, PIG → bk, GORILLA → k, DOG → dk; and /p/→/b/ in PIG → Bk; and /f/ → /v/ in GIRAFFE → v. A targeted investigation of this found that he had some auditory difficulties when discriminating between voice/voiceless pairs, e.g. he did not detect the difference between /s/ (voiceless) and /z/ (voiced) in the spoken words SUE and ZOO and spelt both of them as ZOO.

In retrospect, how could we have known that Luke would go on to have specific reading and spelling problems? If we look back at his speech processing profile at T1 when he was aged 4;04, it looks unremarkable apart from the speech problem for which he was referred to speech and language therapy. Although this did not come out as a significant problem on the Edinburgh Articulation Test (Anthony et al., 1971), he did perform less well than the controls on real word (−3.43) and nonword (−1.74) repetition tasks. It was also noted at the time that his speech errors involved problems with the voice/voiceless contrast. In spite of this, his language skills were age appropriate, and he did not perform significantly differently from the controls on auditory, phonological awareness or letter knowledge tasks.

In many respects he appeared similar to Zara at T1. However, Luke's overt speech difficulty had

FIGURE 5.10

Luke's spelling from pictures at age 5;05 (T2).

only appeared to have resolved by T2 (CA 5;05). He had an underlying and hidden speech processing problem which affected his ability to learn letter sounds and engage in phoneme segmentation tasks. The problem was even more hidden by the fact that he could perform rhyme tasks and general auditory discrimination tasks perfectly well, and had good expressive language skills.

One of the clues that should have alerted us to his potential literacy problems was already there at CA 5;05: his failure to develop his letter sound knowledge in line with his peer group. Table 5.7 charts his letter name and sound knowledge between the ages of 4;04 and 6;05. At T1 when Luke was 4;04 his letter name and sound knowledge were not only in line with each other but also within the normal range of performance. By

T2, although he had made progress with his letter names, he was becoming significantly behind the controls on letter sounds (−1.34). By 6;05, it was clear that he had serious letter sound difficulties which would impair his reading and spelling performance (−5.56). Luke had therefore failed to progress between T2 and T3; the period at school when his peer group took off with their literacy skills, leaving him falling further and further behind.

Luke's case highlights the problem of defining a resolved speech difficulty. Children like him with hidden speech and language difficulties are particularly at risk for longer term educational and psychosocial difficulties because they are not identified early and given appropriate support. Recognising the barriers that can affect literacy

FIGURE 5.11

Luke's spelling from pictures at age 6;05 (T3).

TABLE 5.7

Luke's letter name and sound development between T1 and T3 (z scores)

	Letter name	*Letter sound*
T1 (4;0.4 yr)	−0.86	−0.86
T2 (5;0.5 yr)	−0.23	−1.34
T3 (6;0.5 yr)	−0.33	−5.56

development will help to identify which children are at risk for persisting spoken and written language problems and ensure that remediation is targeted appropriately (see Nathan & Simpson, in press, for an account of Luke's teaching programme).

CONCLUSION

The co-occurrence of spoken and written language difficulties is not a coincidence. Both can stem from deficiencies in the underlying speech processing system. These deficiencies set up barriers to a child's learning of literacy skills, in particular in the auditory, lexical, speech output and phonological awareness domains.

Some children overcome these barriers. Zara is a good example of how a speech difficulty can resolve completely leaving reading and spelling skills intact. For other children, there are too many barriers to get through within the speech input and output channels, and the stored lexical representations. Tom illustrated how reading and spelling might develop in a child with such pervasive speech processing problems. The only advantage for him was that his difficulties were obvious and demanded attention. This was not the case for Luke who represents a worrying group of children who appear to have recovered from their earlier speech difficulties and are often missed on routine screening assessments. However, this recovery is only "illusory". Unfortunately, these children do not have the necessary foundation on which to build their literacy skills and are unprepared for the onset of literacy instruction when they start school. Consequently their problems are compounded by being overloaded with tasks that they are not able to complete.

It is clear from our longitudinal study that the skills of children with specific speech and language difficulties as well as the normally developing controls change over time. This means that the "at risk" signs also change as children get older. Thus, there is no one "magic" test that will help us to identify which children have insurmountable barriers to their literacy development. Rather, we need to be looking for the developmental signs that can alert us to the children who will struggle with their literacy development.

These developmental signs include persisting speech and language difficulties, associated auditory discrimination and lexical difficulties, and a failure to develop skills at the same time as peers, e.g. phonological awareness and letter knowledge. A psycholinguistic approach which uncovers the underlying speech processing skills is necessary to identify which children are at risk for literacy problems and to help plan appropriate intervention for them. Further, this approach ensures that a child's spoken language difficulties have truly resolved and that no residual underlying barriers persist to interfere with the normal course of literacy development.

ACKNOWLEDGEMENTS

A number of people have contributed to this research. I would like to thank the children, teachers, and speech and language therapists in Camden and Islington, Barnet, Enfield and at the Nuffield Hearing and Speech Centre, London who have taken part; also my collaborators Nata Goulandris, Maggie Snowling and Bill Wells. In particular, a special thanks is extended to Liz Nathan who has worked relentlessly on our longitudinal study for the last four years and without whom this chapter would not have been written. The longitudinal study was funded by the North Thames Regional Health Authority Research and Development programme.

REFERENCES

Anthony, A., Bogle., D., Ingram, T.T.S., & McIsaac, M.W. (1971). *The Edinburgh Articulation Test.* Edinburgh, London and New York: Churchill Livingstone.

Bird, J., & Bishop, D.V.M. (1992). Perception and awareness of phonemes in phonologically impaired children. *European Journal of Disorders of Communication, 27,* 289–311.

Bird, J., Bishop D.V.M., & Freeman, N.H. (1995). Phonological awareness and literacy development in children with expressive phonological impairments. *Journal of Speech and Hearing Research, 38,* 446–462.

Bishop, D.V.M. (1985). Spelling ability in congenital dysarthria: Evidence against articulatory coding in translating between phonemes and graphemes. *Cognitive Neuropsychology, 2,* 229–251.

Bishop, D.V.M. (1989). *TROG — Test for Reception of Grammar (2nd ed.).* [Published by D.V.M. Bishop, and available from Age and Cognitive Performance Research Centre, University of Manchester, UK.]

Bishop, D.V.M., & Adams, C. (1990). A prospective study of the relationship between specific language impairment, phonological disorders and reading retardation. *Journal of Child Psychology and Psychiatry, 31,* 1027–1050.

Bridgeman, E., & Snowling, M. (1988). The perception of phoneme sequence: A comparison of dyspraxic and normal children. *British Journal of Disorders of Communication, 23,* 245–252.

Catts, H.W. (1993). The relationship between speech-language impairments and reading disabilities. *Journal of Speech and Hearing Research, 36,* 948–958.

Catts, H.W., Fey, M.E., Zhang, X., & Tomblin, B. (in press). Language basis of reading and reading disabilities: Evidence from a longitudinal investigation. *Scientific Studies of Reading.*

Chiat, S. (1983). Why Mikey's right and my key's wrong: The significance of stress and word boundaries in a child's output system. *Cognition, 14,* 275–300.

Chiat, S., & Hunt, J. (1993). Connections between phonology and semantics: An exploration of lexical processing in a language-impaired child. *Child Language, Teaching and Therapy 9, 3,* 200–213.

Constable, A., Stackhouse, J., & Wells, B. (1997). Developmental word-finding difficulties and phonological processing: The case of the missing handcuffs. *Applied Psycholinguistics, 18,* 507–536.

Dodd, B., Gillon, G., Oerlemans, M., Russell, T., Syrmis, M., & Wilson, H. (1995). Phonological disorder and the acquisition of literacy. In B. Dodd, (Ed.), *Differential diagnosis and treatment of children with speech disorder.* London: Whurr Publishers.

Dodd, B., Russell, T., & Oerlemans, M. (1993). Does a past history of speech disorder predict literacy difficulties? In R.M. Joshi & C.K. Leong (Eds), *Reading disabilities: Diagnosis and component processes,* pp. 199–212. Netherlands: Kluwer Academic Publishers.

Dunn, L.M., Dunn, L., Whetton, C., & Pintilie, D. (1982). *British Picture Vocabulary Scales.* Windsor: NFER-Nelson.

Elbro, C., Borstrom, I., & Peterson, D.K. (1998). Predicting dyslexia from kindergarten: The importance of distinctness of phonological representations of lexical items. *Reading Research Quarterly, 33, 1,* 36–60.

Elliott, C.D. (1992). *British Ability Spelling Scale.* Windsor: NFER-Nelson.

Elliott, C.D., Murray, D.J., & Pearson, L.S. (1983). *British Ability Scales.* Windsor: NFER-Nelson.

Leitao, S., Hogben, J., & Fletcher, J. (1997). Phonological processing skills in speech and language impaired children. *European Journal of Disorders of Communication, 32,* 91–113.

Lewis, B.A., & Freebairn, L. (1992). Residual effects of preschool phonology disorders in grade school, adolescence and adulthood. *Journal of Speech and Hearing Research, 35,* 819–831.

Lewkowicz, N.K. (1980). Phonemic awareness training: What to teach and how to teach it. *Journal of Educational Psychology, 72,* 686–700.

Locke, J. (1980). The inference of speech perception in the phonologically disordered child Part II: Some clinically novel procedures, their use, some findings. *Journal of Speech and Hearing Disorders, 45,* 445–468.

Magnusson, E., & Naucler, K. (1990). Reading and spelling in language disordered children — linguistic and metalinguistic prerequisites: Report on a longitudinal study. *Clinical Linguistics and Phonetics, 4,* 49–61.

Marion, M.J., Sussman, H.M., & Marquardt, T.P. (1993). The perception and production of rhyme in normal and developmentally apraxic children. *Journal of Communication Disorders, 26,* 129–160.

Muter, V., Hulme, C., & Snowling M. (1997). *Phonological abilities test.* London: The Psychological Corporation.

Nathan, L., & Simpson, S. (in press). Designing a literacy programme for a child with a history of speech difficulties. In J. Stackhouse & B. Wells (Eds), *Children's speech and literacy difficulties. 2. Identification and intervention.* London: Whurr Publishers.

Nathan, L., Stackhouse, J., & Goulandris, N. (1998). Speech processing abilities in children with speech vs speech and language difficulties. *International Journal of Language and Communication Disorders, 33,* 457–462.

Nathan, L., Stackhouse, J., & Goulandris, N. (1999). *Literacy outcome of children with specific speech and language difficulties.* Poster presented at AFASIC 3rd International Symposium Speech and Language Impairments: From theory to practice, University of York, UK, 21–25 March 1999.

Nathan, L., Stackhouse, J., Goulandris, N., & Snowling, N. (1999). Identifying early developmental signs of literacy difficulties in children with specific speech impairments.

Neale, M. (1989). *Neale analysis of reading ability (Rev. British ed.).* Windsor, Berks: NFER-Nelson.

Nimmo, E. (1998). *Speech processing and literacy skills in children whose speech difficulties appear to have resolved.* Unpublished MSc thesis. University College London, Department of Human Communication Science.

Renfrew, C. (1989). *Renfrew action picture test*. London: Winslow Press.

Renfrew, C.E. (1995). *The bus story*. London: Winslow Press.

Scarborough, H. (1990). Very early language deficits in dyslexic children. *Child Development, 61*, 1728–1743.

Semel, E., Wiig, E.H., & Secord, W. (1987). *Clinical evaluation of language fundamentals — revised*. London: The Psychological Corporation.

Snowling, M., Hulme, C., Smith, A., & Thomas, J. (1994). The effects of phonetic similarity and list length on children's sound categorization performance. *Journal of Experimental Child Psychology, 58*, 160–180.

Snowling, M., & Nation, K. (1997). Language, phonology and learning to read. In C. Hulme & M. Snowling (Eds), *Dyslexia: Biology, Cognition and intervention*. London: Whurr Publishers.

Snowling, M., Stothard, S.E., & McLean, J. (1996). *The graded nonword reading test*. Bury St Edmunds: Thames Valley Test Publishers.

Snowling, M., van Wagtendonk, B., & Stafford, C. (1988). Object naming deficits in developmental dyslexia. *Journal of Research in Reading, 11*, 67–85.

Stackhouse, J. (1982). An investigation of reading and spelling performance in speech disordered children. *British Journal of Disorders of Communication, 17*, 53–60.

Stackhouse, J. (1997). Phonological awareness: Connecting speech and literacy problems. In B. Hodson & M.L. Edwards (Eds), *Perspectives in applied phonology*. Maryland: Aspen Publishers.

Stackhouse, J., Nathan, L., & Goulandris, N. (1997). Speech processing skills in children with specific speech difficulties: Phase one of a longitudinal study. *Work In Progress, VII*. 95–119. Department of Human Communication Science, University College London.

Stackhouse, J., Nathan, L. & Goulandris, N. (1999). Speech processing, language and emerging literacy skills in 4 year old children with specific speech difficulties. *Journal of Clinical Speech and Language Studies, 9*, 11–34.

Stackhouse, J., Nathan, L., Goulandris, N., & Snowling, M. (1999). *The relationship between speech dis-orders and literacy problems: Identification of the at risk child. Report on a 4-year longitudinal study*. Department of Human Communication Science, University College, London.

Stackhouse J., & Snowling M. (1992). Barriers to literacy development in two cases of developmental verbal dyspraxia. *Cognitive Neuropsychology, 9*, 272–299.

Stackhouse, J., & Wells, B. (1991). Dyslexia: The obvious and hidden speech and language disorder. In M. Snowling & M. Thomson (Eds), *Dyslexia: Integrating theory & practice*. London: Whurr Publishers.

Stackhouse, J., & Wells, B. (1993). Psycholinguistic assessment of developmental speech disorders. *European Journal of Disorders of Communication, 28*, 331–348.

Stackhouse, J., & Wells, B. (1997). *Children's speech and literacy difficulties. 1. A psycholinguistic framework*. London: Whurr Publishers.

Stackhouse, J., & Wells, B. (Eds), (in press). *Children's speech and literacy difficulties. 2. Identification and intervention*. London: Whurr Publishers.

Stothard, S.E., Snowling, M., Bishop, D.V.M., Chipchase, B.B., & Kaplan, C.A. (1998). Language-impaired preschoolers: A follow-up into adolescence. *Journal of Speech, Language and Hearing Research, 41*, 407–418.

Swan, D., & Goswami, U. (1997). Phonological awareness deficits in developmental dyslexia and the phonological representations hypothesis. *Journal of Experimental Child Psychology, 66*, 18–41.

Webster, P.E., & Plante, A.S. (1992). Effects of phonological impairment on word, syllable, and phoneme segmentation and reading. *Language, Speech and Hearing Services in Schools, 23*, 176–182.

Wechsler, D. (1992). *Wechsler preschool and primary scale of intelligence — revised (WPPSI–R UK) (3rd UK ed.)*. London: The Psychological Corporation.

Wells, B., Stackhouse, J., & Vance, M. (1996). A specific deficit in onset-rhyme assembly in a 9 year-old child with speech and literacy difficulties. In T.W. Powell (Ed.), *Pathology of speech and language: Contributions of clinical phonetics and linguistics*. New Orleans, LA: ICPLA.

6

Pragmatic language impairment: A correlate of SLI, a distinct subgroup, or part of the autistic continuum?

Dorothy V.M. Bishop

Specific language impairment (SLI) is diagnosed when a child has selective difficulties in mastering language, but is developing normally in other respects. Most accounts of SLI stress the disproportionate difficulties seen with specific aspects of language structure, but some children have a rather different clinical picture. Communication may be impaired because of pragmatic difficulties, i.e. problems in using language appropriately in a given context. Such children typically evoke one of two reactions from professionals. One response is to regard the pragmatic difficulties as secondary to the structural language difficulties: thus if a child cannot speak intelligibly, find the right words, or formulate a coherent sentence, communication with others breaks down, and a negative spiral ensues whereby people become reluctant to communicate with the child, and attempts at interaction are unrewarding. An alternative response is to regard pragmatic difficulties as an indication that the child has autism or an autistic spectrum disorder, and should therefore properly be classified as a case of pervasive rather than specific developmental disorder. In this chapter, I suggest that, in our current state of knowledge, it may be sterile to debate whether language-impaired children with pragmatic difficulties should be categorised with SLI or autistic disorder: truly intermediate cases may exist. We should be alert to the possibility that a child who presents with language difficulties may have problems that extend beyond the traditional boundaries of SLI, and resemble those seen in autism. Although additional problems can arise as a consequence of oral language difficulties, we should beware of automatically assuming that pragmatic difficulties are secondary problems. Assessment of nonverbal communication can provide valuable information in making diagnostic distinctions.

INTRODUCTION

Accounts of specific language impairment (SLI) emphasise the difficulties that affected children have with mastering the medium of communication: Grammar, vocabulary and, frequently, phonology are learned with difficulty, so the child has to struggle to express what he or she wants to say. Comprehension is often also impaired, such that the child may focus on a few content words and deduce the meaning from these, but make errors in understanding spoken language if this requires complex vocabulary or syntax. It is typically assumed that the affected child has a normal desire to communicate and is developing unremarkably in other respects. As Miller (1991) put it:

"Children with language disorders evidence strengths in conversation skills. They are purposeful and responsive; however communication is limited by their mastery of grammatical form." (p. 6)

However, not all cases of SLI fit this description. Occasionally one sees children whose problems are not confined to language form: content and use of language are also abnormal. Pragmatic difficulties are communicative problems that have to do with the appropriate use of language in a given context. Typically what one sees is a child using utterances that are syntactically well-formed and complex, but which don't appear appropriate in the conversational context in which they occur (see Bishop, 1997, for a fuller account). In addition, such children may display social and behavioural deficits that resemble those seen in autistic

disorder. Strictly speaking, then, they don't seem to fit the category of *specific* language impairment. Most experts will agree that such children exist (although I shall argue that their numbers may be underestimated), but they disagree as to how to respond to them.

A common reaction is to regard the pragmatic difficulties and nonverbal impairments in social or imaginative behaviours that are seen in SLI as secondary to the oral language difficulties. For instance, Brinton and Fujiki (1993) point out that: "Because language skills play a critical role in social interaction, it seems likely that children with language difficulties would be at particular risk for social failure" (p. 195). These authors argue that the traditional diagnosis of SLI by exclusion, with its emphasis on the *specificity* of the impairments in language structure, is misleading and unrealistic. Impairments in language do not occur in a vacuum, but rather have impacts on many aspects of development. According to this viewpoint, associated impairments are to be expected.

A contrasting view points to the central place that pragmatic deficits play in autistic disorder, and proposes that children with serious pragmatic impairments should be regarded as cases of autism, or at least be categorised as having a pervasive developmental disorder, rather than a specific developmental disorder. Of course, both views might be valid in different cases. The problem is that, unless we are able to specify just how and when a language disorder can lead to secondary problems, we confront major diagnostic difficulties every time we see a child who presents with a clinical picture intermediate between autistic disorder and SLI. Furthermore, as Craig (1993) pointed out, until we establish whether social–interactional difficulties in SLI represent a primary deficit in social knowledge or a secondary consequence of poor language skills, our attempts at intervention will be inadequate.

In this chapter, first I review studies that look at social and pragmatic impairments in children with SLI, considering how frequent these are, and how far they can be regarded as secondary consequences of structural language limitations. I then move on to cases of pragmatic language impairment that are more difficult to explain in this way, because the child's use of language is disproportionately poor in relation to structural language skills. For such children, a critical question is whether a diagnosis of autism or autistic spectrum disorder would be appropriate. My conclusion is that there are many children who fall between the diagnostic options of SLI or autism: their developmental difficulties are not restricted to structural aspects of language but, on the other hand, they do not have the full range of pervasive impairments that would warrant a diagnosis of autism.

SOCIAL AND PRAGMATIC DEFICITS AS SECONDARY CONSEQUENCES OF SLI

Several studies of SLI have documented problems with peer relationships and social interaction. For instance, Paul, Spangle Looney and Dahm (1991) found that late-talking 2- and 3-year-olds were impaired on the Socialization Scale of the Vineland Adaptive Behavior Schedule, even if items involving language were excluded from consideration. Nonverbal items included playing social games, imitating complex motor routines in play, using household objects in play, and smiling appropriately. Around one third of the late talkers had receptive language deficits at age 3 years, and all but one of these children was also impaired on the Socialization Scale. Such a study tells us that problems exist, but does not help us sort out cause and effect. Do the language problems lead to poor peer relations, or does the child have a more basic deficit in social cognition or emotional relations?

Empirical evidence to show that a child's language level affects peer relationships was provided in a series of studies by Rice and her

colleagues. Rice, Sell and Hadley (1991) assessed social interactions in a preschool playgroup for four groups of children: those with SLI, those with speech disorders, those with English as a second language (ESL), and a control group of normally-developing children. They found close similarities between the SLI and ESL groups: both were less likely to initiate interactions, and when they did so, they were more likely to communicate with an adult rather than another child. In a related study, Hadley and Rice (1991) found that children with language or speech impairments were half as likely to be addressed by their peers as children with age-appropriate language. When addressed by other children, they were less likely to respond. It is sometimes assumed that children are largely insensitive to the characteristics of their playmates before the age of 7 or 8 years. This study contradicts that view, and shows that even by 3 or 4 years of age, children are aware of the communicative level of others, and prefer to interact with peers who have age-appropriate language skills. These authors concluded that there is a negative interactive spiral, whereby a child becomes increasingly unwilling to engage in interactions with peers after experiencing lack of success.

Gertner, Rice and Hadley (1994) went on to measure children's peer relations more directly, using a sociometric method in which children were asked to nominate which of their classmates they would like to play with, and which they would prefer not to play with. Children with age-appropriate language were by far the most popular group, and level of receptive language was a strong predictor of children's popularity. These authors note that children with English as a second language, like children with SLI, receive fewer positive and more negative nominations from other children. They argued, therefore, that the social difficulties of the SLI group are a direct consequence of their limited language skills, rather than reflecting some constitutional limitation of social cognition that co-occurs with the language impairment. More recently, Redmond and Rice (1998) showed that teachers rated children with SLI as having more social problems than controls whereas parents did not, and concluded that this was further evidence that social impairments were situationally dependent, and not an intrinsic characteristic of the child. Viewed in this light, abnormal use of language by some children with SLI could be a secondary consequence of lack of social experience, which arises as a result of unsuccessful attempts at communication in the early years of life.

PRAGMATIC DIFFICULTIES THAT ARE HARD TO EXPLAIN AS SECONDARY CONSEQUENCES

There is, however, reason to believe that this is not the whole story. I shall focus on three lines of evidence that favour the view that, in at least some children, there are pragmatic and social difficulties that cannot be explained away as direct or indirect effects of poor mastery of structural aspects of language.

1. Children with disproportionate pragmatic difficulties: "semantic–pragmatic disorder"

Perhaps the greatest difficulty for any theory that attempts to explain away pragmatic problems in SLI as consequences of oral language limitations is the heterogeneity of SLI. Some children who present with SLI appear to have particular difficulties with the pragmatic aspects of communication. Their deficits are similar in kind, though typically milder in degree, than those described in high-functioning autism. However, there is no positive correlation between severity of expressive or receptive language limitations and extent of pragmatic difficulties. Problems in the appropriate use of language can co-occur with relatively good mastery of language form.

In the mid 1980s, two descriptive taxonomies of developmental language disorders were published, one (Rapin & Allen, 1983) in the USA, and the other (Bishop & Rosenbloom, 1987) in the UK. Both described a subtype of language impairment in which structural aspects of language (phonology and grammar) were relatively intact, but use of language was abnormal. Rapin

TABLE 6.1
Rapin's 1996 characterisation of semantic pragmatic deficit disorder
Verbosity Comprehension deficits for connected speech Word finding deficits Atypical word choices Phonology and syntax unimpaired Inadequate conversational skills Speaking aloud to no one in particular Poor maintenance of topic Answering besides the point of a question

and Allen coined the term "semantic pragmatic deficit syndrome" to describe this subtype. Bishop and Rosenbloom described a similar clinical picture and, following Rapin and Allen, termed this "semantic–pragmatic disorder". The most recent clinical account by Rapin (1996) lists the clinical characteristics shown in Table 6.1. Although the UK and US accounts have close similarities, there is an important difference in how they use diagnostic labels. Rapin's classification is not designed simply to subtype SLI, but rather to characterise communicative problems arising from any cause. Thus the term "semantic pragmatic deficit disorder" may be applied to children with known organic etiologies, such as those with hydrocephalus or Williams syndrome, and to those with autistic disorder, as well as to a minority of those with SLI. In the UK, "semantic–pragmatic disorder" has been regarded as a subtype of SLI, and typically incorporates the implicit notion that nonverbal IQ is normal, there is no known organic etiology, and the child does not meet diagnostic criteria for autism.

Conti-Ramsden, Crutchley and Botting (1997) assessed a random sample of all 7-year-old children attending language units (special classes for children with SLI) in England, using both teacher report and standardised tests. On cluster analysis, they identified a subgroup of children (cluster 6) whose language profile closely matched Rapin and Allen's "semantic pragmatic deficit syndrome". However, the difficulties of these children only became evident when teacher ratings were taken into account. If reliance were placed solely on standardised test scores, children in this subgroup looked relatively unimpaired, despite the fact that the teachers regarded their communicative difficulties as severe. This study emphasises on the one hand that pragmatic difficulties can be seen in the context of adequate structural language skills, and on the other that there is a lack of assessments that pinpoint pragmatic difficulties.

2. Microanalysis of conversational glitches

Another approach to understanding pragmatic impairments is to look in detail at the communicative behaviours that lead to a child being regarded as a case of "semantic pragmatic disorder". This approach was adopted by Bishop and Adams (1989), who undertook a classification of children's conversational utterances that had been judged "inappropriate". Although some cases could be accounted for by difficulties in sentence formulation, semantic selection, or comprehension of the partner's talk, others were less easy to explain this way. For instance, some children would provide far too little or far too much information to the conversational partner, or would use stereotyped utterances, sometimes with abnormal prosody. More recently, Bishop et al. (2000) have extended this approach, focusing specifically on the extent to which children's conversational responses mesh with an adult's prior solicitation. An attempt was made to subdivide responses into those judged to be adequate (meeting expectations), inadequate (not meeting expectations, but plausibly accounted for by limitations of language expression or comprehension), and pragmatically inappropriate (not meeting expectations, but not readily explained by limitations of language expression or comprehension). After training, raters achieved reasonable agreement in independently coding children's responses in this way, and the method received some validation from the finding that younger normally-developing children made a relatively high rate of inadequate responses, but relatively few pragmatically inappropriate responses. Children with SLI showed wide individual variation in their performance, but on average made a higher rate of both pragmatically inappropriate and inadequate responses compared to age-matched controls. This study, then, represented a direct attempt to distinguish pragmatic problems that could be secondary to structural language limitations from those that could not, and concluded that for some language-impaired children, the latter type of response was relatively common.

3. Impairments of nonverbal communication

Of particular interest is nonverbal communication. It is sometimes assumed that children with SLI will compensate for their oral language deficits by using nonverbal communication. This is exactly what is seen in children with severe hearing impairments. Even if not exposed to a natural sign language, most hearing-impaired children will make heavy use of gesture and facial expression to communicate, and will, if given the opportunity to interact with other hearing-impaired children, develop a sign language *de novo* (Goldin-Meadow & Mylander, 1998). Use of nonverbal communication in children with SLI is much less well documented, though an early study by Bartak, Rutter and Cox (1975) reported that just over 40% of a sample with receptive language impairments did not use gesture. Several clinical accounts have remarked on difficulties experienced by children with SLI in the use of gesture and facial expression, and difficulties in interpreting nonverbal cues emitted by others (see Goldman, 1987, for a brief review). In the recent study described above, Bishop et al. (2000) analysed conversations between language-impaired children and unfamiliar adults, and compared these with adult–child conversations with normally developing children. The language-impaired children had been selected to include some thought to have disproportionate pragmatic problems, and others with more typical SLI. The surprising finding was that *both* these groups made less use of nonverbal responses (e.g. head nodding) than normally developing children. This could not be regarded as communicative immaturity, because younger language-matched control children made

Boxplot showing distribution of nonverbal responses (absolute number per conversation) for four groups of children: Language matched controls (LA con), age matched controls (CA con), typical SLI (SLI-T) and pragmatic language impaired (PLI). The top and bottom of the shaded bar show the 25th and 75th centiles respectively, with the central line indicating the median. The error bars show 10th and 90th centiles, with the range being represented by circular points. See Bishop et al. (2000) for further data.

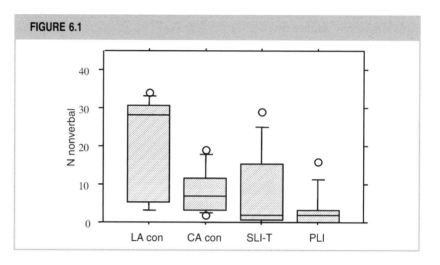

FIGURE 6.1

the highest use of nonverbal responses (see Fig. 6.1).

Overall then, there are several lines of evidence to support the view that some children have pragmatic difficulties that are disproportionate and not readily explained as secondary consequences of SLI. How, then, should we classify such children? One view is that they belong more naturally within the autistic spectrum rather than with SLI. This view needs to be given serious consideration, given that pragmatic difficulties are a hallmark of autistic disorder.

PRAGMATIC PROBLEMS AS SYMPTOMATIC OF AUTISM

The relationship between autism and developmental language disorder was a topic that was much discussed in the 1960s and 1970s. At that time, several experts had suggested that autism was, fundamentally, a form of language disorder, and that the abnormal nonverbal behaviours that are part of the autistic syndrome might simply be

secondary consequences of poor communication skills. However, this view was gradually abandoned as research evidence mounted showing that children with autism had distinctive communicative, social and behavioural difficulties not seen in other conditions that affected language development. As our understanding of autistic disorder increased, a consensus developed that autism and developmental language disorder are qualitatively distinct, a position which is reflected in contemporary diagnostic systems.

The Diagnostic and Statistical Manual (DSM) of the American Psychiatric Association is a case in point. In DSM–IV (American Psychiatric Association, 1994), autistic disorder is identified as a pervasive developmental disorder (PDD), which means that it has two salient characteristics. First, the disorder affects several areas of functioning. In autistic disorder, there is a triad of impairments in language, social relationships and behavioural and imaginative repertoire. Second, the impairments in these domains go beyond simple immaturities, with children showing behaviours that would be abnormal at any age. In contrast, specific language impairment (SLI)

TABLE 6.2

Percentages of children in Bartak et al. (1975) study showing specific behaviours

	Autistic	*Receptive SLI*
Nonverbal		
difficult adaptation to new situations	74	4
quasi-obsessional activities	84	26
ritualistic activities	68	13
resistance to change	42	13
attachment to odd objects	53	22
lacks imaginative play	79	26
Language structure		
no single words by 24 months	58	65
no phrase speech by 30 months	89	83
diminished or abnormal babble	42	65
ever thought deaf	84	65
defects of articulation	53	91
Language use		
pronoun reversal (ever)	58	17
echolalia (ever)	100	26
stereotyped utterances (ever)	63	9
metaphorical language (ever)	37	0
inappropriate remarks	32	0
no spontaneous chat	74	26
fails to respond to questions	63	22
never used gesture	89	43

is a paradigmatic example of a specific developmental disorder. This is diagnosed when there is impairment in a single domain of functioning (in this case language), and the development in this domain is delayed rather than qualitatively abnormal.

The distinction between specific and pervasive developmental disorders was supported by a seminal early study by Bartak et al. (1975). These researchers explicitly compared children with autistic disorder and those with receptive developmental language disorder on both quantitative and qualitative measures of communication and behaviour. The initial goal was to identify children with severe comprehension problems in the context of normal nonverbal ability. Boys aged 5–10 years, with nonverbal IQ of 70 or above, were recruited from specialist centres for children with

autism and/or language disorders. Once suitable children had been found, information from case records was used to subdivide them into those with autistic disorder and those with receptive language disorder. A small proportion of children did not fall clearly into either category and were kept separate. Table 6.2 shows some of the findings of the study. In terms of communication there were some points of similarity between children with autism and those with language disorder, but also clear qualitative differences. Two features in particular stand out: first, almost all the children with autism were reported as not using gesture, whereas this was true for only half of the language-impaired children. Second, in the children with language impairment, the communication difficulties could be described in terms of immaturity and/or lack of communicative skills. In those with autism, there were more qualitative oddities in the use of language that are not normal at any age. For instance, children would use words and phrases with a private, individualised meaning based on their own personal experiences, such that the listener who had not shared the child's experience would have difficulty making sense of the utterance. Kanner (1946), who used the term "metaphorical language" to describe such instances, gave an example of a child who referred to himself as "Blum" whenever his parents questioned whether he was telling the truth. This apparently irrelevant utterance assumed meaning once the parents realised that the child had been reading a large advertising sign which stated "Blum tells the truth". In the study by Bartak et al., cryptic utterances such as these, which become comprehensible only when related to the child's personal experiences, as well as stereotyped use of language, were much more common in children with autism as compared to those with language impairments. The results may be summarised by saying that whereas both groups had major difficulties in mastering language form (syntax and semantics), plus limitations in vocabulary comprehension and understanding of complex sentences, the autistic group had additional impairments in the appropriate use of language, i.e. pragmatics.

The study by Bartak et al. (1975) was important in establishing that the profile of impairments in autism cannot simply be reduced to consequences of poor language comprehension. Over the past two decades, the conceptualism of autistic disorder has changed, with greater emphasis being placed on impairments of joint attention, social interaction, and social cognition. These are all areas where children with autism can be shown to be deficient, even when compared with control groups matched on mental age and/or language level. Furthermore, it is now recognised that pragmatic difficulties are a hallmark of autistic communication, and that other language difficulties are a more variable correlate (Frith, 1989).

Bartak et al. (1977) carried out a series of discriminant function analyses on data from the same sample. Discriminant function analysis is a statistical method that assesses how accurately a set of

measures can be used to assign an individual to a specific group. First, the two groups (in this case those with autism or SLI) are compared on a set of variables, and each measure is assigned a weighting which reflects how well it discriminates between the groups. The weighted measures are then summed for each child; those scoring above a cutoff are allocated to category A, and those below the cutoff to category B. If there is little overlap between the groups on the measured characteristics, then there should be close agreement between this categorical assignment and the original allocation of cases to groups. That is exactly what was found by Bartak et al. (1977). Very few children had scores that were at all ambiguous. Overall then, the study by Bartak et al. (1975) was seen as supporting the distinction between autistic disorder and SLI, with pragmatic difficulties being a characteristic difficulty of the former group, but not the latter.

Does this mean, then, that all children with autistic-like pragmatic difficulties should be regarded as autistic? There are two lines of evidence that caution against leaping to that conclusion. First, the studies concerned with differential diagnosis of autism and SLI, while noting the different clinical pictures of these disorders, also reveal cases that are hard to categorise as one or the other. Second, studies of children who are identified as having semantic–pragmatic disorder reveal that only a subset of them appear to have significant autistic features in nonlinguistic domains.

STUDIES CONTRASTING AUTISTIC DISORDER AND SLI: EVIDENCE FOR INTERMEDIATE CASES

Bartak et al. (1975) noted that while the data showed a clear differentiation between autism and developmental language impairment, five "mixed" cases were important in demonstrating an area of overlap containing children who show some features of both conditions. On the discriminant function analysis, about one fifth of the children could not be unequivocally classified, usually because data from the child's clinical history told a different story than the contemporary information. Some children had moved from an autistic profile to a language-impaired one, whereas others changed in the opposite direction.

Cantwell, Baker, Rutter and Mawhood (1989) carried out a follow-up in middle childhood of 29 of these children. These investigators found that the earlier, clear differentiation between the groups became somewhat blurred at the later age. Although many aspects of communication and behaviour tended to improve in the language-impaired group, there was a subset of children for whom peer relations deteriorated notably. Cantwell et al. commented: "the finding of marked difficulties in friendships in some children whose language was improving raises questions regarding the traditional view that the socioemotional problems are just secondary features that have developed as a response to . . . having a language handicap" (p. 29). Furthermore, at follow-up, 28% of the language-impaired group showed ritualistic behaviour, 36% had stereotyped mannerisms, 21% used metaphorical language, and 31% produced stereotyped utterances. All of these are behaviours that are not typically regarded as part of the clinical picture of SLI but are seen in autism. Mawhood (1995) studied the same sample in adulthood and found that several cases who had been regarded as having a receptive language disorder continued to show evidence of social impairment and restricted interests. Overall, then, both the original study by Bartak et al., and subsequent follow-ups of this sample confirmed that, even when the most detailed and careful diagnostic process is applied, there are children who are difficult to categorise unambiguously as cases of autistic disorder or SLI.

In recent years, the notion of a sharp boundary between autistic disorder and language impairment has come under increasing pressure. In a study of preschool children with mental handicap and very limited language skills, Lord and Pickles (1996) contrasted social behaviour, nonverbal communication, and repetitive behaviours in autistic vs nonautistic cases. They concluded that, although none of the nonautistic group had ever been thought to have a pervasive developmental disorder, they nevertheless had difficulties in social behaviour that were similar to those of the autistic children. They commented on the artificiality of absolute diagnostic distinctions within a population of cognitively delayed, language-impaired young children. The existence of intermediate cases has been emphasised further in studies of parents and siblings of people with autism, which find that although core autism is rare in these relatives, milder difficulties, often involving only one or two of the elements of the autistic triad, are common (Bolton et al., 1994). This has led to the notion of a "lesser variant" of autism being employed in genetic studies.

AUTISTIC FEATURES IN CHILDREN WITH SEMANTIC–PRAGMATIC DISORDER

Although there has been much debate as to whether "semantic–pragmatic disorder" is part of the autistic continuum (e.g. Lister Brook & Bowler, 1992; Boucher, 1998, and associated commentaries on Boucher's paper), there has been little hard evidence on which to base an argument. A recent study using neuropsychological tests and measures of social cognition showed close overlap in test profile between a group with "semantic–pragmatic disorder" and children with high-functioning autism, both of whom contrasted with children with a more typical form of SLI (Shields, Varley, Broks, & Simpson, 1996a, b). However, other studies, including those reviewed above, show that many children with pragmatic difficulties fall short of meeting diagnostic criteria for autistic disorder. So we are left with the question of how to categorise language-impaired children who have pragmatic difficulties which sometimes, but not always, occur in association with mild abnormalities of social interaction or restricted interests.

Part of the problem confronting researchers who wish to address this issue is the lack of clear criteria for defining "semantic–pragmatic disorder", coupled with lack of suitable diagnostic instruments for objectively documenting pragmatic difficulties. With most forms of SLI it is possible to devise operational definitions, selecting children, for instance, whose standardised scores on language tests fall below some specified level. However, the clinical features shown in Table 6.1 are not easy to assess by available tests. As noted above, Conti-Ramsden et al. (1997) found that language tests did not reveal a distinctive pattern of deficits in children who were thought to have semantic–pragmatic disorder: it was only when teacher impression was taken into account that the difficulties of these children could be characterised.

One way of responding to this situation is to make teacher ratings more objective. This approach was adopted by Bishop (1998) in developing the children's communication checklist (CCC). This study had two related goals. On the one hand, it aimed to develop a more objective way of assessing children's pragmatic impairments using ratings by teachers or other professionals who knew the child well. The rationale for adopting this approach was that many pragmatic deficits are rare in occurrence, and/or difficult to elicit in a clinical assessment because they are contextually dependent. A person who interacts with the child regularly might, therefore, be in a better position to evaluate these aspects of behaviour than a professional who sees the child for a single assessment. A second goal of this study was to consider how strongly pragmatic impairments were associated with impairments in other domains, especially problems with social interaction and restricted interests of the kind that are characteristic of autism. In this study, a subset of children from the survey by Conti-Ramsden et al. (1997) were assessed on a checklist that included scales assessing aspects of structural language, pragmatic skills, social interaction, and restricted interests. Items were retained in the checklist if they showed acceptable levels of agreement between independent raters. Diagnostic information from school records was compared with checklist results. Children whose records indicated a definite or possible diagnosis of "semantic–pragmatic disorder" did, as expected, obtain lower scores on the pragmatic scales. None of these children had a diagnosis of autism, but a subset was thought to have possible or definite autistic features or Asperger

syndrome. The latter group showed some impairments on the social and interests scales. However, another subset of the semantic–pragmatic group had never been given any autistic spectrum diagnosis. These children did not differ from a "typical SLI" group in terms of their scores on the social and interests scales. This study, then, supported the view that, while pragmatic impairments and other autistic features tend to co-occur, there are children with significant pragmatic difficulties who do not have any marked difficulties in the domains of peer relations or interests. The checklist gives only a cursory examination of these areas, and in future work it is planned to do a much more detailed analysis of autistic features in language-impaired children with pragmatic problems, using instruments developed for the diagnosis of autism. For the present, though, our data are consistent with those of other studies in suggesting that there is wide variation in the specific clinical profiles shown by children with pragmatic difficulties, and it would be premature to conclude that all of them have a mild form of autistic disorder.

IS THERE A SEPARATE SYNDROME OF SEMANTIC–PRAGMATIC DISORDER?

I have argued that one sees children with pragmatic difficulties that are not just secondary to structural language problems, yet who do not appear to meet criteria for autism either. So where should they be classified? One solution would be to propose "semantic–pragmatic disorder" as a separate diagnostic entity, distinguished from both SLI and autistic disorder. I shall argue that this is not a satisfactory solution, because there is little evidence that the features described in Table 6.1 form a coherent syndrome. Rather, it seems as though pragmatic difficulties are a variable correlate of SLI: they can be found in children who meet the clinical descriptions of semantic–pragmatic disorder and who use fluent, complex language, but they can also be found in other children who have more typical structural language problems. They may be associated with semantic

FIGURE 6.2

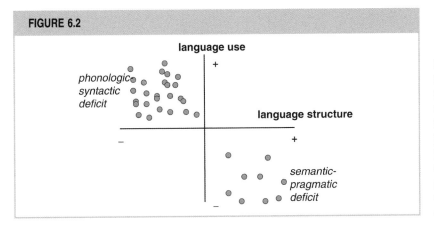

Notional distribution of impairments in language structure and language use, according to a model that allows for opposite profiles in those with phonologic-syntactic deficit and those with semantic–pragmatic deficit. Good skills are shown as +, and deficits as −.

difficulties, but can also be found in children who do not appear to have either word-finding problems or unusual vocabulary.

What is the evidence to support these assertions? One source of data comes from studies I conducted in the 1980s, using experimental methods to assess aspects of pragmatic functioning in language-impaired children. The goal was to contrast children who had the clinical features of semantic pragmatic disorder with other children with more typical SLI. To this end, I developed various tasks that were designed to pinpoint cognitive processes thought to underlie pragmatic problems, anticipating that these would clearly differentiate typical SLI from "semantic–pragmatic disorder". However, assessments that were devised to be sensitive to deficits in cases of semantic–pragmatic disorder typically revealed unexpected deficits in some children with more typical SLI. This proved to be the case with tests of referential communication skill (Bishop & Adams, 1991) and story comprehension (Bishop & Adams, 1992). In the study already described by Bishop et al. (2000), which used detailed analysis of more naturalistic conversational data, the same picture emerged. There was a subset of children who were prone to make pragmatically inappropriate responses, and who were also abnormally restricted in their use of nonverbal responding. However, these children are not necessarily the ones identified by teachers as having characteristics of semantic–pragmatic disorder.

Some of them had structural language limitations as well.

Clinical classifications have stressed the contrast between semantic–pragmatic disorder and more typical SLI, which typically corresponds to what Rapin (1996) would term phonologic–syntactic deficit disorder. On this basis, one anticipates a double dissociation between the two kinds of impairment, as shown in Fig. 6.2. However, in a study using an earlier version of a teacher checklist, Bishop (2000) found results more consistent with the scenario shown in Fig. 6.3. Rather than the predicted inverse relationship between impairments of language form and pragmatic difficulties shown in Fig. 6.2, there was a small *positive* correlation between the two domains. Although there were many children who did resemble the profile in Table 6.1, with relatively good mastery of syntax and phonology and poor pragmatics, and others who showed the opposite picture, there were yet other cases who had a "double deficit", with poor ratings on language form and language use. Taken together, such results begin to question the notion of semantic–pragmatic disorder as a separate syndrome of language impairment. Pragmatic difficulties are a common, though by no means universal, correlate of language impairment. A further result from this study was that there was no positive correlation between semantic and pragmatic difficulties, semantic impairments being common in all language-impaired children.

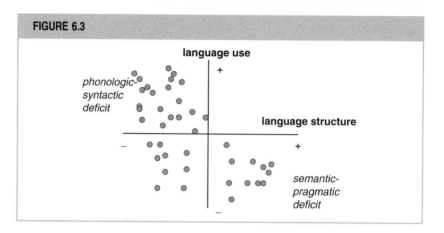

FIGURE 6.3

Alternative model of distribution of impairments, showing additional subgroup with impairment in both language structure and language use.

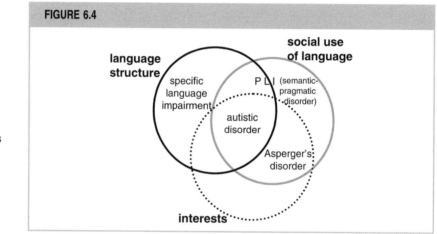

FIGURE 6.4

Model depicting dissociable impairments in language structure, social use of language, and interests, and how particular profiles map onto existing clinical categories.

Bishop (1998, 2000) suggested that the notion of a distinct syndrome of semantic–pragmatic disorder may have come about just because pragmatic problems are much more obvious and hard to explain away when they occur in the context of good formal language skills. Quite simply, children who speak clearly and in complex sentences but who use strange language draw attention to themselves, because on the one hand we can understand what they are saying, and on the other hand we don't expect odd utterances from a child with apparently mature language skills. Data from both conversational analysis and from teacher checklists, however, suggest that there is a wide range of pragmatic competence in children with more limited mastery of language form. However,

we automatically tend to make allowance for pragmatic difficulties in such a child, assuming that this is a secondary consequence of limited powers of expression and comprehension.

Findings such as these do raise questions about a term such as "semantic pragmatic deficit syndrome". The label "pragmatic language impairment" seems preferable. It does not imply that semantic and pragmatic problems will necessarily co-occur, and it is easier to accommodate to a more dimensional view of language impairment, which treats pragmatics as one domain in which communication may be impaired.

The set diagram shown in Fig. 6.4 illustrates this more dimensional view of communication disorders. The three sets have some correspondence with the traditional triad of autistic impairments, but are shown as frequently being dissociated. Different children will have different combinations of symptoms, varying in severity. Autistic disorder is diagnosed when a child has major impairments in all three domains. Asperger's disorder, defined in DSM–IV as a pervasive developmental disorder in which structural language skills develop normally, is shown as involving a combined deficit in the social use of language and restricted interests. Children who have pragmatic problems in the context of relatively good language form would, in this diagram, fit in the area in the top right of the figure, where only the "social/pragmatic" circle is involved. However, as the diagram emphasises, there are no clear boundaries between this disorder and autistic disorder, on the one hand, and SLI on the other. Furthermore, there are children who have a mixed picture of problems with language structure and pragmatics.

PRAGMATIC DIFFICULTIES AND PDDNOS

A dimensional view may be useful in capturing the full range of clinical phenomena, but it can create problems in practice. Quite simply, diagnostic labels are important in ensuring that children obtain access to suitable education and intervention. All too often, the clinical reality is that many children have complex constellations of developmental difficulties, but provision tends to be directed towards the textbook categories. Thus one may be confronted with a stark choice between an educational placement for children with autism, which is geared mainly to the needs of low-functioning children with difficult-to-manage behaviour, or one for children with SLI, where the emphasis is on conventional speech–language therapy.

One diagnosis that is increasingly being adopted in such complex cases is Pervasive Developmental Disorder Not Otherwise Specified, or PDDNOS (see, e.g. O'Hare, Quew, & Aitkin, 1998). This category was introduced in DSM–IV to be used for cases where there is subthreshold symptomatology, or where there is significant

impairment in only one or two of the domains of the autistic triad. However, there are problems with this label. PDDNOS was originally intended as a default diagnosis to be used in rare instances when a child just fell short of diagnostic criteria for autism. It is vaguely described with no clear defining criteria, and potentially incorporates a huge range of clinical profiles. It is too nonspecific a diagnosis to be useful for identifying the kinds of services a child requires (though the label itself may serve a function in ensuring that the child obtains access to *some* kind of services). It may be that, as PDDNOS becomes an increasingly popular diagnosis, better services will be developed for high-functioning children who do not have major behaviour problems but who do have complex difficulties. Some speech-language therapists have developed considerable expertise in working with such cases (e.g. Brinton & Fujiki, 1989; Gallagher, 1991), but many professionals still are seriously challenged by their complex deficits. Although there is some work concerned with facilitating nonverbal communication in children (e.g. Nowicki & Duke, 1992), this has been developed independently by clinical psychologists and there has been little application to language-impaired children.

My own view is that it would be premature to conclude that children with PLI either do or do not properly belong in the autistic spectrum in our current state of knowledge. Future research on etiology or underlying cognitive processes may give clearer answers. Meanwhile, an important message from the research to date is that we need to look carefully at pragmatics when assessing a child with language impairment, and not automatically assume that poor use of communication is a secondary symptom. To date we have been seriously limited by the lack of reliable and practical assessment tools. Methods such as the checklist described by Bishop (1998) may provide a start in alerting practitioners to cases where the child has a wider range of communicative difficulties. In addition, video analysis of nonverbal communication looks like a promising method for identifying the child whose communication difficulties extend beyond oral language. I suspect that ultimately we may need to abandon the sharp distinction between autism and SLI, and move to a more quantitative approach, which depicts PLI as literally intermediate between autistic disorder and SLI, rather than belonging with one or the other. One challenge for the future is to devise more appropriate provision for children with such complex problems.

REFERENCES

American Psychiatric Association. (1994). *Diagnostic and statistical manual of mental disorders, 4th edition. (DSM–IV)*. Washington, DC: American Psychiatric Association.

Bartak, L., Rutter, M., & Cox, A. (1975). A comparative study of infantile autism and specific developmental receptive language disorder: I. The children. *British Journal of Psychiatry, 126*, 127–145.

Bartak, L., Rutter, M., & Cox, A. (1977). A comparative study of infantile autism and specific developmental receptive language disorders. III. Discriminant function analysis. *Journal of Autism and Childhood Schizophrenia, 7*, 383–396.

Bishop, D.V.M. (1997). *Uncommon understanding: Development and disorders of language comprehension in children*. Hove, UK: Psychology Press.

Bishop, D.V.M. (1998). Development of the children's communication checklist (CCC): A method for assessing qualitative aspects of communicative impairment in children. *Journal of Child Psychology and Psychiatry, 39*, 879–892.

Bishop, D.V.M. (2000). What's so special about Asperger syndrome? The need for further exploration of the borderlands of autism. In A. Klin, F.R. Volkmar, & S.S. Sparrow (Eds), *Asperger syndrome* (pp. 254–277). New York: Guilford Press.

Bishop, D.V.M., & Adams, C. (1989). Conversational characteristics of children with semantic–pragmatic disorder. II. What features lead to a judgement of inappropriacy? *British Journal of Disorders of Communication, 24*, 241–263.

Bishop, D.V.M., & Adams, C. (1991). What do referential communication tasks measure? A study of children with specific language impairment. *Applied Psycholinguistics, 12*, 199–215.

Bishop, D.V.M., & Adams, C. (1992). Comprehension problems in children with specific language impairment: Literal and inferential meaning. *Journal of Speech and Hearing Research, 35*, 119–129.

Bishop, D.V.M., Chan, J., Hartley, J., Adams, C., & Weir, F. (2000). Conversational responsiveness in specific language impairment: Evidence of disproportionate pragmatic difficulties in a subset of children. *Development and Psychopathology, 12*, 177–199.

Bishop, D.V.M., & Rosenbloom, L. (1987). Classification of childhood language disorders. In W. Yule & M. Rutter (Eds), *Language development and disorders: Clinics in Developmental Medicine* [double issue]. London: MacKeith Press.

Bolton, P., MacDonald, H., Pickles, A., Rios, P., Goode, S., Crowson, M., Bailey, A., & Rutter, M. (1994). A case-control family history study of autism. *Journal of Child Psychology and Psychiatry, 35*, 877–900.

Boucher, J. (1998). SPD as a distinct diagnostic entity: Logical considerations and directions for future research. *International Journal of Language and Communication Disorders, 33*, 71–81.

Brinton, B., & Fujiki, M. (1989). *Conversational management with language-impaired children: Pragmatic assessment and intervention*. Rockville, MD: Aspen Publishers.

Brinton, B., & Fujiki, M. (1993). Language, social skills, and socioemotional behavior. *Language, Speech, and Hearing Services in Schools, 24*, 194–198.

Cantwell, D., Baker, L., Rutter, M., & Mawhood, L. (1989). Infantile autism and developmental receptive dysphasia: A comparative follow-up into middle childhood. *Journal of Autism and Developmental Disorders, 19*, 19–31.

Conti-Ramsden, G., Crutchley, A., & Botting, N. (1997). The extent to which psychometric tests differentiate subgroups of children with SLI. *Journal of Speech, Language, and Hearing Research, 40*, 765–777.

Craig, H.K. (1993). Social skills of children with specific language impairment: Peer relationships. *Language, Speech, and Hearing Services in Schools, 24*, 206–215.

Frith, U. (1989). A new look at language and communication in autism. *British Journal of Disorders of Communication, 24*, 123–150.

Gallagher, T. (Ed.). (1991). *Pragmatics of language: Clinical practice issues*. San Diego: Singular Publishing Group.

Gertner, B.L., Rice, M.L., & Hadley, P.A. (1994). Influence of communicative competence on peer preferences in a preschool classroom. *Journal of Speech and Hearing Research, 37*, 913–923.

Goldin-Meadow, S., & Mylander, C. (1998). Spontaneous sign systems created by deaf children in two cultures. *Nature, 391*, 279–281.

Goldman, L.G. (1987). Social implications of language disorders. *Reading, Writing and Learning Disabilities, 3*, 119–130.

Hadley, P.A., & Rice, M.L. (1991). Conversational responsiveness of speech and language impaired preschoolers. *Journal of Speech and Hearing Research, 34*, 1308–1317.

Kanner, L. (1946). Irrelevant and metaphorical language in early infantile autism. *American Journal of Psychiatry, 103*, 242–246.

Lister Brook, S., & Bowler, D. (1992). Autism by another name? Semantic and pragmatic impairments in children. *Journal of Autism and Developmental Disorders, 22*, 61–82.

Lord, C., & Pickles, A. (1996). Language level and nonverbal social-communicative behaviors in autistic and language-delayed children. *Journal of the American Academy of Child and Adolescent Psychiatry, 35*, 1542–1550.

Mawhood, L. (1995). Autism and developmental language disorder: Implications from a follow-up in early adult life. Unpublished Ph.D. thesis, University of London, UK.

Miller, J. (1991). Research on language disorders in children: A progress report. In J. Miller (Ed.). *Research on child language disorders* (pp. 3–22). Austin, TX: Pro-Ed.

Nowicki, S., & Duke, M.P. (1992). *Helping the child who doesn't fit in*. Atlanta: Peachtree Publishers.

O'Hare, A.E., Quew, R., & Aitken, K. (1998). The identification of autism in children referred to a tertiary speech and language clinic and the implications for service delivery. *Autism, 2*, 171–180.

Paul, R., Spangle Looney, S., & Dahm, P.S. (1991). Communication and socialization skills at ages 2 and 3 in "late-talking" young children. *Journal of Speech and Hearing Research, 34*, 858–865.

Rapin, I. (1996). Developmental language disorders: A clinical update. *Journal of Child Psychology and Psychiatry, 37*, 643–655.

Rapin, I., & Allen, D. (1983). Developmental language disorders: Nosologic considerations. In U. Kirk (Ed.), *Neuropsychology of language, reading, and spelling* (pp. 155–184). New York: Academic Press.

Redmond, S.M., & Rice, M.L. (1998). The socioemotional behaviors of children with SLI: Social adaptation or social deviance? *Journal of Speech, Language, and Hearing Research, 41*, 688–700.

Rice, M.L., Sell, M.A., & Hadley, P.A. (1991). Social interactions of speech and language impaired children. *Journal of Speech and Hearing Research, 34*, 1299–1307.

Shields, J., Varley, R., Broks, P., & Simpson, A. (1996a). Hemispheric function in developmental language disorders and high-level autism. *Developmental Medicine and Child Neurology, 38*, 473–486.

Shields, J., Varley, R., Broks, P., & Simpson, A. (1996b). Social cognition in developmental language disorders and high-level autism. *Developmental Medicine and Child Neurology, 38*, 487–495.

7

Specific language impairment across languages

Laurence B. Leonard

For many English-speaking children with specific language impairment (SLI), grammatical morphology represents an area of special difficulty. In this chapter, we review the status of grammatical morphology in children with SLI who are acquiring other languages. Several crosslinguistic generalisations can be made about the use of grammatical morphology by children with SLI. These children differ from normally developing peers in the degree to which they use particular grammatical morphemes, not in whether they use these morphemes. When the problematic grammatical morphemes are produced, they are used in appropriate contexts. The errors made are language-specific. For example, in a language in which all verbs are inflected, errors of substitution can occur, but errors of omission do not. Even when grammatical morpheme use is weak, errors reflecting application of rules can often be identified. For example, errors akin to "throwed" can be found in the speech of children with SLI acquiring several different languages. Somewhat surprisingly, children with SLI who are acquiring a language with a rich inflectional morphology seem less impaired in the use of grammatical inflections than their counterparts who are acquiring a language with a sparse inflectional morphology such as English. This advantage of a rich morphology does not seem to apply to function words. The latter seem vulnerable to production factors, such as prosodic limitations, that operate independently of the number or type of grammatical features involved. These findings have implications for intervention with children acquiring English as well as other languages.

INTRODUCTION

The term "specific language impairment" (SLI) is applied to children who exhibit a significant deficit in language ability yet display normal hearing, age-appropriate scores on tests of nonverbal intelligence, and no obvious signs of neurological damage. Children matching this general description have been identified in many different countries, representing many different languages (see Leonard, 1998 for a review). Some of the universal hallmarks of SLI appear to be the late appearance of first words, with a protracted period of lexical development thereafter. Word combinations also appear at a later age than expected. Across languages, many children with SLI are described as having more difficulty with language production than language comprehension, even when comprehension ability is below age level. In languages in which more than a handful of children with SLI have been studied, individual differences among children have been noted.

For many children with SLI, grammatical ability is also quite limited. Grammar is concerned with the syntactic relations of sentence components, as expressed in word order and clausal relations, and the expression of "grammatical morphemes". Grammatical morphemes are grammatical elements such as the inflections that appear at the end of "play" in "Gina plays basketball every day" and "Gina played basketball every day", and function words such as the auxiliary verb *is* and the article *the* in the sentence "Charles *is* watching *the* film".

Grammatical morphology as a vulnerable area

There is a large body of evidence indicating that, in English, grammatical morphology is an especially weak area (e.g. Cleave & Rice, 1997; Hadley & Rice, 1996; Johnston & Kamhi, 1984; Loeb & Leonard, 1991; Marchman, Wulfeck, & Ellis Weismer, 1999; Oetting & Horohov, 1997). Evidence for serious weaknesses in grammatical morphology among German-speaking children

with SLI is also beginning to mount (e.g. Bartke, 1994; Clahsen, 1989; Rice, Noll, & Grimm, 1997). Because grammatical morphology is often so weak in children with SLI, it seems to represent an important piece of the puzzle in our attempt to understand this disorder and to find more effective methods of identification and intervention.

An excellent example of an effort that explores the contribution of grammatical morphology to the condition of SLI is the work of Rice and her colleagues. These researchers are examining the possibility that problems with tense-related grammatical morphology might serve as a clinical marker of SLI. Examples of English morphemes of this type include past *-ed*, present third person singular *-s*, the copula and auxiliary forms *is*, *are* and *am*, and auxiliary *do* forms. Rice (1998, this volume) found that, at age five, a composite measure of these tense-related morphemes distinguished English-speaking children with SLI from typically developing children with a sensitivity of 97% and a specificity of 98%. That is, this measure identified 97% of the children with SLI as being the affected children, and 98% of the typically developing children as being the unaffected children. Using a similar composite measure but with children six months younger on average, Bedore and Leonard (1998) found sensitivity to be a bit lower at 88%, but specificity to be just as high, 100%. There is also evidence that problems with these kinds of morphemes can continue into the school years for many English-speaking children with SLI (e.g. Rice, Wexler, & Hershberger, 1998).

The collaborative project

Given the potential diagnostic significance of grammatical morphology in English, it is important to determine whether serious grammatical morpheme problems represent a universal characteristic of SLI. It will be some time before we can answer this question definitively; however, thanks to researchers in many locations of the world, we have made a good start. In this chapter, I will be reviewing select details of grammatical morphology in children with SLI across several different language families, specifically Germanic,

TABLE 7.1

Mean ages and MLUs of the children with SLI, the normally developing children matched according to age (ND-A), and the normally developing children matched sccording to MLU (ND-MLU) in each language

	SLI	*ND-A*	*ND-MLU*
English			
Age	4;11	4;11	3;0
MLU	3.77		3.68
Italian			
Age	5;2	5;1	3;2
MLU	3.76		3.73
Hebrew			
Age	5;2	5;2	3;2
MLU	3.02		3.06
Spanish			
Age	4;9	4;7	3;6
MLU	3.05		3.04
Swedish			
Age	4;11	4;11	2;11
MLU	3.53		3.39

Romance and Semitic languages. The emphasis will be on data collected as part of a large collaborative project, involving Italian (e.g. Bortolini, Caselli, & Leonard, 1997), Hebrew (e.g. Dromi, Leonard, & Shteiman, 1993; Dromi, Leonard, Adam, & Zadunaisky-Erhlich, 1999), Spanish (Bedore, & Leonard, 1999), Swedish (Hansson, Nettelbladt, & Salameh, 1999), and English (e.g. Leonard, Eyer, Bedore, & Grela, 1997). In this review, we will see some common themes in the SLI data across languages, but also some important differences. I shall try to interpret these findings and, in the end, I will offer some comments on the clinical implications of these similarities and differences.

The studies have employed a similar research design, represented in Table 7.1. A group of children with SLI, 4–7 years of age, were studied along with two comparison groups. One group consisted of normally developing (ND) children matched with the children with SLI according to age. The other group consisted of younger ND

children, who were matched with the children with SLI according to a language measure such as mean length of utterance (MLU). These children were on average almost two years younger than the children with SLI with whom they were matched. By matching according to MLU, researchers are better able to take into account the possible constraining role that reduced utterance length may play in children's use of grammatical morphology.

The MLU values shown in Table 7.1 are computed in terms of words rather than morphemes. We have found that for these particular languages, MLU in words is a useful measure for crosslinguistic comparisons. However, for many withinlanguage comparisons, matching was also done according to MLU in morphemes, employing whatever morpheme measure is in use for that particular language. We have found that for the languages shown in Table 7.1, children with SLI and younger ND children matched according to MLU in words are also quite well matched for a language-specific length measure computed in terms of morphemes. However, we suspect that this will not be true for all languages.

Many of the studies to be reviewed have found that children with SLI use particular grammatical morphemes with lower percentages than younger MLU-matched children as well as same-age peers. When we use terms like "extraordinary problems" with grammatical morphology, or "special difficulty" with grammatical morphology, we are usually making reference to this kind of finding.

We should put these differences into perspective by considering the fact that MLU matching is a conservative technique. Grammatical morphemes influence utterance length. For example, the utterance "Charles is watching the film" and the utterance "Charles watching film" differ in the presence versus absence of two function words, but they also differ in number of words — their utterance length. MLU matching, then, has the potential to remove some of the differences the study was designed to examine.

With this in mind, consider that of the 45 grammatical morphemes on which we have compared children with SLI and younger ND compatriots matched according to MLU, we found statistically significant differences for 24. Perhaps more

FIGURE 7.1

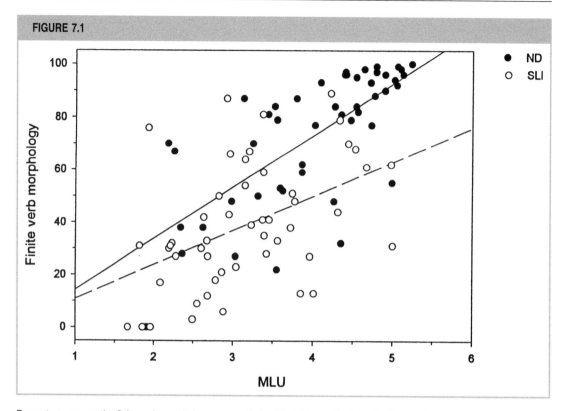

Percentage use on the finite verb morphology composite by 50 children with SLI and 48 normally developing (ND) children, plotted as a function of mean length of utterance (MLU). The solid line is the regression line for the ND children; the broken line is the regression line for the children with SLI.

striking is the fact that all 24 differences were in the same direction; in each case, the children with SLI were weaker in the use of the grammatical morpheme than the younger MLU-matched ND children.

In some studies, similar group differences have been documented without employing a strict MLU matching between children with SLI and younger ND children. In this type of study, the investigator selects younger ND children who simply show a range of MLU that resembles the MLU range of the children with SLI. The children's use of grammatical morphology is then plotted according to MLU. An illustration is shown in Fig. 7.1. These are data from two groups of children, one group of 50 children with SLI, the other a younger group of 48 ND children covering approximately the same MLU range (from Leonard, Miller, & Gerber, 1999). Each circle represents a child's

percentage correct use on a finite verb morphology composite, as described above. In Fig. 7.1. we can see that at any given MLU level, the children with SLI use finite verb morphemes with lower percentages than their younger peers. Put differently, the children with SLI make less use of finite verb morphology than we might expect given the length of the children's utterances.

MAJOR PROPERTIES OF THE GRAMMATICAL MORPHOLOGY OF CHILDREN WITH SLI

Some representative findings

Table 7.2 provides a summary of selected findings from the collaborative project. I have singled out

TABLE 7.2

Children with SLI relative to MLU-matched ND children in four languages

	Present sing	*Past*	*Dir obj clitic/pronoun*
English	"play<u>s</u>"	"play<u>ed</u>"	"Jill saw <u>him</u>"
	21 < 48	32 < 65	93 = 96
Hebrew	"mitgalesh<u>et</u>"	"hitgalsh<u>a</u>"	
	"she slides"	"she slid"	
	84 = 89	77 < 91	
Italian	"dorm<u>e</u>"		"Paula <u>lo</u> vede"
	"sleeps"		"Paula sees him"
	88 = 92		26 < 66
Spanish	"abr<u>e</u>"	"abr<u>ió</u>"	"Lisa <u>lo</u> persigue"
	"opens"	"opened"	"Lisa chases him"
	85 = 91	82 = 84	40 < 60

Note: Values are mean percentages of use in obligatory contexts. "<" indicates a statistically significant difference.

a few of the morphemes that pertain to tense and agreement in some direct or indirect way — present tense singular verb inflections and past verb inflections, and direct object clitic pronouns which, at least in Romance languages, must occupy particular sentence positions depending on whether the verb marks tense or agreement. (In some places, there is a blank because the morpheme type doesn't exist in the language or it hasn't been studied yet.)

It can be seen that for each morpheme type, there are differences across languages — in some languages, children with SLI seem to be poorer than the younger MLU control children; in others, they seem to do as well as the younger control children. Importantly, no morpheme type shows a consistent difference between the two groups of children across languages. This is not true just for these particular morpheme types, but seems to hold for other sets of morphemes as well. On the other hand, in every language we have studied, children with SLI have extraordinary problems with some detail of grammatical morphology. Based on the morpheme types we have examined thus far, it seems that the detail most likely to pose special difficulty for children with SLI is related directly or indirectly to grammatical agreement and/or tense. It may not always be, say, a

verb inflection that marks present tense third person singular, but it is likely to involve agreement and/or tense in some way.

Differences in degree of use

The percentages shown in Table 7.2 illustrate an important point that must be made about the special weaknesses that are found. Even when differences are seen between children with SLI and their younger controls, the differences are in terms of degree of use, not in terms of whether the morphemes are used.

Appropriate use

Of course, occasional correct use does not ensure that the children with SLI have knowledge of the morphemes in question. For example, perhaps children with SLI treat the inflected forms as phonological variants of the noninflected forms of the same word. That is, perhaps the children detect both the inflected and noninflected forms but have no idea of the grammatical function served by the inflected version and therefore they use the two versions at random (Gopnik, 1990). If this were true, the inflected versions should appear with considerable frequency in contexts requiring the noninflected versions. However, this does not appear to be the case. For example, we found that whereas English-speaking children with SLI used third person singular -s in 23.7% of contexts requiring this inflection, they produced this inflection in only 0.8% of contexts for which it was inappropriate. These numbers are similar to numbers reported by others (e.g. Bishop, 1994; Rice, Wexler, & Cleave, 1995); when grammatical morphemes are produced, they are usually appropriate.

Language-specific errors

Another property of the morphosyntactic use of children with SLI is shown in Table 7.3. The most common errors seen in young ND children acquiring a particular language are also seen in children with SLI acquiring that language. Of course, in the children with SLI, the age range over which the errors are seen is extended. Nevertheless, the errors show a clear sensitivity to the type of language being acquired. In English, children with SLI tend to produce a bare stem where an inflected word is required. Such errors as "play" for "plays" might be characterised as omissions of the inflection; however, some investigators, such as Rice, Wexler, and Cleave (1995), view errors of this type as selections of infinitive forms (cf. "I watched Roger play cards"). Such an interpretation receives support from our observation of Swedish. In this language, infinitives are marked by overt inflections, and these are

sometimes used in place of finite verb forms, as in the use of "klippa" for "klipper" shown in Table 7.3. On the other hand, the most frequent errors on finite verbs in Italian and Hebrew are neither bare stems nor infinitives. In these languages, finite inflected forms containing some, but not all, of the appropriate tense and agreement features constitute the most frequent type of error. For example, in Italian, if an error occurs on the present third person plural form, it is most likely to be replaced by the present third person singular form, as in Table 7.3. However, if an error occurs on present first person plural, the present first person singular form is more likely to be the substitute.

Productivity

Another characteristic of the grammatical morphology of children with SLI is that, despite the lower percentages of use of grammatical morphemes by these children, there is often evidence of productivity, that is, productions that seem to have been invented by the children. For example, Leonard et al. (1997) found that a group of nine English-speaking children with SLI used past tense -ed with lower percentages than MLU controls (32% versus 65%). Yet, in spite of this limited use of past -ed forms, six of the nine children with SLI produced overregularisations such as "throwed" for "threw" and "catched" for "caught". Overregularisations of past are also common in the speech of children with SLI acquiring Swedish (Hansson, Nettelbladt, & Salameh, 1999).

A different kind of overregularisation comes from our Italian data. Thus far in our work, the present third person plural inflection seems to be the only one that Italian-speaking children with SLI have more difficulty with than do their MLU-matched compatriots (Bortolini et al., 1997; Leonard, Bortolini, Caselli, McGregor, & Sabbadini, 1992). However, here too we found a type of overregularisation. Some Italian verbs change their stem for certain (but only certain) inflections. For example, "push" is expressed variously as "spindʒere" (to push) "spindʒe" (he or she pushes) "spindʒevo" (I used to push) and "spindʒiamo" (we push). However "they push" is

TABLE 7.3

Common errors by children with SLI and ND children in four languages

Language	Error	
English	plays →	play
Swedish	klipper →	klippa
	he/she cuts	to cut
Italian	dormono →	dorme
	they sleep	he/she sleeps
Hebrew	hitgalsha →	hitgalesh
	she slid	he slid

TABLE 7.4

Mean percentage of use of present singular inflections by children with SLI in four languages

	English	*German*	*Italian*	*Hebrew*
Pres third sing	21	53	94	—
Masc sing	—	—	—	93
Fem sing	—	—	—	88

"spiŋgono", not "spindʒono". Yet, Bortolini et al. (1997) found that 11 of the 12 children with SLI in their study overregularised the stem by saying "spindʒono". Even though it was the stem that was overregularised, these are original forms because the children had never heard the inflection -ono used with this stem. (It should be added that none of the children showed evidence of consonant substitutions of [dʒ] for [g] apart from these stem overregularisations.)

Some of the creative errors seen in our Hebrew data are overregularisations of the verb pattern or "binyan". In Hebrew, the same consonantal root can appear in more than one pattern. For example, for the meaning "she gets dressed", a verb is used in the hitpa'el pattern, and is pronounced as "mitlabeshet". Another pattern is the pa'al pattern, which for this root would be "loveshet", which means "she wears" (for example, a dress). Still another pattern is the pi'el pattern. Several children with SLI used this pattern with the same root as the examples above, resulting in the production "melabeshet". The problem is that this pattern is not used with this root in Hebrew — this was a clear invention by the children.

We have found other examples of overregularisation in the data from Italian, Swedish, Spanish, and Hebrew. They are not difficult to find, and strongly suggest that in spite of weaknesses in using inflected forms, this use reflects a good degree of grammatical knowledge of these forms on the part of children with SLI.

Benefits of rich inflectional morphology

The grammatical morpheme limitations of children with SLI present a paradox. As noted earlier, in every language studied to date children with SLI seem to have extraordinary problems with at least a few details of grammatical morphology. Yet, they seem to do better with grammatical inflections if their language has a lot of them. Grammatical inflections are used in a higher percentage of obligatory contexts by children with SLI in languages with a rich inflectional morphology. Furthermore, fewer differences between children with SLI and younger MLU controls tend to emerge in languages of this type.

Table 7.4 provides an example. Here we have a list of several present-tense inflections with similar though not identical functions. The children have similar MLUs in words. The percentages for English, Italian, and Hebrew come from our collaborative work (Bortolini et al., 1997; Dromi et al., 1999; Leonard et al., 1997). The percentages for German are based on the Roberts and Leonard (1997) analysis of the speech of those children in the Clahsen and Rothweiler (1992) data set with MLUs matching those of the children in our collaborative project. In English, German, and Italian, present-tense inflections make distinctions according to person and number. In Hebrew, present-tense inflections make distinctions according to gender and number. The two languages with the lowest percentages — English and German — are the two in which children with SLI use third singular inflections with lower percentages than younger MLU control children. In contrast, the percentages for the Italian- and Hebrew-speaking children with SLI are not only higher, but no differences are seen between these children and their younger MLU-matched peers. There is no single standard for placing languages on a continuum of inflectional richness, though

TABLE 7.5

Mean percentage of use of past inflections by children with SLI in two languages

	English	Spanish
Past	32	—
First sing	—	90
First plur	—	91
Third sing	—	82
Third plur	—	65

it seems reasonable to say that German probably falls between inflectionally sparse English and inflectionally rich Italian and Hebrew. Roberts and Leonard (1997) found that the present third singular inflection was used with higher percentages by German-speaking children with SLI than by English-speaking children with SLI matched for MLU in words.

Some examples of percentages for past tense inflections appear in Table 7.5. English makes use of a single inflection in past tense — -ed — with no distinction according to person or number. In contrast, Spanish makes use of a distinct past tense inflection for each person–number combination. The Spanish data here come from Bedore and Leonard (1999); only first and third person singular and plural inflections were studied. As can be seen from Table 7.5, even though Spanish-speaking children with SLI must choose an inflection that is appropriate for person and number as well as tense, they appear to be more facile with these inflections than English-speaking children with SLI. Only the past third person plural inflection was somewhat difficult for the Spanish-speaking children with SLI. Yet even this relatively difficult inflection was used with higher percentages than their English-speaking counterparts were able to muster with their lone past inflection, -ed.

This picture of "more is better" might have its limits, however. For the Spanish-speaking children with SLI, the mean percentage correct for past tense inflections across person and number combinations was 82. Furthermore, the Spanish-speaking children did not differ from MLU controls (Bedore & Leonard, 1999). For the Hebrew-speaking children with SLI, the mean percentage correct for past tense inflections was 77, and these children were significantly weaker than their MLU-matched compatriots (Dromi et al., 1999). What might account for these differences between the two languages?

One possibility is that the past tense inflection paradigms of the two languages differ in complexity. In (1) below, we have the essence of the paradigm for Spanish past tense inflections. The italicised letters stand for inflections.

(1)		Singular	Plural
	First	gax*a*	gax*b*
	Second	gax*c*	gax*d*
	Third	gax*e*	gax*f*

It can be seen that distinctions are made for person (first, second and third) and number (singular and plural). In contrast, as we see in (2), some paradigms require a distinction for gender as well as person and number for certain inflections.

(2)		Singular		Plural
	First		gax*a*	gax*b*
	Second	M: gax*c*	F: gax*d*	gax*e*
	Third	M: gax*f*	F: gax*g*	gax*h*

Hebrew is one of these languages. There is a second person masculine singular form, a second person feminine singular form, a third person masculine singular form, and a third person feminine singular form. The remaining distinctions within past tense are distinctions of person and number. Because gender distinctions do not enter into the past tense inflections of Spanish, however, it seems fair to say that the Hebrew paradigm is somewhat more complex. It seems possible that this complexity began to take a toll on the Hebrew-speaking children with SLI. Their percentages for past tense inflections were lower than those for MLU controls even though they resembled these control children in their use of present tense inflections. As noted earlier, the present tense paradigm makes distinctions only according to gender and number.

Even if we find that there are limits to the advantages of a rich inflectional morphology for children with SLI, it seems clear that high levels of complexity will have to be reached before rich morphology becomes a burden rather than a benefit. For example, whereas Hebrew past inflections were used by children with SLI with a mean percentage of 77, the English-speaking children with SLI used past inflections with a mean percentage of only 32.

Status of function words

I have been careful to say that there may be advantages to a rich *inflectional* morphology. We have evidence to suggest that *function words* do not benefit from a rich morphology in the same way. Table 7.6 includes means for three types of function words in Italian studied by Leonard and Bortolini (1998) (see also Leonard et al., 1992). The first type is the auxiliary verb; more precisely, monosyllabic auxiliary verbs such as the auxiliary ha in "Ha comprato un gelato" or è in "È arrivato alle cinque". These forms were used in a smaller percentage of obligatory contexts by Italian-speaking children with SLI than by younger MLU controls. By far the most common error was omission. The same was true for preverb clitics. These are monosyllabic forms such as lo in "Anna lo spinge". (In Table 7.2, summary data

TABLE 7.6

Mean percentages of use of three types of function words and non-morphemic weak syllables by Italian-speaking children with SLI and MLU-matched ND children

	SLI	ND–MLU
Monosyllabic auxiliaries	56	88
Preverb clitics	45	86
Definite articles	68	84
Non-morphemic non-SW weak syllables	86	95

Note: The ND–MLU children's percentages were significantly higher than those of the children with SLI for each of the four forms.

for clitics in Spanish were included, from Bedore & Leonard, 1999.) Here, too, percentages were lower for children with SLI than for MLU controls.

Auxiliaries and clitics are directly or indirectly related to tense and agreement, which we suspect are fragile areas in the grammars of children with SLI. However, the problems that children with SLI have with auxiliaries seem less dramatic when the auxiliaries consist of more than one syllable (e.g. hanno in "Hanno comprato un gelato", (They bought an ice cream) and sono in "Sono arrivato alle cinque", (I arrived at five)). Similarly, when clitics can appear in final, post-infinitival position (e.g. lo in "Mamma vuole comprarlo" (Mamma wants to buy it"), percentages of appropriate use are considerably higher. Differences between children with SLI and younger controls are not apparent for these particular forms (Leonard & Bortolini, 1998). This suggests that the difficulty might be related in part to the use of function words that are monosyllabic and followed by other words in the sentence.

Indeed, problems with non-final monosyllabic function words may not be limited to morphemes pertaining to the verb system. From Table 7.6, it can be seen that Italian-speaking children with SLI also have more difficulty in the use of definite articles than MLU-matched children (Leonard & Bortolini, 1999; see also Leonard et al., 1993). As was true for monosyllabic auxiliaries and preverb clitics, errors on articles were usually omissions. In Italian, articles mark not only definiteness but also number and gender. Relative to English, then, the Italian article system is morphologically rich. Yet, percentages of use of articles by Italian-speaking children with SLI are no higher than those reported for English-speaking children with SLI (e.g. Leonard et al., 1993; Rice & Wexler, 1996).

Prosodic Factors

Why do function words seem to present more difficulty to children with SLI than inflections in a morphologically rich language? One possible contributing factor is prosody. In the languages in which we have seen the most obvious limitations in the use of function words, the dominant stress pattern is trochaic, that is, a strong syllable–weak syllable (SW) pattern as in the English words "Tony" and "tiger". Young, normally-developing children and children with SLI rarely omit weak syllables that follow strong syllables as in these examples. On the other hand, weak syllables that do not follow strong syllables (for example, those in a WS pattern), as in the first syllables of "Jeanette" and "giraffe", are quite likely to be omitted by young children and children with SLI. Investigators such as Gerken (1991, 1994, 1996) have found that the relative advantage of SW syllable sequences over WS syllable sequences seen at the word level also operates between words. This has significant implications for the production of monosyllabic function words. The sentences in (3) are examples of those used by Gerken in one of her studies of young normally developing children:

(3) (a) *He* kissed the bear
     (b) *The* bear kissed him
     (c) The bear kissed *him*
     (d) Pete kissed *the* bear

In (3a) and (3b), the utterance-initial position of "he" and "the" followed by the strong syllable of the next word (he kissed; the bear) create WS sequences at the level of the phonological phrase. In contrast, in (3c) and (3d), "him" and "the" appear in positions of the phonological phrase that are immediately following a strong syllable, "kissed", that begins a phonological phrase (kissed him; kissed the). Thus, these two function words can be organised in an SW sequence. Gerken found that the first two function words were more likely to be omitted than the last two. Of special note here is the fact that such prosodic differences were found even when the function word was held constant, as in (3b) versus (3d). McGregor and Leonard (1994) found the same for children with SLI, along with a higher overall tendency to omit the weak syllable forms compared to control children.

However, difficulty with weak syllables that fall outside SW syllable sequences (hereafter, "non-SW weak syllables") cannot be the complete explanation. In Table 7.6, we can see that

the Italian-speaking children with SLI also had greater difficulty than control children in the use of prosodically similar weak syllables that had no morphemic status. An example would include the first syllable of "farfálla" in the phrase "prende farfálla" (takes butterfly), where the initial weak syllable of "farfálla" is preceded by the final weak syllable of "prénde" and thus cannot be incorporated into an SW sequence. Another example is seen in the word "pécora" (sheep), which has a strong initial syllable followed by two weak syllables. The children with SLI were more likely than their younger, normally-developing peers to omit one of the syllables, resulting in an SW production such as "péca".

Notice, though, that the percentages for both groups are lower for the function words than for the non-morphemic syllables. Omissions of the function words occurred to a greater degree than omissions of the non-SW weak syllables having no morpheme status. We have found the same to be true for English — function words in the form of non-SW weak syllables are more likely to be omitted than non-SW weak syllables that are part of a monomorphemic word (Bortolini & Leonard, 1996). And this seems to be true across several types of function words (e.g. uncontractible copula and auxiliary "be" forms), not just articles. What might account for this difference?

Sentence Production Demands

One possibility is that the sentence production requirements are greater when a weak syllable is a function word. For an illustration, let's assume that we ask children to describe a picture, such as the one shown in Figure 7.2, in response to a question such as "What's happening here?" We are looking for a sentence such as "The ostrich is biting the man", and we want to see if the children are able to include the uncontractible auxiliary "is". That is, do the children say "The ostrich is biting the man" or do they say instead "The ostrich biting the man"? (Of course, there are other weak-syllable function words, such as articles, and we could just as easily examine these.) The auxiliary "is" in this sentence is a weak syllable in a non-SW context given that it immedi-

FIGURE 7.2

A picture used for the target sentence "The ostrich is biting the man."

ately follows a weak syllable (the second syllable of "ostrich"). Hence, if non-SW weak syllables are problematic for the children, the auxiliary "is" should be quite vulnerable.

But there is an additional factor. In sentence production models (see, for example, Bock & Levelt, 1994), it is assumed that when generating a sentence, the speaker retrieves words consistent with the message intended, and then retrieves a syntactic frame that can accommodate the meaning. For a sentence such as "The ostrich is biting the man", the syntactic frame has a hierarchical structure that accommodates a subject, an auxiliary verb, a main verb and an object. The syntactic frame is free of lexical items, which must be inserted. The slot for the auxiliary verb is also empty; this function word must be retrieved as a separate step in the process, from a separate mental store.

We can see, then, that if non-SW weak syllables are already fragile in children with SLI, then they might be even more so if they must be retrieved as a separate operation before being prosodically integrated in the sentence. Weak syllables in multisyllabic words such as "giraffe" and "Jeanette" do not require this extra operation.

SUMMARY AND IMPLICATIONS

Overview of findings

To summarise thus far, children with SLI do not show the same grammatical profile across languages, though extraordinary problems with grammatical morphology can be identified in each language studied. These special weaknesses involve use of grammatical morphemes in fewer obligatory contexts than expected, rather than the complete absence of the morphemes. Errors resemble the errors seen in younger, normally-developing speakers of the same language, and their patterns of use suggest that when the morphemes are used, they are not the product of memorisation or random selection. Productivity as reflected in overregularisation and other systematic, creative errors can also be seen in these children's utterances, across languages.

Paradoxically, children with SLI acquiring languages with a rich inflectional morphology look stronger in the use of inflections than those acquiring a language with a sparse inflectional morphology such as English. This advantage of a rich morphology does not appear to hold for function words such as certain auxiliaries, clitics and articles. Part of the problem with function words might be related to prosodic factors coupled with the fact that function words require additional steps in the sentence production process.

Implications for intervention

The findings from this crosslinguistic work have implications for intervention. Let's consider one of the major findings: that some of the details of grammatical morphology that constitute serious problems for children with SLI in a language such as English are not especially troublesome for children with SLI acquiring other languages. In essence, this finding implies that if a British-born infant at risk for SLI were to find herself suddenly in Italy, over the next few years she would look stronger in her use of certain grammatical inflections — both in a relative as well as in an absolute sense — than if she had remained in the UK and been raised as a speaker of English.

If, as the crosslinguistic evidence suggests, certain grammatical details can be acquired at an earlier point — at the same MLU as ND children — then perhaps there are characteristics of the input that render grammatical morphemes more (or less) accessible. This would indicate that the problem does not reside in grammatical machinery that is damaged or ill-configured but in the identification and interpretation of the evidence in the input that is required by the grammatical machinery.

What do we mean by "problems in the identification and interpretation of the evidence"? Indeed, we do not yet know which are the relevant factors. But here are some possibilities. Consider the present third person singular verb inflection "-s". This form is much more difficult for children with SLI than the corresponding third singular forms in languages such as Italian, Spanish or Hebrew. The English third singular inflection might be problematic because the children hear many more instances of bare stems than do children acquiring these other languages. They occasionally hear "She sleeps" or "He sleeps" but they

also hear "I sleep, we sleep, you sleep, they sleep". "Sleeping", another inflected form, will be heard, but so will "to sleep, will sleep, can sleep", and other noninflected forms. So, these children might regard the inflected forms as marginal at best and might disregard them altogether for an extended period of time.

Another factor that might slow the acquisition of third singular in English is the fact that the inflection -s for third singular is the only overt inflection in the present tense paradigm of English. In some of the other languages, there is a distinct inflection for "I sleep" (e.g. dormo), "we sleep" (dormiamo), "they sleep" (dormono), and so on. So, the fact that overt person and number information should appear with the verb is probably more obvious to children acquiring these other languages. It is also the case that some of the inflections of English, including third singular -s, are consonants and relatively brief in duration, especially given the fact that they appear in the middle of a sentence in about 90% of sentences that adults direct toward young children (see Hsieh, Leonard, & Swanson, 1999). So, these inflections are not perceptually salient either.

Faced with these obstacles, without a clear indication of which obstacles are the most relevant, how can we help English-speaking children with SLI make greater use of inflections such as third singular -s? Put more generally, how can we increase the accessibility of inflections when English is the language being acquired?

There are some sensible things we can do, without violating the properties of English. In our stories and conversations with children in the preschool and therapy settings, we could increase the percentage of our utterances that contain inflected forms. We can't invent inflections that don't exist in the language, but we can at least increase the likelihood that the children will register the inflections that do occur. We could also ensure that adjacent utterances contain the same verbs with a different inflection or, in some cases, no inflection. If along with "She plays" the child hears "I play", "They play", "She played", "Let's see her play", we might facilitate the child's interpretation of the person, number, tense and finiteness role of this inflection and speed up its consolodation in the child's grammar. We could also vary the sentence contexts in which the inflections appear. This is especially helpful for inflections such as third singular -s and possessive 's because these inflections have significantly longer durations in sentence-final position (Hsieh et al., 1999). So, in our stories or conversations with children, we could include sentences that place the inflections in perceptually advantageous positions, as in (5) and (6).

(5) I know what Paula wants. She wants a cookie.
(6) This is Paula's. It's Paula's apple.

The goal, then, is to provide the most optimal input that the language will permit. It would not be a typical input in terms of the frequency of occurrence and sentence position distribution of inflections, but would be well within typical boundaries in terms of meaning and conversational naturalness.

Thus far, the examples have dealt with inflections, prompted by our findings that English-speaking children with SLI seem to be at a disadvantage relative to children with SLI acquiring languages with a pervasive and obligatory inflectional morphology. One of our other major findings was that function words are vulnerable in the speech of children with SLI, even in languages where grammatical inflections are not especially problematic and the function words in the language carry a great deal of morphological information.

I don't think it is coincidental that the function words most likely to be problematic are monosyllabic, weak and non-final. They are brief in duration and thus less salient perceptually. However, as we noted earlier, they may also be problematic because their common prosodic positions make production difficult.

Let's start with an example from Italian, just to highlight the fact that weaknesses in monosyllabic function words are not unique to English. In most instances, direct object clitics such as "lo" precede the verb, as in "Gina lo vede" ("Gina sees him", literally "Gina him sees"). However, it can be placed after an infinitive, if it serves as the direct object of that verb, as in "Gina può vederlo" ("Gina can see him"). In this context, the clitic "lo" is in final position, immediately following a strong syllable, seemingly a more pronounceable prosodic position for children with SLI. It seems like a good idea to ensure that the child has success in producing clitics in these sentence-final, SW contexts before expecting high percentages of use of these forms in non-sentence-final, non-SW positions.

We can also place some of the problematic function words of English in a sentence-final, SW position. For example, we could have scripts with a dialogue such as in (7).

(7) Character 1: Chris is riding a bike. Is Paula riding one too?
Character 2: No, but Gus is. Gus is riding a really big bike.

Some function words cannot be placed in sentence-final position. Articles are probably the most frequently-occurring function word of this type. For these function words, the best we can do is find sentence-internal contexts that are less conducive to weak syllable omission, as in the work of Gerken (1991, 1994) and McGregor and Leonard (1994). An example is shown in (8).

(8) (a) Mary pushed the car
       S   W   S   W   S
    (b) Mary's pushing the car
       S   W   S   W   W   S

The sentence in (8a) is more likely to promote use of "the" than the sentence in (8b) because in the former, the article has the possibility of aligning with the preceding strong syllable, "pushed". Note that we do not have to require accuracy in the problematic past tense inflection or auxiliary "is" to take advantage of this context, as can be seen in (9).

(9) (a) Mary push the car
       S   W   S   W   S
    (b) Mary pushing the car
       S   W   S   W   W   S

If we are interested in promoting production of articles, then sentences such as (8a) would be a good place to start.

Much work remains to be done. Crosslinguistic study has been extremely helpful in narrowing the field of potential factors that might have a detrimental effect on the use of grammatical morphology by children with SLI. Some of the factors that remain as potentially operative might be universal; others may constitute areas of vulnerability that, under optimal input conditions do not cause the degree of difficulty that they do under more typical conditions. Through continued crosslinguistic research, we should be able to increase our precision in identifying the crucial factors. This, in turn, should allow us to better tailor our intervention practices to the point where our activities consistently hit at the heart of the children's problem.

ACKNOWLEDGEMENTS

Much of the research described in this chapter was supported by research grant 5 R01 DC 00-458 from the National Institute on Deafness and Other Communication Disorders, National Institutes of Health. The author offers thanks to Carol Miller for her valuable technical assistance during the preparation of this chapter.

REFERENCES

Bartke, S. (1994). *Dissociations in SLI children's inflectional morphology: New evidence from agreement inflections and noun plurals in German.* Paper presented at the Meeting of the European Group for Child Language Disorders, Garderen, The Netherlands.

Bedore, L., & Leonard, L. (1998). Specific language impairment and grammatical morphology: A discriminant function analysis. *Journal of Speech, Language, and Hearing Research, 41*, 1185–1192.

Bedore, L., & Leonard, L. (1999). *The use of grammatical morphology by Spanish-speaking children with specific language impairment.* Paper presented

at the Annual Meeting of the Society for Research in Child Development, Albuquerque.

Bishop, D. (1994). Grammatical errors in specific language impairment: Competence or performance limitations? *Applied Psycholinguistics, 15*, 507–550.

Bock, K., & Levelt, W. (1994). Grammatical encoding. In M. Gernsbacher (Ed.), *Handbook of Psycholinguistics* (pp. 945–984). San Diego: Academic Press.

Bortolini, U., Caselli, M.C., & Leonard, L. (1997). Grammatical deficits in Italian-speaking children with specific language impairment. *Journal of Speech and Hearing Research, 40*, 809–820.

Bortolini, U., & Leonard, L. (1996). Phonology and grammatical morphology in specific language impairment: Accounting for individual variation in English and Italian. *Applied Psycholinguistics, 17*, 85–104.

Clahsen, H. (1989). The grammatical characterization of developmental dysphasia. *Linguistics, 27*, 897–920.

Clahsen, H., & Rothweiler, M. (1992). Inflectional rules in children's grammars: Evidence from children's participles. In G. Booij & J. van Marle (Eds), *Yearbook of Morphology 1992* (pp. 1–34). Dordrecht, The Netherlands: Kluwer.

Cleave, P., & Rice, M. (1997). An examination of the morpheme BE in children with specific language impairment: The role of contractibility and grammatical form class. *Journal of Speech, Language, and Hearing Research, 40*, 480–492.

Dromi, E., Leonard, L., Adam, G., & Zadunaisky-Ehrlich, S. (1999). Verb agreement morphology in Hebrew-speaking children with specific language impairment. *Journal of Speech, Language, and Hearing Research, 42*, 1414–1431.

Dromi, E., Leonard, L., & Shteiman, M. (1993). The grammatical morphology of Hebrew-speaking children with specific language impairment: Some competing hypotheses. *Journal of Speech and Hearing Research, 36*, 760–771.

Gerken, L.A. (1991). The metrical basis for children's subjectless sentences. *Journal of Memory and Language, 30*, 431–451.

Gerken, L.A. (1994). Young children's representation of prosodic phonology: Evidence from English-speakers' weak syllable productions. *Journal of Memory and Language, 33*, 19–38.

Gerken, L.A. (1996). Prosodic structure in young children's language production. *Language, 72*, 683–712.

Gopnik, M. (1990). Feature blindness: A case study. *Language Acquisition, 1*, 139–164.

Hadley, P., & Rice, M. (1996). Emergent uses of DO and BE: Evidence from children with specific language impairment. *Language Acquisition, 5,* 209–243.

Hansson, K., Nettelbladt, U., & Salameh, E. (1999). *Verb morphology and word order in Swedish-speaking children with specific language impairment.* Paper presented at the Annual Meeting of the Society for Research in Child Development, Albuquerque.

Hsieh, L., Leonard, L., & Swanson, L. (1999). Some differences between English plural noun inflections and third singular verb inflections in the input: The contribution of frequency, sentence position, and duration. *Journal of Child Language, 26,* 531–543.

Johnston, J., & Kamhi, A. (1984). Syntactic and semantic aspects of the utterances of language-impaired children. The same can be less. *Merrill-Palmer Quarterly, 30,* 65–85.

Leonard, L. (1998). *Children with specific language impairment.* Cambridge, MA: MIT Press.

Leonard, L., & Bortolini, U. (1998). Grammatical morphology and the role of weak syllables in the speech of Italian-speaking children with specific language impairment. *Journal of Speech, Language, and Hearing Research, 41,* 1363–1374.

Leonard, L., Bortolini, U., Caselli, M.C., McGregor, K., & Sabbadini, L. (1992). Morphological deficits in children with specific language impairment: The status of features in the underlying grammar. *Language Acquisition, 2,* 151–179.

Leonard, L., Bortolini, U., Caselli, M.C., & Sabbadini, L. (1993). The use of articles by Italian-speaking children with specific language impairment. *Clinical Linguistics and Phonetics, 7,* 19–27.

Leonard, L., Eyer, J., Bedore, L., & Grela, B. (1997). Three accounts of the grammatical morpheme difficulties of English-speaking children with specific language impairment. *Journal of Speech and Hearing Research, 40,* 741–753.

Leonard, L., Miller, C., & Gerber, E. (1999). Grammatical morphology and the lexicon in children with specific language impairment. *Journal of Speech, Language, and Hearing Research, 42,* 678–689.

Loeb, D., & Leonard, L. (1991). Subject case marking and verb morphology in normally developing and specifically language impaired children. *Journal of Speech and Hearing Research, 34,* 340–346.

Marchman, V., Wulfeck, B., & Ellis Weismer, S. (1999). Morphological productivity in children with normal language and SLI: A study of the English past tense. *Journal of Speech, Language, and Hearing Research, 42,* 206–219.

McGregor, K., & Leonard, L. (1994). Subject pronoun and article omissions in the speech of children with specific language impairment: A phonological interpretation. *Journal of Speech and Hearing Research, 37,* 171–181.

Oetting, J., & Horohov, J. (1997). Past tense marking by children with and without specific language impairment. *Journal of Speech and Hearing Research, 40,* 62–74.

Rice, M. (1998). In search of a grammatical marker of language impairment in children. *Division One Newsletter, 5* (1), 3–7. Rockville, MD: American Speech-Language-Hearing Association.

Rice, M., Noll, K.R., & Grimm, H. (1997). An extended optional infinitive stage in German-speaking children with specific language impairment. *Language Acquisition, 6,* 255–295.

Rice, M., & Wexler, K. (1996). Toward tense as a clinical marker of specific language impairment. *Journal of Speech and Hearing Research, 39,* 1239–1257.

Rice, M., Wexler, K., & Cleave, P. (1995). Specific language impairment as a period of extended optional infinitive. *Journal of Speech and Hearing Research, 38,* 850–863.

Rice, M., Wexler, K., & Hershberger, S. (1998). Tense over time: The longitudinal course of tense acquisition in children with specific language impairment. *Journal of Speech, Language, and Hearing Research, 41,* 1412–1431.

Roberts, S., & Leonard, L. (1997). Grammatical deficits in German and English: A crosslinguistic study of children with specific language impairment. *First Language, 17,* 131–150.

8

Experimental studies of language learning impairments: From research to remediation

Paula Tallal

This chapter focuses on the merging of two lines of research to develop a novel remediation strategy (Fast ForWord®) for children with language learning problems resulting from a variety of causes. One line of research has been the study of the etiology of speech and language impairments. This research demonstrated that a reduced capacity for processing rapidly successive information may compromise oral and written language development. The second line of research has been physiological mapping of the cerebral cortex at the cellular level, and experiential factors responsible for remapping sensory maps throughout the lifespan (neuroplasticity). A detailed description of how these two lines of research have been instantiated in this new training method, as well as efficacy data supporting the utility of the method, is presented.

INTRODUCTION

In the final paragraph of her recent book *Uncommon Understanding*, Bishop (1997) concludes her comprehensive review of the research literature on etiology, assessment and treatment of children with receptive language impairments with the following quote:

"The ultimate test of a hypothesis is through experimental manipulation. If one believes one has identified the primary process that is implicated in SLI, then by ameliorating that deficit, one should be able to show beneficial effects on other aspects of language development. Although applications to intervention are frequently cited by researchers as justification for doing experimental studies, all too often the link with clinical practice is never made. It is time for researchers to recognise that intervention studies are not just an optional, applied adjunct to experimental work, but that they provide the best method available for evaluating hypotheses and unconfounding correlated factors. Intervention studies, such as the methods for sharpening discrimination of rapid auditory stimuli, experimental vocabulary training work, and morphological learning studies, are still very new, but they generate excitement precisely because they allow us to test causal theories directly, and to monitor the process of comprehension development as it occurs."

Bishop points out here that not only is it an important aim of research on developmental language disabilities to have this research lead to better assessment and remediation services for affected children but, conversely, remediation research may be one of the strongest means of testing competing research hypotheses. One example mentioned by Bishop, of intervention research that is generating excitement, is the use of acoustically modified speech, coupled with adapted neuroplasticity training, to ameliorate language-based learning disabilities. This research was first published in two papers in *Science* (Tallal et al., 1996; Merzenich et al., 1996) with additional field trial studies published in a series of subsequent papers (Tallal, 1998; Tallal, Merzenich, Miller, & Jenkins, 1998; Tallal, Miller, Jenkins, & Merzenich, 1999; Miller et al., 1999; Merzenich et al., 1999; Merzenich et al., in press). These remediation studies grew out of over 25 years of basic and clinical research in two distinct disciplines. One utilised primarily behavioural methods to study the etiology of developmental language-based learning disabilities. The other utilised primarily physiological methods to study neuroplasticity, that is, physiological changes in the brain driven by behavioural training techniques. These remediation studies,

conducted both in the laboratory as well as in clinics and classrooms across the USA and Canada, have led to the development of a new generation of training programmes, the first of which is called Fast ForWord®. The focus of this chapter will be to review the scientific studies that led to the development of these new remediation techniques, based on neuroplasticity research, as well as the outcome data derived from controlled laboratory studies and field trials aimed at assessing the efficacy of these new training methods.

Early studies focusing on the aetiology of developmental language impairments date back to the early 1960s. In a classic paper, Benton (1964) hypothesised that central auditory processing deficits may characterise many children with developmental dysphasia, now referred to as specific language impairment (SLI). Subsequent studies focused on one aspect of central auditory processing, that is, sequencing or temporal order judgement (TOJ) deficits.

Pursuing these early studies, Tallal and Piercy (1973a; 1973b) set out to investigate further the auditory perceptual abilities of children with developmental dysphasia. In addition to an experimental TOJ task, they included a frequency discrimination task as a control condition. The identical set of stimuli were presented in both the TOJ and the frequency discrimination task. Stimuli consisted of two 75 msec duration complex tones that differed in fundamental frequency (100 Hz vs 305 Hz). All possible combinations of these two stimuli were presented in pairs. The two tones in the pair were separated by a silent interval of varying duration (inter-stimulus interval — ISI). In the TOJ task the child was trained to press two response buttons, to indicate the temporal order of the two tones. If the same tone was presented twice, the button representing that tone was pressed twice. If two different tones were presented, the child was trained to indicate which one came first and which second, using the two-button response panel. In the discrimination task, children were trained on the same two-button response panel to push one button if the two tones in the pair were the same and the other button if they were not the same. Thus, the stimulus set and the response panel were the same across tasks, but only one of the tasks required temporal order judgements. Twelve children with developmental dysphasia (aged 6–9 years) and twelve age- and performance IQ-matched controls participated.

Based on earlier studies it was expected that children with language impairments would perform poorly only on the TOJ task. Surprisingly, this is not what the results showed. Contrary to expectation, these children had no difficulty either on the TOJ or the discrimination task, when the brief (75 msec duration) stimuli were presented relatively slowly (separated by hundreds of milliseconds). Furthermore, they were impaired on both tasks in comparison to matched controls, when these brief stimuli were presented rapidly in succession (separated by tens of milliseconds).

These results changed the interpretation of the auditory processing problems of children with developmental dysphasia from a focus on sequencing (TOJ) deficits *per se*, to a more basic rate processing constraint affecting multiple levels of acoustic analysis (attention, discrimination, sequencing, serial memory).

The finding that children with developmental language learning problems are impaired in their ability to process brief, rapidly successive acoustic stimuli, specifically in the tens of millisecond time window (often referred to as a "temporal processing" deficit, although it is important to keep in mind that the deficit encompasses frequency changes that occur rapidly in time as well), has had significant impact on research on the neurobiological basis of speech perception. These acoustic studies with nonverbal stimuli focused attention on the acoustics of speech, specifically on how the brain processes the brief, rapidly successive acoustic changes (spectral, amplitude and durational) that characterise speech.

We know that the most basic unit of any language is the phoneme, the smallest unit of sound that differentiates meaning. However, we know very little about how the individual phonemes of a language come to be represented neurobiologically in the brain. As the sounds perceived as phonemes are physically complex acoustic stimuli, the role that complex auditory processing plays in the development of phonological systems has been a topic of increased research concentration.

It has been increasingly documented that phonological systems are developed through exposure to the native language (Kuhl et al., 1997). As the infant is exposed to a continuous speech stream from the environment, she must parse the incoming acoustic signal into consistent, replicable chunks that will come to represent the phonemes of her language(s). Clearly the infant does not know which language or languages she will be exposed to. Rather, neural firing patterns that recur most frequently in response to the incoming speech stream will come to be represented as the building blocks, phonemes, of the native language.

Neurophysiologists have mapped the features of the sensory world at the single cell level. This is done by inserting an electrode into a single neuron in the brain and observing which features of a stimulus make the cell fire. This work has shown that within each sensory modality the features that represent the physical world come to be mapped neuronally in a highly organised fashion. For example, in the auditory modality, there is a tonotopic representation of frequency such that the single cells that fire to a specific frequency reside physically right next to the cells that fire to the next higher frequency, in a continuous manner throughout the frequency range (Clopton, Winfield, & Flammino, 1974). That these sensory maps must be learned from environmental exposure is evidenced by neurophysiological research showing the effects of sensory deprivation (Neville, 1985).

Although it was previously thought that environmental exposure had to occur during critical periods of development and, once established, these maps were immutable, more recent research has challenged that perspective. For example, Jenkins, Merzenich, and colleagues have recently conducted a series of elegant studies in adult monkeys that have shown that the neural representations for the fingers on the hand can be significantly altered through training (Jenkins et al., 1990). Figure 8.1 shows the results of a prototypical training study. This study begins by mapping the somatosensory region that represents the primate hand, neuron by neuron. Here we see that the fingers of the hand are represented topographically at the neuronal level in a manner similar to the spatial representation of the fingers on the hand

FIGURE 8.1

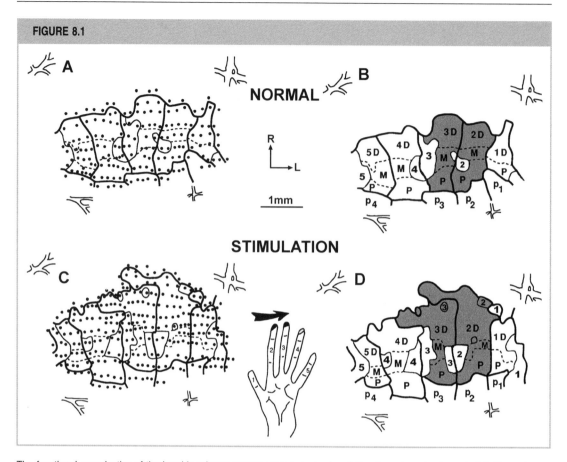

The functional organisation of the hand in primary somatosensory cortex in adult owl monkeys is shown in this figure. In A each dot represents a single cell. In B the cells that fire when each finger on the hand is stimulated are shown, labelled as 1 = thumb and 5 = little finger. In C and D, changes that occur after behaviourally controlled tactile stimulation training, involving only fingers 2 and 3, are shown. The significant expansion in the area representing finger 2 and 3 on the organisational neural map that occurs following training, is observed by comparing the shaded areas shown in B (that represent fingers 2 and 3 before training) with those shown in D, that represent fingers 2 and 3 after training. (Figure adapted from Jenkins et al., 1990)

on the animal's body. In this figure, the thumb is labelled as digit 1 and the little finger as digit 5. The top half of the figure shows the neurons that fire when each of the fingers is individually stimulated. The neurons that fire for stimulation to touches on fingers 2 and 3 are shaded. The bottom half of the figure shows the change in neuronal representation that occurs after the animal has engaged in intensive training that requires it to focus its attention on stimulation presented in rapid succession to digits 2 and 3. As can be seen, after training the number of cells that

respond to stimulation on digits 2 and 3 have significantly increased. These changes in the sensory map are the physical instantiation of sensory learning in the brain.

What aspects of learning are necessary to drive these physiological changes? Behavioural training studies coupled with physiological recording at the level of the single neuron have shown that there are several components of the learning process that are critical. First, the subject must attend closely to features of a sensory task. Second, in order for attention to be maintained, the subject

FIGURE 8.2

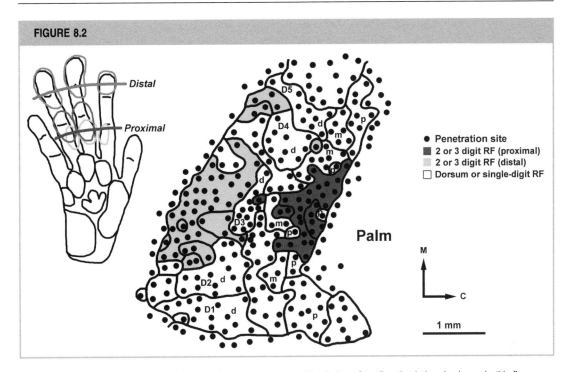

The remodelling of hand representation in adult cortex, determined by timing of tactile stimulation, is shown in this figure. After training to a task that presented stimulation either simultaneously only to the distal or proximal regions of the fingers, the neural representation of the fingers is remodelled. Instead of normal representation of each individual finger, the fingers stimulated simultaneously in time are now grouped such that only distal and proximal regions across simulated fingers are represented (as indicated by shaded areas). (Figure adapted from Wang et al., 1995)

must be able to perform the task at a high level of accuracy. If the task is too difficult, learning cannot be achieved and changes in the sensory map do not occur. Behaviour must be reinforced in a highly consistent and rewarding manner to maintain motivation and drive learning through corrective feedback. Highly consistent, repetitive input must be given over an intense period of time so that consistent patterns of neuronal activation occur repetitively, sharpening specific stimulation patterns to "represent" this input from the environment in the brain. Finally, having established a behaviour that can be responded to accurately and consistently, learning can be driven most effectively by systematically increasing the difficulty of the task as the subject's performance improves. Merzenich and colleagues have referred to these features of the learning process as "scientific learning principles" and have demon-

strated that neuroplasticity at the neuronal level accompanies behavioural learning (Merzenich & Jenkins, 1998).

What can our understanding of learning in the somatosensory system in the hand of the monkey teach us about the development of speech perception? After all, the physical relationship of the fingers of the hand occurs in an invariant way on the body of the animal, which is certainly not the case for the phonemes that are the building blocks of languages. How do we know that the animal is not born with distinct neuronal connections already in place to represent each part of the body? A second experiment by Wang, Merzenich, Sameshima, and Jenkins. (1995), addresses this important issue. In this experiment, illustrated in Fig. 8.2, the monkey is trained in a different task. Instead of receiving individual touches in rapid succession to fingers 2 and 3, as was the case in the first experiment, in this experiment the monkey receives simultaneous stimulation across all four fingers (excluding the thumb), either to the tips of the fingers or to the base, near the palm. Imagine a pencil striking the tips of all four fingers simultaneously, followed by the base, then the tips, then the base. However, on occasion, instead of alternating the location of stimulation, the pencil strikes the same location twice in a row — either the base and the base again, or the tips and the tips again. The task is to detect this change. When the "scientific learning principles" were applied to this training procedure in awake behaving adult monkeys, something quite remarkable occurred in the monkey's brain. As can be seen in Fig. 8.2, instead of the individual fingers being represented as five distinct entities, after training all four fingers were represented as a single entity in two groupings, tips and base, separated by inhibitory neurons between these two groupings.

Importantly, this experiment demonstrates the fundamental role of learning in building neural representation from sensory input. Even for body parts, complex neural representations are learned through experience, and can be altered throughout the lifetime with training. This experiment also demonstrates another basic organising principle underlying the development and maintenance of neural representations, that is, the profound impact of input timing of neural stimulation on the development and maintenance of sensory maps. When sensory inputs enter the nervous system differentially in time, as is the case when the five fingers of the hand move separately one from the other, and hence receive information differentially in time, the neuronal representation for each finger develops as distinct and separable. However, when information enters the nervous system either simultaneously, or within a critical window of time (tens of milliseconds) that is too rapid to separate, the information is "bound" together and thus is neurally coded as a unit. It has been hypothesised that it is in this way that the many different physical features of a complex stimulus, such as speech, are combined (bind together) to form a unified percept (Llinas, Ribary, & Tallal, 1998; Ribary et al., 1998).

As speech is at its essence a complex sensory signal, these neurophysiological sensory mapping

studies tell us a great deal about how the brain may come to represent it. Think about the processes that occur in the brain of the infant as she experiences the ongoing acoustic waveform of speech. It is widely held that language is an innate capacity that develops automatically, without the need for explicit training. However, recent cross-linguistic research shows that this is not the case (Kuhl et al., 1997), at least for phonology. As each language has its own set of phonemes, and as the infant has no way of knowing which native language he will be born into, the phonemes of the native language must indeed be explicitly learned from environmental exposure to the native language and represented as distinct firing patterns in the auditory cortex. It is important to note here that explicit training does not refer to conscious teaching, but rather explicit, repetitive environmental exposure.

But how does this representation occur? As is the case in all other sensory modalities, the complex acoustic information within the waveform of speech is broken down into its distinct physical features, each of which is represented in fine grained detail in the auditory system (Kraus, McGee, Carrell, & Sharma, 1995). The neural mechanisms underlying the development of representations for complex sensory or motor patterns were elegantly described by Hebb. According to Hebb (1949), when a complex signal occurs, all of the neurons that are activated by this complex series of features, per unit time, fire simultaneously. Repeated exposure to consistent sensory input features will result in that input pattern being neurally represented as a unified percept. The likelihood that a particular pattern will come to be represented increases with each additional exposure of a firing pattern ensemble.

It would be a simple matter to understand how the individual phonemes come to be represented in this way if they occurred one at a time, in an invariant acoustic pattern, with distinct boundaries separating the end of one from the beginning of another. However, none of this is the case. Rather, speech occurs in an ongoing acoustic stream (waveform) without distinct boundaries. The acoustic patterns produced by the articulators differ from utterance to utterance, especially within different phoneme contexts (Liberman, Cooper,

TABLE 8.1

Studies that demonstrate that individuals with language learning impairment have deficits in processing brief, rapidly successive acoustic cues in non-verbal stimuli

Lowe & Campbell, 1965	Tallal, 1980	Benasich & Tallal, 1996
Stark, 1967	McCrosky & Kidder, 1980	Ribary et al., 1996
Aten & Davis, 1968	Tallal et al., 1981	McAnally & Stein, 1997
Griffith, 1972	Thal & Barone, 1983	Wright et al., 1997
Tallal & Piercy, 1973a	Robin et al., 1989	Protopapas et al., 1997
Tallal & Piercy, 1973b	Stefanatos et al., 1989	Llinas et al., 1998
Kracke, 1975	Lincoln et al., 1992	Witton et al., 1998
Lea, 1975	Tomblin et al., 1992	Nagarajan et al., 1999
Tallal et al., 1976	Neville et al., 1993	
Haggerty & Stamm, 1978	Hari & Kiesilä, 1996	

Shankweiler, & Studdert-Kennedy, 1967), with the acoustic features of one phoneme affecting and co-occurring with those of adjacent ones. This is called coarticulation. For example, the acoustic pattern produced by the phoneme /b/, differs markedly depending on the differing vowel contexts in which it can occur. Further, in ongoing speech there is no distinct boundary that tells the brain where one phoneme ends and the next one begins. In learning to represent the acoustic world of speech the brain must segment the ongoing speech stream into chunks of time, and then seek consistencies in the neural firing patterns that result from these segmented chunks. Consistencies can be derived from chunking across various units of time. Smaller chunking units (in the tens of millisecond time window) will result in representations consistent with individual phonemes within a language. Chunking across a larger time window (hundreds of milliseconds) will equally result in consistent firing patterns, but in this case the firing patterns will be consistent with syllable level representations rather than phoneme representations.

The experiments described above showed that whether the fingers of the hand are represented in the brain as distinct, individual units, or more broadly (like a paw), is based primarily on the timing inputs of sensory stimulation. Similarly, speech may be represented in fine grain phonetic precision or more coarse grained syllabic precision, depending on temporal parameters of segmentation applied to the ongoing speech stream.

SPECIFIC LANGUAGE IMPAIRMENTS

Now, let us return our focus to studies of individuals with phonological processing problems that affect either oral and/or written language learning. Over the past 30 years, substantial evidence has been reported in the scientific literature that demonstrates that many individuals with language learning impairments integrate information across a longer (hundreds of milliseconds) time window, whereas those with typical language and reading abilities are capable of integrating within a more fine grained (tens of millisecond) time window. This rate processing constraint occurs across sensory modalities (auditory, visual, somatosensory). Table 8.1 lists some of the many studies demonstrating this finding, when non-verbal stimuli are used. Farmer and Klein (1995) and Leonard (1998) provide excellent reviews of this literature. But how does this processing rate constraint specifically impact speech perception? Figure 8.3 shows two sets of speech syllables. The first set are examples of vowels that incorporate acoustic spectra that differed one from the other across hundreds of milliseconds, such as the vowels /a/ as in the word "body" (US English) vs /ae/ as in the word "bat". The second set are the two stop-consonant vowel syllables /ba/ as in the word "body" vs /da/ as in the word "dot". These syllables begin with a brief segment, composed of a 40 msec duration formant transition followed

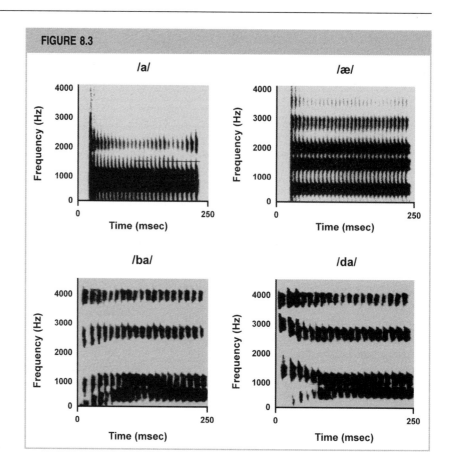

Spectrogram for vowel stimuli /ɑ/ and /ae/ and consonant-vowel (CV) syllables /bɑ/ and /bɑ/.

rapidly in succession by the steady-state vowel formants. Discrimination between these syllables depends on the ability to process the brief duration formant transitions (which incorporate coarticulated information about both the consonant and following vowel) within the context of the rapidly successive vowel formants. Numerous studies across many laboratories have demonstrated that children with language learning impairments are often most impaired in discriminating speech syllables that incorporate brief, rapidly successive acoustic changes intra-syllabically (see Table 8.2). It is important to emphasise that these studies show deficits that occur in processing rapid acoustic changes that occur intra-syllabically (within the syllable), not inter-syllabically (between syllables or words). Several recent studies, notably Mody, Studdert-Kennedy and Brady (1997) have misinterpreted these findings and have

manipulated intervals between syllables, rather than rates of change within syllables, focusing on TOJ rather than discrimination. Although short ISIs have been problematic for children with language learning limitations in studies employing brief tones as stimuli, this has not been the variable manipulated in the speech studies listed in Table 8.2. Therefore, a failure to find TOJ deficits with speech stimuli should not be interpreted as a failure to replicate previous studies. (For a scholarly critique of Mody et al., 1997, see Denenberg, 1999.)

That discrimination deficits for phonological contrasts which incorporate brief, rapidly successive acoustic changes are specifically related to the duration of intra-syllabic acoustic cues was demonstrated initially by Tallal and Piercy (1975). In this experiment the duration of the formant transition within the syllables /bɑ/ and /dɑ/ was

TABLE 8.2

Studies that demonstrate that individuals with language learning impairment have deficits in processing brief, rapidly successive acoustic cues in verbal stimuli

McReynolds, 1966	Alexander & Frost, 1982
Rosenthal, 1972	Werker & Tees, 1987
Tallal & Piercy, 1974	Elliott & Hammer, 1988
Tallal & Piercy, 1975	Elliott et al., 1989
Henderson, 1978	Reed, 1989
Thibodeau & Sussman, 1979	Leonard et al., 1992
Frumkin & Rapin, 1980	Sussman, 1993
Tallal et al., 1980a,b	Kraus et al., 1995
Tallal & Stark, 1981	Kraus et al., 1996
Godfrey et al., 1981	Stark & Heinz, 1996

extended from 40 to 80 msec, while the duration of the following steady-state portion representing the vowel was reduced from 210 to 170 msec. This acoustic modification resulted in highly significant improvement in discrimination. The significant benefit of acoustically extending the brief intra-syllabic cues within the speech waveform has been replicated across several studies (Frumkin & Rapin, 1980; Alexander & Frost, 1982).

The studies listed in Tables 8.1 and 8.2 demonstrate a concurrent relationship in young school age children between language disorders and rate processing constraints. However, they do not allow us to look at developmental interactions, prospectively. However, a recent series of studies has demonstrated that acoustic segmentation rates in infancy may play a fundamental role in the rate of normal as well as abnormal language development (Benasich & Tallal, 1996; Benasich & Tallal, 1998). In these studies the auditory temporal integration threshold of infants born into families with a history of language learning problems was assessed at six months and compared to that of infants born into families with no history of language or learning problems. Figure 8.4 shows an example of the significant difference in the auditory temporal processing threshold obtained in a representative family history positive as compared to a family history negative child.

The familial nature of language learning problems has been established in a number of studies (Tallal, Ross, & Curtiss, 1989 a, b; Gilger, Borecki,

DeFries, & Pennington, 1994; Tomblin, Freese, & Records, 1992; see Leonard, 1998 for review). An autosomal dominant mode of genetic transmission appears to be most consistent with these data. This entails that every infant with an affected parent or sibling will have a 50% chance of also having a language learning problem. Spitz, Tallal, Flax, and Benasich (1997) found that, at six months of age, approximately half of the infants in a family history positive group had auditory temporal integration thresholds in the hundreds of millisecond time window (similar to that shown for a representative infant born into a family with a positive history of language impairment in Fig. 8.4), whereas the other half had integration thresholds in the tens of millisecond time window, similar to the threshold shown in Fig. 8.4 for a representative infant with a negative family history. These infants have been followed prospectively by Benasich and colleagues and their language development has been assessed longitudinally using the MacArthur Child Development Inventory (Fenson et al., 1993). Importantly, the auditory temporal integration thresholds established at six months of age, for both groups of infants, have proven to be highly predictive of subsequent receptive and expressive language development. These data show that those infants with slow temporal integration rates are developing laguage more slowly than those with more rapid integration rates (Benasich & Tallal, 1996, 1998). A similar finding has been reported by Trehub

FIGURE 8.4

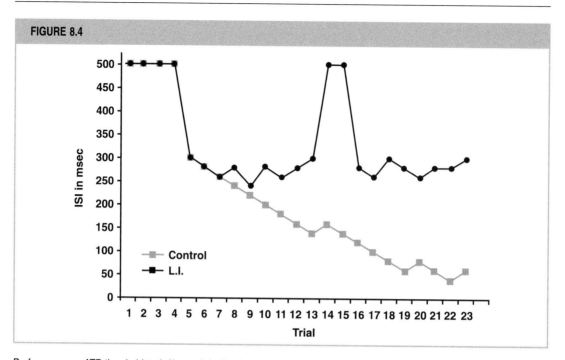

Performance on ATP threshold task (6 months). This figure shows performance on an adaptive two-alternate forced choice auditory temporal processing (ATP) threshold task using head turn responses. Plots of two individual infants, control and family history of language impairment (LI) show inter-stimulus-intervals (ISI) for different trials. Following a series of correct responses at 500 ms, ISI is decreased to 300 ms. ISI is decreased for correct responses and increased for incorrect responses (*) in 20 ms steps while ISI remains the same for no response. Probe trials are delivered at 500 ms if there are 3 consecutive incorrect responses. The probes verify the child is still performing the task. This figure shows the significant difference in auditory temporal processing threshold obtained in a representative family history of LI as compared to control infant. (Figure adapted from Benasich & Tallal, 1998)

and Henderson (1996) using a measure of gap detection threshold in a large cohort of normally developing infants. These findings suggest that individual differences in acoustic information processing rates, present within the first months of life, play a significant role in language learning. Preliminary results suggest that the infants with both the slowest processing rates, and who also have a family history of language learning impairments, are most at risk to become language learning impaired.

THE LANGUAGE LITERACY CONTINUUM

There has been a good deal of discussion about the possible relationship between oral language and written language deficits. As part of this discussion, it has been hypothesised that children who segment speech in larger time chunks will not only experience difficulties learning phonological skills necessary for oral language development, but also for written language. Specifically, they may be expected to have considerable difficulty being able to learn to segment words into the finer grain phonetic units important for developing phonological awareness skills that are necessary for establishing letter to sound correspondence rules so important for learning to read. To investigate this hypothesis, the processing rate of individuals experiencing written language problems (dyslexics) has been studied extensively and also related to those of children with oral specific language deficits (SLI) (see Stark & Tallal, 1988 and Farmer & Klein, 1995 for reviews). Results

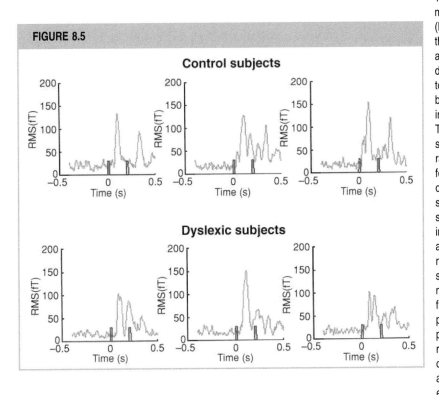

FIGURE 8.5

This figure shows magnetoencephalographic (MEG) recordings from three control subjects (top) as compared to three dyslexic subjects (bottom) to the presentation of two brief tones (onset times indicated along X axis). The controls each show a sharp positive peak and rapid recovery to base line following the presentation of each of the two distinct, successive acoustic stimuli, separated by a 200 msec interval. For the dyslexics, although the neural response to the first stimulus is initiated normally, the recovery from this response is prolonged well into the period in which the second response should have, but does not occur. (Figure adapted from Nagarajan et al., 1999)

across many studies have shown a highly significant correlation between difficulty with phonological decoding, and a slow rate of information processing. For example, an early study by Tallal (1980) showed a highly significant correlation between the rate of processing brief, rapidly successive tones differing in frequency, and error rates for reading nonsense words in dyslexic children. Importantly, it was shown in this study that not all dyslexic children showed rate processing constraints. What was striking was the relationship between rate processing constraints and reading decoding skills. Those dyslexic children who did not demonstrate rate processing constraints also were not impaired in either reading decoding skills or oral language comprehension abilities. They did have reading problems, but these did not seem to be based on phonological processing or awareness deficits. More recently, Witton et al. (1998) have shown a very similar correlation between

processing rapidly modulating tones, as well as visual transient stimuli, and nonsense word reading in adults with a history of dyslexia.

Deficits in responding to rapidly successive acoustic stimuli also have been demonstrated physiologically in a recent study using magnetoencephalography (MEG), a neuroimaging technique that records magnetic signals emitted from the surface of the skull with excellent spatial as well as temporal precision (Nagarajan et al., 1999). Figure 8.5 shows the neurophysiological MEG response to two brief acoustic stimuli presented with differing inter-stimulus intervals (ISIs). The top half of the graph shows the neurophysiological response of normal adults without a history of language or reading problems. Here it is seen that two distinct, positive neural responses (indicated by a sharp positive peak in the recording) occur for each of two distinct, successive acoustic stimuli separated by a 200 msec ISI. The bottom of this graph shows the brain responses to the same stimuli for adults with dyslexia. It is seen clearly that although the neural response to the first stimulus is initiated normally (as indicated by a sharp positive peak in the recording), this response is prolonged over time (as indicated by the period of time taken to return to baseline). For the dyslexic subjects, this prolonged response to the first stimulus continues well into the period in which the second response (seen in the recordings from the control subjects as a second sharp peak) should have, but does not, occur. In this study it was found that the dyslexic subjects required several hundred milliseconds before a second neural response occurred. These neurophysiological data mirrored these subjects' behavioural perception of whether they heard one or two successive tones. These results demonstrate that when brief, rapidly successive acoustic stimuli converge in the nervous system within tens of milliseconds, these signals are not processed normally in the brains of people with dyslexia.

These results taken in aggregate demonstrate that certain individuals begin life as slow acoustic processors and this information processing rate constraint continues throughout the life span. In addition to slow processing rates, these same individuals are generally characterised by both oral and written language deficits. After comprehensively reviewing the extensive research literature pertaining to the aetiology of specific developmental language impairments (SLI) in children, Leonard (1998) finds that:

> "The conclusion that children with SLI have difficulty processing brief or rapidly presented stimuli seems indisputable. These findings are so consistent and demonstrable across tasks and stimulus variations that it is difficult to imagine that they are not an important piece of the SLI puzzle." (p. 145)

Given the consistency of these findings across so many studies and laboratories, it is important to try to determine why a few recent studies have reported difficulty replicating these results (Bishop et al., 1999; Mody et al., 1997; Nittrouer, 1999). These discrepancies can probably be related to differences in subject selection criteria and im-

portant stimulus design and other methodological differences between studies. Difficulty of psychophysical tasks, attentional demands and reinforcement schedules must also be carefully compared across studies with children, especially when failure to replicate previous studies depends on findings that rely entirely on failure to reject the null hypothesis (see Denenberg, 1999, for a critique). Understanding these differences, rather than simply viewing them as a failure to confirm past research, will help to extend and refine our understanding of the perceptual constraints of individuals with language learning impairment and how they relate to the language and reading problems of these individuals.

Whereas the direct effect that acoustic rate processing constraints may play on the development of fine grain phonological representations has been extensively studied, the extent to which a general rate processing constraint can affect higher level aspects of linguistic development has received far less experimental attention. Leonard (1998) (see also Leonard, Chapter 7, this volume) addressed this issue in considerable detail. Leonard comprehensively reviewed cross-linguistic studies that focus on the linguistic error patterns of children with specific language impairment (SLI) learning a variety of different languages. It was expected that cross-linguistic data would replicate the pattern of linguistic deficits that have been reported so consistently for English-speaking children with SLI (see Rice & Wexler, 1996 for review, and also Rice, Chapter 2, this volume). Leonard hypothesised that if children with SLI have a deficit in linguistic knowledge, as has been proposed as the basis of SLI, then a consistent pattern of linguistic deficits should be seen, regardless of the language that a child is learning. Despite the broadly held view that SLI represents primary and specific linguistic deficits, extensive cross-linguistic studies have failed, on the whole, to support this hypothesis. That is, few specific linguistic patterns of errors have been found that are consistent across all languages. For example, Rice and Wexler (1996) have suggested that children with SLI have a specific deficit in grammatical morphology, particularly past tense verbs. However, children with SLI learning more highly-inflected languages, such as Italian, fail to show a similar pattern of errors. After reviewing an extensive literature focusing on the linguistic patterns of errors of children with SLI learning a variety of languages, Leonard concluded that there is little support for a linguistic specific deficit in these children. Rather, children across all of these languages show a protracted rate of language development, following much the same pattern of language development as younger children learning that language.

Leonard goes on to make a strong case for a different interpretation of linguistic data obtained cross-linguistically from children with SLI. He discusses two plausible and compatible hypotheses. One of these — the morphological richness hypothesis — pertains to the frequency and obligatory nature of inflections in the target language. The other is the surface hypothesis. According to this hypothesis, whichever linguistic structures in a particular language are acoustically brief and of weak phonetic substance are most difficult for all children to learn, and are particularly problematic for individuals with SLI. Fellbaum, Miller, Curtiss, and Tallal (1995) designed a study in English-speaking children to address this hypothesis directly. Specific English morphologic structures were selected that are brief and have weak phonetic substance including plural (-s); regular past tense (-ed); nominative case pronouns (he, she, they); modal auxiliary (will); possessive ('s). These were compared to linguistic structures, typically learned by children across the same age range, that in the most frequent obligatory contexts are acoustically longer, stronger and hence have more phonetic salience (including: object pronouns (him, her); comparative (more), comparative (er). The results of this study, seen in Fig. 8.6, were striking. In comparison to children with typical language development, English-speaking children with SLI make significantly more errors on the brief, phonetically non-salient morphological structures as compared to the longer morphological structures. These results support the surface hypothesis.

Leonard concluded his recent, comprehensive review of the literature on SLI by proposing an integrating theory that best seems to account for the acoustic, perceptual, conceptual, neuroscientific and linguistic data in this field.

According to this review, much of the data, regardless of scientific approach used, fit parsimoniously with a general information processing constraint that specifically affects the rate of information processing across sensory modalities, and affects both verbal and non-verbal information processing.

REMEDIATION STUDIES

If language learning problems are characterised by a basic processing constraint in the rate at which incoming sensory information is segmented and represented (Tallal's rate processing hypothesis and Leonard's 2nd hypothesis), and also is affected by the frequency and obligatory nature of morphological structures in a target language (Leonard's 1st hypothesis) these factors should have important implications for the design of remediation strategies. Recently, Tallal, Merzenich, Miller and Jenkins (1998) hypothesised that the "scientific learning principles", that had been shown in studies with monkeys to drive neuroplasticity, might be adapted to ameliorate the rate processing constraints of children with language learning problems, while simultaneously using neuroplasticity training procedures to train linguistic skills based on frequency of obligatory occurrence. Specifically, a hierarchy of computer-based training exercises now called Fast ForWord® was developed:

1. To attempt to drive neural processing of rapidly successive acoustic stimuli to faster and faster rates,
2. To improve speech perception, phonological analysis and awareness and language comprehension by providing intensive training exercises within various linguistic contexts (phonological, morphological, semantic and syntactic) that utilise speech stimuli that have been acoustically modified to amplify and temporally extend the brief, rapidly successive (phonetically non-salient) intrasyllabic cues (see Nagarajan et al., 1998 for a detailed description of the speech modification algorithm).

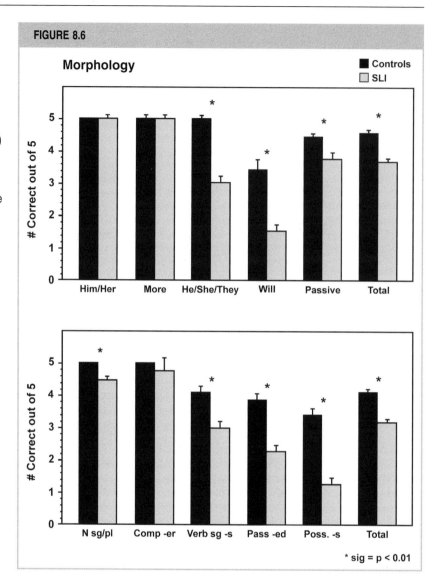

FIGURE 8.6

The performance of children with specific language impairment (SLI) and matched controls is shown for grammatical structures that are acoustically brief and have weak phonetic substance (plural -s; regular past tense -ed; nominative case pronouns he/she/they; modal auxiliary will, possessive -s) as compared to structures that are acoustically longer, stronger and have more phonetic salience (object pronouns him/her; comparative more; comparative -er). Significant group differences (*p* < .01, indicated by an *) were found for all of the acoustically brief, phonetically non-salient morphological structures, and none of the acoustically longer, stronger morphemes. (Figure adapted from Fellbaum et al., 1995)

Seven training exercises were developed in the form of computer games. The exercises were programmed to be individually adaptive. That is, the goal was to find for each child a level of acoustic and linguistic functioning that could be responded to at a high rate of accuracy, through the use of acoustically modified speech. Once established, the exercises were programmed to adaptively change trial by trial, based on each individual child's responses. That is, trials got more difficult (moving towards more rapid and less amplified, natural speech) following correct linguistic responses or more simplified (more acoustically modified) following incorrect responses. The goal was to move the individual child from a reliance on the acoustically modified speech towards the ability to process more and more complex linguistic tasks with rapidly successive, natural speech. Similarly, adaptive training was also undertaken to directly affect temporal integration thresholds for rapidly

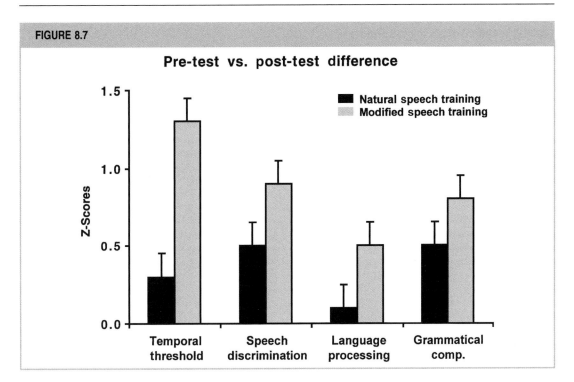

FIGURE 8.7

Difference *z* scores (post-training minus pre-training) are shown for LLI subjects who received speech and language training with either acoustically modified or natural speech. Difference *z* scores are presented for measures of temporal threshold, speech discrimination (GFW), language processing (Token Test), and grammatical comprehension (CYCLE-R). To facilitate group comparisons across each of the measures, raw scores were converted to *z* scores on the basis of the pre-training performance of all subjects on each individual test. Mean and standard error values for each measure demonstrate that significantly larger improvements were achieved by the LLI children receiving the acoustically modified speech training (grey bars) as compared with the performance improvements recorded for the subjects receiving natural speech training (black bars). The temporal threshold values were converted to positive values for display purposes. (Figure adapted from Tallal et al., 1996)

successive acoustic sweep tones. The goal was to drive, through adaptive training, each child into the normal processing rate of tens of milliseconds, while simultaneously increasing each child's ability to process linguistic structures in their most frequent, naturally occurring, obligatory contexts.

Two initial laboratory studies demonstrated dramatic success with a prototype of this training method (Merzenich et al., 1996; Tallal et al., 1996). The results seen in Fig. 8.7 showed that intensive daily training (approximately two hours a day five days a week for four weeks) resulted in highly significant improvements in temporal integration rates, speech discrimination, language processing and grammatical understanding. This controlled laboratory study demonstrated the specificity of this training method. A control group received essentially identical language training, but using natural, unmodified speech. In addition, they played computer games for an equivalent period of time. However, these computer games were visual, not auditory, and were not temporally adaptive. Both groups received the same amount of training, reinforcement and rewards for performance. The results showed that the control group demonstrated significantly poorer outcomes than the group that received the acoustically modified speech and rate processing training.

Moving research from the laboratory to clinics and classrooms

Based on these initial promising results from controlled laboratory studies, two large-scale field trials have been conducted to assess the efficacy of the Fast ForWord training programme in clinical and educational settings. The purpose of the first trial was to determine whether the efficacy that was demonstrated in the laboratory could be replicated in clinics and classrooms under the supervision of clinicians and teachers (rather than trained researchers). This is a difficult, but an essential first step in the process of moving research from the laboratory into clinics and classrooms. In order to assure consistency in programme delivery, data collection and analysis, and quality control across multiple sites and long distances, the adaptive training programmes were created in the form of a CD-Rom which could be activated and monitored through data exchange over the Internet. Trial by trial responses for each of the seven exercises in the programme are recorded on the hard drive of the computer each child uses to play the games. These responses are sent daily, coded by individual client ID numbers, over the Internet to Scientific Learning Corporation (the company that produces the programmes) where they are analysed, tabulated, and then returned to the professional supervising the training for each child (for more details see www.scientificlearning.com).

The first field trial included over 500 children identified by 60 professionals at 35 clinical or educational sites. Clinicians were instructed to use standardised speech and language assessment tests to include children who were at least one or more standard deviations below the mean in the area of central auditory processing, speech discrimination and/or language comprehension. Clinicians were encouraged to select a battery of standardised speech, language and central auditory processing tests that they used most commonly in their own clinical practice. Case history records indicated that children who met these study criteria had one or more of the following diagnostic classifications: specific language impairment (SLI), attention deficit disorder (ADD), pervasive developmental disability (PDD), autism, central auditory pro-

cessing disorder (CAPD), dyslexia or learning disability (LD).

The goals of the first clinical trial were to determine

1. whether or not the results obtained in the laboratory could be replicated, by the clinicians/educators who most often treat children with language/learning problems,
2. whether the result obtained in the laboratory with children with SLI would generalise to a broader population of children with a variety of speech, oral and written language and central auditory processing disorders, and
3. whether efficacy would generalise to the wide variety of standardised receptive and expressive speech, language and central auditory processing tests that are most commonly used clinically, or just to items similar to those that were directly trained in Fast ForWord.

Results of this field trial represented the first phase of moving this research programme from the laboratory into practical use. As such, it was not a controlled trial. This is important because, if the results failed to replicate those found in the controlled laboratory study, it would not be possible to determine whether improved performance resulted from practice or placebo effects, rather than the specific aspects of the training programme. However, if the results did replicate those found in the controlled laboratory study, we could rule out these factors as explanatory, as they had already been controlled for in the laboratory studies. As the cost of running such a large-scale trial in the field with controls was prohibitive, it was determined that the first step should be an attempt to replicate and extend the results of the previous controlled laboratory studies in "real-world" clinical and classroom settings, using a standardised programme presented via CD-Rom, with monitoring over the Internet. A detailed report of the design and results of this first field study is reported elsewhere (Merzenich et al., in press).

A summary of results is shown in Figs 8.8, 8.9 and 8.10 comparing pre-Fast ForWord training

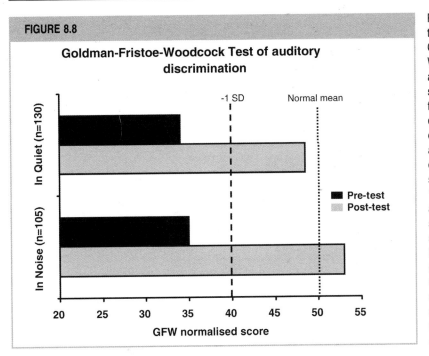

FIGURE 8.8

Pre- vs post-Fast ForWord training results for the Goldman Fristoe Woodcock (GFW) test of auditory discrimination are shown. The test is normed for presentation either in quiet or noise. The group of children in this study assessed with the GFW demonstrated mean test scores approximately 1.5 SDs below the mean at pre-test. Post-test scores demonstrated a significant improvement in both the quiet and noise conditions ($p < .00005$) after training, with average scores approaching or exceeding the mean. (Figure adapted from Tallal & Merzenich, 1997)

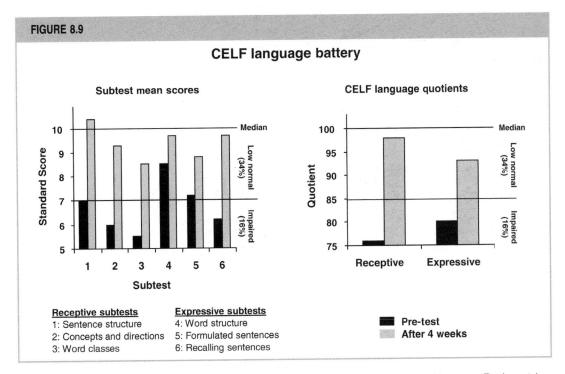

FIGURE 8.9

Pre- and post-Fast ForWord training standardised scores are shown for the Clinical Evaluation of Language Fundamentals (CELF) language battery. Each receptive and expressive sub-test standard score is shown on the left-hand side of the figure. The right-hand side of the figure shows composite receptive and expressive language quotients derived from performance on the complete test battery. (Figure adapted from Merzenich et al., in press)

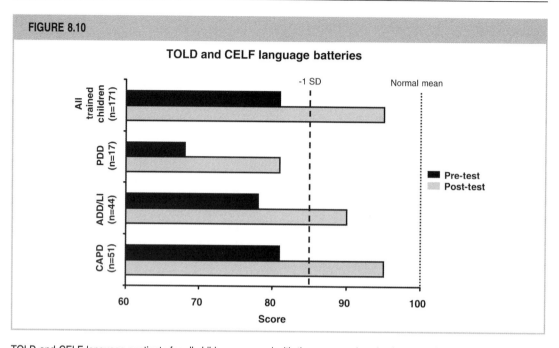

FIGURE 8.10

TOLD and CELF language quotients for all children assessed with these comprehensive language batteries are shown for pre-test as well as post-Fast ForWord training. Scores are shown for all children with language impairments (LI) combined; as well as for LI children diagnosed as having pervasive developmental disorder (PDD), or with co-morbid diagnoses of attention deficit disorder (ADD), or central auditory processing disorder (CAPD). Although the degree of language deficit differed at pre-test among these groups of children (with children diagnosed as PDD having the most severe language disorder and CAPD having the least severe), there were no significant differences in the magnitude of improvement across groups achieved with training. All groups were 1 or more SD below the mean at pre-test and showed significant improvement ($p < .0001$) from pre- to post-testing. Although the PDD group improved significantly following training, they still remained more than 1 SD below the mean following training, based on these test batteries. The children with language impairments co-morbid for ADD or CAPD entered the study with pre-test scores more than 1 SD below the mean, while their average post-test scores approached the normal median. (Adapted from Tallal et al., 1998)

standardised test scores to post-test standard scores for each child. Figures 8.8 and 8.9 demonstrate that the laboratory results were replicated in clinics and classrooms, and thus can be considered a replication of the controlled laboratory studies. Significant efficacy was obtained in areas of central auditory processing, speech discrimination and language comprehension, the areas targeted by Fast ForWord training. However, in addition, results showed that efficacy extended to include improved expressive language abilities as well, although only receptive language skills were directly trained using the Fast ForWord method. Overall, the results of this field trial demonstrated that approximately 90% of children who complied with the study protocol showed significantly improved

performance (at least one standardised deviation change from pre-training to post-training) on standardised speech, language and/or auditory processing measures, regardless of the precise clinical measures selected by each professional.

There was considerable variability across children as to the degree and pattern of improvements they made across domains, as would be expected, based on the variety of symptomatology and clinical classifications of this large heterogeneous group of children with language learning problems. Figure 8.10 shows that significant efficacy was obtained for a much broader group of children than had been included in the initial laboratory studies. Furthermore, the significant difference in the degree of efficacy was not found to be based on the child's clinical diagnostic classification or classifications, age, gender or degree of impairment. On average, the language skills of children who completed the protocol improved by a year and a half following six weeks of training. These results are significant not only in magnitude of improvement, but specifically in light of the very brief period of time (weeks rather than years) over which the intervention (training) was provided.

Clearly both the controlled laboratory and clinical field trial results indicate the immediate efficacy of this new training approach. However, it is also very important to determine the longer term effectiveness of this brief, but intensive, training. Figure 8.11 shows follow-up results for the SLI subjects who participated in the original controlled laboratory study (Bedi et al., 1999). This graph shows that training results were sustained at follow-up at both six weeks and six months, without additional training. Children who received the experimental training in the controlled laboratory studies clearly maintained their advantage over their matched controls. These significant improvements and group differences were maintained out to six months. Longer term follow-up is currently in progress.

In a second field trial the potential use of these neuroplasticity-based training programmes for preventing language-based learning problems was investigated (Miller et al., 1998). Regular classroom elementary teachers at 19 different public schools in the United States were instructed to select children who they identified as "at risk for academic failure". The reason for being identified as "at risk" was not specified in this study to relate solely to language-based problems.

This second trial represents the second phase of bringing this research out of the laboratory and into the public domain. As such, it was a randomised control trial with children randomly assigned to receive Fast ForWord training, as compared to receiving additional educational services being provided in their public school for "at risk" children, for a comparable period of time (one hour and forty minutes a day, five days a week for six weeks). All participants also received a battery of standardised tests both pre- and post-training. One

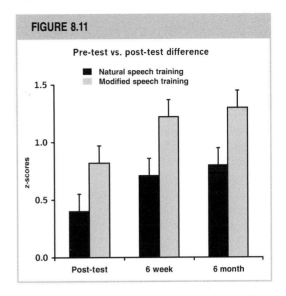

FIGURE 8.11

Pre-test vs. post-test difference

■ Natural speech training
▨ Modified speech training

Longitudinal follow-up data of change scores (z-scores) from baseline: immediately after 4 weeks of training (post-test); 6 weeks after training was completed; and 6 months after training. Change scores are shown (grey bars) for children receiving language training using modified speech and adaptive computer games compared to a matched control group of children who received the same language training, but with natural speech and non-adaptive computer games (black bars). The results immediately following the training (post-test) have been published previously in *Science* (Tallal et al., 1996). The modified speech group showed significantly greater improvement than the natural speech group ($p < .015$). Follow-up testing 6 weeks and 6 months after training show that both groups continue to improve, with the difference between the groups continuing to be significant. (Adapted from Bedi et al., 1999)

of the most striking results of this field trial of school children selected as academically "at risk" was the finding that these children's oral language was their most significant problem, based on pre-training test scores. These results are very interesting in that they show that classroom teachers identified children as academically "at risk", who upon testing were found to be performing at a lower level on standardised measures of oral language. This is an important finding as these teachers were not instructed or encouraged to select children based on oral language impairment, but rather based on their intuition that a child was "at risk" for academic failure. Nonetheless, on testing, these children as a group showed oral language performance skewed towards the lower range of normal.

This result is consistent with a striking finding from a recently published epidemiological study on the incidence of SLI. Tomblin et al. (1997) report that on testing 7.4% of kindergarten children were found to be more than one and a quarter standard deviations below the mean in oral language skills. Perhaps the most striking finding, however, was that only 29% of the parents or teachers of these children had ever identified oral language problems in these children with SLI. This finding suggests that 71% of oral language deficits may remain undetected and untreated at the time a child enters school. Our school study shows that, although teachers are quite accurate in identifying children who are "at risk for academic failure", they do not select "language comprehension deficit" on a check list when indicating why they think the child is "at risk for academic failure". This suggests that they are not aware that it may be weak receptive language skills that they are actually recognising in these children. As a result, only a minority of children with weak language development are ever identified or given speech therapy or other oral language interventions. Rather, the majority of these children with weak oral language skills enter our school systems unidentified and, indeed, at risk for academic failure, which may first appear as a problem learning to read, write and spell.

The results of this field study showed that before training, over half of the subjects identified by their teachers as "academically at risk" scored one or more standard deviations below the mean in oral language comprehension. After Fast ForWord training, post-testing results showed that the oral language comprehension performance of these "academically at risk" children substantially and significantly improved, shifting substantially to within the normal distribution. Furthermore, improvements were significantly greater in children receiving Fast ForWord training as compared to the control group (Miller et al., 1998). Children in both groups are now being followed longitudinally in their public schools to deter-

mine the longer term efficacy of Fast ForWord as a "prevention" for subsequent reading problems in "academically at risk" children.

CONCLUSIONS

Our laboratory research over the past 25 years has been based on questions pertaining to the possible etiologies of specific language-based learning disabilities. That research led to the development of a hypothesis that one potential basis for SLI is a pervasive rate processing constraint that particularly affects the development of normal phonological processing and grammatical morphology, leading to both oral and, in many cases, written language deficits. This hypothesis led us recently to develop a series of laboratory studies that aimed to evaluate the effects of attempting to ameliorate the underlying rate processing constraints while simultaneously directly training many aspects of speech and language, using an acoustically modified signal. The results showed that dramatic improvements in temporal integration rates, as well as language processing and comprehension, could be achieved in a short period of time using these new methods.

It is important to note that the specific role of each of the variables manipulated in these initial studies has not as yet been studied separately. As such, we cannot determine which specific variable(s) contribute to the improvements we reported. It is also important to note that the magnitude of the improvements we observed led us away from our previous focus on aetiology, to a new focus on the development of practical and efficacious remediation techniques. The nature of the questions posed when developing new remediation techniques are, by their very nature, different from the theoretical concerns that are at the heart of study focused on aetiology. It is fair to say that the initial concerns in developing remediation techniques is demonstrating efficacy, not in working out which specific theory best explains the results. As such, the methods of laboratory research, of carefully changing a single variable at a time and seeing the effect, are not efficient for the initial stages of the development of training programmes such as Fast ForWord. To the contrary, the goal is to develop the most effective, generalisable programme, by "cross training" as many skills as possible together, in the briefest period of time, to get the greatest improvements across the largest and most heterogeneous population. Once a programme is found to be effective, it is a reiterative process to determine what specific training components are most effective, so that the programme can be improved. It is at this stage that issues pertaining to theory, that is, what is responsible for the changes in specific targeted areas, can become the focus of research. It is anticipated that many future studies will address these issues.

This report outlines the steps we have taken to date to use data obtained in controlled laboratory studies to develop new diagnostic and treatment approaches for language learning problems, and to move this research from the laboratory to "real world" clinics and classrooms. It is important to emphasise that when we refer to the Fast ForWord training programme as "proven", this is intended to refer to its clinical effectiveness, based on standardised test results and clinical reports, rather than to suggest that it proves any particular theory. It is our primary goal that this line of research will lead to increased progress in improving diagnostic, remediation and educational programmes for the millions of individuals affected with developmental language learning problems worldwide. It is also our hope that future theoretical and aetiological research also will be stimulated by these efforts.

ACKNOWLEDGEMENTS

The research discussed in this chapter was funded by the National Institute of Deafness and Communication Disorders, the March of Dimes, Rutgers University, University of California at San Francisco, Santa Fe Institute and Scientific Learning Corporation. Paula Tallal is a co-founder of Scientific Learning Corporation, the company that developed the Fast ForWord training programme.

REFERENCES

Aten, J., & Davis, J. (1968). Disturbance in the perception of auditory sequence in children with minimal cerebral dysfunction. *Journal of Speech and Hearing Research, 11,* 236–245.

Alexander, D.W., & Frost, B.P. (1982). Decelerated synthesized speech as a means of shaping speed of auditory processing of children with delayed language. *Perceptual and Motor Skills, 55,* 783–792.

Bedi, G., Miller, S., Merzenich, M., Jenkins, W.M., & Tallal, P. (1999). *Efficacy of neuroscience-based training for receptive language and auditory discrimination deficits in language-learning impaired children: A follow up study.* Paper presented at the Cognitive Neuroscience Society Meeting, Washington, DC.

Benasich, A.A., & Tallal, P. (1996). Auditory temporal processing thresholds, habituation, and recognition memory over the first year. *Infant Behavior and Development, 19,* 339–357.

Benasich, A.A., & Tallal, P. (1998). Infant processing of auditory temporal information: Links to family history and later language outcome. *Society for Neuroscience Abstract, 24,* 819.

Benton, A. (1964). Developmental aphasia and brain damage. *Cortex, 1,* 40–52.

Bishop, D.V.M. (1997). *Uncommon understanding,* Hove, UK: Psychology Press.

Bishop, D.V.M., Carlyon, R.P., Deeks, J.M., & Bishop, S.J. (1999). Auditory temporal processing impairment: Neither necessary nor sufficient for causing language impairment in children. *Journal of Speech, Language, and Hearing Research, 42,* 1295–1310.

Clopton, B.M., Winfield, J.A., & Flammino, F.J. (1974). Tonotopic organization: Review and analysis. *Brain Research, 76,* 1–20.

Denenberg, V.H. (1999). A critique of Mody, Studdert-Kennedy, and Brady's "Speech perception deficits in poor readers: Auditory processing or phonological coding?" *Journal of Learning Disabilities, 32,* 379–383.

Elliott, L., & Hammer, M. (1988). Longitudinal changes in auditory discrimination in normal children and children with language-learning problems. *Journal of Speech and Hearing Disorders, 53,* 467–474.

Elliott, L.L., Hammer, M.A., & Scholl, M.E. (1989). Fine-grained auditory discrimination in normal children and children with language learning problems.

Journal of Speech and Hearing Research, 32, 112–119.

Farmer, M., & Klein, R.M. (1995). The evidence for temporal processing deficit linked to dyslexia: A review. *Psychonomic Bulletin and Review, 2*, 460–493.

Fellbaum, C., Miller, S., Curtiss, S., & Tallal, P. (1995). Auditory processing deficits as a possible source of SLI. In D. MacLaughlin & S. McEwen (Eds), *Proceedings of the 19th Annual Boston University Conference on Language Development* (pp. 1204–1215). Somerville, MA: Cascadilla Press.

Fenson, L., Dale, P.S., Reznick, J.S., Thal, D., Bates, E., Hartung, J.P., Pethick, S., & Reilly, J.S. (1993). *Technical manual for the MacArthur communicative development inventory.* San Diego, CA: Singular Publishing Group Inc.

Frumkin, B., & Rapin, I. (1980). Perception of vowels and consonant-vowels of varying duration in language impaired children, *Neuropsychologia, 18*, 443–454.

Gilger, J.W., Borecki, I.B., DeFries, J.C., & Pennington, B.F. (1994). Comingling and segregation analysis of reading performance in families of normal reading probands. *Behavior Genetics, 24*, 345–355.

Godfrey, J.J., Syrdal-Lasky, A.K., Millay, K.K., & Knox, J. (1981). Performance of dyslexic children on speech perception tests. *Journal of Experimental Child Psychology, 32*, 401–424.

Griffith, D. (1972). *Developmental aphasia: An introduction.* London: Invalid Children's Aid Association.

Haggerty, R., & Stamm, J.S. (1978). Dichotic auditory fusion levels in children with learning difficulties. *Neuropsychologia, 16*, 349–360.

Hari, R., & Kiesilä, P. (1996). Deficit of temporal auditory processing in dyslexic adults. *Neuroscience Letters, 205*, 138–140.

Hebb, D.O. (1949). *The organization of behavior: A neuropsychological theory.* New York: Wiley.

Henderson, B. (1978). *Older language impaired children's processing of rapidly changing acoustic signals.* San Francisco, CA: Convention of the American Speech-Language-Hearing Association.

Jenkins, W.M., Merzenich, M.M., Ochs, M.T., Allard, T., & Guic, R.E. (1990). Functional reorganization of primary somatosensory cortex in adult owl monkeys after behaviorally controlled tactile stimulation. *Journal of Neurophysiology, 63*, 82–104.

Kracke, I. (1975). Perception of rhythmic sequences by receptive aphasic and deaf children. *British Journal of Disorders of Communication, 10*, 43–51.

Kraus, N., McGee, T., Carrell, T.D., & Sharma, A. (1995). Neurophysiologic bases of speech discrimination. *Ear and Hearing, 16*, 19–37.

Kraus, N., McGee, T.J., Carrell, T.D., Zecker, S.G., Nicol, T.G., & Koch, D.B. (1996). Auditory neurophysiologic responses and discrimination deficits in children with learning problems. *Science, 273*, 971–3.

Kuhl, P.K., Andruski, J.E., Chistovich, I.A., Chistovich, L.A., Kozhevnikova, E.V., Ryskina, V.L., Stolyarova, E.I., Sundberg, U., & Francisco, L. (1997). Cross-language analysis of phonetic units in language addressed to infants. *Science, 277*, 684–686.

Lea, J. (1975). *An investigation into the association between rhythmic ability and language ability in a group of children with severe speech and language disorders.* Master's thesis, University of London.

Leonard, L.B. (1998). *Children with specific language impairment.* Cambridge, MA: MIT Press.

Leonard, L.B., McGregor, K., & Allen, G. (1992). Grammatical morphology and speech perception in children with specific language impairment. *Journal of Speech and Hearing Research, 35*, 1076–1085.

Liberman, A.M., Cooper, F.S., Shankweiler, D.P., & Studdert-Kennedy, M. (1967). Perception of the speech code. *Psychological Review, 74*, 431–461.

Lincoln, A., Dickstein, P., Courchesne, E., Elmasian, R., & Tallal, P. (1992). Auditory processing abilities in non-retarded adolescents and young adults with developmental receptive language disorder and autism. *Brain and Language, 43*, 613–622.

Llinas, R., Ribary, U., & Tallal, P. (1998). Dyschronic language-based learning disability, In C. von Euler (Ed.), *Basic mechanisms in cognition and language.* Stockholm: Werner-Gren International Series, 70.

Lowe, A., & Campbell, R. (1965). Temporal discrimination in aphasic and normal children. *Journal of Speech and Hearing Research, 8*, 313–314.

McAnally, K.I., & Stein, J.F. (1997). Scalp potentials evoked by amplitude-modulated tones in dyslexia, *Journal of Speech, Language and Hearing Research, 40*, 939–945.

McCrosky, R., & Kidder, H. (1980). Auditory fusion among learning disabled, reading disabled, and normal children. *Journal of Learning Disabilities, 13*, 69–76.

McReynolds, L.V. (1966) Operant conditioning for investigating speech sound discrimination in aphasic children. *Journal of Speech and Hearing Research, 9*, 519–528.

Merzenich, M.M., Jenkins, W.M., Johnston, P., Schreiner, C., Miller, S.L., & Tallal, P. (1996). Temporal processing deficits of language-learning impaired children ameliorated by training. *Science, 271(5245)*, 77–81.

Merzenich, M.M., & Jenkins, W.M. (1998). Cortical plasticity, learning, and learning dysfunction. In B. Julesz, & I. Kovacs (Eds), *Maturational windows and adult cortical plasticity* (pp. 247–272). New York: Addison-Wesley Pub. Co.

Merzenich, M.M., Tallal, P., Peterson, B., Miller, S.L., & Jenkins, W.M. (1999). Some neurological principles relevant to the origins of — and the cortical plasticity based remediation of — language learning impairments. In J. Grafman (Ed.), *Neuroplasticity: Building a bridge from the laboratory to the clinic*, (pp. 169–187). Amsterdam: Elsevier.

Merzenich, M.M., Miller, S., Jenkins, W.M., Protopapas, A., Saunders, G., Peterson, B., Ahissar, M., & Tallal, P. (in press). A novel training strategy for amelioration of language learning impairments: Initial results of a large field trial. *Journal of Learning Disabilities*.

Miller, S.L., DeVivo, K., LaRossa, K., Pycha, A., Peterson, B.E., Tallal, P., Merzenich, M.M., & Jenkins, W.M. (1998). Acoustically modified speech and language training reduces risk for academic difficulties. *Society for Neuroscience Abstract, 24*, 923.

Miller, S.L., Linn, N., Tallal, P., Merzenich, M.M., & Jenkins, W.M. (1999). Acoustically modified speech and language training: A relationship between auditory word discrimination training and measures of language outcome, *Speech and Language Therapy*, Special Issue "Reeducation Orthophonique", N197, Paris, France.

Mody, M., Studdert-Kennedy, M., Brady, S. (1997). Speech perception deficits in poor readers: Auditory processing or phonological coding? *Journal of Experimental Child Psychology, 64*, 199–231.

Nagarajan, S.S., Wang, X., Merzenich, M.M., Schreiner, C.E., Johnston, P., Jenkins, W.M., Miller, S., & Tallal, P. (1998). Speech modifications algorithms used for training language learning-impaired children. *IEEE Transactions on Rehabilitation Engineering, 6*, 257–268.

Nagarajan, S.S., Mahncke, H.M., Salz, T., Tallal, P., Roberts, T., & Merzenich, M.M. (1999). Cortical auditory signal processing in poor reading adults. *Proceedings of the National Academy of Sciences, 96*, 6483–6488.

Neville, H., Coffey, S., Holcomb, P., & Tallal, P. (1993). The neurobiology of sensory and language processing in language-impaired children. *Journal of Cognitive Neuroscience, 5*, 235–253.

Neville, H.J. (1985). Effects of early sensory and language experience on the development of the human brain. In J. Mehler & R. Fox (Eds), *Neonate cognition: Beyond the blooming buzzing confusion*, pp. 349–363. Hillsdale, NJ: Lawrence Erlbaum Associates.

Nittrouer, S. (1999) Do temporal processing deficits cause phonological processing problems? *Journal of Speech, Language and Hearing Research, 42*, 925–942.

Protopapas, A., Ahissar, M., & Merzenich, M.M. (1997). Auditory processing deficits in adults with a history of reading difficulties. *Society for Neuroscience, 23*, 491.

Reed, M.A. (1989). Speech perception and the discrimination of brief auditory cues in reading disabled children. *Journal of Experimental Child Psychology, 48*, 270–292.

Ribary, U., Jolot, M., Miller, S.L., Kronberg, E., Cappell, J., Tallal, P., & Llinas, R. (1996). Cognitive temporal binding and its relation to 40Hz activity in humans: Alteration during dyslexia. In C. Woods, Y. Okada, & C. Aine (Eds), *Biomag '96 advances in biomagnetism research*. Heidelberg: Springer Verlag.

Rice, M.L., & Wexler, K. (1996). Tense as a clinical marker of specific language impairment in English-speaking children. *Journal of Speech and Hearing Research, 39*, 1239–1257.

Robin, D., Tomblin, J.B., Kearney, A., & Hug, L. (1989). Auditory temporal pattern learning in children with severe speech and language impairment. *Brain and Language, 36*, 604–613.

Rosenthal, W. (1972). Auditory and linguistic interaction in developmental aphasia: Evidence from two studies of auditory processing. *Papers and Reports on Child Language Development, 4*, 19–34.

Spitz, R.V., Tallal, P., Flax, J., & Benasich A. (1997). Look who's talking: A prospective study of familial transmission of language impairments. *Journal of Speech and Hearing Research, 40*, 990–1001.

Stark, J. (1967). A comparison of the performance of aphasic children on three sequencing tests. *Journal of Communication Disorders, 1*, 31–34.

Stark, R.E., & Heinz, J.M. (1996). Perception of stop consonants in children with expressive and receptive-expressive language impairments. *Journal of Speech and Hearing Research, 39*, 676–686.

Stark, R.E., & Tallal, P. (1988). *Language, speech, and reading disorders in children: Neuropsychological studies*. Boston, MA: Little, Brown and Co., Inc.

Stefanatos, G.A., Green, G.G.R., & Ratcliff, G.G. (1989). Neurophysiological evidence of auditory channel anomalies in developmental dysphasia. *Archives of Neurology, 46*, 871–875.

Sussman, J. (1993). Perception of formant transition cues to place of articulation in children with language impairments. *Journal of Speech and Hearing Research, 36*, 1286–1299.

Tallal, P. (1980). Auditory temporal perception, phonics, and reading disabilities in children. *Brain and Language, 9*, 182–198.

Tallal, P. (1998). Language learning impairment: Integrating research and remediation. *Scandinavian Journal of Psychology, 39*, 195–197.

Tallal, P., & Merzenich, M. (1997). *Fast ForWord training for children with language-learning problems: Results from a national field study by 35 independent facilities*. Paper presented at the annual meeting of American Speech-Language-Hearing Association, Boston, MA. November.

Tallal, P., Merzenich, M., Miller, S., & Jenkins, W. (1998). Language learning impairments: Integrating basic science, technology and remediation. *Experimental Brain Research, 123*, 210–219.

Tallal, P., Miller, S.L., Bedi, G., Byma, G., Wang, X., Nagarajan, S.S., Schreiner, C., Jenkins, W.M., & Merzenich, M.M. (1996). Language comprehension in language-learning impaired children improved with acoustically modified speech. *Science, 271(5245)*, 81–84.

Tallal, P., Miller, S., Jenkins, W.M., & Merzenich, M.M. (1999). Moving research from the laboratory to clinics and classrooms. In D. Duane (Ed.), *Reading and attention disorders: Neurobiological sources of co-morbidity*. San Diego: York Press.

Tallal, P., & Piercy, M. (1973a). Defects of non-verbal auditory perception in children with developmental aphasia. *Nature, 241*, 468–469.

Tallal, P., & Piercy, M. (1973b). Developmental aphasia: Impaired rate of non-verbal processing as a function of sensory modality. *Neuropsychologia, 11*, 389–398.

Tallal, P., & Piercy, M. (1974). Developmental aphasia: Rate of auditory processing and selective impairment of consonant perception. *Neuropsychologia, 12*, 83–93.

Tallal, P., & Piercy, M. (1975). Developmental aphasia: the perception of brief vowels and extended stop consonants. *Neuropsychologia, 13*, 69–74.

Tallal, P., Ross, R., & Curtiss, S. (1989a). Familial aggregation in specific language impairment. *Journal of Speech and Hearing Disorders, 54*, 167–173.

Tallal, P., Ross, R., & Curtiss, S. (1989b). Unexpected sex-ratios in families of language/learning impaired children. *Neuropsychologia, 27*, 987–998.

Tallal, P., & Stark, R. (1981). Speech acoustic cue discrimination abilities of normally developing and language impaired children. *Journal of the Acoustical Society of America, 69*, 568–574.

Tallal, P., Stark, R.E., & Curtiss, B. (1976). Relation between speech perception and speech production impairment in children with developmental dysphasia. *Brain and Language, 3*, 305–317.

Tallal, P., Stark, R., Kallman, C., & Mellits, D. (1980a). Perceptual constancy for phonemic categories: A developmental study with normal and language impaired children. *Applied Psycholinguistics, 1*, 49–64.

Tallal, P., Stark, R., Kallman, C., & Mellits, D. (1980b). Developmental aphasia: The relation between acoustic processing deficits and verbal processing. *Neuropsychologia, 18*, 273–284.

Tallal, P., Stark, R., Kallman, C., & Mellits, D. (1981). A reexamination of some nonverbal perceptual abilities of language-impaired and normal children as a function of age and sensory modality. *Journal of Speech and Hearing Research, 24*, 351–357.

Thal, D.J., & Barone, P. (1983). Auditory processing and language impairment in children: Stimulus considerations for intervention. *Journal of Speech and Hearing Disorders, 48*, 18–24.

Thibodeau, L., & Sussman, H. (1979). Performance on a test of categorical perception of speech in normal and communicatively disordered children. *Journal of Phonetics, 7*, 375–391.

Tomblin, J.B., Freese, P., & Records, N. (1992). Diagnosing specific language impairment in adults for the purpose of pedigree analysis. *Journal of Speech and Hearing Research, 35*, 832–843.

Tomblin, J.B., Records, N.L., Buckwalter, P., Zhang, X., Smith, E., & O'Brien, M. (1997). Prevalence of specific language impairment in kindergarten children. *Journal of Speech and Hearing Research, 40*, 1245–1260.

Trehub, S.E., & Henderson, J.L. (1996). Temporal resolution in infancy and subsequent language development. *Journal of Speech and Hearing Research, 39*, 1315–1320.

Wang, X., Merzenich, M.M., Sameshima, K., & Jenkins, W.M. (1995). Remodeling of hand representation in adult cortex determined by timing of tactile stimulation. *Nature, 378*, 71–75.

Werker, J.F., & Tees, R.C. (1987). Speech perception in severely disabled and average reading children. *Canadian Journal of Psychology, 41*, 48–61.

Witton, C., Talcott, J.B., Hansen, P.C., Richardson, A.J., Griffiths, T.D., Rees, A., Stein, J.F., & Green, G.G.R. (1998). Sensitivity to dynamic auditory and visual stimuli predicts nonword reading ability in both dyslexic and normal readers. *Current Biology, 8*, 791–797.

Wright, B.A., Lombardino, L.J., King, W.M., Puranik, C.S., Leonard, C.M., & Merzenich, M.M. (1997). Deficits in auditory temporal and spectral resolution in language-impaired children. *Nature, 387*, 176–178.

9

Intervention for children with developmental language delay

Susan Ellis Weismer

Children with language delay in the absence of other developmental disabilities have been shown to benefit from various language intervention approaches. Discussion will briefly focus on toddlers with late onset of language (late talkers), followed by a more in-depth consideration of intervention approaches for pre-school and school-aged children with specific language impairment (SLI). A synopsis of current empirical findings from treatment investigations with late talkers will be provided, along with a discussion of the debate surrounding the pros and cons of providing early language intervention for this population. A new longitudinal project examining linguistic processing abilities of late talkers will be described, and potential contributions of this investigation relative to intervention issues will be discussed. Next, treatment implications of a processing capacity limitation account of SLI will be considered. After briefly reviewing recent empirical studies supporting this view, possible clinical ramifications will be detailed. This will include presenting evidence of linguistic trade-off effects in spontaneous production and discussing how this behavioural pattern might be taken into account when planning expressive language goals. Treatment implications will be drawn from experimental tasks involving novel word and morpheme learning that have examined the effects of various modifications of the linguistic input (including variations in speaking rate or use of differing stress patterns), as well as tasks involving manipulations of "wait time," i.e. the pauses separating speakers' conversational turns, especially within question–answer sequences. Finally, the effectiveness of script-based intervention approaches, which are hypothesised to reduce cognitive processing load through the introduction of targeted language forms within a familiar routine, will be considered.

In this chapter, I shall consider intervention approaches for children who have language delay in the absence of other developmental disabilities. The primary focus of the discussion will be toddlers with late onset of language, and preschool and school-age children with specific language impairment (SLI). In many cases, delays in language development are accompanied by cognitive, sensory or motor deficits. However, there is a group of toddlers, often identified within the literature as "late talkers" (cf. Rescorla, 1989; Ellis Weismer, Murray-Branch, & Miller, 1993, 1994), whose delays appear to be mainly confined to language. Similarly, the term specific language impairment (SLI) refers to somewhat older children (usually at least 3 years of age) who demonstrate significant limitations in language skills without any clearly identifiable aetiology. Key characteristics of this population are delayed onset and acquisition of language, normal nonverbal cognition, normal hearing, and absence of emotional disturbance or frank neurological deficits (cf. Leonard, 1998). This chapter will focus initially on late talkers, followed by a discussion of children with SLI.

INTERVENTION WITH LATE TALKERS

Three key questions about intervention for late talkers are:

- Is it effective?
- Is it important?
- Can we predict who will benefit?

In order to consider these questions, it is necessary to briefly review outcome findings from investigations of late talkers. Toddlers have been classified as late talkers on the basis of their early restricted expressive language abilities (Paul, 1991; Rescorla, 1989, 1991; Thal, 1991; Thal & Bates, 1988), though some of these children have also been reported to exhibit delays in receptive language abilities, socialisation, and phonological skills (Paul, 1991; Rescorla & Ratner, 1996; Stoel-Gammon, 1991; Thal & Bates, 1988; Thal, Oroz,

& McCaw, 1995). Follow-up studies have found that approximately half of the toddlers who display late onset of talking at 2 years catch up to their peers by 3 years and exhibit no further language problems (Paul, 1991; Rescorla & Schwartz, 1990; Rescorla, Roberts, & Dahlsgaard, 1997). Other late talkers continue to exhibit production delays, even after vocabulary moves into normal range, in other areas including phonology, morphology/syntax, and narrative abilities (Paul, 1991; Paul, Hernandez, Taylor, & Johnson, 1996; Paul & Smith, 1993; Rescorla & Schwartz, 1990; Rescorla et al., 1997; Roberts, Rescorla, Giroux, & Stevens, 1998). Several longer-term follow-up investigations have reported that the majority of late talkers meet normative expectations on language assessment measures and measures of early reading abilities by the elementary school period (Paul, 1996; Paul, Murray, Clancy, & Andrews, 1997; Rescorla, 1993; Whitehurst et al., 1991); however, these children score significantly below controls matched on age, SES, and nonverbal cognition in various areas of linguistic functioning (Paul, 1996; Rescorla, 1993).

On the surface, the positive outcomes for most late talkers seem to be at odds with other research which indicates that a substantial proportion of preschoolers identified as having language impairment at 3 to 4 years of age experience continued language delay that may additionally be manifested in terms of difficulties with reading and academic achievement (Aram, Ekelman, & Nation, 1984; Bishop & Adams, 1990; Bishop & Edmundson, 1987; Catts, 1993; Catts & Kamhi, 1986, 1999; Silva, McGee, & Williams, 1983; Silva, Williams, & McGee, 1987). There also appears to be a mismatch when one considers the prevalence of late talkers at age 2 (10–14%) and their high percentage of resolution of language delay, on the one hand, compared to the prevalence of SLI at 5 years (7.4%, based on an epidemiological study by Tomblin et al., 1997). However, most of the studies of late talkers have not included all children likely to develop SLI, since children with receptive-expressive delays have been excluded either intentionally or inadvertently by assessing cognitive ability using instruments that include verbal as well as nonverbal items.

Given that there is no evidence that children with SLI demonstrate a regression in language skills or a pattern involving an initial period of normal development followed by an extended plateau, most cases of SLI will have come from the ranks of those toddlers identified as late talkers.

Debate concerning clinical management

There is considerable debate regarding the clinical management of late talkers (Ellis Weismer, 1999; Olswang & Bain, 1991; Olswang, Rodriguez, & Timler, 1998; Paul, 1996, 1997; Robertson & Ellis Weismer, 1999; Thal & Katich, 1996; van Kleeck, Gillam, & Davis, 1997; Whitehurst et al., 1991; Whitehurst & Fischel, 1994). A range of options might be adopted. For example, the child might be allowed to develop further, with intervention occurring at a later point only if persistent problems are apparent. Alternatively, the child's progress might be periodically monitored following a set of guidelines for when to initiate treatment as needed. Other options include providing early language intervention through direct clinician-implemented programmes or through programmes in which parents are trained to stimulate their children's language development. Whitehurst and colleagues (1991) have advocated a wait-and-see approach for toddlers with specific expressive language delays, based on the lack of differences they observed for late talkers and controls on language assessment measures at kindergarten. Paul (1996) has recommended a watch-and-see policy, suggesting that late talkers who do not evidence additional risk factors (such as poverty, hearing impairment or serious medical problems) could be monitored throughout development as an alternative to intervention. If the problem becomes worse or deficits are noted in other areas, intervention would then be indicated. Although Paul (1996) contends that careful monitoring seems to be the most cost-effective approach, she allows that early intervention might be provided for late talkers in cases where the necessary resources are available and parents wish to pursue this option. In these cases, Paul (1996) has recommended that parents be counselled regarding the likelihood of the effectiveness of

intervention based on current research. In chapter 11 of this volume, Paul goes so far as to suggest that early intervention can be counterproductive for some late talking children.

Effectiveness and importance of early intervention

There are relatively few empirical studies that have investigated the effectiveness (or importance) of early intervention with this population. Whitehurst et al. (1991) investigated the effectiveness of a parent-implemented treatment programme in facilitating vocabulary use in 2-year-olds whom they identified as having specific expressive language delay. The treatment involved training parents to promote their children's language development at home through the use of milieu teaching techniques, which take advantage of the child's interests (e.g. commenting on a toy the child is playing with), and include naturalistic reinforcement for communicating (e.g. providing a requested object) (cf. Warren & Kaiser, 1986; Kaiser, Yoder, & Keetz, 1992). This approach resulted in significant improvement in toddlers' expressive language skills compared to those of a control group of late talkers who did not receive treatment. Despite the evidence for short-term gains, Whitehurst and colleagues (1991) questioned the importance of early language intervention for this group of children in light of follow-up findings indicating similar outcomes for the two groups at age 5. They did note that the immediate positive effects appeared to reassure parents concerning the child's developmental status and probably resulted in improved parent–child interactions but yet concluded that, on balance, the early intervention did not influence later outcomes.

Girolametto, Pearce, and Weitzman (1996) assessed the effectiveness of a parent-implemented intervention that employed a focused stimulation approach to promote vocabulary development in late talking toddlers who were between 23 and 33 months of age. Children were randomly assigned to a treatment or control/delayed treatment group; those in the treatment group received an 11-week intervention adapted from the Hanen Program for Parents. Results indicated significant differences between the treatment and control groups in both maternal interactional behaviour and child linguistic skills. Following the treatment, the language input that mothers provided to their toddlers was less complex, presented at a slower rate, and focused more on target vocabulary. Significant gains in children's linguistic skills included increases in vocabulary abilities (vocabulary size, total number of different words used in interactions, number of different target words used in interactions, number of control words used in interactions) and in multiword utterances. In a separate study investigating the influence of this lexical treatment programme on phonological abilities of late talkers, Girolametto, Pearce, and Weitzman (1997) reported significant increases in speech sound inventories and the variety of complex syllable shapes produced.

The relative effectiveness of two clinician-implemented treatment techniques stemming from an interactive approach to language intervention was investigated by Ellis Weismer et al. (1993). This study employed an alternating treatment, single-case design to compare the two treatment methods of interest, modelling only versus modelling plus evoked production. The late talkers in this study came from a longitudinal investigation of language development from the prelinguistic period to multiword productions (Ellis Weismer et al., 1994); they ranged from 27 to 28 months of age at the beginning of the 3-month treatment programme. Children were taught different sets of words under the two treatment methods during group and individual instruction. Two of the children differed as to which particular treatment method resulted in better vocabulary development. Neither treatment method was effective for the third child who exhibited minimal gains in the targeted vocabulary over the course of the programme. This child had clearly delayed language at 3 years. Follow-up assessments at 4 years also indicated that this child, unlike the other two late talkers, evidenced continued language deficits characteristic of SLI.

Recently, Robertson and Ellis Weismer (1999) have examined the effects of a clinician-implemented early language intervention programme on various linguistic and social skills of

late talking toddlers, as well as assessing the impact of treatment on parental stress. Twenty-one late talkers (21–30 months of age) were randomly assigned to an experimental group (n = 11) or a control (delayed treatment) group (n = 10). The cohort of late talkers in this study included several children with both receptive and expressive delays, though the majority of children exhibited only expressive delays. The treatment consisted of an interactive, child-centred approach that provided general language stimulation emphasising vocabulary development and use of multiword combinations within a social context. Treatment was administered within a centre-based birth-to-three programme, where toddlers in the experimental group attended 75-minute sessions twice a week for a period of 12 weeks. The treatment programme incorporated features designed to reduce linguistic processing demands (which will be discussed in more depth later in the chapter).

The experimental and control groups were compared at pre- and post-test on five linguistic variables, as well as on measures of socialisation and parental stress. Data for four of the linguistic variables were obtained from spontaneous language samples analysed using SALT (Systematic Analysis of Language Transcripts) (Miller & Chapman, 1996). These included: mean length of utterance in morphemes (MLU), total number of words, number of different words, and percentage of intelligible utterances. Vocabulary size was assessed using a parent report measure, the McArthur Communicative Development Inventory (CDI) (Fenson et al., 1993). In order to explore the effects of early intervention on social skills of late talkers, the Socialisation Domain of the Vineland Adaptive Behaviour Scales (VABS, Interview Edition, Expanded Form) (Sparrow, Balla, & Cicchetti, 1984) was administered. Parental stress was assessed with the Parenting Stress Index (PSI) — Child Domain (Abidin, 1995), which has been used previously to examine the effect of early language intervention on parental stress levels (Tannock, Girolametto, & Siegel, 1992).

This investigation revealed significant facilitating effects of the treatment (with large effect sizes) for each of the variables. Children in the experimental group, compared to those in the control group, evidenced significantly greater increases in MLU, total number of words, number of different words, reported lexical repertoire on the CDI, and percentage of intelligible utterances. The increase in socialisation skills was also significantly higher for the experimental group than the controls. An additional analysis of the language-loaded versus non-language items on the VABS suggested that the improvements in socialisation skills of the experimental group were not merely reflective of gains in language. Finally, the parental stress was significantly reduced in the experimental group compared to the control group. These findings provide evidence for the effectiveness of early language intervention in facilitating short-term linguistic gains, as well as impacting more broadly on other areas, including socialisation and parental concerns, which may weigh into decisions concerning appropriate clinical management of late talkers.

In those cases where we do opt to provide early intervention, it is important to at least have evidence of the immediate effectiveness of this approach. Each of the studies that have been reported is consistent in demonstrating positive, short-term effects of early language intervention with late talkers. The conclusions drawn from these investigations differ, however, with respect to the importance of this intervention. Varying perspectives on the role of early intervention for late talkers appear to stem from different views on how the importance of treatment should be gauged. One way is to compare the long-term outcomes across those children with and without a history of late onset of language development and/or across treated versus untreated groups; this was the approach adopted by Whitehurst and colleagues (1991). Alternatively, importance could be measured by the breadth of short-term changes noted in treated versus untreated groups (as in the Robertson and Ellis Weismer, 1999, study); that is, the value of early intervention might be assessed not only with respect to its ability to move children into normal range linguistic functioning as soon as possible, but also in terms of its immediate impact on related areas such as socialisation and parental concerns (cf. Olswang & Bain, 1991; Olswang et al., 1998).

Predicting who needs treatment

The optimal situation would be one in which it was possible to determine early on whether a particular child was likely to have persistent language problems so that clinical services could be concentrated only on those children who were truly in need of intervention. Researchers have attempted to determine predictors of language outcome in late talkers in order to identify factors that are indicative of recovery versus continued delay (Ellis Weismer et al., 1994; Paul, Spangle-Looney, & Dahm, 1991; Rescorla & Schwartz, 1990; Rescorla et al., 1997; Thal et al., 1991; Thal & Tobias, 1992; Whitehurst, Fischel, Arnold, & Lonigan, 1992). Short-term predictors at varying points in development have been reported, but these differ across studies (cf. Ellis Weismer et al., 1994; Rescorla et al., 1997). To date, no clear predictor or set of predictors has been established to indicate long-term outcomes for late talkers. However, Olswang, Rodriguez, and Timler (1998) have recently provided an excellent summary of findings from investigations of late talkers and attempted to highlight converging evidence indicating various risk factors and predictors of change; they argue that toddlers who display few positive predictors of change and many risk factors are the ones for whom intervention should be recommended.

My colleagues and I have recently begun a longitudinal investigation focused on examining the link between late onset of language and SLI. We aim to extend what is known about processing limitations in SLI to late talking toddlers in an effort to determine if early linguistic processing skills can serve as useful predictors of language outcomes. Preliminary data have been obtained on a novel word learning task with ten 3-year-olds (who were participating in a longitudinal investigation of variability in language development being conducted by Virginia Marchman). Four of these children had normal language (NL) development and the other six children had been identified as late talkers at 18 months of age based on their performance on the McArthur CDI parent checklist (Fenson et al., 1993). By age 3, however, these late talkers were catching up to their

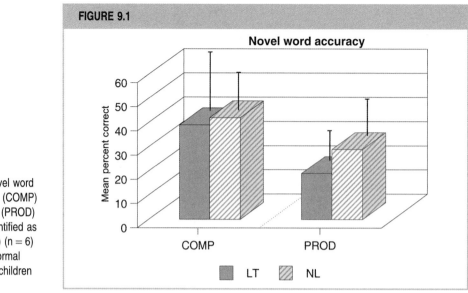

Mean percent accuracy of novel word comprehension (COMP) and production (PROD) for children identified as late talkers (LT) (n = 6) compared to normal language (NL) children (n = 4).

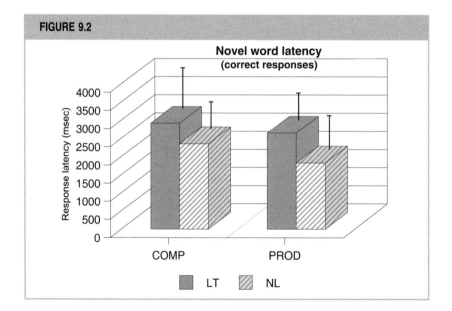

Response latency (msec) for correct novel word comprehension (COMP) and production (PROD) for children identified as late talkers (LT) (n = 6) compared to normal language (NL) children (n = 4).

peers in terms of reported productive vocabulary on the CDI. Despite the fact that the children who had been late talkers were reported by parents to have normal range vocabulary skills at the time of testing, differences between the groups were noted in processing and acquisition of novel words. The late talkers demonstrated increased variability for comprehension and lower mean accuracy for production of novel words compared to the NL children (Fig. 9.1). They also were slower to give correct responses than the NL children, particularly for production of novel words (Fig. 9.2). These data suggest that children with late onset of language development may have relatively less proficiency in linguistic processing than NL children, even as their scores on clinical assessment measures move into normal range in certain areas. We are interested in determining whether performance on these types of linguistic processing tasks (which we have now adapted for use with 2-year-olds) can assist in identifying those children whose language difficulties are likely to persist and who therefore may be candidates for early intervention.

INTERVENTION WITH CHILDREN WITH SPECIFIC LANGUAGE IMPAIRMENT: A LIMITED PROCESSING CAPACITY PERSPECTIVE

In contrast to the small number of treatment studies with late talkers, there has been a considerable amount of research investigating the effectiveness of various intervention approaches for children with SLI. Recent reviews of this research include those by Leonard (1998) and Brinton and Fujiki (1995). Rather than providing a general overview, this discussion will focus specifically on studies that can be interpreted from the perspective that children with SLI have a limited processing capacity.

The notion of a limited capacity system has been incorporated in various models of language processing (Baddeley, 1986, 1996; Bloom, 1993; Bock & Levelt, 1994; Gathercole & Martin, 1996; Just & Carpenter, 1992). The main premise of these models is that cognitive resources which can be allocated to different tasks are limited and when demands exceed available resources, the processing and storage of linguistic information is compromised. Evidence of linguistic interactions and trade-offs comes from experimental studies with adults (Baddeley & Hitch, 1974; Carpenter & Just, 1989; MacDonald, Just, & Carpenter, 1992; Miyake, Carpenter, & Just, 1994) and from the language acquisition literature (Bloom, Lightbown, & Hood, 1974; Gershkoff-Stowe & Smith, 1997). For instance, increased naming errors in young children co-occur with rapid growth in productive vocabulary and increased rates of speaking (Gershkoff-Stowe & Smith, 1997). Just and Carpenter and colleagues (Carpenter, Miyake,

& Just, 1994; Just & Carpenter, 1992) contend that individual differences in cognitive capacity constrain language processing more in some people than in others. A number of investigators have proposed that children with SLI have particular limitations in their capacity to process and store information (Bishop, 1992, 1994; Ellis Weismer, 1996, 1997; Ellis Weismer & Hesketh, 1996; Gathercole & Baddeley, 1990, 1993; Johnston, 1994; Leonard, 1994, 1998; Montgomery, 1995, 1996). Given that there is evidence suggesting that children with SLI have unusual restrictions in processing capacity (see Leonard, 1998, for a review), it would be useful to discover ways to reduce the processing demands of the language learning task for these children.

Influence of input modifications on language processing and learning

In a series of recent investigations, Ellis Weismer and colleagues have examined factors influencing lexical and morphological learning by children with SLI within a limited processing capacity framework (Ellis Weismer, 1996, 1997; Ellis Weismer & Hesketh, 1993, 1996, 1998); most of this work has centred on lexical learning and processing, which will be the focus of this discussion. In these investigations, various factors posited to impact on the cognitive load of the linguistic processing task were manipulated, including a) rate of speech, b) vocal stress, and c) use of visual cues accompanying spoken language. It was hypothesised that presentation of linguistic stimuli at fast speaking rates may exceed children's capacity limitations and lead to reduced lexical learning whereas the additional processing time afforded by slow speaking rates may facilitate linguistic computation and storage of lexical items. Use of emphatic stress on target forms was hypothesised to reduce processing demands by cueing listeners to important information to which they should allocate attentional resources. Similarly, it was posited that visual cues may serve to highlight target words, enhancing attention and memory.

The basic paradigm was the same in all of these studies, consisting of a novel word learning task. Use of novel target forms ensures equivalent levels of knowledge of the targets prior to training. Children were shown a toy figure identified as Sam the outerspace man and told that they would learn some "funny-sounding" words in Sam's outerspace language to refer to his toys. Modelling procedures were used during one to two training sessions such that the novel target forms were repeatedly paired with a particular unusual object. Novel target words consisted of either consonant-vowel-consonant (CVC) forms (e.g. "koob") or consonant-vowel-consonant-consonant (CVCC) forms (e.g. "bimp"). These target words were presented within 5-syllable sentence frames ("Sam is by the koob") under linguistic input conditions that involved varying speaking rates, either slow (2.8 syll/sec), normal (4.4 syll/sec), or fast (5.9 syll/sec), use of emphatic or neutral stress on target forms, or supplemental visual cues (gestures). Each novel word was consistently presented under a certain input condition (e.g. fast speaking rate) for a particular child and this variable was counterbalanced across children. Stimuli consisted of natural speech that had been tape recorded and digitised. Rate and stress variations were documented via acoustic measurements and perceptual judgements by adult listeners. The task in these experiments included exposure trials, followed by production probes ("What's this?") and comprehension probes (e.g. "Put Sam by the koob").

In the initial investigation by Ellis Weismer and Hesketh (1993), the acquisition of novel words by 5- and 6-year-old children (N = 16, 8 SLI, 8 NL) was examined under linguistic input conditions that varied in terms of rate of speech, vocal stress and use of visual cues. Acquisition of novel words by both groups was significantly affected by alterations in speaking rate and by the use of gestures accompanying spoken language. That is, children demonstrated significantly better understanding of novel words trained at slow rate than at fast rate. In addition, both groups correctly produced significantly more novel words trained at slow rate than fast rate and significantly more words trained at normal rate than fast rate. Although the group x rate interaction did not reach statistical significance in this relatively small sample, there was a clear trend for the group with

SLI to exhibit more pronounced effects in response to rate variations than the NL group in both comprehension and production. With respect to visual cues, both groups demonstrated significantly better comprehension of words trained with accompanying gestures than those without gestures. There were no statistically significant effects for the stress manipulations, although children with SLI tended to produce correctly novel words that had received emphatic stress during training more often than words presented with neutral stress. Results from this preliminary investigation suggested that it is important to consider how the manner of presentation of the linguistic signal influences the processing and acquisition of language and indicated that additional study of this issue was warranted.

A subsequent study by Ellis Weismer and Hesketh (1996) further investigated 7- and 8-year-old children's novel word learning when speaking rate was varied. There were 16 children with SLI, 16 controls matched on mental age (MA), and a subset of children (the older children with SLI and younger controls) who were matched on receptive vocabulary abilities. No significant rate effects were found for comprehension of novel words, with all children performing at relatively high levels of accuracy (70–83%). In terms of production of novel words, a significant group × rate interaction was found in which children with SLI had more difficulty with fast rate words than normal language (NL) controls matched on MA (Fig. 9.3) or vocabulary level (Fig. 9.4). Contrary to expectations, presentation of novel words at slow rate did not result in significantly better performance for the group with SLI. However, individual subject analyses indicated that 38% of the subjects in the SLI group evidenced benefits of slower speaking rates in comprehension, whereas no NL subjects demonstrated consistent benefits of slower rate in terms of their comprehension scores. For production, difference scores across rates also indicated that 50% of the children with SLI demonstrated improved performance under slow rate, as did a few of the younger NL subjects.

In this study, rate manipulations primarily impacted upon production of novel words, rather than comprehension of the words. Examination of the overall levels of accuracy for the SLI and NL

FIGURE 9.3

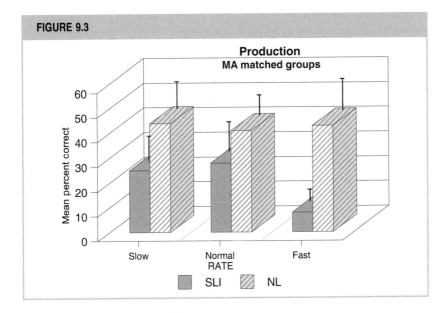

Mean percent correct production of novel words trained at slow, normal, or fast speaking rate for children with specific language impairment (SLI) and normal language (NL) controls matched on mental age (MA). Adapted from Ellis Weismer and Hesketh (1996).

FIGURE 9.4

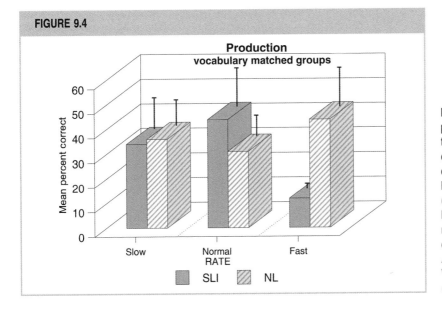

Mean percent correct production of novel words trained at slow, normal, or fast speaking rate for children with specific language impairment (SLI) and normal language (NL) controls matched on vocabulary comprehension abilities. Adapted from Ellis Weismer and Hesketh (1996).

groups on comprehension and production items (70–83% compared to 20–43%) provided insight into this pattern of results. Adjustments in the rate of linguistic input appeared to have the greatest effect on the most difficult items (i.e. least accurate), namely the production items. Consistent with these findings, one would predict on the basis of a limited capacity model that presentation rate

modifications would have the greatest impact as cognitive demands of the task increased and as available resources were stretched to the limits of capacity. Although rate effects were observed for comprehension in the initial study (Ellis Weismer & Hesketh, 1993), the overall level of accuracy was lower than in the second study, suggesting that comprehension items were more cognitively demanding for the younger, kindergarten children who participated in the initial investigation. In summary, these results support the conclusion that rate manipulations of the linguistic input influence language learning in children with SLI such that limitations in processing rapidly presented verbal information translate into difficulties in lexical learning.

Ellis Weismer and colleagues (Ellis Weismer, 1997; Ellis Weismer & Hesketh, 1998) further examined the role of emphatic stress in school-age children's lexical processing and acquisition using the same novel word learning task. They assessed 20 children with SLI and 20 MA matched controls ranging in age from 6 to 9 years, as well as a subset compared on vocabulary level. The MA controls performed significantly better than the SLI group for both comprehension and production of novel words. It is important to note that all children demonstrated relatively high levels of comprehension accuracy on this lexical learning task, with comprehension being considerably better than production accuracy (75–90% compared to 36–61%). A significant stress effect was observed for production such that target words that had been presented with emphatic stress during training were produced correctly more often than those presented with neutral stress. This finding held for the MA comparison as well as the vocabulary level comparison group. As was the case for the study of speaking rate variations (Ellis Weismer & Hesketh, 1996), adjustments in the linguistic input had the greatest effect on the most difficult items, namely those requiring children to produce rather than comprehend the novel words. This result is consistent with predictions based on a limited capacity framework. That is, it is only when cognitive resources are sufficiently taxed that manipulations of the linguistic input designed to reduce processing demands would be expected to have a notable influence on performance. The present findings can be viewed as the complement to results indicating that capacity restrictions can result in trade-offs leading to decrements in certain aspects of linguistic performance. In this case, adjustments in the linguistic signal which heighten the saliency of key information apparently can serve to free up cognitive resources, facilitating enhanced processing of new linguistic material.

Contrary to our original expectations and the trends observed in the initial investigation (Ellis Weismer & Hesketh, 1993), the NL and SLI groups obtained similar benefits from cues signalling important new information to which they should attend. The tendency for the children with SLI in the prior study (Ellis Weismer & Hesketh, 1993) to demonstrate greater responsiveness to stress variations than the NL controls may have been related to the increased difficulty those younger children experienced in producing novel words compared to the older school-age children in the current study. The lack of a differential pattern of performance by the NL and SLI groups in this study might be viewed as failure to support the claim that children with SLI have special restrictions in processing capacity. Alternately, it may be the case that the relatively small boost in performance afforded by emphatic stress on this task had a limited effect with respect to freeing cognitive resources and therefore did not provide an adequate test of differential processing abilities under varying conditions of cognitive load for the children with and without language impairment. It is possible to hypothesise that certain cognitive processes contributing to the efficiency or total capacity for language processing (cf. Just & Carpenter, 1992) are more vulnerable than others in children with SLI. Thus, one can speculate that temporal processing constraints may play a more central role in the capacity limitations in children with SLI than allocation processes. In other words, speed of computations may be more of a factor in language processing for these children than the ability to deploy cognitive resources effectively. In an ongoing investigation we are examining this issue more directly through the use of a dual processing comprehension task in which children with SLI and NL controls are required to shift their attention between two speakers in following oral directions that are presented simultaneously.

Wait time effects on language processing

In addition to thinking about ways in which we might adjust the speech signal to facilitate language processing and learning, we can consider ways of manipulating the communicative exchange at the discourse level to promote linguistic processing. The term "wait time" has been used to refer to the duration of pauses separating speakers' utterances, particularly across speaker turns within question-answer sequences. Wait time has been investigated extensively within the educational literature with respect to classroom discourse. The effects of wait time have been examined for school-age children as well as university students for a variety of academic subjects (cf. Kaplan & Kies, 1994; Tobin, 1987). Research has shown that average teacher wait times following questions are one second or less (cf. Tobin, 1986). In naturally occurring interactions, longer wait times have been observed following higher cognitive level questions (involving synthesis of information or evaluation rather than basic knowledge or comprehension) or after divergent rather than convergent questions (Ellsworth, Duell, & Velotta, 1991; Jones, 1980). When teachers are trained to maintain an average wait time of approximately three seconds or longer, various desirable changes have been found in children's performance, including: longer responses and increased amounts of discourse; more initiations; increases in the complexity and cognitive level of response; and higher levels of achievement and retention of information (cf. Ellis Weismer & Schraeder, 1993).

There are a limited number of studies in which the influence of wait time on children with disabilities has been examined either within classroom discourse or dyadic discourse contexts. A few studies have investigated naturally occurring wait times for mothers' interactions with young children with developmental disabilities (Marfo, 1992; Vettel & Windsor, 1997). For instance, Vettel and Windsor (1997) found that mothers allowed longer wait time for language-age matched controls than for children with Down syndrome following questions that children did not answer. Other investigations have explored the effects of manipulating wait time upon the performance of children with disabilities. One study found that preschool children with developmental disabilities gave substantially more responses across three different tasks under a condition involving a 5-sec teacher wait time compared to a 1-sec wait time (Lee, O'Shea, & Dykes, 1987). Findings from another study indicated that school-age children with multiple handicaps gave more accurate responses in instructional contexts employing long wait time (10 sec) as opposed to short wait time (1 sec) (Valcante, Roberson, Reid, & Wolking, 1989).

Ellis Weismer and Schraeder (1993) investigated wait time in terms of discourse characteristics and verbal reasoning in school-age children with language disorders. These children (who were 8–9 years old) exhibited both specific language impairments and problems with written language; children with this combination of difficulties have been referred to as having language-learning disabilities (LLD) (cf., Wallach & Miller, 1988; Wallach & Butler, 1994). Wait time was examined within the context of dyadic (clinician-student) interactions using experiential and narrative tasks. Children's responses to varying cognitive levels of questions were evaluated under both natural and manipulated wait time conditions for each task. The manipulated wait time condition involved imposing at least a 3-sec pause prior to a response opportunity. (A pencil tap on the table was used to signal the end of the three-second interval as determined by a digital stopwatch; pretraining was conducted to ensure that children responded only after the pencil tap for the manipulated wait time condition.) The two kinds of tasks (experiential and narrative) provided an opportunity for the use of language relating to the here and now and for more decontextualised language characteristic of classroom discourse (cf. Nelson, 1991) which is assumed to impose a higher cognitive load than contextualised language.

Effects of manipulating wait time were observed only for the narrative task, which was the more difficult of the two tasks as evidenced by accuracy and response latency measures. This is consistent with a limited processing capacity model and is similar to the results from the novel word learning tasks discussed previously (Ellis Weismer & Hesketh, 1996, 1998). Findings indicated that manipulated wait time, where the child was required to pause at least 3 seconds before responding, promoted accuracy of responses to

Mean percent accuracy of responses to lower level, knowledge (KNWL) questions (e.g. Who were the main characters in the story?) and higher level, synthesis (SYN) questions (e.g. What is another thing Serendipity could do with the garbage in the sea?) under manipulated and natural wait time (WT) on the narrative task, for children with language-learning disabilities (LLD) and age-matched normal language (NL) controls. Adapted from Ellis Weismer and Schraeder (1993).

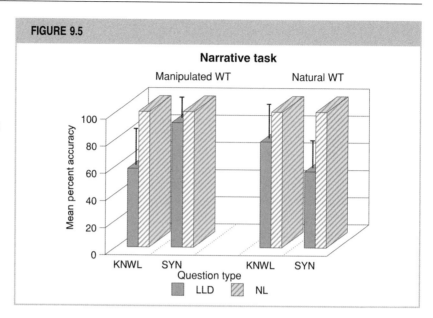

FIGURE 9.5

higher cognitive level questions for the group with LLD but had no significant impact on lower cognitive level questions (Fig. 9.5). This result is consistent with prior research that has found an interaction between wait time and cognitive level of questioning, such that extended wait times are associated with increased achievement when higher cognitive level processes are evoked whereas achievement/accuracy decreases when longer wait times are used with factual questions (Riley, 1986; Tobin, 1986).

Another question addressed by this study pertained to the degree of verbal fluency in responses formulated under natural wait time versus manipulated wait time. Verbal fluency was measured in terms of the occurrence of mazes or communication breakdowns. These include whole or part-word repetitions, phrase repetitions, sentence reformulations, filled pauses and abandoned utterances (cf. Leadholm & Miller, 1992; Loban, 1976). On the narrative task, increased wait time significantly improved verbal fluency (i.e. resulting in fewer mazes) for both groups of children. Children produced an average of one maze every two to three responses when an extended wait time was imposed, compared to more than one maze per response without the extended wait time. Although the group × wait time interaction did

not reach statistical significance, there was a clear trend for the children with language disorders to exhibit proportionately greater benefit from the manipulated wait time than the controls. It is important to note that the possible confound of differences in utterance length and number of utterances per answer was examined and it was determined that differences in the occurrence of mazes under the two wait time conditions were not attributable to varying lengths of answers.

Scripts

Another way in which processing demands might be reduced during language intervention is through the use of scripts. Scripts have been proposed as a model of event representation in memory; more specifically, scripts entail generalised representations of familiar events or routines organised around a temporal-causal sequence of acts (cf. Nelson, 1986). It is assumed that scripts are learned as an outgrowth of children's everyday experiences. For instance, most young children have scripts for common events or routines such as bathtime, bedtime and birthday parties. One of the assumptions underlying the use of script-based treatment approaches is that intervention conducted within the context of a familiar routine will reduce children's cognitive load so they can focus on language targets (Constable, 1986; McCormick, 1997). In other words, when new language forms are presented within scripted contexts, children have clear expectations about the sequence of events, roles that different people assume, and use of appropriate props to carry out the activities. This event knowledge presumably allows children to direct fewer cognitive resources toward the activity itself, thereby increasing resources that can be applied to the linguistic demands of the task. Within scripted event contexts, young children have been found to use more semantically complex language, including more frequent references to past and future events and references to more topic types. Further, they have been reported to answer questions better in scripted than in nonscripted event contexts (cf. Lucariello, Kyratzis, & Engel, 1986; Ross & Berg, 1990).

Robertson and Ellis Weismer (1997) examined the effects of peer modelling during sociodramatic play upon the play scripts of children with SLI. Thirty preschool children (4- and 5-year-olds) participated in the first study, including 20 children with SLI and 10 age-matched peers with normal language abilities. The children were enrolled in an early childhood classroom, where those without language problems were serving as typical peer models. Children with SLI were randomly assigned to either the experimental group (SLI-E) or to the control group (SLI-C). Children in the SLI-E group participated in four, 15-minute play sessions in which they were paired with a normal language peer model and instructed to play house using the various props provided within the house centre. Children in the SLI-C group continued to participate in their classroom activities, but were not paired with peer models for play sessions centred around a playing house script.

The influence of this experimental treatment was evaluated by examining four variables within language samples in which the children described how to play house. These included number of words, different words, play theme-related acts and linguistic markers. Number of words was selected as a general measure of verbal productivity. Mean number of different words was used

to assess variability in the content of the verbal scripts. Play-theme-related acts provided a measure of the commonality across children's scripts in terms of the description of particular action sequences. In order to obtain a set of behaviours that children at this developmental level associate with playing house, verbal scripts for playing house were elicited from the peer models as well as 20 additional 5-year-olds with normal language. Common themes extracted from these verbal scripts included descriptions of acts related to food preparation and consumption, role playing, cleaning, doll play, dress up and social interaction. Linguistic markers served as an index of grammatical complexity and included terms denoting temporal sequences (e.g. first, later), conditionals (e.g. or, if), or other conjunctions (e.g. but, because). Significant effects were found for each of the variables at post-test as well as follow-up, three weeks after treatment. Children with SLI who participated in the experimental treatment demonstrated significantly higher gains than the control group of children with SLI (from pre- treatment to post-treatment and pre-treatment to follow-up) in terms of mean number of words, number of different words, number of play-theme-related acts and linguistic markers. Results of a second study provided additional support for the contention that play interactions with normal language peers facilitates the development of play scripts in children with SLI and promotes higher levels of language use associated with these scripts.

Several investigations have examined the use of script-based intervention approaches for children with language disorders. Constable (1986) reported that a script-based approach implemented within a preschool setting was successful in addressing various semantic, syntactic and pragmatic language goals for a group of children with SLI. Goldstein and colleagues (Goldstein & Cisar, 1992; Goldstein et al., 1988) found that sociodramatic script training resulted in improvements in social and communicative interactions among typically developing children and children who had language disorders associated with developmental disabilities.

In an investigation by Kim and Lombardino (1991), the effects of script-based treatment were compared to a nonscripted approach within an alternating treatment, single-case design study. The treatment consisted of three script routines and three nonscripted activities that targeted comprehension of two semantic constructions (agent-action-object and action-object-location). Repeated probes across the alternations of the two types of treatment demonstrated a consistent pattern in which the script-based treatment was more effective in promoting comprehension of the semantic constructions than the nonscript approach for three of the four children with language delay. Clinical applications of script-based intervention approaches have been described in detail by Bunce and Watkins (1995) and McCormick (1997). Although script treatments have typically focused on preschool children and early levels of language functioning, Paul (1995) has discussed how this approach could also be used to facilitate acquisition of more advanced language targets in school-age children with language impairment.

CONCLUSIONS: TREATMENT IMPLICATIONS OF A LIMITED PROCESSING CAPACITY ACCOUNT OF SLI

There are various treatment implications that stem from limited capacity models of language processing and from the claim that children with SLI have particular restrictions in processing capacity. First, clinicians should analyse the cognitive demands of a specific task and attempt to reduce processing loads when introducing new language targets. By ensuring that other aspects of the task require minimal cognitive resources, a greater proportion of the child's available resources can be allocated to the processing and storage of the new information. For instance, the evidence regarding linguistic interactions and trade-offs should be taken into account when addressing productive language goals. In teaching new vocabulary, these findings indicate that it would be best to start with words containing sounds that the child can readily produce rather than those with more complex phonetic forms. Instead of selecting sounds that are generally considered to be early develop-

ing for most children, "in phonology" words should be established on an individual basis for each child (Schwartz & Leonard, 1982, 1984, 1985). When targeting new syntactic structures, highly familiar vocabulary should be used so that processing resources can be focused primarily on the grammatical aspect of the utterance. Similar recommendations have been made by Lahey and Bloom (1994) with respect to facilitating narrative use in older school-age children with language disorders. They have suggested that the initial stages of intervention directed at narrative development should focus on mental models that are easily constructed, use earlier acquired vocabulary and simple syntactic constructions, and deal with material that is neutral with respect to affect rather than emotionally charged. (In order to maintain interest, beginning levels of narrative intervention might focus on personal anecdotes of everyday activities that the child would be motivated to recount, such as describing interactions with friends at play.) These variables can then be adjusted as therapy progresses so that the child has the opportunity to produce narratives under increasingly complex and demanding conditions.

During instructional interactions, processing demands might also be reduced through certain adjustments in the manner in which linguistic models are presented, through manipulations of communicative exchanges at the discourse level, or through features of the nonlinguistic event context.

For instance, results from the input manipulation studies indicate that variations in the speaking rate at which linguistic models are presented and the prosodic features of those models, as well as use of supplemental gestural cues, affect children's ability to process and learn language. This suggests that clinicians should attend not only to the *content* of the models provided during intervention, but also to the *manner* in which models are presented. This is especially important since modelling is one of the primary teaching techniques used in a variety of language intervention approaches. Paul (1995) has similarly emphasised the critical importance of linguistic input in promoting language growth and suggested that the properties of the input and ways of adapting it should be considered in order to make it the most effective and efficient mechanism of change possible.

In terms of speaking rate modifications, children with SLI appear to have particular difficulty processing and storing verbal information presented at rapid rates; therefore, speaking rates should be carefully monitored in instructional situations. Although children with SLI, as a group, do not demonstrate better word learning with slow presentation rate, individual analyses indicate that some children with SLI do benefit from models presented at slowed speaking rates. Use of emphatic stress on target words apparently helps direct children's cognitive resources to the new information to be learned, improving their ability to recall novel words later. This approach might be useful for various lexical and grammatical targets (as has been described by Ellis Weismer, 1997). Group findings from experimental tasks such as these can serve as a general guide for determining the impact of certain variables on children's language learning. However, there may be considerable variability in children's responses to variations in linguistic input; therefore, individual trial teaching would be warranted to assess the effect of such modifications on a particular child's language learning.

These types of techniques would presumably be used only in the initial stages of addressing particular language goals and would be phased out as language targets were practised and became automatised.

Findings from the wait time studies indicate that manipulations of the extent of the pause following questions can influence accuracy and fluency of children's responses. In determining appropriate wait times within discourse contexts, it is important to take into account the cognitive level of the information to be processed. Longer wait times appear to facilitate accuracy of responses to higher level questions requiring synthesis of information but do not increase correct responses to lower level factual questions. Additional findings from the Ellis Weismer and Schraeder (1993) investigation (not reviewed previously) indicated that children with LLD generally responded quickly and did not appear to adjust

spontaneously the amount of processing time for differing levels of cognitive questions. Therefore, the use of an imposed wait time of at least 3 seconds may be an effective teaching strategy with these children when the focus is on the comprehension of more cognitively complex information. Extended wait time also has been shown to impact on the clarity with which children express their messages, with additional wait time leading to fewer mazes. Thus, it appears that certain discourse level manipulations involving the use of extended wait time can facilitate children's linguistic processing.

Clinicians can also establish teaching contexts that are designed to reduce processing loads by embedding language targets within highly familiar routines or scripts. Scripts that the child has already constructed might be utilised or new scripts can be developed by establishing certain routines within the intervention setting. Once a script is well established, violations of that script can be used to prompt comments about changes in the expected routine or to demonstrate possible variations within a particular script context (cf. Ellis Weismer, 1999; Paul, 1995).

Another way in which processing capacity limitations in children with SLI might be mitigated is by working to increase automaticity in the use of recently acquired linguistic abilities. As various aspects of linguistic processing become fairly automatic, fewer resources are used such that the net effect is increased capacity. Automaticity is achieved through practice, which might take several forms. In some cases, practice might entail the use of structured, drill-type activities; however, as Lahey and Bloom (1994) have noted, clinicians can also promote automaticity by providing repeated, focused opportunities for meaningful use of particular language forms and functions within naturalistic contexts. Finally, automaticity can be promoted by ensuring that language skills are firmly established within a particular context before advancing to new goals. By considering the processing demands of instructional interactions and accommodating potential processing capacity limitations in children with SLI in these ways, it should be possible to promote better language learning.

ACKNOWLEDGEMENTS

The preparation of this manuscript was supported by funding from the National Institutes of Health, NIDCD 5 P50 CD02746-04, Midwest Collaboration on Specific Language Impairment, and NIDCD 1 R01 DC03731-01A1, Linguistic Processing in Specific Language Delay.

REFERENCES

Abidin, R. (1995). *The parenting stress index.* Charlottesville, VA: Pediatric Psychological Press.

Aram, D., Ekelman, B.L., & Nation, J.E. (1984). Preschoolers with language disorders: 10 years later. *Journal of Speech and Hearing Research, 27,* 232–244.

Baddeley, A.D. (1986). *Working memory.* New York: Oxford University Press.

Baddeley, A.D. (1996). The concept of working memory. In S. Gathercole (Ed.), *Models of short-term memory* (pp. 1–27). Hove, UK: Psychology Press.

Baddeley, A.D., & Hitch, G. (1974). Working memory. In G.H. Bower (Ed.), *The psychology of learning and motivation* (Vol. 8, pp. 47–89). New York: Academic Press.

Bishop, D.V.M. (1992). The underlying nature of specific language impairment. *Journal of Child Psychology and Psychiatry, 33,* 3–66.

Bishop, D.V.M. (1994). Grammatical errors in specific language impairment: Competence or performance limitations? *Applied Psycholinguistics, 15,* 507–550.

Bishop, D.V.M., & Adams, C. (1990). A prospective study of the relationship between specific language impairment, phonological disorders and reading retention. *Journal of Child Psychology and Psychiatry, 31,* 1027–1050.

Bishop, D.V.M., & Edmundson, A. (1987). Language-impaired 4-year-olds: Distinguishing transient from persistent impairment. *Journal of Speech and Hearing Disorders, 52,* 156–173.

Bloom, L. (1993). *The transition from infancy to language: Acquiring the power of expression.* Cambridge, UK: Cambridge University Press.

Bloom, L., Lightbown, P., & Hood, L. (1974). Structure and variation in child language. *Monographs for the Society for Research on Child Development, 40,* (2), 1–97.

Bock, K., & Levelt, W. (1994). Language production: Grammatical encoding. In M. Gernsbacher (Ed.), *The handbook of psycholinguistics* (pp. 945–984). San Diego, CA: Academic Press Inc.

Brinton, B., & Fujiki, M. (1995). Conversational intervention with children with specific language impairment. In M. Fey, J. Windsor, & S. Warren (Eds), *Language intervention: Preschool through the elementary years* (pp. 183–212). Baltimore, MD: Paul H. Brookes.

Bunce, B.H., & Watkins, R.V. (1995). Language intervention in a preschool classroom: Implementing a language-focused curriculum. In M.L. Rice & K.A. Wilcox (Eds), *Building a language-focused curriculum for the preschool classroom* (pp. 39–72). Baltimore, MD: Paul H. Brookes.

Carpenter, P., & Just, M. (1989). The role of working memory in language comprehension. In D. Klahr & K. Kotovsky (Eds), *Complex information processing: The impact of Herbert A. Simon* (pp. 31–68). Hillsdale, NJ: Lawrence Erlbaum Associates Inc.

Carpenter, P., Miyake, A., & Just, M. (1994). Working memory constraints in comprehension: Evidence from individual differences, aphasia, and aging. In M.A. Gernsbacher (Ed.), *Handbook of Psycholinguistics* (pp. 1075–1122). San Diego: Academic Press.

Catts, H. (1993). The relationship between speech-language impairments and reading disabilities. *Journal of Speech and Hearing Research, 36,* 948–958.

Catts, H., & Kamhi, A. (1986). The linguistic basis for reading disorders: Implications for the speech-language pathologist. *Language, Speech, and Hearing Services in Schools, 17,* 329–341.

Catts, H., & Kamhi, A. (1999). *Language and reading disabilities.* Needham Heights, MA: Allyn & Bacon.

Constable, C. (1986). The application of scripts in the organization of language intervention contexts. In K. Nelson (Ed.), *Event knowledge: Structure and function in development* (pp. 205–230). Hillsdale, NJ: Lawrence Erlbaum Associates Inc.

Ellis Weismer, S. (1996). Capacity limitations in working memory: The impact on lexical and morphological learning by children with language impairment. *Topics in Language Disorders, 17,* 33–44.

Ellis Weismer, S. (1997). The role of stress in language processing and intervention. *Topics in Language Disorders, 18,* 41–52.

Ellis Weismer, S. (1999). Language intervention for young children with language impairment. In L. Watson, T. Layton, & E. Crais (Eds), *Handbook of early language impairments in children: Volume II,*

Assessment and Treatment (pp. 173–198). Albany, NY: Thomson Learning.

Ellis Weismer, S., & Hesketh, L. (1993). The influence of prosodic and gestural cues on novel word acquisition by children with specific language impairment. *Journal of Speech and Hearing Research, 36,* 1013–1025.

Ellis Weismer, S., & Hesketh, L. (1996). Lexical learning by children with specific language impairment: Effects of linguistic input presented at varying speaking rates. *Journal of Speech and Hearing Research, 39,* 177–190.

Ellis Weismer, S., & Hesketh, L. (1998). The impact of emphatic stress on novel word learning by children with specific language impairment. *Journal of Speech, Language, and Hearing Research, 41,* 1444–1458.

Ellis Weismer, S., Murray-Branch, J., & Miller, J. (1993). Comparison of two methods for promoting productive vocabulary in late talkers. *Journal of Speech and Hearing Research, 36,* 1037–1050.

Ellis Weismer, S., Murray-Branch, J., & Miller, J. (1994). A prospective longitudinal study of language development in late talkers. *Journal of Speech and Hearing Research, 37,* 852–867.

Ellis Weismer, S., & Schraeder, T. (1993). Discourse characteristics and verbal reasoning: Wait time effects on the performance of children with language learning disabilities. *Exceptionality Education Canada, 3,* 71–92.

Ellsworth, R., Duell, O., & Velotta, C. (1991). Length of wait-times used by college students given unlimited wait-time intervals. *Contemporary Educational Psychology, 16,* 265–271.

Fenson, L., Resznick, S., Thal, D., Bates, E., Hartung, J., Pethick, S., & Reilly, J. (1993). *The MacArthur Communicative Development Inventory.* San Diego, CA: Singular Publishing Group, Inc.

Gathercole, S.E., & Baddeley, A. (1990). Phonological memory deficits in language disordered children: Is there a causal connection? *Journal of Memory and Language, 29,* 336–360.

Gathercole, S., & Baddeley, A. (1993). *Working memory and language processing.* Hove, UK: Lawrence Erlbaum Associates Ltd.

Gathercole, S., & Martin, A. (1996). Interactive processes in phonological memory. In S. Gathercole (Ed.), *Models of short-term memory* (pp. 73–100). Hove, UK: Psychology Press.

Gershkoff-Stowe, L., & Smith, L.B. (1997). A curvilinear trend in naming errors as a function of early vocabulary growth. *Cognitive Psychology, 34,* 37–71.

Girolametto, L., Pearce, P., & Weitzman, E. (1996). Interactive focused stimulation for toddlers with expressive vocabulary delays. *Journal of Speech and Hearing Research, 39,* 1274–1283.

Girolametto, L., Pearce, P., & Weitzman, E. (1997). Effects of lexical intervention on the phonology of late talkers. *Journal of Speech, Language, and Hearing Research, 40,* 378–388.

Goldstein, H., & Cisar, C.L. (1992). Promoting interaction during sociodramatic play: Teaching scripts to typical preschoolers and classmates with disabilities. *Journal of Applied Behavior Analysis, 25,* 265–280.

Goldstein, H., Wickstrom, S., Hoyson, M., Jamieson, B., & Odom, S.L. (1988). Effects of sociodramatic script training on social and communicative interaction. *Education and Treatment of Children, 11,* 97–117.

Johnston, J. (1994). Cognitive abilities of children with language impairment. In R. Watkins and M. Rice (Eds), *Specific language impairment in children* (pp. 107–121). Baltimore, MD: Brookes Pub. Co.

Jones, N.A. (1980). The effect of type and complexity of teacher questions on student response wait time. (Doctoral dissertation, University of Pittsburgh). *Dissertation Abstracts International, 41,* 529–A.

Just, M.A., & Carpenter, P.A. (1992). A capacity theory of comprehension: Individual differences in working memory. *Psychological Review, 99,* 1–28.

Kaiser, A., Yoder, P., & Keetz, A. (1992). Evaluating milieu teaching. In S. Warren & J. Reichle (Eds), *Communication and language intervention series: Vol. 1. Causes and effects in communication and language intervention* (pp. 9–47). Baltimore: Brookes Publishing.

Kaplan, J., & Kies, D. (1994). Strategies to increase critical thinking in the undergraduate classroom. *College Student Journal, 28,* 24–31.

Kim, Y., & Lombardino, L. (1991). The efficacy of script context in language comprehension intervention with children who have mental retardation. *Journal of Speech and Hearing Research, 34,* 845–857.

Lahey, M., & Bloom, L. (1994). Variability and language learning disabilities. In G. Wallach and K. Butler (Eds), *Language learning disabilities in school-age children and adolescents* (pp. 354–372). New York: Macmillan.

Leadholm, B., & Miller, J. (1992). *Language sample analysis: The Wisconsin Guide.* Madison, WI: Wisconsin Department of Public Instruction.

Lee, J., O'Shea, L.J., & Dykes, M.K. (1987). Teacher wait-time: Task performance of developmentally delayed and non-delayed young children. *Education and Training in Mental Retardation, 22,* 176–184.

Leonard, L. (1994). Some problems facing accounts of morphological deficits in children with specific language impairments. In R.V. Watkins & M.L. Rice (Eds), *Specific language impairments in children. Communication and language intervention series, Vol. 4.* (pp. 91–105). Baltimore, MA: Brookes Publishing.

Leonard, L. (1998). *Children with specific language impairment.* Cambridge, MA: MIT Press.

Loban, W. (1976). *Language development: Kindergarten through grade twelve.* (Research Rep. No.18). National Council of Teachers of English.

Lucariello, J., Krytatzis, A., & Engel, S. (1986). Event representations, context, and language. In K. Nelson (Ed.), *Event knowledge: Structure and function in development.* Hillsdale, NJ: Lawrence Erlbaum Associates Inc.

MacDonald, M., Just, M., & Carpenter, P. (1992). Working memory constraints on the processing of syntactic ambiguity. *Cognitive Psychology, 24,* 56–98.

Marfo, K. (1992). Correlates of maternal directiveness with children who are developmentally delayed. *American Journal of Orthopsychiatry, 62,* 219–233.

McCormick, L. (1997). Language intervention and support. In L. McCormick, D. Frome Loeb, & R. Schiefelbusch (Eds), *Supporting children with communication difficulties in inclusive settings: School-based language intervention* (pp. 257–306). Needham Heights, MA: Allyn & Bacon.

Miller, J. & Chapman, R. (1996). SALT: *Systematic analysis of language transcripts* (Computer software). Language Analysis Laboratory, Waisman Center, University of Wisconsin-Madison.

Miyake, A., Carpenter, P., & Just, M. (1994). A capacity approach to syntactic comprehension disorders: Making normal adults perform like aphasic patients. *Cognitive Neuropsychology, 11,* 671–717.

Montgomery, J.W. (1995). Sentence comprehension in children with specific language impairment: The role of phonological working memory. *Journal of Speech and Hearing Research, 38,* 187–199.

Montgomery, J.W. (1996). Sentence comprehension and working memory in children with specific language impairment. *Topics in Language Disorders, 17,* 19–32.

Nelson, K. (1986). *Event knowledge: Structure and function in development.* Hillsdale, NJ: Lawrence Erlbaum Associates Inc.

Nelson, N.W. (1991). Teacher talk and child listening — fostering a better match. In C.S. Simon (Ed.), *Communication skills and classroom success* (pp. 78–105). Eau Claire, WI: Thinking Publications.

Olswang, L.B., & Bain, B.A. (1991). Treatment efficacy: When to recommend intervention. *Language, Speech, and Hearing Services in the Schools, 22,* 255–263.

Olswang, L.B., Rodriguez, B., & Timler, G. (1998). Recommending intervention for toddlers with specific language learning difficulties: We may not have all the answers, but we know a lot. *American Journal of Speech-Language Pathology, 7,* 23–32.

Paul, R. (1991). Profiles of toddlers with slow expressive language development. *Topics in Language Disorders, 11,* 1–13.

Paul, R. (1995). *Language disorders from infancy through adolescence: Assessment and intervention.* St. Louis: Mosby.

Paul, R. (1996). Clinical implications of the natural history of slow expressive language development. *American Journal of Speech Language Pathology, 5,* 5–21.

Paul, R. (1997). Understanding language delay: A response to van Kleeck, Gillam, and Davis. *American Journal of Speech-Language Pathology, 6,* 40–49.

Paul, R., Hernandez, R., Taylor, L., & Johnson, K. (1996). Narrative development in late talkers: Early school age. *Journal of Speech and Hearing Research, 39,* 1295–1303.

Paul, R., Murray, C., Clancy, K., & Andrews, D. (1997). Reading and metaphonological outcomes in late talkers. *Journal of Speech, Language, and Hearing Research, 40,* 1037–1047.

Paul, R., & Smith, R. (1993). Narrative skills in 4-year-olds with normal, impaired, and late-developing language. *Journal of Speech and Hearing Research, 36,* 592–598.

Paul, R., Spangle-Looney, S., & Dahm, P. (1991). Communication and socialization skills at age 2 and 3 in "late talking" young children. *Journal of Speech and Hearing Research, 34,* 858–865.

Rescorla, L. (1989). The language development survey. A screening tool for delayed language in toddlers. *Journal of Speech and Hearing Disorders, 11,* 14–21.

Rescorla, L. (1991). Identifying expressive language delay at age two. *Topics in Language Disorders, 11,* 14–20.

Rescorla, L. (1993). *Outcome of toddlers with specific expressive delay (SELD) at ages 3, 4, 5, 7, & 8.* Poster presented at the Biennial Meeting of Society for Research in Child Development, New Orleans.

Rescorla, L., & Ratner, N. (1996). Phonetic profiles of toddlers with specific expressive language impairment (SLI-E). *Journal of Speech and Hearing Research, 39,* 153–165.

Rescorla, L., Roberts, J., & Dahlsgaard, K. (1997). Late talkers at 2: Outcome at age 3. *Journal of Speech, Language, and Hearing Research, 40,* 556–566.

Rescorla, L., & Schwartz, E. (1990). Outcome of toddlers with specific expressive language delay. *Applied Psycholinguistics, 11,* 393–407.

Riley II, J. (1986). The effects of teachers' wait-time and knowledge comprehension questioning on science achievement. *Journal of Research in Science Teaching, 23,* 335–342.

Roberts, J., Rescorla, L., Giroux, J., & Stevens, L. (1998). Phonological skills of children with specific expressive language impairment (SLI-E): Outcome at age 3. *Journal of Speech, Language, and Hearing Research, 41,* 374–384.

Robertson, S.B., & Ellis Weismer, S. (1997). The influence of peer models on the play scripts of children with specific language impairment. *Journal of Speech, Language, and Hearing Research, 40,* 49–61.

Robertson, S.B., & Ellis Weismer, S. (1999). Effects of treatment on linguistic and social skills in toddlers with delayed language development. *Journal of Speech, Language, and Hearing Research, 42,* 1234–1248.

Ross, B.L., & Berg, C.A. (1990). Individual differences in script reports: Implications for language assessment. *Topics in Language Disorders, 10,* 30–44.

Schwartz, R., & Leonard, L. (1982). Do children pick and choose? An examination of phonological selection and avoidance in early lexical acquisition. *Journal of Child Language, 9,* 319–336.

Schwartz, R., & Leonard, L. (1984). Words, objects, and actions in early lexical acquisition. *Journal of Speech and Hearing Research, 27,* 119–127.

Schwartz, R., & Leonard, L. (1985). Lexical imitation and acquisition in language-impaired children. *Journal of Speech and Hearing Disorders, 50,* 141–149.

Silva, P.A., McGee, R., & Williams, S. (1983). Developmental language delay from three to seven years and its significance for low intelligence and reading difficulties at age seven. *Developmental Medicine and Child Neurology, 25,* 783–793.

Silva, P., Williams, S., & McGee, R. (1987). A longitudinal study of children with developmental language delay at age three: Later intelligence, reading and behavior problems. *Developmental Medicine and Child Neurology, 29,* 630–640.

Sparrow, S.S., Balla, D.A., & Cicchetti, D.V. (1984). *Vineland Adaptive Behavior Scales.* Circle Pines, MN: American Guidance Service.

Stoel-Gammon, C. (1991). Normal and disordered phonology in two-year-olds. *Topics in Language Disorders, 11,* 21–32.

Tannock, R., Girolametto, L., & Siegel, L. (1992). Language intervention with children who have developmental delays: Effects of an interactive approach. *American Journal of Mental Retardation, 97,* 145–160.

Thal, D. (1991). Language and cognition in normal and late-talking toddlers. *Topics in Language Disorders, 11,* 33–42.

Thal, D., & Bates, E. (1988). Language and gesture in late talkers. *Journal of Speech and Hearing Research, 31,* 115–123.

Thal, D., & Katich, J. (1996). Predicaments in early identification of specific language impairment: Does the early bird always catch the worm? In P.S. Dale (Ed.), *Assessment of communication and language: Vol. 6. Communication and language intervention series* (pp. 1–28). Baltimore: Paul H. Brookes.

Thal, D., & Tobias, S. (1992). Communicative gestures in children with delayed onset of oral expressive vocabulary. *Journal of Speech and Hearing Research, 35,* 1281–1289.

Thal, D., Oroz, M., McCaw, V. (1995). Phonological and lexical development in normal and late-talking toddlers. *Applied Psycholinguistics, 16,* 407–424.

Thal, D., Tobias, S., & Morrison, D. (1991). Language and gesture in late talkers: A 1-year follow-up. *Journal of Speech and Hearing Research, 34,* 604–612.

Tobin, K. (1986). Effects of teacher wait time on discourse characteristics in mathematics and language arts classes. *American Educational Research Journal, 23,* 191–200.

Tobin, K. (1987). The role of wait time in higher cognitive level learning. *Review of Educational Research, 57,* 69–95.

Tomblin, J.B., Records, N.L., Buckwalter, P., Zhang, X., Smith, E., & O'Brien, M. (1997). The prevalence of specific language impairment in kindergarten children. *Journal of Speech, Language and Hearing Research, 40,* 1245–1260.

Valcante, G., Roberson, W., Reid, W., & Wolking, W. (1989). Effects of wait-time and intertrial interval durations on learning by children with multiple handicaps. *Journal of Applied Behavior Analysis*, *22*, 43–55.

van Kleeck, A., Gillam, R.B., & Davis, B. (1997). When is "watch and see" warranted? A response to Paul's 1996 article, "Clinical implications of the natural history of slow expressive language development". *American Journal of Speech-Language Pathology*, *6*, 34–39.

Vettel, J.K., & Windsor, J. (1997). Maternal wait-time after questions for children with and without Down syndrome. *Research in Developmental Disabilities*, *18*, 93–100.

Wallach, G., & Butler, K. (1994). *Language learning disabilities in school-age children and adolescents*. New York: Macmillan College Publishing Company.

Wallach, G., & Miller, L. (1988). *Language intervention and academic success*. Boston, MA: College-Hill.

Warren, S.F., & Kaiser, A.P. (1986). Incidental language teaching: A critical review. *Journal of Speech and Hearing Disorders*, *51*, 291–299.

Whitehurst, G.J., & Fischel, J.E. (1994). Early developmental language delay: What, if anything, should the clinician do about it? *Journal of Child Psychology and Psychiatry*, *35*, 613–648.

Whitehurst, G.J., Fischel, J.E., Arnold, D.S., & Lonigan, C.J. (1992). Evaluating outcomes with children with expressive language delay. In S. Warren & J. Reichle (Eds), *Causes and effects in communication and language intervention* (pp. 277–313). Baltimore, MA: Paul H. Brooks Publishing.

Whitehurst, G.J., Fischel, J.E., Lonigan, C.J., Valdez-Menchaca, M.C., Arnold, D.S., & Smith, M. (1991). Treatment of early expressive language delay: If, when, and how. *Topics in Language Disorders*, *11*, 55–68.

10

Recasting, elicited imitation and modelling in grammar intervention for children with specific language impairments

Marc E. Fey and Kerry Proctor-Williams

In this chapter, we examine the potential of three language intervention procedures — sentence recasting, elicited imitation, and modelling — for teaching grammatical form to children with specific language impairment (SLI). Recasting is currently used by many clinicians with children with SLI. In part, this is because of recent evidence that children with SLI can benefit from the procedure. In addition, recasts are desirable because they can be used unobtrusively in naturally occurring discourse contexts. Imitation and modelling have long histories of efficacy in teaching syntactic and morphological forms to children. Despite this well-documented success, these procedures have been abandoned by many clinicians, based on evidence that the learning they produce frequently does not generalise to typical communicative contexts. Furthermore, the structured imitation and modelling approaches used in experimental investigations are found by many clinicians to be too restrictive and "unnatural". We propose that imitation and modelling procedures be reconsidered. Their use is defensible not only on the basis of the experimental record, but also on the grounds that they are highly consistent with six principles of grammar facilitation. With appropriate modifications, these procedures can complement recasting in comprehensive approaches to the treatment of the grammatical problems of children with SLI.

In speech and language intervention, the procedures are the techniques that are presumed to have a direct, positive influence on the child's ability to understand or use the intervention target (Fey, 1986). When the intervention target is grammatical knowledge or use, the procedures are designed to help children:

(a)   attend to a new or unmastered language form or operation in the input,

(b)   recognise the semantic, pragmatic and/or grammatical functions of the new form,

(c)   relate the new form or operation to their existing grammatical systems and modify their grammars accordingly, and/or

(d)   access and produce the new structure more quickly and reliably after it is generated by their underlying grammars.

It is the procedures, then, that supply the essential power to change a child's underlying language knowledge and/or overt linguistic performance. In this chapter, we focus on three procedures that have been widely used to facilitate grammatical development in children with SLI: sentence recasting, elicited imitation, and modelling. Sentence recasting can be used in naturally occurring communicative contexts without intruding significantly on the child's agenda (Fey, Catts, & Larrivee, 1995). It finds its way into many different types of modern, pragmatically enlightened, grammar facilitation programmes. In contrast, elicited imitation and modelling are direct instruction procedures that can be highly intrusive. Consequently, they have fallen into disfavour among many researchers and clinicians.

Our primary thesis in this chapter is that elicited imitation and modelling were abandoned prematurely and that they still have important roles to play in language intervention. To support this position, we first examine some of the properties of grammatical forms that children typically find difficult to acquire and use. Next, we discuss the key components of imitation and modelling and show how they can be modified in ways that are more consistent with contemporary intervention principles. We then take a brief look at research that directly compares imitation, modelling and

recasting. We conclude that the most effective intervention approaches are likely to be those that combine these procedures in complementary fashion.

SIX PRINCIPLES OF GRAMMAR FACILITATION

For any language, it is possible to predict with some accuracy which morphosyntactic features will be acquired earlier and which will be acquired later. For example, all other things being equal, forms will be relatively difficult for children to acquire and/or use consistently if they

(a)   are relatively infrequent in the input;

(b)   have semantic correlates that are weak, unclear or cognitively complex;

(c)   are used inconsistently or in an irregular manner with many exceptions;

(d)   are brief in duration and unstressed;

(e)   contain sounds and/or sound sequences that are typically late acquisitions; and

(f)   typically occur in sentence contexts in which they are represented as weak syllables that do not follow strong syllables and, therefore, are prone to being omitted.

Clearly, these principles do not operate in an all-or-none fashion. Instead, the claim is that forms with many of these properties will generally be later acquisitions than forms with few or none of the features. For example, some forms that are frequent in children's learning environments, such as English copulas and articles, are relatively late acquisitions. Presumably, this is because they are unstressed forms that frequently do not follow stressed syllables and do not bear a strong semantic burden.

Leonard (1998) reviewed a substantial body of evidence that indicates that the grammatical forms that display these properties are especially difficult for children with SLI. Leonard hypothesised that complexities introduced by these features, combined with the slow processing abilities of children with SLI, are key factors in their language profiles. Based on this reasoning, we assume that intervention will be successful to the extent that we can

(a) make target forms more frequent in the input;

(b) clarify the semantic correlates of target forms;

(c) help the child identify the conditions governing irregular or exceptional rule use;

(d) make weak, unstressed forms appear in contexts in which they are stronger and perhaps even stressed emphatically;

(e) give the child practice in producing forms that challenge their phonological knowledge and phonetic abilities; and

(f) give the children practice in production of forms in contexts in which they are vulnerable to omission.

For us, these principles form a sort of road map for language intervention. Procedures that serve these principles should lead most directly to the ultimate destination: competent use of grammar in oral and written modalities and in comprehension as well as production.

SENTENCE RECASTING, ELICITED IMITATION AND MODELLING IN GRAMMAR FACILITATION

Before we can examine the potential utility of recasting, imitation and modelling in modern approaches to grammar facilitation, we need to examine briefly the key features of each procedure and the rationales used to explain their use in language intervention.

Sentence recasting

Sentence recasts are adult responses that immediately follow a child's utterance and share referential contexts, referents and major lexical items with that utterance, while maintaining the child's original meaning. At the same time, recasts modify

TABLE 10.1

Examples of corrective and non-corrective recasts

Child platform	Adult recast
It his teeth.	*It's* his teeth.
He need it.	He need*s* it.
This him hat.	*His* hat?
This James.	*Is* this James?
It fit in there.	It fit*s* in there?
Fall down there.	*She has to* fall down there?

one or more of the child's sentence constituents (i.e. subject, verb, object, complement) or change the sentence modality (e.g. affirmative to negative; declarative to interrogative). These types of modifications, illustrated in Table 10.1, often correct errors in the child's utterance.

In contrast to elicited imitation and modelling, sentence recasting was not designed as a didactic intervention technique. Rather, it is a naturally occurring feature of communication interactions between adults and young children (Cross, 1978; Farrar, 1990). Consequently, it has been developed as a non-intrusive, conversational procedure to be utilised during typical adult-child activities, such as play and joint storybook reading. Instead of the clinician initiating a teaching episode, the child must provide the initial stimulus for a recast.

Recasts have been hypothesised to facilitate grammatical development by creating an optimal environment for a child to actively compare target forms with structures generated by the existing grammar. The immediate contrast of the child's attempt and the adult's recast focuses the child's attention on the specific grammatical features in the adult utterance that differ from those produced by the child. Processing resources that might otherwise have been dedicated to shifting attentional focus and to parsing and computing the adult's meaning can be focused instead on the analysis of target forms highlighted in the recast. In other words, even though the clinician does nothing to make the form louder or longer, it may become more perceptible and analysable by virtue of its placement in a sentence that is relatively simple to decode.

No efforts are made to get the child to produce the target. In fact, requests to imitate are contraindicated, because the child's efforts to imitate could interfere with the processes necessary to analyse the new form and incorporate it into the extant grammar (Camarata & Nelson, 1992; Nelson, Welsh, Camarata, Butkovsky, & Camarata, 1995).

Because recasts occur naturally in the language environments of most children, one might ask what their use in intervention is expected to accomplish. If children with SLI have been exposed to recasts and still have not learned as well as their peers, why should recasts be expected to enhance learning in a clinical programme? In fact, some researchers have observed that children with SLI do not receive recasts as frequently as do children with typical language (Conti-Ramsden, 1990; Conti-Ramsden, Hutcheson, & Grove, 1995; Nelson et al., 1995). Based on this evidence and several reports that children with SLI respond well to recasts (Camarata & Nelson, 1992; Camarata, Nelson, & Camarata, 1994; Nelson, Camarata, Welsh, Butkovsky, & Camarata, 1996), Nelson and Welsh (1998) took the strong position that much of the language learning problems of children with SLI can be attributed to their language-learning environments rather than to their learning capabilities. However, in our own investigation with 3-year-old children with SLI, we were unable to replicate the finding that these children are exposed to fewer recasts in their interactions with their caregivers (Fey, Krulik, Loeb, & Proctor-Williams, 1999). In our study, caregivers of children with SLI produced rates of recasts equivalent to those of the caregivers of younger children developing typically who were at the same stage of expressive language development. Furthermore, this similarity was observed at two points in time separated by a period of 8 months. It seems unlikely that the language delays found in these children are due to inadequacies of their learning environments.

We find it much more likely that children with SLI require rates of recasts that are much greater than those typically found in everyday interactions. There is evidence of two types that supports this position. First, we taught parents to use more recasts as one part of a broader parent-directed grammar intervention package (Fey, Cleave, & Long, 1997; Fey, Cleave, Long, & Hughes, 1993). After 10 months of intervention, the parents whose children had made the most gains over the 5 previous months used approximately two recasts per minute in interactions with their children. In contrast, children who made small or no gains over this period received an average of less than one recast per minute. Furthermore, based on estimates we derived from the reports of Conti-Ramsden and her colleagues (Conti-Ramsden, 1990; Conti-Ramsden et al., 1995) and from our own data (Fey et al., 1999), preschool children with typical language received approximately 1–1.3 recasts per minute in interactions with their parents. This is approximately half the average rate used by our most successful parents. Thus, children who gained the most over the intervention period appeared to receive up to twice as many recasts as is common in interactions with typical children.

In addition, Camarata and colleagues (1994) observed that the use of recasts focused on specific grammatical targets of children with SLI was highly effective in fostering the development of the targeted language forms. Each child's target was produced in an adult sentence recast approximately .8 times per minute of clinician/child interaction. In our own studies of children with typical language and those with SLI in play interactions with their parents, however, recasts targeting articles and copulas were found only approximately .25 times per minute on average (Fey et al., 1999). Thus, to have a significant impact on children with SLI, it appears not to be enough just to recast the children's utterances at rates found in their environment. Instead, successful intervention efforts involving recasts have increased the rates by approximately 2–4 times those observed in naturalistic contexts.

Elicited imitation

Elicited imitation is probably the most frequently studied grammar facilitation procedure. A prototypical example of this is given in Table 10.2. The fundamental components of elicited imitation are:

TABLE 10.2

A prototypical example of elicited imitation focusing on the copula, *is*

Adult:	Tell me about this picture. Say, *The sun is hot.*
Child:	*Sun is hot.*
Adult:	Good, now, look at this picture and say, *The apple is red.*
Child:	*Apple red.*
Adult:	No, try again. Say, *The apple is red.*
Child:	*Apple is red.*
Adult:	That's it. Very good.

(a) presentation of a nonverbal stimulus, such as a picture, along with a verbal request for a response, such as a question (e.g. "What's happening in this picture?");

(b) an imitative stimulus that corresponds to the nonverbal stimuli and contains the target form; and

(c) reinforcement contingent upon the correct use of the target.

Ultimately, the imitative stimuli and extrinsic reinforcement are removed, and the child produces the target correctly in response to the nonverbal stimuli and/or to the non-imitative verbal stimuli, (cf. Connell, 1987a; Gray & Ryan, 1973; Hegde & Gierut, 1979).

This didactic procedure differs from recasting in at least two very significant ways. First, the adult, rather than the child, chooses the nonverbal and verbal stimuli and determines what will be an acceptable response. Second, the child is required to follow the imitative stimulus with a correct response. These elements of control are often viewed as negative characteristics of clinician-oriented procedures. However, this control may be highly desirable with respect to our learning principles. For example, by carefully selecting targets that highlight aspects of the form that may make it difficult to learn, clinicians can clarify relationships between different forms in the sentences (e.g. auxiliaries *is* versus *are*, to indicate present or habitual actions, to form interrogatives,

and so on), and between specific forms and their underlying meanings and functions (e.g. auxiliary *are* to redundantly mark the plurality of the subject noun phrase). Learning contexts with such idealised stimuli arise all too infrequently in natural learning contexts. In addition, the intensive production practice provided by imitation tasks can be highly desirable for reasons discussed below.

There are many variations on the basic elicited imitation theme. Some investigators present the imitative stimulus immediately, so the child imitates the model before any attempts to produce the target spontaneously (Connell, 1982, 1986b, 1987a; Courtright & Courtright, 1976, 1979). In other approaches, the clinician first arranges a nonverbal context, such as a picture, and produces a question or other verbal stimulus. A request to imitate is used only if the child's response fails to include the target morpheme or structure (Camarata & Nelson, 1992; Culatta & Horn, 1982; Hegde & Gierut, 1979; Hester & Hendrickson, 1977; Kaiser, Yoder, & Keetz, 1992; Lee, Koenigsknecht, & Mulhern, 1975; Warren, McQuarter, & Rogers-Warren, 1984). It should be noted that when this occurs, the imitative prompt takes on some of the teaching properties of a corrective recast. The child's effort omits or misuses the target form, which immediately results in the presentation of an imitative model.

Imitation of new forms may be difficult when a new goal is first introduced. Therefore, some approaches "shape" a complete response by first accepting or even intentionally eliciting a partial response. For example, the approach developed by Gray and his colleagues (Gray & Fygetakis, 1968; Gray & Ryan, 1973) is illustrated in Table 10.3. In this module for teaching the copula, *is*, the child is first required to imitate only *is*, then *is* + complement (e.g. *is red*), then subject + *is* + complement (e.g. *ball is red*). This approach clearly identifies the target form for the child and results in a high frequency of correct responses. These are highly desirable consequences in an operant conditioning programme. On the other hand, it is peculiar to require the child to produce a grammatical functor like copula *BE*-forms or auxiliary verbs or infinitive particles in isolation.

TABLE 10.3

An example of elicited imitation using shaping, as in Gray and Ryan (1973)

Step 1 — work to a 10/10 criterion, using different pictures
    Adult: Tell me about this picture. Say, *is.*
    Child: *is.*
Step 2 — work to a 10/10 criterion, using different pictures
    Adult: Good, now, look at this picture and say, *is jumping.*
    Child: *is jumping.*
Step 3 — work to a 10/10 criterion, using different pictures
    Adult: Good, now, look at this picture and say, *The rabbit is jumping.*
    Child: *The rabbit is jumping.*

TABLE 10.4

A modification of Gray and Ryan's shaping procedure, based on Leonard (1975a)

Step 1 — work to a 10/10 criterion, using different pictures
    Adult: Tell me about this picture. Say, *jumping.*
    Child: *jumping.*
Step 2 — work to a 10/10 criterion, using different pictures
    Adult: Good, now, look at this picture and say, *rabbit jumping.*
    Child: *rabbit jumping.*
Step 3 — work to a 10/10 criterion, using different pictures
    Adult: Good, now, look at this picture and say, *The rabbit is jumping.*
    Child: *The rabbit is jumping.*

It seems unlikely that this non-developmental sequence could encourage the child to compute the necessary relationships between such grammatical morphemes and related sentence constituents.

Leonard (1975a) proposed an alternative developmental sequence that would require the child to imitate only meaningful utterances. An example of this type of developmental approach for teaching the copula, *is*, is provided in Table 10.4. This example illustrates how this modification captures another desirable characteristic of recasts. At step 2, the child is required to produce forms resembling her own productions. Step 3 involves only the addition of the target morpheme, much like a simple recast often adds a single element of complexity to the child's platform utterance. If part of the child's difficulty lies in computing the relationships between grammat-

ical functors and other sentence constituents, this type of technique might help to highlight these relationships.

The basic mechanisms for learning assumed by most users of elicited imitation have been the stimulus-response associations of operant theory (cf. Fey, 1986). Reinforcement of the child's production of the imitated target form under appropriate stimulus conditions is presumed to make the child more likely to produce the form again under similar circumstances. By fading the imitative stimuli and reinforcement, the discriminative stimuli for the correct form become more like those occurring in the naturally occurring environment. Because this operant approach seems incompatible with the current emphasis on pragmatics and intervention in naturalistic contexts, many clinicians have abandoned the use of imita-

TABLE 10.5

An example of modelling, focusing on the use of relative clauses

Step 1 — Provide 10–20 models without interruption

Adult: Here's a boy *who is wearing a raincoat.*
  And here's another one *who is wearing a sweatshirt.*
  This girl knows the boy *who's wearing a sweatshirt.*
  She doesn't know the *boy wearing the raincoat.*
  Now I see some children *who are hungry.*
  And some other children *who are thirsty.*
  The children *who are hungry* are getting some biscuits.
  The children *who are thirsty* are drinking juice.

Step 2 — work to a 10/10 criterion

Child: There's some boys wearing coats.
  And these ones are wearing sweatshirts.

Adult: Who will be the warmest?
  The ones *who are wearing sweatshirts.*

Adult: And who will stay dry?

Child: The boys *what are wearing the raincoats.*

Adult: Talk in your special way. Who will be driest? The boys *who are wearing raincoats* or the boys *who are wearing sweatshirts?*

Child: The boys *who are wearing raincoats.*

tion entirely, while others have sought to implement the approach in more naturalistic contexts (see Fey, 1986; Kaiser et al., 1992).

Nevertheless, imitation has potential value in its ability to

(a) dramatically increase the frequency of target forms by comparison to rates found in the typical learning environment;

(b) call attention to grammatical forms assumed not to be readily perceived, remembered, or grammaticised by children with SLI (e.g. Fygetakis & Ingram, 1973);

(c) clarify the general patterns underlying the use of new forms by removing distracting sentences that have unrelated forms (Connell, 1982, 1986b, 1987a); and

(d) provide production practice that might strengthen and stabilise representations of morphemes and syntactic representations and enhance their accessibility during on-line sentence production (Connell & Stone, 1992).

The first two of these functions seem to be served rather well by sentence recasting. The latter two pose special advantages for imitation over recasting. We believe that, with some modifications of the approach, discussed later, clinicians can further enhance the ability of imitation to serve these functions. In sum, although we reject the use of elicited imitation for the purposes outlined by operant theory, we believe that it has an important role to play in modern grammar facilitation approaches.

Modelling

The modelling we refer to in this paper is sometimes called imitative modelling or observational modelling. Like elicited imitation, modelling approaches often really comprise several procedures, and these have been combined differently by different investigators. The essential steps, as illustrated in Table 10.5, are:

(a) the clinician or a confederate produces 10 or 20 sentences containing the target grammatical form. The sentences are descriptions of pictures or taped or live actions and/or are responses to verbal stimuli, such as questions;

(b) the child listens quietly without producing the target until the entire set of training stimuli has been modelled;

(c) the child is then instructed to respond to the same or a different set of stimuli in the same manner just modelled.

As with imitation, the child often is informed when responses are correct and may be reminded to use "the special way of talking" when errors are made (Goldstein, 1984; Leonard, 1975b).

As with elicited imitation, there are many variations on this theme. For example, in some modelling approaches, the child may hear as many as 20 models of the target structure before a response is required (Connell, 1987a; Leonard, 1975a, 1975d). In others, the models may be distributed among other language forms, as is more typical in non-intervention contexts (Culatta & Horn, 1982). Most users of the approach have stressed that when a new form is being introduced, it is important to present the models without interfering stimuli that might compete for the child's cognitive resources. However, to maintain experimental control, some investigators have required children to produce a verbal response that does not contain the target form after each model. For example, in their comparison of imitation and modelling procedures, Connell and Stone (1992) asked children to imitate the phrase, "Pick *it* up", following each model of the target form.

As was the case for elicited imitation, production of complete responses can be shaped by first modelling short responses, then gradually lengthening the models as the child reaches a predetermined criterion and, finally, presenting exemplars of the complete target utterance. Leonard (1975a) reported that modelling that shaped responses in a developmental progression like that found in Table 10.4 was more effective in getting children to produce subject — verb sentences with the auxiliaries *is* and *don't* than was an unnatural sequence like that illustrated in Table 10.3.

The theoretical basis for modelling is different from that which originally motivated elicited imitation procedures. Modelled utterances contain dense concentrations of the target form, but the semantic content of each modelled sentence differs from every other. Under these conditions, it may be easier for the child to observe the underlying grammatical commonalities across the utterances and to readily represent these patterns in the form of language rules (Courtright & Courtright, 1976, 1979; Leonard, 1975b). This being the case, any distractions from the processing of the common linguistic pattern, such as that resulting from a request to imitate, may be contraindicated.

As with elicited imitation, modelling differs from recasting in many ways, most notably in that the clinician has control over the verbal and nonverbal stimuli and the response required. Consequently, modelling as we have described in this section seems to have lost favour among clinical researchers and, we suspect, most clinicians as well. Still, this clinician control can be construed as an advantage for the clinical process. For example, like imitation, modelling provides clinicians with the opportunity to select ideal target stimuli designed to challenge the child in ways that reflect their underlying problems with specific grammatical forms. Furthermore, in many respects, modelling seems more like natural language learning than imitation, and it could be that it prepares the child for natural language learning better than does imitation.

EXPERIMENTAL COMPARISONS OF THE PROCEDURES

Numerous experimental investigations have provided evidence that elicited imitation (Connell, 1986a, b, Connell, 1987a; Connell & Stone, 1992; Fygetakis & Ingram, 1973; Gray & Fygetakis, 1968; Gray & Ryan, 1973), modelling (Courtright & Courtright, 1976, 1979; Ellis Weismer & Murray-Branch, 1989; Goldstein, 1984; Leonard, 1975c; Wilcox & Leonard, 1978), and recasting (Camarata & Nelson, 1992; Camarata et al., 1994; Fey et al., 1997; Fey et al., 1993; Nelson et al.,

1996) facilitate the development of grammatical forms in children with SLI. Even though, in several of these studies, success was measured as responses in untrained utterances under conditions much like the intervention setting, they all represent cases in which the children produced utterances that were consistent with the rule being taught. Rather than baulking at the artificiality of some of these exercises and of the rules that were learned, our position is that we should look for ways to enhance the procedures' teaching properties. Before considering some of these enhancements, however, we must consider whether there are empirical reasons for preferring one of these procedures over another. In this section, then, we evaluate several studies that have directly compared the effectiveness of these approaches to grammatical interventions for children with SLI.

Evidence that modelling is superior to imitation

Courtright and Courtright (1976, 1979) hypothesised that modelling should be superior to elicited imitation because rule induction draws heavily upon the child's cognitive resources. When a child imitates an adult utterance, the formulation of the imitative response interferes with the underlying memory and computational processes that are needed to incorporate the modelled form into the grammar. Courtright and Courtright's predictions were confirmed by the results of their experiments. Their 4–7-year-old participants with SLI used the pronoun, *they* (Courtright & Courtright, 1976), and an artificial language form (Courtright & Courtright, 1979) more reliably following modelling than following an elicited imitation treatment.

It is important to note, however, that Courtright and Courtright (1976, 1979) did not use imitation in either of their studies in the same manner as others who have had greater success. For example, they did nothing to shape correct responses (cf. Tables 10.3 and 10.4). Furthermore, they did not systematically remove their imitative stimuli or fade their reinforcement. Thus, despite some encouraging results supporting the use of model-

ling, it is difficult to conclude that modelling is superior to imitation, based on these findings.

Evidence that imitation is superior to modelling

In direct contrast with the findings of Courtright and Courtright (1976, 1979), Connell and his colleagues (Connell, 1987a; Connell & Stone, 1992; Roseberry & Connell, 1991) have reported that imitation not only is effective, it leads to higher rates of target morpheme production than does observational modelling for children with SLI. The goal in these studies was an artificial derivational suffix, represented by a syllable (e.g. *-a*, *-um*) and having a meaning such as "part of" or "broken". For example, a broken TV was referred to as *TV-um*. Interestingly, in these studies Connell and his colleagues observed an advantage for imitation over modelling only for the children with SLI, not for children with typical language. Furthermore, the imitation advantage for children with SLI was seen only in production and not in comprehension. Based on this collection of findings, Connell and Stone argued that children with SLI have difficulty with the access of grammatical morphemes from memory. Imitation may be more effective than modelling, then, not because of its superiority in teaching derivational morphology, but because the practice it provides helps the child to build a more stable, accessible representation in long-term memory.

Although this is an intriguing possibility, as pointed out previously, the modelling procedures employed by Connell and Stone (1992) differed in an important way from those recommended by Courtright and Courtright (1976, 1979) and Leonard (1975b). In this study, after each model was presented by an animated ghost character on a computer screen, the child was required to tell another animated ghost character to "pick it up". This procedure was an important aspect of experimental control because subjects who received the imitation treatment were required to give a similar command that included the target label (i.e. "pick up the chair-um"). Unfortunately, this procedure violates an important assumption of modelling — that the child must be able to hear the entire set of models without interference caused by the execution of production processes. This may well have reduced the children's rate of learning in the modelling condition.

Even if Connell and Stone's conclusions are correct, it may be that the presumed inferiority of modelling can be compensated for easily in the clinic if the clinician provides the child with an opportunity to produce the targets following presentation of a set of models and presents corrective feedback following incorrect responses. These modifications would seem to provide the child with production practice roughly equivalent to that of imitation and may render modelling similarly effective.

Evidence for the superiority of recasting

An assumption made by proponents of language intervention procedures in natural settings like conversations, shared bookreading, play and classroom activities, has always been that these approaches lead to more generalised use of targets in communicative contexts. Camarata and Nelson have reported a series of studies in which they compared a conversational intervention approach based on recasting with a didactic approach based on imitation (Camarata & Nelson, 1992; Camarata et al., 1994; Nelson et al., 1996). They took strides to ensure that their 4–7-year-old subjects with SLI and the younger, MLU-matched subjects with typical language (Nelson et al., 1996) were not using grammatical forms selected as targets prior to the intervention. Their outcome measures included the number of sessions to first spontaneous use of the target and the number of spontaneous uses of the target during play.

In the collaborations of Camarata, Nelson and their colleagues (Camarata & Nelson, 1992; Camarata et al., 1994; Nelson et al., 1996), both imitation and recasting led to spontaneous use of the target structures and were judged to cause changes in the children's spontaneous language performance. The recast treatment, however, resulted in more spontaneous productions in non-treatment play contexts than did the imitation treatment. In addition, the first spontaneous use of a target was attained more rapidly in the recast treatment than with imitation. Thus, conversational recasting was judged to be the superior procedure for these children.

It is important to point out, however, that the imitation procedure used by Camarata and Nelson and their colleagues did not contain the feature of contrastive alternation described below and demonstrated by Connell (1986b) to be effective in teaching rule-governed language behaviour by children with SLI. As with the other comparisons, then, it is difficult to conclude that recasting is inherently better than one of the other procedures when the most exemplary models of each procedure have not been compared.

In addition, Nelson and colleagues (1996) noted that grammatical targets that were partially mastered prior to the study were used frequently in spontaneous contexts at the end of the treatment period, even when they had not been treated. On the basis of this evidence, Nelson and colleagues claimed that it may not be necessary to teach to high levels of accuracy in obligatory contexts; once children with SLI acquire productive use of a morphosyntactic form, they may be likely to master that form on their own without further intervention. Although this is possible, it must be remembered that a prolonged period from initial acquisition of grammatical forms to mastery has been a hallmark feature of SLI (Leonard, 1998; Rice, Wexler, & Hershberger, 1998). It is not unusual to observe a child with SLI making highly productive use of a specific morpheme (e.g. as determined by over-regularisation, as in *taked* and *goed*) at the same time the child most frequently omits the morpheme in connected speech (Bishop, 1994; Leonard, 1994). Therefore, this claim is in need of much further study. In fact, we believe there are good reasons, presented below, to think that when stimulus sentences are carefully selected, production practice stimulated through imitation or modelling in structured contexts may facilitate development from the point of initial acquisition to mastery of grammatical forms.

Despite their preference for the use of recasting in conversational contexts, even Camarata and Nelson (1992) have suggested that there is a place for such didactic procedures. For example, some forms, like gerunds (e.g. *Learning is fun*; *I don't like his teasing*), occur naturally with such low frequency that direct instruction approaches may pose significant advantages over conversational approaches in efforts to facilitate their development. Camarata and Nelson also have pointed out that imitation might have a role in helping children first to attend to the target structure in the input and then to produce it. This initial didactic phase of intervention could then be followed by recasting in less intrusive contexts to facilitate productive use of the target form in spontaneous, naturally occurring communicative contexts (Camarata & Nelson, 1992; Camarata et al., 1994; Nelson et al., 1996).

MANIPULATING ELICITED IMITATION AND MODELLING PROCEDURES ACCORDING TO THE INTERVENTION PRINCIPLES

The greatest dissatisfaction with elicited imitation and modelling approaches has been that their effects often were limited to the teaching context (e.g., Culatta & Horn, 1982; Fey, 1986; Leonard, 1981; Mulac & Tomlinson, 1977). In fact, clinicians who expected these procedures to do the whole job (this includes the first author) dramatically underestimated the complexity of what children have to learn. We also overestimated clinicians' ability to provide children with all of the relevant examples needed for development of functional language rules through the use of didactic exercises. Today, we know that, by increasing the frequency of target-specific recasts in otherwise relatively naturally occurring contexts, we can facilitate the use of previously absent grammatical forms. Our quest, then, is for complementary procedures that might enhance the effects of recasting in fostering earlier acquisition and speedier transitions from initial acquisition to eventual mastery of grammatical forms. In this final section, we introduce three general ways to manipulate traditional imitation and modelling procedures in accordance with the intervention principles introduced earlier in this paper. These

include (a) structured contrasts of grammatically related forms; (b) modifying the activity to make the didactic context more like connected discourse; and (c) planning production of forms in challenging metrical contexts.

Using imitation and modelling to contrast related forms

Connell has criticised the imitation and modelling procedures used by many clinicians and researchers on the grounds that each modelled or imitated sentence presents only the target form; neither the training sentences nor the probes typically require the participants to produce utterances containing alternative forms. Connell (Connell, Gardner-Gletty, Dejewski, & Parks-Reinick, 1981; Connell, 1982, 1987b) argued that such training may well teach a rule that is not inherently linguistic. For example, consider teaching the English copula in a sentence such as "The apple is red", using an approach like that found in Tables 10.3 and 10.4. With these procedures, the child could learn a rule like, "Say the name of an animate or inanimate object. Then, say *is*, and then produce a modifier that describes the object." This strategy would result in a perfect score even with new probes not used in training, as long as all of the pictured objects were singular rather than plural, were not pictures of the child or intervention agent (i.e. requiring 1st or 2nd person), in the present and not past tense or future modality, and so on. If the probes offered any of these other options, the child would exhibit overuse of *is* and limited true knowledge of its distribution in the language.

Connell's solution to this problem is to contrast the child's target with some other form that is semantically and/or grammatically related. Thus, in his studies, nominative case pronoun targets (e.g. *he, she*) are contrasted with their accusative counterparts (e.g. *him, her*) (Connell, 1986b), and stem forms of nouns are contrasted with the derived forms (e.g. *chair* versus the artificial form, *chair-a* to mean "part of a chair") (Connell, 1987a; Connell & Stone, 1992). Similarly, past tense forms of verbs (e.g. *verb + ed*, as in *walked*) could be contrasted with present tense (e.g. 3rd *person verb + s*, as in *walks*), present progressive

---

TABLE 10.6

An illustration of the planned contrasting of bare stem first person and non-finite verb forms and third person present tense singular -s, in an imitation procedure

Adult: This man says, I (like to) eat apples. Say, *I (like to) eat apples.*
Child: *I (like to) eat apples.*
Adult: Okay, good. He eats apples. Say, *He eats apples.*
Child: *He eat apples.*
Adult: No, listen again. *He eats apples.*
Child: *He eats apples.*
Adult: This monkey says, I need to swing. Say, *I (need to) swing all day.*
Child: *I (need to) swing all day.*
Adult: Yeah, *he swings all day.*
Child: *He swings all day.*
Adult: This boy says, I want to cook hamburgers. Say, *I (want to) cook hamburgers.*
Child: *I (want to) cook hamburgers.*
Adult: Say, *he cooks hamburgers.*
Child: *He cook hamburgers.*
Adult: No, say, *He cooks hamburgers.*
Child: *He cooks hamburgers.*

(e.g. *verb + ing*, as in *walking*), future modality (e.g. *will + verb*, as in *will walk*), or infinitive forms (e.g. *to + verb*, as in *to walk*) (Connell, 1982, 1987b).

In our own intervention research (Cleave & Fey, 1997; Fey et al., 1997; Fey et al., 1993), we began each individual session with contrastive imitation exercises. Ten models of one target form were presented first, followed by 10 models of the contrast target. After these models, the child was required to alternate targets, one after the other. We made no effort to continue this exercise to any learning criterion. Rather, we reasoned that this contrastive drill might focus the child's language learning resources on the target form. Following this 10-minute activity, we proceeded to play with the child in more naturalistic activities and provided opportunities to model the target form frequently and to recast the child's sentences using the target form.

An example of this type of contrast is illustrated in Table 10.6, which contrasts 3rd person, present forms with infinitival forms of the same verb. Third person singular, present tense forms in English are commonly omitted by children with SLI (Leonard, Eyer, Bedore, & Grela, 1997; Rice

& Wexler, 1996; Rice et al., 1998). This type of alternation in elicited imitation and modelling would require children to focus more carefully on the models and imitative prompts. It also may encourage them to listen more closely to the phonetic shape of the target form(s) than is necessary in standard non-contrastive exercises. Furthermore, the contrast should encourage the child to examine more closely the semantic and syntactic cues associated with the use of the target and the contrasted form. For example, the alternation of nonfinite targets with 3rd person present tense forms as shown in Table 10.6 might help the child to appreciate that tense cannot be marked in nonfinite clauses (a fact that is probably already known by children with SLI who omit tense markers) and that it *must* be marked in matrix clauses (a fact that seems not to be well appreciated by these children). Note that in this task, the child cannot assume that the use of the -s marker is optional (e.g. Rice & Wexler, 1996); productions that do not contain the marker will not be reinforced and may be followed by another request to imitate the 3rd person form. Still, this structured contrasting is not likely literally to teach the child all aspects of the complex rules involved. Instead, it is expected to challenge the child's existing grammar and to activate the child's learning mechanisms. This should sensitise the child to relevant models in other, more naturalistic, intervention and extra-intervention contexts, where the complete array of cues associated with the target form are present.

The effectiveness of this modification of direct instruction imitation and modelling approaches has not been studied, to the best of our knowledge. In one important study, however, Connell (1986b) demonstrated that children with SLI made marked improvements in their spontaneous use of target pronouns during play following this type of alternating target, elicited imitation approach. More importantly, the children also began to use other forms theoretically related to nominative case marking (e.g. 3rd person singular -*s*, inversion of subject and auxiliary/copula) with no additional intervention.

Making responses in imitation and modelling more pragmatically appropriate

Both elicited imitation and modelling can be implemented in less didactic and more naturalistic activities, such as during play at home or in the classroom or during the telling of stories. In fact, these are the forms in which these procedures are most commonly found today. For example, the intervention models categorised as milieu approaches are heavily dependent on imitation and child-selected reinforcement (Kaiser et al., 1992). The interactive language development teaching approach of Lee and her colleagues (Lee et al., 1975) relies on modelling in the context of story telling and also makes frequent use of immediate and delayed imitation. Culatta and Horn (1982) developed and tested an approach to foster mastery of already acquired grammatical forms that is based primarily on the systematic fading of models in otherwise relatively naturalistic play conditions. These approaches all involve greater distribution of the target form, however, and sacrifice the high-density, low-distraction characteristics of the didactic methods we have described. Consequently, these approaches may be more useful in teaching words and early grammatical

constructions than more complex morphosyntactic forms (see, for example, Yoder, Kaiser, & Alpert, 1991). Alternatively, they are useful in facilitating generalisation of later-developing forms once they have been acquired (Culatta & Horn, 1982).

Clinicians who wish to use elicited imitation and modelling do not need to sacrifice pragmatic propriety altogether. Both approaches can be made more pragmatically appropriate with some surprisingly simple modifications in the nonverbal and verbal stimuli used to evoke the child's responses. Many examples of these modifications can be found elsewhere (see also Ellis Weismer & Murray-Branch, 1989; Fey, 1986).

Table 10.7 contains an illustration of an alternating contrast approach in an activity in which the same theme is carried over multiple models and requests to imitate. Because of this, cohesive devices are used to connect sentences into a thematic whole, much as they are in connected discourse. A very natural extension of this sort of activity is to use published storybooks or create new stories (see Cleave & Fey, 1997) that place a contrastive focus on the child's specific targets. We have included an example of such a story in the Appendix. A broad range of individual and group intervention activities based on such stories can be developed to provide opportunities for imitative and non-imitative productions of the child's target forms. These range from the children's creation of pictures for their own storybooks to dramatic play based on the story's theme.

Didactic language instruction as production practice

There is considerable evidence that, even after their grammars reflect underlying knowledge of certain morphemes and how they are used, these forms frequently will be omitted by children with SLI (Leonard, 1998). The final two grammar intervention principles discussed earlier in this chapter allude to observations regarding the effects of production processes. First, forms that are segmentally complex may be more likely to be omitted than forms that are more easily produced (see Leonard, Sabbadini, Volterra, & Leonard,

---

TABLE 10.7

An example of planned contrasting of uninflected and third person present tense singular -s in a more coherent and cohesive activity

Adult:	This puppet likes to cook hamburgers. First, he's going to tell us what he does. Then, we'll make a list, so we can cook burgers, too.
Puppet:	First, I have to take out my pan. Say, *first, you take out the pan.*
Child:	*You take out the pan.*
Puppet:	Then, I have to get the meat out. Say, *next, you get the meat out.*
Child:	*You get out the meat.*
Puppet:	Next, I need to roll the meat into a ball. Say, *you have to roll the meat.*
Child:	*You have roll the meat.*
Puppet:	Then, I have to press it flat. Say, *then, you press it flat.*
Child:	*You press it flat.*
Adult:	Okay, now let's start our list of everything he does to get ready to cook.
Adult:	First, he takes out the pan. Say, *he takes out the pan.*
Child:	*He take out the pan.*
Adult:	No, say, *he takes out the pan.*
Child:	*He takes out the pan.*
Adult:	Yeah, then he gets the meat out. Say, *He gets the meat out.*
Child:	*He gets the meat out.*
Adult:	Then, he rolls it into a ball. Say, *he rolls it into a ball.*
Child:	*He roll it into a ball.*
Adult:	No, *he rolls it into a ball.*
Child:	*He rolls it into a ball.*

1988). Second, some forms that are represented by weak syllables are especially prone to omission, even when they have been projected by the child's underlying grammar. For example, although weakly stressed syllables are generally at risk in children's productions of words and sentences, there is a great deal of evidence that children learning English favour weak syllables that follow stressed ones (Gerken & McGregor, 1998). Consider the sentence, *He ate the cookies, I think.* In this sentence, the pronoun, *he*, is weakly stressed, and it precedes a stressed syllable. Because it does not follow a stressed syllable, it is expected to be especially vulnerable to omission. In the related sentence, *I **think** he ate a cookie*, the same morpheme, *he*, follows the stressed word, *think.* Consequently, we can predict that uses of this form will be omitted more frequently in contexts like the first case than the last (McGregor & Leonard, 1994). Now consider the sentence, *John is **work-ing***. In this sentence, *is* attaches to *John* as part of a strong-weak sequence. The same form follows a weak syllable in the related sentence, ***Helen is working***, however. We would predict, then, that a child with knowledge of *is* would be more likely to omit it in contexts like the second sentence than those like the first.

These same factors can influence perception. That is, we might assume that target forms that commonly appear as weak syllables which do not follow strong syllables present a greater challenge to the child's perceptual mechanisms, making them more difficult to acquire. Several investigators have suggested that to help children acquire certain forms such as auxiliary verbs, copulas and pronouns in English, the verbal context should be manipulated to increase the frequency of these forms in positions in which they receive greater stress and/or follow stressed syllables (Bedore & Leonard, 1995; Fey, 1986; Gerken & McGregor, 1998). Thus, we might encourage the presentation of auxiliaries and copulas in sentence final position, where they are naturally lengthened and may even be stressed (e.g. *Yes, he **is**. Sure, he **will***). Alternatively, the clinician can create contexts requiring that these target morphemes be stressed emphatically (e.g. *Here is a boy and a girl. **He's** not working but **she** is*).

These techniques should render the forms more perceptible and may ensure that the child processes them completely and incorporates them into their grammars. Unfortunately, the same techniques would seem to do little for the child assumed already to have the requisite knowledge for these forms. Recall that these children tend to omit weak forms that do not follow strong forms, even when the forms clearly are part of their underlying grammars. It seems to us that what these children need is practice in the production of the target forms in the very contexts in which they are most likely to be omitted for reasons of production difficulties. Consider the examples in Table 10.8. The stimuli in this exercise have been designed to give the child practice in producing the auxiliaries, *is* and *are*, in contexts in which the subjects are disyllabic. Thus, in every case, the auxiliary is weak and does not follow a strong syllable. Practice, using stimuli such as these, should inform the child of the necessity to include these forms even in contexts that present challenges to output processes. Furthermore, the exercises should help to automatise the production of syllables in these disfavoured contexts.

CONCLUSION

We believe that no single procedure will optimise the development of difficult morphological and syntactic forms among children with SLI. Once goals are selected, the clinician must decide how didactic and naturalistic teaching procedures will be combined. We have no evidence on how this can be done to the greatest effect. Our best hunch is that forms should first be introduced in didactic teaching exercises, using modelling and/or imitation. After a brief period of practising in these contexts, focused stimulation, using recasts in typically occurring conversational and bookreading activities, can begin. Because we suspect that the didactic procedures offer advantages over recasting in natural settings both for the acquisition of previously absent forms and for the progression towards mastery following acquisition, we would alternate the didactic and naturalistic procedures across different sessions and/or within the same sessions until the child mastered the form in spontaneous contexts.

Research is needed to test our hypothesis that imitation and modelling can be used to complement recasting to maximise the effectiveness and efficiency of grammatical intervention. Until we find evidence to show that this hypothesis is wrong, however, we are not ready to put these time-tested procedures to rest.

ACKNOWLEDGEMENTS

The writing of this chapter was supported (in part) by research grant number R01 DC 01817 from the National Institute on Deafness and Other Communication Disorders and by center grant HD02528 from the National Institute on Child Health and Human Development.

REFERENCES

Bedore, L.M., & Leonard, L.B. (1995). Prosodic and syntactic bootstrapping and their applications: A

TABLE 10.8

Practice sentences requiring the auxiliary *is* in weak syllables that do not follow stressed syllables and are likely to be omitted

This baby is sleeping.
This baby is crying.
This lion is roaring.
This lion is smiling.
Mummy is driving the car.
Now, Daddy is driving the car.
A monster is chasing this lady.
Now, the lady is chasing the monster.

tutorial. *American Journal of Speech-Language Pathology, 4*, (February), 66–72.

Bishop, D.V.M. (1994). Grammatical errors in specific language impairment: Competence or performance limitations? *Applied Psycholinguistics, 15*, 507–550.

Camarata, S.M., & Nelson, K.E. (1992). Treatment efficiency as a function of target selection in the remediation of child language disorders. *Clinical Linguistics and Phonetics, 6*, 167–178.

Camarata, S.M., Nelson, K.E., & Camarata, M.N. (1994). Comparison of conversational-recasting and imitative procedures for training grammatical structures in children with specific language impairment. *Journal of Speech and Hearing Research, 37*, 1414–1423.

Cleave, P.L., & Fey, M.E. (1997). Two approaches to the facilitation of grammar in children with language impairments: Rationale and description. *American Journal of Speech-Language Pathology, 6*, (February), 22–32.

Connell, P., Gardner-Gletty, D., Dejewski, J., & Parks-Reinick, L. (1981). Response to Courtright and Courtright [letter]. *Journal of Speech and Hearing Research, 24*, 146–150.

Connell, P.J. (1982). On training language rules. *Language, Speech and Hearing Services in Schools, 13*, 231–248.

Connell, P.J. (1986a). Acquisition of semantic role by language-disordered children: Differences between production and comprehension. *Journal of Speech and Hearing Research, 29*, 366–374.

Connell, P.J. (1986b). Teaching subjecthood to language-disordered children. *Journal of Speech and Hearing Research, 29*, 481–492.

Connell, P.J. (1987a). An effect of modelling and imitation teaching procedures on children with and without specific language impairment. *Journal of Speech and Hearing Research, 30*, 105–113.

Connell, P.J. (1987b). Teaching language rules as solutions to language problems: A baseball analogy. *Language, Speech, and Hearing Services in Schools, 18*, 194–205.

Connell, P.J., & Stone, C.A. (1992). Morpheme learning of children with specific language impairment under controlled instructional conditions. *Journal of Speech and Hearing Research, 35*, 844–852.

Conti-Ramsden, G. (1990). Maternal recasts and other contingent replies to language-impaired children. *Journal of Speech and Hearing Disorders, 55*, 262–274.

Conti-Ramsden, G., Hutcheson, G.D., & Grove, J. (1995). Contingency and breakdown: Children with SLI and their conversations with mothers and fathers. *Journal of Speech and Hearing Research, 38*, 1290–1302.

Courtright, J.A., & Courtright, I.C. (1976). Imitative modelling as a theoretical base for instructing language-disordered children. *Journal of Speech and Hearing Research, 19*, 655–663.

Courtright, J.A., & Courtright, I.C. (1979). Imitative modelling as a language intervention strategy: The effects of two mediating variables. *Journal of Speech and Hearing Research, 22*, 389–402.

Cross, T. (1978). Mothers' speech and its association with rate of syntactic acquisition in young children. In N. Waterson & C. Snow (Eds), *The development of communication*. New York: John Wiley and Sons.

Culatta, B., & Horn, D. (1982). A program for achieving generalization of grammatical rules to spontaneous discourse. *Journal of Speech and Hearing Disorders, 47*, 174–180.

Ellis Weismer, S.E., & Murray-Branch, J. (1989). Modelling versus modelling plus evoked production training: A comparison of two language intervention methods. *Journal of Speech and Hearing Disorders, 54*, 269–281.

Farrar, M.J. (1990). Discourse and the acquisition of grammatical morphemes. *Journal of Child Language, 17*, 607–624.

Fey, M.E. (1986). *Language intervention with young children*. Austin, TX: Pro-Ed.

Fey, M.E., Catts, H.W., & Larrivee, L.S. (1995). Preparing preschoolers for the academic and social challenges of school. In M.E. Fey, J. Windsor, & S.F. Warren (Eds), *Language intervention: Preschool through the elementary years* (pp. 3–38). Baltimore: Paul H. Brookes.

Fey, M.E., Cleave, P.L., & Long, S.H. (1997). Two models of grammar facilitation in children with language impairments: Phase 2. *Journal of Speech, Language, and Hearing Research, 40*, 5–19.

Fey, M.E., Cleave, P.L., Long, S.H., & Hughes, D.L. (1993). Two approaches to the facilitation of grammar in children with language impairment: An experimental evaluation. *Journal of Speech and Hearing Research, 36*, 141–157.

Fey, M.E., Krulik, T.E., Loeb, D.F., & Proctor-Williams, K. (1999). Sentence recast use by parents of children with typical language and specific language impairment. *American Journal of Speech-Language Pathology, 8*, 273–286.

Fygetakis, L.J., & Ingram, D. (1973). Language rehabilitation and programmed conditioning: A case study. *Journal of Learning Disabilities, 6*, 60–64.

Gerken, L., & McGregor, K. (1998). An overview of prosody and its role in normal and disordered child language. *American Journal of Speech-Language Pathology*, *7*, (May), 38–48.

Goldstein, H. (1984). Effects of modelling and corrected practice on generative language learning of preschool children. *Journal of Speech and Hearing Disorders*, *49*, 389–398.

Gray, B., & Ryan, B. (1973). *A language program for the nonlanguage child*. Champaign, IL: Research Press.

Gray, B.B., & Fygetakis, L. (1968). Mediated language acquisition for dysphasic children. *Behavior Research and Therapy*, *6*, 263–280.

Hegde, M.N., & Gierut, J. (1979). The operant training and generalization of pronouns and a verb form in a language delayed child. *Journal of Communication Disorders*, *12*, 23–34.

Hester, P., & Hendrickson, J. (1977). Training functional expressive language: The acquisition and generalization of five-element syntactic responses. *Journal of Applied Behavior Analysis*, *10*, 316.

Kaiser, A.P., Yoder, P.J., & Keetz, A. (1992). Evaluating milieu teaching. In S.F. Warren & J. Reichle (Eds), *Causes and effects in communication and language intervention* (pp. 9–47). Baltimore: Paul H. Brookes.

Lee, L., Koenigsknecht, R., & Mulhern, S. (1975). *Interactive language development teaching*. Evanston, IL: Northwestern University Press.

Leonard, L.B. (1975a). Developmental considerations in the management of language disabled children. *Journal of Learning Disabilities*, *8*, 222–237.

Leonard, L.B. (1975b). Modelling as a clinical procedure in language training. *Language, Speech, and Hearing Services in Schools*, *6*, 72–85.

Leonard, L.B. (1975c). Relational meaning and the facilitation of slow-learning children's language. *American Journal of Mental Deficiency*, *80*, 180–185.

Leonard, L.B. (1975d). The role of nonlinguistic stimuli and semantic relations in children's acquisition of grammatical utterances. *Journal of Experimental Child Psychology*, *19*, 346–357.

Leonard, L.B. (1981). Facilitating linguistic skills in children with specific language impairment. *Applied Psycholinguistics*, *2*, 89–118.

Leonard, L.B. (1994). Some problems facing accounts of morphological deficits in children with specific language impairments. In R.V. Watkins & M.L. Rice (Eds), *Specific language impairments in children* (pp. 91–105). Baltimore: Paul H. Brookes.

Leonard, L.B. (1998). *Children with specific language impairment*. Cambridge, MA: MIT Press.

Leonard, L.B., Eyer, J.A., Bedore, L.M., & Grela, B.G. (1997). Three accounts of the grammatical morpheme difficulties of English-speaking children with specific language impairment. *Journal of Speech, Language, and Hearing Research*, *40*, 741–753.

Leonard, L.B., Sabbadini, L., Volterra, V., & Leonard, J. (1988). Some influences on the grammar of English- and Italian-speaking children with specific language impairment. *Applied Psycholinguistics*, *9*, 39–57.

McGregor, K.K., & Leonard, L.B. (1994). Subject pronoun and article omissions in the speech of children with specific language impairment: A phonological interpretation. *Journal of Speech and Hearing Research*, *37*, 171–181.

Mulac, A., & Tomlinson, C.N. (1977). Generalization of an operant remediation program for syntax with language delayed children. *Journal of Communication Disorders*, *10*, 231–243.

Nelson, K.E., Camarata, S.M., Welsh, J., Butkovsky, L., & Camarata, M. (1996). Effects of imitative and conversational recasting treatment on the acquisition of grammar in children with specific language impairment and younger language-normal children. *Journal of Speech and Hearing Research*, *39*, 850–859.

Nelson, K.E., & Welsh, J.A. (1998). Progress in multiple language domains by deaf children and hearing children: Discussions within a rare event transactional model of language delay. In R. Paul (Ed.), *Exploring the speech-language connection* (Vol. 8, pp. 179–225). Baltimore: Paul H. Brookes.

Nelson, K.E., Welsh, J., Camarata, S., Butkovsky, L., & Camarata, M. (1995). Available input for language-impaired children and younger children of matched language levels. *First Language*, *43*, 1–18.

Rice, M.L., & Wexler, K. (1996). Toward tense as a clinical marker of specific language impairment in English-speaking children. *Journal of Speech and Hearing Research*, *39*, 1239–1257.

Rice, M.L., Wexler, K., & Hershberger, S. (1998). Tense over time: The longitudinal course of tense acquisition in children with specific language impairment. *Journal of Speech, Language, and Hearing Research*, *41*, 1412–1431.

Roseberry, C.A., & Connell, P.J. (1991). The use of an invented language rule in the differentiation of normal and language-impaired Spanish-speaking children. *Journal of Speech and Hearing Research*, *34*, 596–603.

Warren, S.F., McQuarter, R.J., & Rogers-Warren, A.K. (1984). The effects of mands and models on the speech of unresponsive language-delayed preschool children. *Journal of Speech and Hearing Disorders, 49*, 43–52.

Wilcox, M.J., & Leonard, L.B. (1978). Experimental acquisition of wh-questions in language-disordered children. *Journal of Speech and Hearing Research, 21*, 220–239.

Yoder, P.J., Kaiser, A.P., & Alpert, C.L. (1991). An exploratory study of the interaction between language teaching methods and child characteristics. *Journal of Speech and Hearing Research, 34*, 155–167.

APPENDIX

A story created to provide focus on the modal, *will*, as contrasted with the past tense.

One day, Brian and his mum were out walking.
Brian found a little seed.
He picked it up.
He looked at it carefully.
I know, said Brian.
I will plant this seed.
It will grow.
It will grow this tall.
Will you water it every day? asked Brian's mum.
Yes, I **will**, answered Brian.
I will take good care of it.
But what is it, mum? Brian asked.
What will this seed be?
I won't tell you now, responded his mum.
We will see.
Brian showed the seed to his friend, Michael.
Look, Michael, I found this seed.
Tomorrow, I will plant it.
I will plant it in my back yard.
Then it will grow.

Will you help me, Michael?
Will you?
I don't think it will grow, said Michael.
That seed will not grow.
Yes, it **will**, said Brian.
I will take care of it.
It will get very big.
You will see.
The next day, Brian planted the seed.
He planted it in the garden.
And he watered it every day.
It **won't** grow, said Michael.
It **will** grow, shouted Brian.
I just know it will.
Two weeks passed.
Everyone forgot about the seed.
Everyone, except Brian.
He watered the seed.
He talked to it.
You will grow.
You **will**.
I just know you will.
Then, one day, Brian heard his mum shouting.
Brian, come here, come here!
Brian hurried to the back door.
Then he rushed outside.
He looked on the ground where his seed was.
But his seed wasn't there.
Instead, there was a little green plant.
It is growing, Mum, said Brian.
I knew it would.
What will it be?
What will it be?
Well, said Brian's mum.
You planted a sunflower seed.
It will grow very tall.
It will have a big, yellow flower.
You will see.
You will see.
But now Brian was dreaming about that flower.
No, Mum, he said.
I can see it already.

11

Predicting outcomes of early expressive language delay: Ethical implications

Rhea Paul

To the loving memory of my husband, Charles Isenberg.

This chapter reports data from a longitudinal study of language development in children who presented as "late talkers" in the second and third year of life. Patterns of development through the preschool years and outcomes in early school age are described. Factors present at age 2 that are significant predictors of outcome at school age are discussed. These findings suggest that prediction of long-term outcome in children with circumscribed language delay is difficult because only a small amount of the variance in outcome is accounted for by performance on communication and related assessments that can be measured early on. The implications of these findings for making decisions as to whether to provide early intervention to young children with slow language development are discussed from an ethics viewpoint. Potential benefits and possible harmful effects of intervention are addressed. The results of these analyses are used to argue that for children from functional families with circumscribed language delays and no other risk factors, parent training to optimise language input will be the intervention of choice, along with careful and frequent monitoring of linguistic progress.

Children with slow expressive language development (SELD), who at age 2 appear normal in every way but fail to begin talking, are often of concern to their parents and the clinicians their parents consult. It is well-established that children with learning disabilities frequently have histories of slow language growth (Catts & Kamhi, 1986; Maxwell & Wallach, 1984; Weiner, 1985). It is also known that older preschoolers with delayed language tend to have chronic deficits (Aram, Ekelman, & Nation, 1984; Aram & Nation, 1980; Garvey & Gordon, 1973; Griffiths, 1969; Hall & Tomblin, 1978; King, Jones, & Lasky, 1982). Until recently, however, there have been few data on which to base prognostic statements for children under three who appear to be normal in every way, except for the expression of words and sentences. The condition of circumscribed language delay in very young children is relatively common, though. Rescorla (1989) reported that 10–15% of middle class toddlers failed to produce more than 50 words or use two word combinations at 24 months of age.

Recently, several research groups have followed the development of children who present with SELD before age three (Paul, 1993; Rescorla & Schwartz, 1990; Scarborough & Dobrich, 1990; Thal, Tobias & Morrison, 1991; Ellis Weismer, Murray-Branch & Miller, 1994; Whitehurst, Fischel, Arnold, & Lonigan, 1992). SELD is defined in these studies as a small expressive vocabulary size (usually less than 50 words) during the third year of life. Vocabulary size is generally ascertained by parent report. Both the *MacArthur Communication Development Inventory* (CDI; Fenson et al., 1993) and the *Language Development Survey* (LDS; Rescorla, 1989) are parent report instruments that have been used for this purpose.

Outcome studies of these children who had small vocabularies as toddlers (summarised by Paul, 1996) suggest that many retain deficits throughout the preschool period. These deficits, while appearing as an overall delay at age two, become more focused later in the preschool years to a few areas of language production, including phonology, syntax and narrative skills. By school entry, the majority of these children perform within the normal range of expressive language.

Nevertheless, many clinicians (e.g. Nippold & Schwarz, 1996) continue to express concern about the long-term development of these children and their risk for later academic difficulties.

The Portland Language Development Project (PLDP) has been following a group of these children with SELD, and a control group of peers with normal language history, since they were toddlers (see Paul, 1991 a, b for details). The purpose of the PLDP has been twofold:

1. to track the development of children who present with small expressive vocabularies in the third year of life, and
2. to identify factors that will help to predict outcome in such children.

In the present report, a brief outline of the school-age outcomes of these children will be presented, reviewing data from previously published reports. Results of regression and discriminant function analyses used to predict school age language outcome from variables collected at intake will be reported. Finally, the implications of these findings for thinking about early language delays will be discussed.

THE PORTLAND LANGUAGE DEVELOPMENT PROJECT

Table 11.1 shows the characteristics of children participating in the PLDP. Children were recruited to the project as cases of SELD if, between the ages of 20 and 34 months, they produced fewer than 50 different words, by parent report. This criterion was chosen to select the lower end of the normal distribution of language development. Nelson (1973) has shown that the majority of middle-class children produce more than 50 different words by 20 months of age. Dale, Bates, Reznick and Morisset (1989) reported that average expressive vocabulary size at 20 months (in a large sample of children geographically and socioeconomically similar to the PLDP) is 155 words with a standard deviation of 87. Thus an expressive vocabulary size of 50 words at 20 months falls more than one standard deviation below the norm in their sample.

Rescorla's (1989) *Language Development Survey* (LDS), a parent checklist consisting of 300 of the most common words in children's early vocabularies, was used to assess expressive vocabulary size. Reznick and Goldsmith (1989) found that a parent checklist is a valid indicator of expressive vocabulary size in the third year of life. Rescorla has shown high reliability, validity, specificity and sensitivity for the LDS when used to identify expressive language delay in toddlers.

Thirty-six children between the ages of 20 and 34 months who were diagnosed as SELD by this criterion were identified by means of preliminary questionnaires distributed in pediatricians' offices and through radio and newspaper advertising. All the children passed hearing screening at 15 dB or threshold testing at 25 dB. All had IQs on the *Bayley Scales of Infant Development* (Bayley, 1969) of 85 or better. All children passed informal observational screening for neurological disorders and autism. All came from middle-class homes, as indicated by the socioeconomic status (SES) score, derived from parents questionnaires using Myers and Bean's (1968) modification of Hollingshead's four factor scale of social position.

Intake assessment: Predictor variables

Children were seen for intensive assessment of language and related skills at intake into the study, when they were between 20 and 34 months of age. Table 11.1 presents measures collected during the intake assessment that were used to predict school age language outcome, as well as demographic data on the two groups. The intake assessment covered the following areas.

Nonverbal cognition. The *Bayley Scales of Infant Development* — Mental Scale (Bayley, 1969) was used to assess developmental cognitive level. In addition to computing a score for this measure, the number of nonverbal items on which the child scored correctly was also computed. About half the items at the 18–30-month level on the *Bayley* involve nonverbal performance. The score

on these items was taken as an index of nonverbal cognition.

Adaptive behaviour. The *Vineland Adaptive Behavior Scales* (VABS; Sparrow, Balla, & Cicchetti, 1984) were used to assess adaptive behaviour. The VABS assess several areas of adaptive behaviour using a structured parent interview format. In addition to assessing social, daily living, gross and fine motor skills through parent interview, the VABS also assesses communication skills in both expressive and receptive areas. This assessment of communication differs from direct assessments in that it looks at adaptive uses of expressive and receptive skills, such as whether the child can deliver a message to a third person, or understand a simple direction, rather than at the production or comprehension of specific language forms. Each subscale on the Vineland was entered as a separate predictor in the analyses.

Phonological production. Phonological skills were indexed by the number of different consonant types produced during a ten-minute parent-child interaction (Paul & Jennings, 1992). The interactions were videotaped, and research assistants derived phonetic inventories for each by recording the first appearance of each consonant production heard, in either intelligible or unintelligible utterances. The number of consonants in the inventory comprised this measure for each subject.

Expressive vocabulary. The size of expressive vocabulary was computed by counting the number of items indicated by parents on the LDS (Rescorla, 1989). All subjects with SELD had fewer than 50 words at intake into the study on this measure.

Maladaptive behaviour. A maladaptive behaviour questionnaire was also administered to the parents at the intake assessment. This measure was described in Paul (1991a). It listed a series of problem behaviours and asked parents to indicate which ones constituted "no problem" (rated as 0), "some problem" (rated as 1), or "major problem" (rated as 2) for their child. A high score on this measure indicated a high level of parental perception of problem behaviours. The behaviours on

TABLE 11.1

Areas assessed, assessment instruments and values for variables used to predict outcomes from intake evaluation data

Area assessed	Instrument	SELD group mean (and s.d.)	NL group mean (and s.d.)
Age (months)		25.4 (4.6)	25.2 (4.0)
Developmental quotient	*Bayley Scale of Mental Development* (Bayley, 1969)	102.9 (10.6)	116.3 (17.6)
Nonverbal cognitive raw score	*Bayley Scale of Mental Development* — nonverbal items (Paul, 1991a)	15.2 (3.8)	15.4 (3.4)
Adaptive behaviour age equivalent (mo): Communication	*Vineland Adaptive Behavior Scales* (Sparrow, Balla, & Cicchetti, 1984)		
Expressive		11.0 (3.4)	29.5 (9.8)
Receptive		19.8 (2.3)	22.5 (1.6)
Motor skills			
Gross motor		21.8 (3.1)	34.7 (3.9)
Fine motor		19.3 (3.7)	36.8 (4.4)
Social skills		17.3 (2.6)	44.2 (4.3)
Daily living skills		31.5 (6.8)	35.7 (4.4)
Expressive vocabulary size	*Language Development Survey* (Rescorla, 1989)	26.2 (23.3)	203.8 (68.9)
Number of consonant types produced	Phonetic inventory (Paul & Jennings, 1992)	8.2 (4.5)	16.5 (2.8)
Number of maladaptive behaviours	Parent questionnaire (Paul, 1991a)	6.1 (4.5)	4.4 (3.5)
Birth order	Parent questionnaire	1.7 (0.9)	1.8 (1.0)
Socioeconomic status (SES)*	Parent questionnaire (Myers & Bean, 1968)	2.8 (1.0)	2.5 (1.4)
Proportion of males		76	69

* on a scale from 1 to 5, with 1 being the highest, based on Myers and Bean's (1968) modification of the Hollingshead four factor scale of social status

the questionnaire included poor eye contact, impulsivity, temper tantrums and sleeping difficulties.

Outcome variables

In second grade, when the children were aged around 7 years, outcome measures of language, temperament and school achievement were collected. The outcome measure used in the prediction equation was the Developmental Sentence Score (DSS; Lee, 1974), which assesses expressive syntactic and morphological abilities. The DSS was chosen as the primary index of expressive language ability: first, because it had proved to be the most sensitive measure of differences between children with SELD and those with normal language histories in earlier studies of this sample (Paul, 1993); second, it was considered an ecologically more valid measure of language production than a score on a standardised test, as it involves spontaneous conversation.

Using DSS scores, the subjects with a history of SELD were subdivided into two groups at second grade. Children who were originally placed in the SELD group at intake and had DSS scores at or above 8.11 (the tenth percentile for age 6–6) were referred to as the History of Expressive Language Delay (HELD) group. Twenty-seven (84%) of the 32 original subjects with SELD comprised this subgroup. The remaining five (16%) subjects from the original SELD group scored below 8.11 on the DSS and were considered the chronic Expressive Language Delay group (ELD). All subjects originally classified as having normal language (NL) had DSS scores above 8.11 in second grade.

Other variables collected when the children were 7–8 years of age were as follows:

The McCarthy Scales of Children's Abilities (McCarthy, 1972). The McCarthy is a standardised IQ test that yields both verbal and performance IQ. It was administered in second grade as a measure of cognitive function. Scores are reported as T-scores with a mean of 50 and a standard deviation of 10.

Test of Language Development — Primary (TOLD; Newcomer & Hammill, 1988). The TOLD-P was administered to all children as a standardised measure of oral language. The TOLD-P consists of subtests that measure semantics, syntax and phonology in both expressive and receptive modalities. In this report, mean standard scores (and standard deviations) for each diagnostic group will be reported for two composite scores: speaking quotient and listening quotient. The speaking quotient (SQ), is a composite of scores on the expressive language subtests and includes measures of expressive syntax, semantics and phonology. The listening quotient (LQ) is a composite of scores on the language comprehension subtests and includes measures of receptive syntax, semantics, and phonology.

Percent Consonants Correct (PCC; Shriberg & Kwiatkowski, 1982). PCC was employed as a quantitative measure of speech intelligibility. The middle 100 words in each speech sample were used, and phonemic transcriptions for each consonant produced by the children were derived from the audiotaped speech samples. PCC was derived by counting the number of correct consonants (relative to the target consonants in words in the orthographic transcriptions) and dividing by the number of correct plus number of incorrect consonants (relative to the target consonants in words in the orthographic transcriptions) in the 100 word sample.

Lindamood Auditory Conceptualization Test (LAC; Lindamood & Lindamood, 1979). In second grade, subjects were administered the LAC as a measure of metaphonological skill. This instrument measures the ability to segment nonsense words into phonemes and to manipulate the order of the segmented phonemes. This task was chosen as an assessment procedure for second grade both because it would be sensitive to group differences of interest, and because it provides norm-referenced data suitable for comparison to other measures used in the study. The LAC involves practice trials associating different coloured blocks randomly with phonemes (this [blue] is /i/; this [red] is /f/; this [green] is /s/). Subjects are then told, "If this (red-blue-green) is /fis/, what is /sif/?" The child's task is to rearrange the blocks to correspond to the phonemes in the new item (e.g. /sif/; green-blue-red). The LAC provides norm-referenced scores for kindergarten through sixth grade. Responses are scored as "correct" only if the child rearranges the blocks accurately to represent each of the phonemes in the stimulus. (For example, if the child produced green-red-blue for the item above, this response would be scored as incorrect.)

Peabody Individual Achievement Test (PIAT; Dunn & Markwardt, 1970). The PIAT was employed as a measure of school achievement. The test provides standardised scores in the areas of reading recognition (word identification), reading comprehension, spelling, mathematics and general information.

Temperament Assessment Battery for Children (TABC; Martin, 1988). According to Thomas and Chess (1977), "temperament" is the "how" of behaviour, or an individual's inherent behavioural style. Temperament is thought to be a stable, constitutional characteristic that influences the manner and intensity with which individuals respond to stimuli they encounter. The TABC consists of three scales: a parent form, a teacher form, and a clinician form. For the sake of brevity, and because results on the other forms were similar, data on the clinician ratings only will be presented here. Clinician ratings were obtained, as per instructions in the manual, by having graduate student research assistants rate the subjects following an intensive two-hour observation of the child, during which time they worked with the children, administering a variety of assessments.

The form contains 24 items, divided into five scales: activity, adaptability, approach/withdrawal, persistence and distractibility. Each item is scored on a 7-point scale. Scores given for each item are summed for each scale and converted to T-scores based on normative data in the TABC manual. Because our aim was to examine temperamental factors in the groups with a history of slow expressive language development as a whole, the SELD group was not subdivided into two subgroups in terms of this variable.

School age outcomes

Table 11.2 presents the outcome data for the three subgroups in second grade, in terms of verbal and nonverbal IQ, oral language skills (TOLD), speech intelligibility (PCC), school achievement (PIAT) and phonological awareness (LAC). As can be seen here, the ELD group scored significantly lower than the other two groups in both verbal and nonverbal IQ. Both subgroups with a history of SELD scored significantly lower (though within the normal range, again) in expressive language, though there were no differences in terms of receptive language. There were no significant differences in terms of word identification, reading comprehension or spelling, but the normal group scored significantly higher than either of the SELD groups in general information and higher than the ELD group in mathematics. Again, however, average scores for all groups were in the normal range on all these measures. Our measure of metaphonology also revealed that the ELD group scored significantly lower than the other two. Even their scores on this measure, though, were within the low average range. Finally, temperament data indicate that children with a history of SELD score within the normal range on all temperament scales. However, they are rated as significantly more shy by their parents than were their peers with normal language histories.

Regression analyses

To determine the long-term effects of early language delay on second grade DSS score, outcome DSS data for the group with a history of SELD were analysed in two ways. First, step-wise regressions were performed, using scores from the intake variables in Table 11.1 as predictors of second grade DSS. This procedure allows us to determine which factors at the early point in development significantly contribute to predicting DSS score at age 7. Second, stepwise linear discriminant analyses were used to predict "successful" DSS scores. This procedure provides a more qualitative assessment of outcome. It shows which variables at age 2 predict either "success" or "failure" in syntactic achievement at age 7. "Suc-

TABLE 11.2

Mean (and s.d.) IQ, language, speech, school achievement, metaphonology, and temperament outcome scores in three groups in second grade (age 7–8)

Task	Group NL (n = 27)	HELD (n = 27)	ELD (n = 5)
McCarthy Test of Children's Abilities T-scores			
Verbal*	55.5 (11.4)[1]	50.2 (11.5)[1]	39.4 (6.3)[2]
Performance*	54.9 (10.7)[1]	51.3 (11.9)[1]	43.2 (8.1)[2]
TOLD[a] Standard scores			
Speaking quotient*	109.1 (9.2)[1]	98.2 (14.9)[2]	91.0 (9.8)[2]
Listening quotient	108.1 (9.6)	106.5 (11.0)	101.2 (7.4)
PCC[b] %	98.6 (2.1)	93.7 (13.7)	96.8 (3.6)
PIAT[c] Standard Scores			
Reading recognition	114.4 (14.5)	112.3 (16.8)	100.8 (21.3)
Reading comprehension	114.0 (12.4)	108.1 (14.2)	103.1 (11.8)
Spelling	106.9 (11.6)	108.5 (12.5)	103.4 (18.4)
Mathematics*	113.1 (11.3)[1]	111.3 (12.0)[1]	93.2 (10.3)[2]
General information*	116.2 (12.8)[1]	111.3 (13.7)[1,2]	99.6 (9.3)[2]
LAC[d] * Raw score	75.3 (17.6)[1]	71.2 (16.9)[1]	49.4 (18.4)[2]
TABC[e] T-scores	NL	SELD	
Activity	49.4 (8.0)	48.9 (8.2)	
Adaptability	50.3 (6.2)	47.9 (8.4)	
Approach/withdrawal*	50.8 (5.0)	46.8 (5.3)	
Distractibility	51.3 (8.7)	53.5 (9.3)	
Persistence	54.3 (5.0)	54.1 (5.6)	

* significant differences found among groups using Kruskal-Wallis non-parametric Analysis of Variance: Groups with differing superscripts are significantly different on Mann-Whitney U testing; those with the same superscripts are not different.
[a] *Test of Language Development — Primary* (Newcomer & Hammill, 1988)
[b] Percent consonants correct (Shriberg & Kwiatkowski, 1982)
[c] *Peabody Individual Achievement Test* (Dunn & Markwardt, 1970)
[d] *Lindamood Auditory Conceptualization Test* (Lindamood & Lindamood, 1979)
[e] *Temperament Assessment Battery for Children* (Martin, 1988)

cess" was defined as a score above 8.1 on the DSS, the cut-off for the tenth percentile for children 6.5 years of age. In these procedures the .1 level of significance was used for both forward and backward steps.

As Table 11.3 shows, the stepwise procedure yielded only two significant predictors: socioeconomic status (SES) and VABS Expressive score.

Using the discriminant analysis, intake SES, VABS Expressive score and VABS Gross Motor score were significant predictors of "success" on the DSS in second grade. This yielded a sensitivity (proportion of successes correctly classified) of 96.2%, and a specificity (proportion of failures correctly classified) of 90%. Overall correct classification rate using these measures was 94.4%.

TABLE 11.3

Regression and discriminant function analyses of DSS outcome in children with SELD: second grade

	Significant predictors	R^2	Effect size	Sensitivity	Specificity	Overall correct classification
Step-wise regression — all SELD	SES; *VABS* expressive score	.27	Small*	–	–	–
Discriminant function — all SELD	SES; *VABS* expressive score; *VABS* gross motor score	–	–	96.2%	90%	94.4%

* Meline & Schmitt, 1997

Discussion

These data indicate that 16% of children with a history of SELD had syntactic production deficits in spontaneous speech at second grade. The overriding finding of this study, though, was that children with a history of SELD performed within the normal range on standardised measures of language and school achievement at second grade. This was the case even though the second graders with ELD scored significantly below peers with normal language on a nonverbal cognitive measure. Paul (1996) reported that in kindergarten, when 26% of the children with a history of SELD were classified as ELD, there were significant differences on verbal McCarthy scores, but not on the nonverbal scale. The children who still remain in the ELD group as late as second grade, however, comprise only 16% of the original SELD group, and these children would appear to be the ones with lower general cognitive abilities. Still, it should be noted that the nonverbal T-scores of the children with ELD were within (though at the low end of) the normal range (40–60). And even these children with persistent ELD and lower general nonverbal "intelligence" still operated within the normal range of school achievement at the primary level.

There were few statistically significant differences among the groups in school achievement.

There were no differences in the areas most closely related to literacy: reading recognition, reading comprehension or spelling achievement. The groups differed on the LAC metaphonological task, with the NL and HELD groups performing significantly better than the ELD. Nonetheless, the LAC scores for the ELD group were well within the normal range. On the other measures for which there were significant differences between NL and ELD groups (TOLD speaking quotient, mathematics, general information, LAC), again none of the children with ELD scored below the normal range.

The data on temperament indicated that these children were not perceived as overly active or difficult to manage, but they did seem more withdrawn than peers. It is interesting to note that Paul and James (1990) reported that parents did see these children as overly active, moody and difficult to manage when they were toddlers. These behaviour problems do not appear to persist, and may be more a result of their frustration with their communicative difficulties than a cause. Caulfield (1989) reported that parents also rated their late-talking toddlers as more shy and fearful than normally speaking peers. It appears that this difference in outgoingness, unlike the overactivity and moodiness, is a persistent one.

Overall, these findings suggest that the best predictors at 20–34 months of second grade spontaneous language production outcome in this sample of children with a history of SELD are early expressive communication skill (as indexed by parent report of adaptive communication ability), and socioeconomic status. To predict "success" on the spontaneous language measure; i.e. whether the child's score will fall above the tenth percentile at second grade, parent report of early gross motor skills provides some additional information.

It is interesting to note which variables did *not* contribute any significant prediction. Parent report of receptive communication on the VABS did not provide any significant prediction, although this may be due to the difficulty parents have in accurately rating children's understanding of language. Most studies using direct measures of language comprehension do find better outcomes in children with higher levels of comprehension (Bishop, 1997). Although studies of short-term prediction (Thal, Tobias, & Morrison, 1991) did report better expressive outcomes one year after diagnosis of SELD in children with higher receptive skills at age 2, this study of long-term outcome does not support the predictive value of early receptive performance. These findings are more in accord with those reported by Tallal (1988), in which few differences based on receptive skills were found among children diagnosed with specific language disorders.

Phonological production skills at age 2 also failed to predict long-term outcome. Although Paul and Jennings (1992) found significant differences between toddlers with normal and delayed language in terms of the phonetic inventory size, syllable structure level and percent consonants correct, the degree of early phonological delay does not appear to predict outcome.

Nonverbal cognitive skills did not contribute significant prediction to long-term outcome. Although nonverbal cognitive skills of SELD children who continued to score below the tenth percentile on the DSS in second grade were lower than those of children whose DSS scores moved into the normal range by that time, early nonverbal skills do not appear to be reliable predictors of this outcome. This finding is related to the known difficulty of using early IQ scores to predict later performance (Honzik, 1983; McCall,

1983; Rose, Feldman, Wallace, & McCarton, 1989). Early nonverbal IQ measures simply are not reliable in predicting long-range intellectual functioning. They are, apparently, also unreliable in predicting language outcome in the SELD population.

Similarly, the amount of maladaptive behaviour reported by parents of toddlers with SELD does not predict outcome. These findings strengthen the suggestion that the early maladaptive behaviours shown by these children were most likely to be a result of their frustration at being unable to communicate. As their communication skills grew, this frustration and its attendant behaviour ameliorated. However, their more stable, temperamental shyness stays with them.

Birth order and gender also failed to predict outcome in this study. About 40% of the SELD children were first-borns (Paul, 1991a), and a comparable proportion of the normally speaking children in the control group were first borns as well. Although popular wisdom holds that later borns talk late because their siblings "talk for them" and would therefore be more likely than first born late talkers to eventually outgrow their delay, there is no support for this position in the present data. Birth order does not appear to be related to long-term outcome in this sample. The same can be said for gender. Although there are more males with SELD than females, sex does not seem to have a significant effect on long-term outcome.

What does appear to predict language outcome, at least to a small degree, in late talkers is socioeconomic status (SES). This is striking in that *all* the children within this sample are middle class. Although not all the families in our sample would be considered professional, they ranged from lower- to upper-middle class in terms of occupational and educational levels. The finding that SES predicts outcome within this narrow range suggests that even small differences in SES can affect outcome for children with mild language delays. Again, it is important to remember that the effect sizes are small, and the effect is not of SES alone, but in combination with early adaptive expressive ability, as well as with other unidentified factors. Nevertheless, the finding tends to accord with those of Hart and Risley (1995), who found that higher SES is associated with better language outcomes in typically developing children, as a function of parent input and interactional style. Although Hart and Risley looked at rather broad SES categories (welfare, working class, professional) it appears from these data that even relatively small differences in SES within the middle class families in this sample, presumably mediated by mother's educational level, can affect outcome. These findings have, I think, some important implications for dealing clinically with children who present as SELD, to which we will return.

Early adaptive use of expressive communication is an additional significant predictor. This predictive power may be related to the temperament findings. Children with SELD tend to have a mild but stable tendency toward shyness both at early and later ages. This tendency may be manifested in early years by less frequent or less persistent attempts to convey expressive communication through a variety of channels, which parents may perceive and reflect in their reports on the VABS expressive communication. In any case it would appear that children who are more successful as toddlers at engaging in expressive communication with their parents, even when their linguistic means for doing so are limited, have an advantage in overcoming early language delays.

The finding that gross motor skills have some role in predicting later language outcome is of interest as it relates to current theories regarding the source of language delay. Bishop and Edmundson (1987) have argued for seeing SLI as not truly specific, but rather a reflection of a general neurodevelopmental lag that affects a variety of areas of development, including motor skills (Powell & Bishop, 1992). The small role that motor skills appear to play in predicting outcomes for this sample suggest that for children with SELD, we may be witnessing a process of neurodevelopmental lag. The findings suggesting that these children perform at the low end of the normal range in both language and school achievement by second grade accord with a view of this sample as representing a developmental delay, rather than a *bona fide* pathology.

Implications

Middle-class children with slow expressive language development as toddlers seem, on the basis of these results, to have a good chance of performing within the normal range in terms of language and academic achievement by the time they reach school age, even in the absence of intensive intervention. These findings led me at first to argue for a public policy of "watch and see" with regard to these otherwise normal children with SELD. That is, I suggested that otherwise healthy, normal, late talkers should be monitored yearly during the preschool years in order to insure that:

1. language continues to be the only concern. Cognitive, behavioural, hearing, medical and neurological development proceeds normally. Both expressive and receptive language should be carefully monitored during this period. Receptive language should function broadly within the normal range by the time the child is three (Paul, 1991a).

2. significant progress is made in sentence length, intelligibility and conversational skill. Even if the child continues to score below the normal range in these areas through the preschool period, there should be evidence of growth.

3. the child's speech can be understood by family, friends and peers.

It is important to note that these findings are limited to children from stable, relatively advantaged families with no additional risk factors. For children from more deprived backgrounds, or who have any degree of sensory, neurological or motor deficits, early intervention is clearly warranted and known to be effective (Guralnick, 1997). Similarly, it is important to remember that children who have persistent language impairments (the SLI population) show patterns of early development very like those seen in the late talkers. Data from several sources (e.g. Rescorla & Lee, in press; Stothard et al., 1998) suggest that children with language delays that persist to age 4 or 5 do show risk for chronic impairments. Rescorla and

Lee (in press) advocate calling children SELD until age 4 and labelling those with persistent disorders at this age as SLI. These children with persistent disorders in the late preschool period should receive higher priority for intervention services.

Many would argue, though, that even the middle class, otherwise typical late talkers described here should be given intervention to increase the rate of their entrance into the normal range. This argument is made on the basis of the need to take advantage of the critical period for brain development and the optimal degree of neural plasticity that is present before 3 years of age. In fact, when I recommended that monitoring rather than direct intervention is the management of choice, my recommendation has been criticised on just these grounds. But I would like to take the opportunity here at least to raise the question as to whether there might be another side to this argument. Let us consider a review of a book recently published by a mother of a child diagnosed at 30 months with Pervasive Developmental Disorder (Kephart, 1998). The reviewer, Margaret Talbot (1999, p. 5) wrote in the *New York Times Book Review*:

Childhood these days is often a land of diagnoses. Detours from the developmental path can easily get a kid tagged with one new syndrome or another. And as far as many parents [and clinicians] are concerned, this is an unmitigated good. These parents . . . are grateful to have an explanation . . . and are relieved to know that they are not alone. We don't hear quite as much from parents [or clinicians] who react to such labels with tortured ambivalence, who wonder whether their child's individuality has been reduced to pathology and what might be lost if it has.

What has been lost? Is there any cost to providing intervention to children who, if left to the natural contingencies of language acquisition, would sooner or later find their way more or less into the normal range? Do we run any risk of derailing developments about which we know very little, and for which we do not test, by focusing the child's attention on language through therapy?

If we invoke the concept of multiple intelligences (Gardner, 1983), might we perhaps in forcing the child to concentrate on developing language ability, deflect attentional resources from the development of other kinds of intelligence that may be unique to him and on which we, as a culture, place less value? Although we certainly want to capitalise on the known neural plasticity present in the very early years of life, we might, in taking advantage of that plasticity, actually recruit neural power to language development that was originally programmed for the development of the child's more singular abilities. This might result in better performance in school down the line. But in doing such recruiting, might we be reducing the child's chance to develop some unique set of abilities, some artistic or musical or intrapersonal talent that, granted, would not be rewarded in the school setting, but would enrich the personality of the child and the experience of everyone with whom he comes in contact? I don't know the answer to these questions; I'm only speculating. But the point I want to make is that hurrying up the language development of a child who is on a slow language development course may not, as Talbot suggests, be an "unmitigated good". While we know, as Whitehurst et al.'s (1992) research has told us, that we can effect short term change in language performance, we may want to consider what else we might be doing inadvertently. Could it be that working with a professional might send a meta-message to the child? A message such as, "You're different. This stuff you do with the therapist is special, more important than other stuff, and you're bad at it." Apart from learning the language forms taught in the intervention, the child may learn other things about himself — we don't know, but we might consider these possible costs, when we compute the benefits of intervention for children with circumscribed language delays under the age of three.

A related consideration concerns the temperamental data presented. The consistent finding of mild shyness in this population suggests that these are children for whom interaction may not be the highest priority, at least at certain points in development. Redmond and Rice (1998) have argued that this is a result of the child's language disorder, but I would suggest that it may also be the case that the withdrawn quality came first, and the slower rate of language acquisition follows, as the child is less driven to seek interaction and devotes attention to other aspects of growing more attuned to his temperament.

I have argued elsewhere (Paul, 1996) that these children who function within, but at the low end of the normal range of language ability, may not do "well enough" to be left without help. This argument is made on the basis of our knowledge that children of similar social class and economic status perform higher, as the NL subjects in this study do, on measures of language function. Now, if the SELD subjects were from more deprived backgrounds, their standard scores of 80–90 would represent nothing unusual. But in the middle-class academic environments in which they must function, all the children, like the ones from Garrison Keillor's mythical Lake Wobegon, are above average. We might say, then, that even though children with SELD are statistically within the normal range, they are functionally impaired because of the reference group of students with whom they will be compared.

This may very well be true. It may be true, further, that as our society becomes more knowledge- and technology-dependent, the language and verbal reasoning skills in which these children are shaky (as reflected, I think, in their low mathematics scores on the PIAT) are just the ones that are crucial for academic and vocational success. This may, as Leonard (1991) has suggested, be sufficient reason to provide intervention to children with "weak" language skills, even when they do not have a pathological condition.

But I would like to take the opportunity here to play the Devil's Advocate; to engage in a small thought experiment. Suppose for a moment that we were to discover a drug that specifically provided a mild stimulus to language development, without side-effects or long-term dangers. Suppose that an agent was found that affected language learning in much the way Prozac affects mood, or Ritalin affects attention, or growth hormone affects stature. Would we want to see children with language disorders take this drug? Most of us would probably say "yes". Language skills are important in life; of course we would want to maximise them in any way possible. Would we want our late talking 2-year-olds to be given them? I imagine many people would also answer "yes", but perhaps a somewhat smaller majority. We have a conditioned wariness about giving drugs to children to do the same things we have no qualms trying to affect with behavioural interventions. But what if a parent of a child with perfectly normal language development asked us for it? Or the parent of a normal but very quiet child? Would these children, too, be appropriate candidates for our wonder drug? I think many of us would feel uncomfortable about these cases. We tend to feel uneasy about using drugs to ameliorate performance in people without handicaps. It is this uneasiness that prompted Peter Kramer, in writing about Prozac, to coin the term "cosmetic psychopharmocology" to discuss our ambivalence about this kind of intervention. And we see this ambivalence in the distressed reaction of many Americans, for example, on learning that Mark McGuire, the baseball hero who set a new Major League record for homeruns in 1998, used (legal, non-prescription) anabolic steroids to enhance his performance. My point is that prescribing early intervention for otherwise normal, middle-class late talkers with a good prognosis for more-or-less normal outcome gives me the same kind of uneasiness. My disquiet may be misguided, based on a romantic notion of individuality and of childhood as a time of dreamy, unhurried meandering, unhampered by the rigorous scheduling and pursuit of goals to which our adult lives are devoted. And surely my neurological metaphors have no basis in fact that I know of. I want only to ask that we think outside our frame of reference as "language pathologists" at times, and entertain the possibility that there may indeed be something lost, both to our subdued little late talkers, and to our culture, which tends to expect rigid scheduling of development early in life.

I don't mean to imply that this tendency is, either, an "unmitigated evil". There is much to celebrate in our society's attempt to make literacy, academic advancement and the economic opportunity these make possible available to all our children; and in its willingness to devote resources to remediating whatever might be getting in the way of these achievements. I want to suggest only that we think about our behavioural interventions a bit more critically and realise that they may be as powerful, in ways we cannot always fully predict, as the chemical interventions about which we would think so hard before recommending.

Now, if we could continue our thought experiment for a moment, suppose that instead of discovering a drug like the one I just described, we were to find out that a naturally occurring nutrient, present in certain foods, provided the same sort of mild stimulus to language development. Would we feel more comfortable in suggesting to parents that they try to get their language-impaired children to eat more of these foods? Might we also feel more at ease about suggesting that parents of late talkers increase their presence in the children's diet? Would we try to feed more of them to our own normally-developing children? I suspect we probably would answer "yes" to all of these questions. I would like to suggest, further, that we do have such a nutrient available to us — it is parent-child interaction. The context of parent-child play, even when done consciously and intensively with modifications in its form like those suggested by Ellis Weismer (this volume) and Fey (this volume), may convey through its emotional content more acceptance of the child and his natural pace. And this is an intervention we could offer to any parent who wanted it. Although it is clearly not a comfortable role for all parents, and should not be advocated unless the parent feels s/he wants to do it, for some parents this form of readily accessible language "nutrition" provides a naturalistic opportunity for them to feel some sense of contribution to their child's development. Encouraging parents to play and talk more with their children is unlikely to cause discomfort in even the most easily disturbed clinician's mind. Girolametto, Pearce and Weitzman (1996) provided an interactive focused stimulation programme to parents of

children like those with SELD. They found positive effects on the quality of parent language, size of child vocabulary and number of multiword combinations as a result, when children receiving treatment were compared to a delayed-treatment control group. Perhaps a combination of parent education and careful monitoring of progress toward typical language use could provide unmitigated good to middle-class children with no other risk factors who present as late talkers under the age of three.

ACKNOWLEDGEMENTS

This research was supported by grants from NIDCD (DC00793), the Meyer Memorial Trust, the American Speech-Language Hearing Foundation and Portland State University.

REFERENCES

Aram, D., & Nation, J. (1980). Preschool language disorders and subsequent language and academic difficulties. *Journal of Communication Disorders*, *13*, 159–170.

Aram, D., Ekelman, B., & Nation, J. (1984). Preschoolers with language disorders: 10 years later. *Journal of Speech and Hearing Research, 27*, 232–244.

Bayley, N. (1969). *Scales of infant mental development*. NY: Psychological Corp.

Bishop, D.V.M. (1997). *Uncommon understanding: Development and disorders of language comprehension in children*. Hove, UK: Psychology Press.

Bishop, D.V.M., & Edmundson, A. (1987). Specific language impairment as a maturational lag: Evidence from longitudinal data on language and motor development. *Developmental Medicine and Child Neurology, 29*, 442–459.

Catts, H., & Kamhi, A. (1986). The linguistic basis for reading disorders: Implications for the speech-language pathologist. *Language, Speech, and Hearing Services in Schools, 17*, 329–341.

Caulfield, M. (1989). Communication difficulty: A model of the relation of language delay and behavior problems. *SRCD Abstracts, 7*, 212.

Dale, P., Bates, E., Reznick, J., & Morisset, C. (1989). The validity of a parent report instrument of child language at twenty months. *Journal of Child Language*, *16* (2), 239–249.

Dunn, L., & Markwardt, F. (1970). *Peabody individual achievement test.* Circle Pines, MN: AGS.

Elllis Weismer, S., Murray-Branch, J., & Miller, J. (1994). A prospective longitudinal study of language development in late talkers. *Journal of Speech and Hearing Research*, *37*, 852–867.

Fenson, L., Dale, P., Reznick, S., Thal, D., Bates, E., Hartung, J., Pethick, S., & Reilly, J. (1993). *MacArthur Communicative Development Inventories.* San Diego: Singular Publishing Group.

Gardner, H. (1983). *Frames of mind: The theory of multiple intelligences.* New York: Basic Books.

Garvey, M., & Gordon, N. (1973). A follow-up of children with disorders of speech development. *British Journal of Disorders of Communication*, *8*, 17–28.

Girolametto, L., Pearce, P., & Weitzman, E. (1996). Interactive focused stimulation for toddlers with expressive vocabulary delays. *Journal of Speech and Hearing Research*, *39*, 1274–1283.

Griffiths, C. (1969). A follow-up study of children with disorders of speech. *British Journal of Disorders of Communication*, *4*, 46–56.

Guralnick, M. (1997). *The effectiveness of early intervention.* Baltimore: Paul H. Brookes.

Hall, K., & Tomblin, J. (1978). A follow-up study of children with articulation and language disorders. *Journal of Speech and Hearing Disorders*, *43*, 227–241.

Hart, N., & Risley, T. (1995). *Meaningful differences in the everyday experience of young American children.* Baltimore: Paul H. Brookes.

Honzik, M. (1983). Measuring mental abilities in infancy: The value and limitations. In M. Lewis (Ed.), *Origins of intelligence: Infancy and early childhood* (2nd. ed.). New York: Plenum.

Kephart, M. (1998). *A slant of the sun.* New York: Norton.

King, R., Jones, D., & Lasky, E. (1982). In retrospect: A fifteen year follow-up of speech-language disordered children. *Language, Speech, and Hearing Services in Schools*, *13*, 24–32.

Lee, L. (1974). *Developmental sentence analysis.* Evanston, IL: Northwestern University Press.

Leonard, L. (1991). Specific language impairment as a clinical category. *Language, Speech, and Hearing Services in Schools*, *22*, 66–68.

Lindamood, C., & Lindamood, P. (1979). *Lindamood auditory conceptualization test.* Allen, TX: DLM.

Martin, R. (1988). *The temperament assessment battery for children.* Brandon, VT: Clinical Psychology.

Maxwell, S., & Wallach, G. (1984). The language-learning disabilities connection: Symptoms of early language disability change over time. In G. Wallach & K. Butler (Eds.), *Language and learning disabilities in school-aged children.* Baltimore: Williams & Wilkins.

McCall, B. (1983). A conceptual approach to early mental development. In M. Lewis (Ed.), *Origins of intelligence: Infancy and early childhood* (2nd. ed.). New York: Plenum.

McCarthy, D. (1972). *McCarthy scales of children's abilities.* New York: Psychological Corp.

Meline, T., & Schmitt, J. (1997). Case studies for evaluating statistical significance in group designs. *American Journal of Speech-Language Pathology*, *6*, 33–41.

Myers, J., & Bean, L. (1968). *A decade later: A follow-up of social class and mental illness.* New York: Wiley & Sons.

Nelson, K. (1973). Structure and strategy in learning to talk. *Monographs of the Society for Research in Child Development*, *38* (Serial No. 149). Chicago, IL: University of Chicago Press.

Newcomer, P., & Hammill, D. (1988). *Test of Language Development — Primary.* Austin, TX: Pro-Ed.

Nippold, M., & Schwarz, I. (1996). Children with slow expressive language development: What is the forecast for school achievement? *American Journal of Speech-Language Pathology*, *5*, 20–25.

Paul, R. (1991a). Profiles of toddlers with slow expressive language development. *Topics in Language Disorders*, *11*, 1–13.

Paul, R. (1991b). Assessing communication in toddlers. *Clinics in Communication Disorders*, *1*, 7–24.

Paul, R. (1993). Outcomes of early expressive language delay. *Journal of Childhood Communication Disorders*, *15*, 7–14.

Paul, R. (1996). Clinical implications of the natural history of slow expressive language development. *American Journal of Speech-Language Pathology*, *5*, 5–30.

Paul, R., & James, D. (1990). Language delay and parental perceptions. *Journal of the American Academy of Child and Adolescent Psychiatry*, *29*, 669–670.

Paul, R., & Jennings, P. (1992). Phonological behavior in toddlers with slow expressive language development. *Journal of Speech and Hearing Research*, *35*, 99–107.

Powell, R., & Bishop, D. (1992). Clumsiness and perceptual problems in children with specific language impairment. *Developmental Medicine and Child Neurology, 34,* 755–765.

Redmond, S., & Rice, M. (1998). The socioemotional behaviors of children with SLI: Social adaptation or social deviance? *Journal of Speech, Hearing, and Language Research, 41,* 688–700.

Rescorla, L. (1989). The Language Development Survey: A screening tool for delayed language in toddlers. *Journal of Speech and Hearing Disorders, 54,* 587–599.

Rescorla, L. (1993). *Outcome of toddlers with specific expressive delay at ages 3, 4, 5, 6, 7, & 8.* Paper presented at the Biennial Meeting of the Society for Research in Child Development, New Orleans, LA.

Rescorla, L., & Lee, E. (in press). Language impairment in young children. In T. Layton, E. Cruis, & L. Watson (Eds), *Handbook of early language impairment in children: Nature* (pp. 11–55). Albany, NY: Delmar.

Rescorla, L., & Schwartz, E. (1990). Outcome of toddlers with specific expressive language delay. *Applied Psycholinguistics, 11,* 393–407.

Reznick, S., & Goldsmith, L. (1989). A multiple form word production checklist for assessing early language. *Journal of Child Language, 16,* 91–100.

Rose, S., Feldman, A., Wallace, I., & McCarton, C. (1989). Infant visual attention: Relation to birth status and developmental outcome during the first five years. *Developmental Psychology, 25,* 560–576.

Scarborough, H., & Dobrich, W. (1990). Development of children with early language delay. *Journal of Speech and Hearing Disorders, 33,* 70–83.

Shriberg, L., & Kwiatkowski, J. (1982). Phonological disorders III: A procedure for assessing severity of involvement. *Journal of Speech and Hearing Disorders, 47,* 256–270.

Sparrow, S., Balla, D., & Cicchetti, D. (1984). *Vineland adaptive behavior scales.* Minneapolis, MN: American Guidance Service.

Stothard, S., Snowling, M., Bishop, D.V.D., Chipchase, B., & Kaplan, C. (1998). Language-impaired preschoolers: A follow-up into adolescence. *Journal of Speech, Language, and Hearing Research, 41,* 407–418.

Talbot, M. (1999, January 3). *New York Times Book Review* [A review of Beth Kepthart's (1998) *A slant of the sun.* New York: Norton] p. 5.

Tallal, P. (1988). Developmental language disorders. In J.F. Kavanagh & T.J. Truss, Jr. (Eds), *Learning disabilities: Proceedings of the national conference.* (pp. 181–272). Parkton, MD: York Press.

Thal, D., Tobias, S., & Morrison, D. (1991). Language and gesture in late-talkers: A 1 year follow-up. *Journal of Speech and Hearing Research, 34,* 604–612.

Thal, D., & Katich, J. (1997). Issues in early identification of language impairment: Does the early bird always catch the worm? In K. Cole, P. Dale, & D. Thal (Eds), *Assessment of communication and language.* Baltimore: Paul H. Brookes.

Thomas, A., & Chess, S. (1977). *Temperament and development.* New York: Bruner/Mazel.

Weiner, P. (1985). The value of follow-up studies. *Topics in Language Disorders, 5,* 78–92.

Whitehurst, G., & Fischel, J. (1994). Early developmental language delay: What, if anything, should the clinician do about it? *Journal of Child Psychology and Psychiatry, 35,* 613–648.

Whitehurst, G., Fischel, J., Arnold, D., & Lonigan, C. (1992). Evaluating outcomes with children with expressive language delay. In S. Warren & J. Reichle (Eds), *Causes and effects in communication and language intervention* (pp. 277–314). Baltimore: Paul H. Brookes.

12

Educational placements for children with specific language impairments

Gina Conti-Ramsden and Nicola Botting

SLI is an exclusion-based description of children who have language impairments, but also have normal cognitive ability and no identifiable cause for their difficulties. SLI includes a wide range of different profiles of impairment. SLI profiles may develop in each individual over time to give a changing pattern of impairment. Only one fifth of children thought to have SLI are receiving specialist language provision (1% out of the incidence figure of 5%). Specialist language placements began appearing in the 1960s in the form of a few residential schools. Since then hundreds have been founded, the main type being language units. A number of factors determine whether a child is placed in a language unit, including child-based reasons, practical considerations and policy. Language units are classes (usually) attached to mainstream schools. They have on average a specialist teacher, a nursery nurse or other assistant, and half time speech therapy. The classes have about 10 children and offer intensive language input with the aim of returning children to mainstream. Of children in language units, 98% are placed appropriately (i.e. they appear to have SLI and not global cognitive delays). Almost half the children attending language units have very poor scores on at least one test of language. Language units appear to be providing for those children with severe expressive and/or receptive difficulties and those with complex difficulties rather than those with more specific speech problems. Different models of provision exist for children with language impairment including withdrawal from class, in-class support, reverse integration and specific interventions. No uniform system or method of intervention has been adopted in the educational system for children with SLI in the UK. The most likely alternative placement for children who are recommended specialist language provision but for whom such a placement is not available is a mainstream school setting (usually with speech therapy monitoring or clinic attendance). Communication centres may provide a better placement for some of these children, especially those with more pervasive difficulties. This would also enable a proportion of language units to offer effective, short-term intervention to children with more transient difficulties who will integrate to mainstream education within primary education. Professionals report that language units appear to be providing for a different population from that of some years ago. They feel the children have more complex and severe difficulties and that the "turnover" of the units is harder to maintain.

INTRODUCTION

Specific language impairment (SLI) is not a homogenous disorder but a term currently used to describe children with a range of different profiles, all of which include marked language difficulties in the context of normal cognitive abilities, where no identifiable cause is present (Bishop, 1997; Leonard, 1998). Thus, the definition of SLI excludes children with autism, general cognitive deficits, and physical or neurological damage (such as cleft palate, cerebral palsy or head injury). Although SLI has been studied and treated in some form or another for over one hundred years, precise definitions of this disorder have not been agreed upon. This is in part due to the varying profiles arising from combinations of deficits in particular areas of communication (phonology, morphology, syntax, semantics and pragmatics).

The profiles of children with SLI can change over time. That is, children who are identified as having a certain pattern of difficulty may improve in some areas and not in others, creating a different profile from year to year. We found, for example, that although the same profiles of SLI could be identified at different age levels, the particular children displaying the profile were not the same across time (Conti-Ramsden & Botting, 1999b). This variation and developmental change in the

SLI population makes it particularly important to investigate the educational placements provided for these children at various stages in their school history. This chapter attempts to provide a picture of the educational provision in Britain for children with SLI. We include in this discussion the characteristics of language units and the children who attend them, alternative placements for children with SLI, and potential problems and strengths of different placement types.

Much of this chapter will refer to a nationwide study based at Manchester (led by the first author) and funded by the Nuffield Foundation. The project recognised the need at this stage in the development of specialist education for children with SLI to "map out" the characteristics of children attending language units, examine their educational moves and outcomes and to investigate some of the processes behind these outcomes. The central aim of the Nuffield Foundation Study was to examine the placements of children *following* language unit placement. Using a randomly selected sample, half of the Year 2 children attending units of this sort in England were recruited into the study. This age group (7-year-olds) was of particular interest to us, because it is at this age that many children move from infant to junior years (4–7 years and 8–11 years respectively). This often involves a change of school, and many language units provide only for infant attenders. We aimed not only to examine placements for the whole group, but also to look particularly at those children who were not placed in the type of establishment recommended by the child's teacher and speech-language therapist. During pilot interviews we established that this was not only where language provision "runs out" (as we had expected), but also it sometimes occurred when children remained in the unit, contrary to the professionals' recommendations.

THE DEVELOPMENT OF SPECIALIST PLACEMENTS

Educational placements for children with SLI have changed drastically over the last 40 years and are still changing today. With an estimated prevalence of 5–7% (see Law et al., 1998, chapter 3 for a full review; see also Leonard, 1998; for prevalence among kindergarten children see Beitchman, Nair, Clegg, & Patel, 1986 and Tomblin, Records, & Zhang, 1996), these language impairments represent one of the most problematic areas for special educational needs services. The specific nature of children's problems means they cannot easily be educated in schools for those with moderate learning difficulties.[1] Yet because language is so vital to the development of social, educational and cognitive abilities, children with SLI are also difficult to support in an extra-curricular way and often need a more intensive environment for language learning. This balance of specialist need and integration into mainstream education was not realised in legislation in Britain until the 1981 Education Act, whereas the US and some European countries assigned this duty to local authorities much earlier (Conti-Ramsden, 1993).

One of the earliest reports on the types of placements available for children with SLI was conducted by Hutt and Donlan (1987) for Invalid Children's Aid Nationwide (ICAN: a body which provides and supports specialist language schools in Britain[2]). These authors emphasised the huge increase in specialist places for children with SLI, from about four residential schools offering 60 places in 1962, to 240 language units and schools across the UK in the late 1980s. The lan-

guage unit has now become the most widely-used form of educational placement when difficulties are severe enough to warrant a Statement of Educational Needs. Language units will be described later in this chapter.

Summary of current placements for children with SLI

If we assume, following Law and colleagues (1998), that SLI affects 5% of all children in Britain at any given age, along with Hutt and Donlan's (1987) and Conti-Ramsden's (1993) reports of the proportions of children attending certain types of placement, rough estimates of the current educational distribution of Year 2 children with SLI can be produced. Statistics supplied by the Department for Education and Environment regarding schools in England (DfEE, 1996) provide information on children attending school for the age band 5–10 years. If we divide this figure by year group we can estimate the number of children attending Year 2 in 1996. Based on these statistics, approximately 715,000 children were attending Year 2 in England, i.e. there were approximately 715,000 seven-year-olds in schools in England in 1996. With a prevalence figure of 5%, there would be approximately 36,000 Year 2 children with SLI in England in 1996. Our study found that approximately 500 Year 2 children were attending language units in England at that time, representing 0.07% of all Year 2 children (Lindsay & Dockrell, 1998). Furthermore, we can estimate that around 50 seven-year-olds (Year 2 children) would have been attending special language schools, representing 0.01% of the Year 2 population. Approximately 4700 Year 2 children were withdrawn from class for language support in mainstream schools (any type of withdrawal), representing 0.7% of the Year 2 population. Finally, approximately 1400 Year 2 children were identified as SLI in mainstream schools and were catered for via modifications in the school curriculum and a whole school approach. This represents 0.2% of the Year 2 population. Taken together, these figures suggest that 1% of the entire Year 2 primary school population is identified and receive special educational provision specifically designed for children with

SLI, leaving 4% with other educational arrangements. Thus, we estimate that 80% of children with SLI are not receiving specialist educational provision.

It is likely that a large number of these children have problems that are not severe enough to warrant specialist educational input, and are equally well provided for by regular attendance at a speech-language therapy clinic, either at a local centre or nearby hospital. Others may attend schools for children with moderate learning difficulties (henceforth referred to as MLD schools) whose changing role is discussed more fully below. Yet another subgroup may be children with pragmatic language impairment, who may begin by being identified by speech-language therapy services, but later show a more pervasive difficulty. These children may be placed in mainstream schools with non-language support or attend schools for children with autism or communication disorders. As mentioned later, there may also be children who are not identified, or who have been fully integrated into mainstream education despite their language impairment.

What is a "language unit"?

Language units are classes, usually within mainstream schools, which offer an intensive language learning environment. In the recent Nuffield Foundation Study involving 118 language units in England (Botting, Conti-Ramsden, & Crutchley, 1998), we found that these units usually have a class teacher who is experienced and/or specially trained in the difficulties of children with SLI, a classroom assistant or other auxiliary in each class (sometimes more than one) and a class size of about 8–10 children. Importantly, language units also have the expertise of a speech-language therapist for half the school week (on average — units vary significantly from only half a day to full-time speech therapy staff). A few units also have their own midday assistant or speech therapy assistant.

As can be seen from this description, the ratio and level of expertise is substantial in these units and although all children follow the National Curriculum there is more opportunity in language units for individualised teaching programmes and to build language learning into all activities. Typically, children spend their school day in the language class and integrate as they are able with the mainstream classes. For about a quarter of the children, this is only during assembly and break-times. For others it may be half the school day. Often, teachers are able to integrate children into the year below the child's chronological age to enable learning and prevent feelings of failure. Children are sometimes integrated into their local school to aid smooth return to a mainstream school in their area. Many units aid language development by using a signing system (Makaton or Paget-Gorman are the most widely used) in order to support learning; others have a symbol or colour system to enhance communication. Some even have specialised computer equipment with voice systems enabling children to relate written text to spoken language, to copy speech sounds from the computer or to hear their own words repeated back.

The children attending language units

Children attending language units vary enormously, both across units and within units. Some centres have stricter entry criteria than others, leading to a more homogeneous group of children. One advantage of the Nuffield Foundation Study was that we were able to gain an average national picture and produce some overall descriptions.

COGNITIVE ABILITY

Since units try to establish that all children have normal cognitive abilities before they are given a place, it stands to reason that most children should score within the normal range on a test of nonverbal ability. We found that 88% of the children with SLI in the Nuffield study were within 1 SD of the normal level for their age in a test of nonverbal skills. A further 10% were between 1 and 2 SD of this norm and thus fell into a borderline range. This left only 2% who showed signs of a

FIGURE 12.1

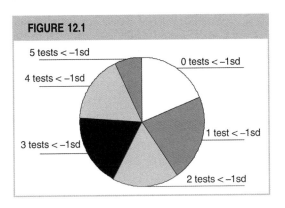

5 tests < –1sd
4 tests < –1sd
3 tests < –1sd
0 tests < –1sd
1 test < –1sd
2 tests < –1sd

Proportions of children with different degrees of SLI severity, showing number of test scores 1 SD or more below the mean.

more global delay affecting not just language but other areas of development (Conti-Ramsden & Botting, 1999a).

Severity of impairment

The majority of children in language units have a number of different language difficulties. Indeed, several professionals working in these centres reported that this is increasingly the case. In the Nuffield Foundation Study, 81% of children had impaired skills on more than one test of oral language abilities. The breakdown of severity of impairment is shown in Fig. 12.1.

Interestingly, about a fifth of children (19%) did not have any language scores falling below the normal range. However, nearly all of this group (98%) had a very large discrepancy between cognitive ability and language skill (40 centiles[3]), indicating that they are communicating well below the level expected according to intellect. As Fig. 12.1 shows, approximately 22% of the children had at least one test 1 standard deviation (SD) below the mean, 17% had 2 tests below –1 SD, 18% had 3 tests below –1 SD, 17% had 4 tests below –1 SD, and 7% had 5 tests below –1 SD. Another way of looking at severity is taking –2 SD as the cut-off point. Less than half the children in the cohort (42%) had very poor scores (below –2 SD) on at least one test. Thirty percent scored below –2 SD on one test only, 8% scored very poorly on two tests and a further 4% scored below –2 SD on three tests of language. Only one child scored below this threshold on four out of the five tests used in the analysis.

Types of impairments

Seven aspects of language skill were assessed in the Nuffield Foundation Study. Table 12.1 summarises how many children in the sample had difficulties with each area, including two measures (number skills, word reading) that were not measures of oral language. Numbers do not total 242 (sample size) and percentages do not add to

TABLE 12.1

Proportions of children with SLI showing difficulties in specific skill areas

Area of impairment	Proportion (number) below –1 SD	Proportion (number) below –2 SD
Number skills/concepts[†]	66% (159/241)	24% (57/241)
Understanding grammar	49% (119/242)	14% (33/242)
Producing correct grammar	59% (116/197)	34% (64/197)
Story retelling	55% (128/231)	52% (119/231)*
Word reading[+]	58% (139/239)	20% (48/239)
Phonology/articulation	32% (75/237)	11% (25/237)
Naming objects	32% (77/241)	9% (22/241)

* proportion below 5th centile — not possible to calculate more accurately given test information.
[+] not oral-language tests

100 since, as we have seen above, children often have more than one area of difficulty.

As can be seen, a large proportion of children with SLI had difficulty with number skills at this age, possibly reflecting the receptive language skills required for the task. About half of the children in language units scored below the normal range on the understanding and expression of grammar, story retelling and word reading. Interestingly, only a third of children showed difficulties with phonology/articulation or with naming objects.

We were interested to see what proportion of children showed different combinations of impairments. Five unique profiles of difficulty (and one including children with normal scores) could be identified to describe the children, based on the assessments carried out. One profile involved children with SLI who performed poorly in all tests and appeared to have severe difficulties across all areas of language, a group we currently refer to as children with severe Expressive and Receptive Impairments. The second profile consisted of children with SLI who had difficulties retelling a story in the context of good phonology, good expressive vocabulary, good word reading and adequate comprehension of grammar. The teachers of these children considered their problems to be tied to the social use of language. This group we currently refer to as children with Pragmatic Language Impairments. A third profile entailed children with SLI who had difficulties with the comprehension of grammar, word reading and retelling a story in the context of good phonology and adequate expressive vocabulary. This group we currently refer to as children with Complex Multi-word Deficits. Fourth were children with SLI who had difficulties with word reading, phonology, and retelling a story in the context of good expressive vocabulary and adequate comprehension of grammar. This group we refer to as children with Expressive-Phonological Impairments. A fifth group of children were very similar to children with Expressive-Phonological SLI but their expressive vocabulary was not as good as the children with Expressive-Phonological SLI. We refer to this group as children with Phonological and Single Word Deficits. The largest group was the first of

these — Expressive and Receptive Impairments — which included 84 of the 242 children in the study (Conti-Ramsden, Crutchley, & Botting, 1997).

It was also possible to classify each child according to more general terminology based on currently-used clinical descriptions, namely, "expressive" (problems with producing language) and "receptive" (problems in understanding language). Just over half of the children in the study had a mixture of expressive and receptive impairments (ER–SLI), while 38% had mainly expressive difficulties (E–SLI). A smaller group appeared to have difficulties both with understanding language and also with the social use of language or pragmatic skills and these children are referred to as children with complex impairments (C–SLI) (Conti-Ramsden & Botting, 1999a).

These results suggest that language units are largely addressing the needs of children who have severe and mixed impairments rather than individuals presenting with circumscribed deficits such as speech impairments or word-finding difficulties. In addition, teachers and speech-language therapists reported an impression that they were dealing with increasing numbers of children with complex, pragmatic problems. Thus, it may well be that the proportions of children with different profiles of impairment attending language units are changing.

OTHER DIFFICULTIES

Behavioural difficulties are not unusual in children with language impairment, but presumably such difficulties must be secondary to the linguistic difficulties for a child to fall into the diagnostic category of SLI. In the Nuffield Foundation Study we found that about 40% of the children had anti-social or emotional problems in addition to their language impairment. These may arise from frustration about not being able to communicate effectively. For the teachers and staff, they represent a serious management issue, both within the language unit and especially when integration is considered. Social difficulties were also prevalent in the cohort of children we studied. This was especially true for children with severe Express-ive and Receptive Impairments and those with Pragmatic Language Impairments. As children grow older and become more aware of their com-munication difficulties, behavioural problems can become a major concern. As with most impaired groups, bullying is thought to be a frequent prob-lem for children with SLI. In our current Nuffield Foundation Study we are documenting more precisely the incidence of being bullied amongst 11-year-olds who attended language units at age 7 years.

Other difficulties often co-occur with SLI, particularly regarding motor control and medical conditions (unrelated to the cause of the lan-guage deficits). Twenty-five percent of children in the Nuffield Foundation Study were receiv-ing additional physio- or occupational therapy, whilst 27% received other medical treatment or consultations.

What determines the type of educational placement for children with SLI in England?

The educational placement of a child with SLI is a complex process. The majority of those attending language units will have a Statement of Educational Needs (95% of those in the Nuffield Foundation Study) which states the child's needs from the perspective of the key individuals in-volved in his or her education. However, there are a number of factors that contribute to this document and the way in which it is put into practice. Table 12.2 lists seven main influences (both explicit and implicit) on the decision-making process in England.

Child's language impairment and additional difficulties

Obviously, the child's own needs and develop-mental level should be foremost in any decision about educational placement. In most areas, some kind of formal criterion is in operation which specifies how severe a language impairment must be to receive language unit provision. This level is usually set at there being at least one aspect of

TABLE 12.2
Educational placement: Influences on the decision-making process
1. Child's language impairment
2. Child's additional difficulties
3. Local Statementing process
4. Area policy and professional beliefs
5. Availability of provision
6. Practical considerations (e.g. transport)
7. Parental attitude

language development more than 1 SD below the mean for the child's age. In addition, most units insist that non-verbal cognitive development be normal or above (i.e. between one SD below the population mean and two SDs above the mean). Some units also specify other criteria such that only children with comprehension difficulties or only those with speech or mild expressive impair-ments be allowed a place. Although English as a second language (ESL) is sometimes used as an exclusionary criterion in units, our team does not believe that this should be the case as long as SLI can be shown. This may be identified through both English and another language showing delay or disorder, through satisfactory bilingual testing or within schools that have a large ESL popula-tion and are experienced at recognising the dif-ference between this type of delay and one caused by SLI. There are serious doubts about the validity of regular English standardised tests with bilingual populations, even when an inter-preter is present (Crutchley, Botting, & Conti-Ramsden, 1997; Crutchley, Conti-Ramsden, & Botting, 1997).

Severe behavioural difficulties or a diagnosis of autism are also factors which prevent children from getting a language unit place although, especially with the latter, the cut-off levels are diffi-cult to establish (see Botting, 1998; and Botting & Conti-Ramsden, 1999). Recently, administra-tion of placements has been executed by a "panel" of experts working for the Local Educational Authorities (LEA). This has frustrated some lan-guage unit staff, many of whom used to make their own decisions about who entered. In particular, they now have little influence over the *balance* of children with different problems they take on or over the mix of gender and age within their class, which inevitably makes the job of the professionals much harder.

We were unable to "pin down" exactly what model was adopted by educationalists in moving children from the language units. However, we could identify a number of factors that were linked to those children who moved. First, a set of key skills was revealed in children who moved. These included good number skills, articulation and expressive skills (naming and grammar). Interestingly, the children who moved did not have higher non-verbal scores, fewer behavioural difficulties or better social skills than children who remained in language units. This suggests that children were selected for the units correctly (i.e. just on the basis of language difficulties) as reported in Conti-Ramsden and Botting (1999a), and that language skills were the underlying basis for changes in children's placements. It seems intuitive that articulation might be a key factor in deciding to move a child from a language unit, since unintelligibility represents a major obstacle in accessing mainstream school both educationally and socially. The other factors are less obvious. Number skills may be a salient expectation of the receiving schools who often worry about the level of competence of other, non-language aspects of the curriculum. A more likely explanation is that the particular test of number skills used is actually also a good assessment of complex understanding and pragmatic ability. For example, this test requires children to understand the terms "more", "less", "shared by", and to grasp changes in question format.

As well as child-based factors, children who had been in the unit longer were also more likely to move at 8 years. We believe that this is not a reflection of pressure to move children and a policy of "first in, first out", since the majority of units could and did keep children on their registers, even in some cases beyond the official age limit of the unit. Rather, we feel it gives some indication of the efficacy of the language unit. Children who had been in the unit longer have had a chance

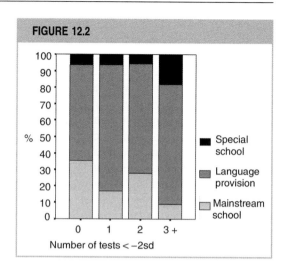

FIGURE 12.2

Number of tests < –2sd

Placement after language unit by impairment *severity*.

to work and develop their language skills enough to warrant integration.

The severity of the language impairment did not affect whether the child moved out of the unit. This is because children with mild impairments moved to mainstream, whilst children with severe difficulties moved to other special placements, e.g. special schools. Hence severity determined in part the *type* of placement the children attended after the unit. Those with three or more language tests below –2 SD (n = 11) were more likely than others to be in the small group of children (14 in total) who moved to special school. Figure 12.2 shows the proportions of severity in each placement type. The general type of language impairment (as outlined earlier) also affected placement as seen in Fig. 12.3. Children with complex language difficulties were more likely to attend special school.

Statementing methods and area policy

Educational placements for children with special needs in England are decided upon in a non-uniform manner across counties and at different times. The vast majority of children needing special help for language will have been subject to the process in which a Statement of Educational Needs is drawn up. Several LEAs prefer State-

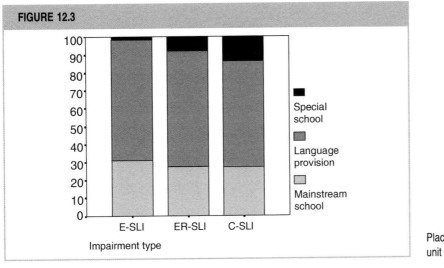

FIGURE 12.3

Placement after language
unit by impairment *type.*

ments to be available only after certain ages or key stages. Most areas now have a "panel" system in which a group decision is made by a collection of professionals whilst others have a professional employed specifically to allocate places. There have been occasions in which the Statementing process takes so long to complete that unfilled places are available in the local unit, but appropriate children are not able to attend without the completed paperwork. In areas where there are strong beliefs about placements and labelling, decisions may be biased towards a particular educational option. This is particularly true where the professional bodies concerned are keen to highlight autistic features or where much time, money and interest have been channelled into schools for those with autism or into autism "teams". Elsewhere, the authority may be strongly in favour of total integration, with special placements reserved only for children with very severe difficulties.

Availability of provision

Even if the Statementing policy in an area allows for recommendation of a language unit or school placement for a child, the number of places available in an authority are limited and waiting lists are a common feature of specialist provision. This presents obvious difficulties since the waiting children continue in mainstream settings, possibly experiencing increasing failure and frustration. As with many services, waiting lists are also not a straightforward turn-over of waiting individuals, but are accessed according to severity of difficulty and suitability of available placements. Hence a child with a relatively mild difficulty may continually be put back and might never gain a place. As already mentioned, there has been a great increase in specialist placements available. However, the current trend for inclusion into mainstream has made it difficult for new units to be justified. The most obvious dearth of language unit places occurs at secondary school age, when most children must be placed elsewhere. It used to be thought that children suited to language units would improve sufficiently by this age. However, there seems to be an increasing number of children in language units who have complex language impairments such as pragmatic difficulties or lexical-syntactic deficits that are both expressive and receptive, and these children have no special provision made for them. Our current Nuffield Foundation study is investigating the educational moves of children in the original cohort from primary to secondary education with a view to documenting the educational outcomes of children who originally attended language units at age 7 years.

Practical considerations

Rural counties present a further complication. In some areas, the recommended language unit is more than one hour's drive from the child's home, and it is therefore impractical to offer a place to the child. Even in areas where the unit is reachable, children travel by taxi or bus on journeys of up to an hour. This journey considerably lengthens the child's school day, and some parents are not willing to let very young children travel so far. Without personal transport, the language unit place becomes untenable for such families.

Parental attitudes

One of the most important factors in the placement of a child with SLI is the understanding and attitude of the parents. It is quite usual for parents initially to reject the idea of a specialist placement of any kind, and language units often invite new parents to see the school and language base for themselves. Parental attitude can also work in the opposite direction when a child comes to leave the unit. Many parents fight the decision to fully integrate because by this time their child has established a positive attitude toward the unit, is gaining language skills and has the benefits of a high teacher-child ratio. Although sometimes the child does require more help and support is removed too early, quite often parents are pleasantly surprised at how well their child copes in mainstream schooling.

Another factor noted during the Nuffield Foundation Study was that the determination and knowledge of the parent may affect the placement process. Some parents told us that they had written or telephoned the LEA with almost immediate results. One mother even employed a solicitor and gained a place for her son the following day. On the other hand, some parents also told us how they had waited years before they realised specialist provision existed and only then persuaded schools to ask for a full assessment. Other parents have told us that they did not ask for help because they did not know that language units, educational psychologists or Statements existed, or because they believed that the right to extra help was time-limited. Although these are only anecdotal histories, it is obviously vitally important that persuasion or parents' educational level should not dictate whether there is a fair process of placement.

It is very important that parents are properly informed about educational placements, including the process, the ideal placement and the realistic options. The charity Afasic, who run a telephone help-line for parents of children with SLI, told us that often families feel that they are being cheated of a better deal when, in fact, they are waiting the usual time for an appropriate place but have not been informed realistically of the process or options.

Potential difficulties in language unit placement

One of the major practical implications of attending a language unit is that the child's school is unlikely to be local. This means that, for families with more than one child, the siblings must attend different establishments, causing both social and practical problems. Most authorities provide a taxi or coach service to transport the child to the language unit, but often this journey can take an hour each way (especially with dropping off or collecting other children) and parents sometimes express concern that their child is simply exhausted from the sheer length of the school day. The additional difficulties of rural counties have already been discussed.

A large number of language units are mixed age classes because of the small numbers of pupils. Sometimes parents worry that this does not provide an appropriate developmental environment, especially where children find themselves at the top end of the age range (e.g. 11 years) with a group of new entrants (e.g. 5 years). However, these worries are usually unfounded and a mixed age group can be an advantage if managed sensitively. Headteachers and sometimes parents feel that children in language units are falling behind on the National Curriculum because they are too isolated from mainstream education or because there is too much emphasis on language skills (see also later discussion under alternative models). Although individuals placed in this provision are indeed often delayed in their educational progress, it is very difficult to separate the effect of severe language impairment on educational progress from that caused by exclusion from mainstream teaching, and it is more than likely that the former is the reason for falling behind. If this is the case, it is even more imperative that the language skills of children with SLI are brought up to sufficient levels as efficiently as possible.

DIFFERENT MODELS OF EDUCATIONAL PROVISION FOR CHILDREN WITH SLI

As mentioned earlier, the majority of children with some kind of SLI are not being educated in language units at Year 2. This may be because they do not have severe enough problems to warrant a full-time language unit place, or because they didn't meet entry criteria or because the identification process is not accurate enough, allowing some to "slip through the net". There are also other, less direct, causes discussed elsewhere in this chapter such as local authority pressure or parental opinions. The main different forms of placements for children with SLI who require extra educational help including language unit are shown below.

Withdrawal and support systems versus intensive language bases

In general, it is the belief of most speech and language therapists that an intensive language base gives a child with SLI the best chance of learning to communicate effectively. However, apart from the problems described earlier in this chapter, there are also other factors that suggest the withdrawal methods and in-class support methods may have their own advantages worth considering.

First, there is the financial aspect. Intensive language units are costly to set up and to run on a daily basis. Second, many mainstream teachers and headteachers believe that keeping the children within the mainstream class has a better outcome both in terms of social and educational skills, although this has not been systematically investigated. This is an ongoing disagreement especially where reintegration of children from language units is concerned. Headteachers may feel that the mainstream member of staff is not experienced enough with the child's difficulties or that the child has simply "missed too much of the curriculum" to be able to function well within the class. In addition, language units effectively make it possible for the schools to be free from the added concern of a number of children with more or less severe SLI.

Reverse integration

Some language units or bases practise reverse integration. In these bases, children from the mainstream school are invited in small groups to join the language class for some activities. The advantages to this approach are many. First, the children attending the unit feel socially and educationally united with the mainstream classes; they are able to make friends in a structured environment with whom they can then mix successfully in (less structured) all-school sessions such as playtime or assembly. At the same time, the numbers of children joining the language base are small enough not to frighten, intimidate or overwhelm the children with SLI, as can happen when children participate in regular integration activities in mainstream school (Conti-Ramsden, 1993; Hurtford & Hart, 1979). To aid this process, the guest children may be peers or children from a younger class. Reverse integration also has potential benefits for the guest children and for general school-language unit relations, in breaking down barriers and prejudice that may exist between the two bases and indeed between non-impaired and impaired individuals of all types. Unfortunately, during the course of the Nuffield Foundation Study very few schools were operating this system, largely because of the extra time and organisation that is required of already hard-pressed teaching staff.

LANGUAGE UNIT TECHNIQUES
AND ORGANISATION

At present, there is no model of language unit intervention that is universally adopted. Each base uses its own system of therapy and education depending on class size, resources and personal beliefs. A few units have adopted a particular system and use a strict methodology, but these are the exception and most use a hybrid of different models and training. These may include imitation (child directly copies therapist), modelling (therapist models correct form but child does not imitate; instead he observes or generates a new example), or recasting (therapist uses play situations using the child's utterances and recasts them to include a target word (Camarata, Nelson, & Camarata, 1994; Nelson et al., 1996; Fey & Proctor-Williams, chapter 10, this volume)). These methods are discussed fully in Leonard (1998) in the form of experimental techniques where subtle differences are preserved. In many cases, language units combine these systems to provide a more flexible mixture of these effective interventions. "Milieu" teaching (which involves creating a setting which encourages communication and in which responses by professionals maximise language use) is probably an accurate description of most language classrooms, with the therapist and teacher working together on this language-intensive style and co-running some group work (Yoder, Kaiser, & Alpert, 1991). In addition, most units use the speech-language therapist on a one-to-one basis where children are given individual time once (or more) a week using more specific techniques. Occasionally, intervention style is very formal with the therapist working almost independently, withdrawing the child from the language base. In a few classes, therapists do almost no individual sessions and work jointly alongside the teacher for much of their time. This variation in situation makes the efficacy of specific types of intervention particularly difficult to assess in practice. It would be very helpful to language bases, especially those just setting up, to have a summary of which systems are most effective. However, no such overall picture exists yet.

Another factor is the amount of speech-language therapy time available. This varies from school to school. Most therapists are funded through the Regional Health Authority, which means that they have different line management and sometimes different aims from the teacher. This funding arrangement also means that the therapist has a regular caseload of individuals at the hospital base, and therapists are often over-stretched regarding the workload and different roles they are expected to perform. Many of the specific techniques tested experimentally require more therapist input per child than is currently available in language units. In the few schools where therapists are funded through education, the posts are full time.

Educational placements for children who do not attend the placement of choice

In actuality, places at language units are limited. Sometimes children do not gain a place in one of these classes simply because there are "more deserving cases", or because parents have not pushed as hard as others or are reluctant for the child to attend special provision. In other circumstances, units have an upper age limit so that children are inevitably moved into an alternative placement. This last reason is most common at secondary school age, when the number of places within unit provision becomes very small indeed. A range of other provisions are used for children who do not get their placement of choice in a language unit.

First, schools for those with moderate learning difficulties (MLD) may be used. There has been concern about children with SLI being placed in an environment designed for children with general learning difficulties. This concern is appropriate since children with SLI are of normal intelligence. However, the level of speech-language therapy available, the advantageous class sizes and generally supportive environment can make this a successful placement, if the school staff understand the child's specific needs. In addition, some schools for children with MLD have explicitly changed their provision, aiming to address general communication difficulties of varying natures and aetiologies and accepting that their population is changing to accommodate children whose needs cannot be met in mainstream schooling. In the Nuffield Foundation Study, of the 128 children whose teachers felt they should stay in language provision, only 3 were placed in units or schools targeting moderate learning delays.

For children who show more pervasive difficulties, including the social use of language and poor conversational skills, schools for children with autism may be considered the best alternative. However, there are potential problems with this approach because of the high motivation to communicate in children with SLI, compared to peers with autism. Furthermore, the key issue of availability of normal models for peer interaction is also of concern. Information about how best to provide meaningful educational experiences for children with SLI with more pervasive difficulties in the social use of language is lacking at present.

Mainstream school with auxiliary support in class, or with regular visits to the speech-language therapy clinic may be sufficient for children whose difficulties are of borderline severity. In our study, 14 of 128 children for whom a continued language unit place was recommended were attending mainstream school one year later. Children who have some other educational needs (even with language as the main impairment) may attend special classes sometimes called "success classes" which operate in mainstream schools in a similar way to language units but which address a general mix of educational needs.

CONCLUSION

Do language units work as an educational placement?

The efficacy of treatment for children with SLI is very difficult to assess. As in other areas of research, results may be influenced by such factors as social class, gender and age. There may also be "protective factors" of a general kind that boost some children's progress. Often these are notoriously difficult to explicate and may include positive parental attitudes to education, motivation to change, good peer relations, and problem-solving ability. Some factors that may also be protective are more tangible, such as high maternal education, high non-verbal IQ and positive self image.

There are other factors in research with SLI that make efficacy studies particularly difficult. First, SLI is a heterogeneous condition that includes individuals with varying types and degree of difficulty (Conti-Ramsden et al., 1997). Second, the definitions or criteria of these subgroups (and indeed of SLI itself) are still developing, with poor agreement across researchers and clinicians alike. Third, as mentioned at the start of this chapter, SLI is a dynamic impairment. Children with these difficulties develop to some extent with or without intervention, either resolving their difficulties or moving from one subgroup of difficulties to another (Conti-Ramsden & Botting, 1999b). Lastly, interventions for children with SLI, unlike medical equivalents which may be reasonably standardised nationwide, vary from unit to unit. Studies examining so-called "waiting list controls" (children recommended for a language unit but waiting for a place) need to be conducted to assess the degree to which such children improve without intensive input compared to varying types of intervention. There needs to be an emphasis on assessing these techniques in real clinical practice as well as in the more controlled experimental environments. In the current Nuffield Foundation study we are also hoping to contribute to the language unit efficacy debate by investigating children with SLI who had similar profiles at age 7 and comparing those who went to mainstream education versus those who remained in language units. In this way we aim to ascertain whether these two groups of children differ in their educational outcomes at age 11 years.

In a recent review of the literature addressing screening for SLI, Law and colleagues conclude that intervention for primary age children is indeed effective. This is true for articulation and phonology, expressive language, receptive language and phoneme awareness (Law et al., 1998). Several different approaches were confirmed as useful by this report, including didactic and naturalistic approaches. Interestingly, parent-led interventions for improving delays in language were found to be as effective as clinician-administered ones. In contrast, for articulation or phonology problems, clinician-led interventions were clearly superior to parent-led interventions. Very few studies have been conducted of receptive language difficulties. This is particularly surprising and of concern given that the Nuffield Study found a large, and expanding, group of such children attending language units. A question of great interest is whether gains seen during intervention have a long-term robustness. Gains seen initially can sometimes be "washed-out" over time (Whitehurst et al., 1991). Without doubt, further research is needed in this area and with particular reference to the forms of treatment used currently in language units.

Studies examining specific techniques are plentiful, but these often have conflicting results or find similar gains across techniques. In another meta-analysis, for example, Nye, Foster and Seaman (1987) examined different types of intervention. Effect sizes were large for all types of intervention and there were no differences between approaches. Leonard (1998) concluded in his chapter on the subject that "we have not reached a point of knowing which approaches are the most effective . . ." (p. 204). It appears, therefore, that some of the most effective intervention is best suited to children who did not feature in large numbers in the Nuffield Foundation Study (i.e. those with speech-related disorders) and hence are infrequently found in language unit provision. Moreover, indirect therapy is reported by Law and colleagues as being equally as effective for children with broader, more receptive, profiles of impairment. This raises important questions for how and why children are selected for entry into language unit provision.

It is our opinion that language units provide an interesting natural experiment where different types of intervention can be evaluated. But, as mentioned at the beginning of the chapter, language units provide services for a relatively small proportion of children with SLI. In addition, the role of language units themselves needs to be re-examined in light of the increasing number of children with more complex and pervasive problems. Currently language units are conceived as short-term "booster" placements that offer effective intervention for children with SLI. The "short-term" aspect of language units may need to be re-examined in light of our findings of persistent problems in a proportion of children with SLI with complex and severe language difficulties. One possible model that could be adopted could involve setting up communication centres similar to those adopted by some schools for children with moderate learning difficulties. Such communication centres could cater specifically for children with a wide range of language difficulties of a complex and pervasive kind. Such centres or units could develop expertise in working with these children. This approach would allow a proportion of language units to maintain their model of a short-term "booster" placement for those children who are able to develop their language skills within the first years of primary education.

ACKNOWLEDGEMENTS

The authors gratefully acknowledge the support of the Nuffield Foundation for Grant No. AT251[OD] and Brian Faragher for his statistical advice.

NOTES

1. In the UK, the term "learning difficulties" refers to global delay in cognitive development rather than specific difficulties.
2. ICAN. ICAN Central office, Barbican Citygate, 1–3 Dufferin Street, London EC1Y 8NA. ICAN is a registered charity.
3. This figure was worked out by a statistician to represent a clinically significant difference even across the most frequent centile score range on a normal distribution.

REFERENCES

Beitchman, J.H., Nair, R., Clegg, M., & Patel, P.G. (1986). Prevalence of speech and language disorders in 5 year old kindergarten children in the Ottawa-Carleton region. *Journal of Speech and Hearing Disorders, 51*, 98–110.

Bishop, D.V.M. (1997). *Uncommon understanding: Development and disorders of language comprehension in children.* Hove, UK: Psychology Press.

Botting, N., & Conti-Ramsden, G. (1999). Pragmatic language impairment without autism: The children in question. *Autism, 3*, 371–396.

Botting, N. (1998). Semantic-pragmatic disorder as a distinct diagnostic entity: Making sense of the boundaries (a comment on Boucher). *International Journal of Language and Communication Disorders, 33*, 71–108.

Botting, N., Conti-Ramsden, G., & Crutchley, A. (1998). Educational transitions from a clinical perspective: A reply to commentaries. *International Journal of Language and Communication Disorders, 33*, 215–220.

Camarata, S.M., Nelson, K.E., & Camarata, M.N. (1994). Comparison of conversational recasting and imitative procedures for training grammatical structures in children with specific language impairment. *Journal of Speech and Hearing Research, 37*, 1414–1423.

Conti-Ramsden, G., & Botting, N. (1999a). Classification of children with specific language impairment. *Journal of Speech, Language, and Hearing Research, 42*, 1195–1204.

Conti-Ramsden, G., & Botting, N. (1999b). Characteristics of children attending language units in England: A national study of 7-year-olds. *International Journal of Language and Communication Disorders, 34*, 359–366.

Conti-Ramsden, G., Crutchley, A., & Botting, N. (1997). The extent to which psychometric tests differentiate subgroups of children with specific language impairment. *Journal of Speech, Language, and Hearing Research, 40*, 765–777.

Conti-Ramsden, G. (1993). Integration of children with specific language impairments. *European Journal of Special Needs Education, 8*, 240–248.

Crutchley, A., Botting, N., & Conti-Ramsden, G. (1997). Bilingualism and specific language impairment in children attending language units. *European Journal of Disorders of Communication, 32*, 267–276.

Crutchley, A., Conti-Ramsden, G., & Botting, N. (1997). Bilingual children with specific language impairment and standardised assessments: Preliminary findings from a study of children in language units. *International Journal of Bilingualism, 1*, 117–134.

Department of Education and Environment (1996). *Statistics of Education: Schools in England.* London: DfEE.

Hurtford, A., & Hart, D. (1979). Social integration in a language unit. *Special Education Forward Trends, 8*, 8–10.

Hutt, E., & Donlan, C. (1987). *Adequate provision? A survey of language units.* London: ICAN.

Law, J., Boyle, J., Harris, F., Harkness, A., & Nye, C. (1998). Screening for speech and language delay: A systematic review of the literature. *Health Technology Assessment, 2*, 1–184.

Leonard, L. (1998). *Children with specific language impairment.* Cambridge, MA: MIT Press.

Lindsay, G., & Dockrell, J.E. (1998). What's in a transition? A reply to Botting, Crutchley and Conti-Ramsden. *International Journal of Language and Communication Disorders, 33*, 198–207.

Nelson, K.E., Camarata, S.H., Welsh, J., Butkovsky, L., & Camarata, M. (1996). Effects of imitative and conversational recasting treatment on the acquisition of grammar in children with specific language impairment and younger language-normal children. *Journal of Speech, Language, and Hearing Research, 39*, 850–859.

Nye, C., Foster, S., & Seaman, D. (1987). Effectiveness of language intervention with the language/learning disabled. *Journal of Speech and Hearing Disorders, 52*, 348–357.

Tomblin, J.B., Records, N.L., & Zhang, X. (1996). A system for the diagnosis of specific language impairment in kindergarten children. *Journal of Speech, Language, and Hearing Research, 39*, 1284–1294.

Whitehurst, G.J., Fischel, J.E., Lonigan, C.J., Valdez-Menchaca, M.C., Arnold, D.S., & Smith, M. (1991). Treatment of early expressive language delay: If, when and how. *Topics in Language Disorders, 11*, 55–68.

Yoder, P.J., Kaiser, A.P., & Alpert, C.L. (1991). An exploratory study of the interaction between language teaching methods and child characteristics. *Journal of Speech, and Hearing Research, 34*, 155–167.

13

Language difficulties and psychopathology

Ian M. Goodyer

Children with speech and language difficulties (SLD) have an increased rate of emotional and behavioural disorders compared with the community at large. In the pre-school years, over-activity, attentional difficulties, wetting and soiling are particularly evident. At school age, attentional difficulties persist, but other emotional and behavioural problems also become apparent. Antisocial behaviour may be seen in those language-impaired children who go on to develop literacy problems. Furthermore, many children referred to psychiatric clinics have un-detected language difficulties. There are several possible explanations for an association between language and behavioural difficulties. Some behavioural problems in young children with SLD may be indicative of underlying neurodevelopmental immaturity. Common environmental risk factors may lead to a constellation of developmental difficulties. In other cases, the adverse experience of communication difficulty may put the child at risk for emotional or antisocial disorders. The relationship between linguistic and nonlinguistic difficulties is likely to change with age, and may be influenced by the child's social environment. Behavioural symptoms and syndromes are not usually considered when classifying SLD. It is proposed that when subtyping speech and language disorders it may be helpful to incorporate non-linguistic as well as linguistic features, taking into account the degree of personal impairment experienced by the child, as well as performance on standardised tests.

INTRODUCTION

Over the past three decades it has become apparent that around 50% of children with speech and language difficulties have a range of associated emotional and behavioural problems, a rate that is at least three times higher than that in the community at large (Beitchman, Hood, & Inglis, 1990; Beitchman, Hood, Rochon, & Peterson, 1989a). For some young children these associated difficulties appear to be an understandable consequence of their speech and language impairment, such as persistent frustration at failing to make their needs and desires understood. For others, however, the reasons for associated problems, such as social disinterest and/or impulsiveness, are less clear and may be present even when the child is not engaged in attempts at communicating with another person. Those reported most frequently are soiling, wetting, temper tantrums, general worry, social withdrawal and/or disinterest in peers (Stevenson, 1996). Although these co-existing clinical features have been frequently recorded, there have been few studies designed to systematically characterise the concurrent patterns of signs and symptoms in language and behaviour, or to investigate the mechanisms and processes linking language difficulties and psychopathology. It remains possible that the phenotypic differences in both linguistic and behavioural terms indicate potentially distinct types of disorder with differing causes and outcomes. If this were true, then the associated behavioural difficulties would not be merely a consequence of communication frustration but in some cases reflect a different underlying developmental or possible disease process. To determine the validity of these ideas requires concurrent investigation of the nature and characteristics of emotional and behavioural features together with those of speech and language. This chapter reviews the findings of this field of inquiry and considers the implications of current knowledge for clinical practice and future research. The acronym SLI is used to refer to children who have received a particular diagnosis of specific language impairment, and SLD when the broader notion of children with speech and language difficulties is being discussed.

Measuring language and behaviour

Concurrent measurement of emotions and behaviour is not straightforward in a population where communication with and comprehension of others is a major focus of difficulty. There are a number of methodological hurdles that need to be taken into account when designing such projects (Rutter & Mawhood, 1991). First, there is clear evidence that language disorders are heterogeneous in type and in severity. Second, studies have to take into account the effects of other factors that may influence language and behavioural development, such as variations in general intelligence within the normal range. Third, there needs to be concurrent measurement of behaviours using procedures that can distinguish language-related and non-related symptoms.

Ideally, studies should be community based and longitudinal in design, to prevent the bias inherent in studying clinical samples and to take into account the effects of development on both speech and language acquisition and the behavioural phenotype. Community samples are, however, likely to contain a smaller proportion of complex cases, and studies may benefit from incorporating clinically-based populations (so-called "enriched studies"), using the same methods. Attention also needs to be paid to obtaining the appropriate control group. For example, if the investigation is determining the nature and characteristics and outcome of SLI populations then comparisons are required between three samples of children, one with language difficulties alone, a second with associated behaviour problems, and a third with behaviour problems alone. Variations in development may affect both language and behaviour, and narrowing the age range of populations studied may provide clearer evidence of specific language-behaviour patterns. This may also result in more helpful information for clinical services, which are frequently structured around the age and developmental stage of the child.

DEVELOPMENTAL EPIDEMIOLOGY

Specific language impairments

Clues about the potential relations between SLI and behavioural disorders can be obtained from epidemiological studies of their respective clinical features. Whitehurst and Fischel (1994) recently concluded that language impairments are most prevalent in 2-year-olds (9–17%), dropping to between 3–8% by 3 years and 1–3% by 5 years. By contrast, Tomblin and colleagues (1997) reported an estimated overall prevalence rate of 7.4% for specific language impairments in 4–5-year-old children attending a monolingual English-speaking kindergarten in the Mid West of the United States. The prevalence estimates were 8% for boys and 6% for girls and less than one third of the parents of this sample had previously been informed that their child had a speech or language problem. These results suggest SLI is more prevalent amongst girls than previously reported and than clinical detection remains low amongst 5-year-olds. There are few data concerning the characteristics or prevalence of general speech and language impairments in school-age samples and precise estimates of SLD in middle childhood and adolescence are not known. Beitchman and colleagues (1994) followed up a community ascertained sample of 5-year-old children with SLI and reported that by 12 years of age more than 70% of these children had some kind of persisting impairment in speech and/or language. This suggests a prevalence estimate of SLI between 3–6% by early adolescence. Overall, the epidemiological findings, whilst not entirely consistent, suggest a moderate declining rate of SLI by late childhood/early adolescence. It is possible that many "early cases" of SLI may reflect a "neuro-developmental immaturity" that is resolved by the school-age years. That is to say, the general neural structure and associated cognitive functions that are required for subsequent speech and language are intact but the pace of development is slow even in the presence of an adequate speech and language environment. The data regarding which clinical characteristics in early childhood predict a good prognosis by adolescence are also unclear. Whilst some authorities suggest that relatively "pure" phonological problems are more likely to recover than other forms of SLI, recent longitudinal data suggest that such difficulties in early childhood do not always carry a positive outcome (Beitchman et al., 1996b; Stothard et al., 1998; see also Stackhouse, this volume, for detailed discussion of phonology and related issues). There may be at least two broadly distinct early onset populations of SLI children: i) a developmentally mediated group of disorders characterised by speech difficulties with a relatively high rate of remission, and ii) a large group with wider linguistic dysfunction including phonological impairments and comprehension difficulties and, in some cases, problems with social discourse. Those in this second broad group are particularly likely to be heterogeneous in their characteristics and outcome and have symptoms that persist into school age.

There may also be a group whose difficulties are less apparent until school age. The major feature of these children is their deficits in social communication rather than phonological or syntactic difficulties. Such cases show an inability to engage in everyday discourse and appear to fail to understand the perspective of the other person during a conversation. These deficits in pragmatic communication are complex and have only recently been the subject of reliable systematic inquiry (Bishop, 1998; chapter 6, this volume). Whether or not rates in older children reflect entirely persistent "early onset" disorders with subsequent social communication difficulties or a combination of early and later onset with different characteristics is not known. To date, there are no epidemiological studies of pragmatic language difficulties in school-age children or adolescents.

Behavioural and emotional syndromes

The prevalence rates of the common emotional and behavioural syndromes also vary with age (Costello et al., 1996b; Verhulst & Koot, 1995; Verhulst, van der Ende, Ferdinand, & Kasius, 1997). For example, attention deficit hyperactivity disorder (ADHD) is more prevalent in young children than adolescents, whereas the reverse is true for major depression. Anxiety disorders are relatively common throughout childhood and adolescence but separation anxiety disorder (around 6%) is significantly more likely in childhood, and agoraphobia and panic disorders in adolescence (for an overview of developmental epidemiology see Verhulst et al., 1997). As with some forms of SLI, alterations in rates of behavioural phenotypes may reflect maturational processes of the central nervous system. For example, at the age of six, 5% of the population suffer from enuresis whereas after the age of seven the rate is less than 1%. Similarly, ADHD shows a marked decline in prevalence with age for both child and parent informants, with reported rates by 12–14 years of age being half those of 6–8 year olds (Breton et al., 1999). The combination of phonological disorder and separation anxiety disorder in the pre-school child might be expected to occur by chance if both are frequently found in the pre-school population. Of course, pre-school children with SLI have reasons for staying closer to a known caregiver and such "proximity seeking behaviour" on its own has a protective function and is not indicative of psychopathology unless other signs and symptoms are also present. For example, pre-school children presenting with a combination of enuresis, poor attentional skills and speech difficulties who are unwilling to be separated from their parents may be demonstrating multisystem developmental immaturity and delay in the acquisition of skills, or suffering from a phonological disorder with comorbid ADHD or anxiety syndromes. These comorbid features may be a result of neurodevelopmental immaturities, environmental difficulties secondary to SLD or reflect an increased genetic risk for both anxiety disorders as well as language difficulties. What needs to be established is whether or not the co-occurrence of these features is greater than each alone in the population at large, in order to establish that chance is not the explanation. If significant co-occurrence is established, this might reflect a truly comorbid condition, with potentially different aetiologies for comorbid and "pure", non-comorbid types.

If we do find rates of co-occurrence greater than chance, then there may be a number of dif-ferent aetiological explanations. First, there may be two independent sets of neurodevelopmental factors that result in an increased risk for concurrent language and non-language difficulties; second, a set of shared brain-based factors may increase the risk for both groups of symptoms; third, there may be a set whose direct effects increase one set of symptoms which itself increases the risks for the other. Finally, the influence of the family environment on both the development of language difficulties and behavioural deviance may moderate the liability for symptoms, particularly in groups at risk for these disorders, such as the offspring of parents with a history of SLI, psychopathology or both. (The term "moderate" indicates environmental factors that may influence how a genetic risk is expressed. The direction of these environmental effects depends on their qualities, which may be positive or negative, reducing or increasing overall risk accordingly.)

SPECIFICITY OF LANGUAGE AND BEHAVIOUR SYNDROMES

The possibility that there are different relationships between particular types of language difficulty and forms of behavioural psychopathology has only recently been addressed. There is a notion that some types of SLI reflect a general developmental delay of language, motor and behavioural skills, rather than a specific disorder (Beitchman et al., 1989a, 1989b; Tallal, Dukette, & Curtiss, 1989). In these cases it is suggested that impairments are not independent coexisting disorders but reflect widespread dysfunctional effects of neurodevelopmental delay. The evidence for this is based on relatively few studies and focused almost entirely on 3–7 year old populations ascertained for SLD. As already noted, for example the highest prevalence rates for ADHD (8–13%) are somewhat greater than for SLD and occur in somewhat older populations (Breton et al., 1999). Since the prevalence rates of developmental difficulties vary with age, it is important to compare the co-occurrence of disorders in populations ascertained for both conditions and to note their stability over time.

Attempts to sub-type the associations between language and behaviour difficulties looking for specific sub-syndromes have recently been reported. First, there is a consistent body of evidence confirming that significant behaviour problems are more often associated with comprehension deficits than with speech disorders (Cantwell & Baker, 1987; Rapin, 1996; Stevenson, 1996; Stevenson, Richman, & Graham, 1985). Children presenting with behaviour disorders are also more likely to have higher rates of other developmental difficulties often associated with lower general intelligence within the normal range, which may include problems with speech and language (Cohen, 1996; Goodman, Simonoff, & Stevenson, 1995). Beitchman and colleagues have proposed that expressive language delay is more associated with ADHD-type symptoms than receptive language delay which appears to have less distinctive behavioural correlates (Beitchman et al., 1989a, 1989b, 1996a). Children with a combination of language and ADHD problems were also noted to have lower IQs and greater difficulties with visuo-motor integration than psychiatric comparison groups of ADHD and non-ADHD behaviour disorders (Beitchman et al., 1994). Unfortunately, there was no comparison with SLI alone, so the argument for a separate sub-group with combined language delay/ADHD, is not, as yet, proven. Indeed, the alternative explanation that these represent simply more severe cases of either or both disorders with the same aetiologies as either alone, is equally as likely.

General intelligence

A number of studies of language-impaired populations have reported that behavioural deviance is increased if the language-impaired group has lower IQ (within the normal range) (Baker & Cantwell, 1987a, 1987b; Beitchman et al., 1989a; Silva, Justin, McGee, & Williams, 1984). It is also clear that the general liability for behavioural deviance is greater among all children with lower IQs within the normal range (Goodman et al., 1995). Lower IQ may indicate a general vulnerability for both language and behaviour problems rather than a specific correlate of either. As yet there is no

clear-cut evidence that there are unique associations between IQ and either behaviour disorders or SLD alone, since few studies have yet reported the relations between behavioural deviance, language function and general intelligence using measures that are reasonably independent of each other. It may be, for example, that in the pre-school child the liabilities for either language or behaviour difficulties arise from a common set of factors indexed by lower IQ. Furthermore, since few studies have taken into account the effects of language impairments on a child's performance on general intelligence tests at any age, it is unclear if other co-occurring syndromes, such as emotional disorders in middle childhood, arise because of factors associated with general intelligence rather than SLD.

The social environment

Two studies have investigated whether there are particular environmental correlates that distinguish between SLI subtypes with and without behaviour disorders. Both studies used young cohorts and confined themselves to rather general psychopathological statements. Beitchman et al. (1989b) found no differences in family background or social class in a large (n = 1655) sample of children ascertained for SLI with and without behaviour problems. By contrast, in a clinical sample Baker and Cantwell (1987b) showed that general psychosocial stresses (marital and family problems, increased daily hassles within the family) were related to behavioural disorders within the language group, which consisted of children with a mixture of speech and language difficulties of varying characteristics and severity. As yet, no firm conclusions can be drawn about the role of general environmental adversities in the onset, course or outcome of complex SLI/behavioural syndromes.

SPEECH AND LANGUAGE DIFFICULTIES IN PSYCHIATRIC POPULATIONS

Cohen and colleagues screened 399 4–12-year-old children attending psychiatric outpatient clinics, excluding children with neurological disorders or pervasive developmental syndromes (Cohen et al., 1993). Using standardised measures of phonology, syntax, semantics, auditory verbal memory and pragmatic skills, they identified three sub-groups: those with previously identified SLI (28%); unsuspected SLI (34%); and a language normal group (62%). The finding that over a third of the psychiatric sample had unsuspected SLI was remarkable.

The authors noted that, compared with the unknown, the known SLI subjects had more severe expressive language and social communication difficulties. There were no differences, however, in their receptive language skills. The authors reasonably concluded that adults' attention was attracted to the more overt expressive language difficulties. It seems likely that covert subtle receptive language problems risk being overlooked in children presenting to psychiatric clinics with behaviour syndromes.

Comparison between all SLI children (suspected and unsuspected) with behavioural disorder and the psychiatric comparison group revealed no substantial differences in the characteristics of their psychopathology. As one would predict, there were high rates of developmental immaturities and ADHD symptoms. However, comparisons between overt known, and covert previously hidden, language difficulty groups revealed significant differences in psychopathology. Overt SLI cases were rated as more socially withdrawn and anxious by their parents whereas the covert group were rated as more aggressive and depressed. These differences appear to be due to the consequences of others knowing, or not knowing, that a child has a language difficulty. Attributing behavioural difficulties to a "linguistic cause" appears likely to alter adult behaviour towards the child for the better. These findings indicate that there are serious psychiatric consequences in overlooking SLI in behaviourally disturbed populations, and that the nature of the behavioural phenotype can be influenced by interpersonal factors. Children's receptive language skills are seldom evaluated when a child with behavioural or emotional symptoms presents for assessment. An important clinical conclusion from this study

is that mental health professionals should consider including language evaluation in their assessment strategies.

In addition to the characteristics within the children themselves, Cohen's group reported higher rates of psychosocial disadvantage (e.g. lower income, poorer housing, greater employment problems amongst parents) for both overt and covert language groups compared to children whose behaviour problems occurred in the context of normally-developing language. The importance of these adverse circumstances is not clear, but for some cases environmental adversities may constrict not just behavioural but also language development. It may be that there are common genetic components that will be expressed as a familial effect. Also, language and cognitive deficits in a parent may limit the direct help they can give their children.

LONG-TERM OUTCOME

A substantial proportion of pre-school children with SLD show persisting language impairments which are not associated with low non-verbal IQ (Leonard, 1991). A longitudinal study of 156 children with such impairment referred to a specialist education centre showed that, as they moved through the school from 6–11 years, the high rates of concurrent overt behavioural disturbance in the younger years declined quite rapidly with age (Haynes & Naidoo, 1991). By contrast, more subtle emotional difficulties characterised by low self-confidence and social withdrawal remained or possibly developed as the children moved into middle childhood. Whether or not this group contained children with new or persisting difficulties with social pragmatics is not known. As with the majority of studies, children with "pure" speech impairments had fewer concurrent or longer term emotional or behaviour problems compared to those with any type of language impairment.

In the clinical sample of Baker and Cantwell (1987b), 202 children with SLI were followed up four years after initial referral. Persistent psychiatric disturbance was predicted by both the severity of the initial SLI and by subsequent social adversities at follow-up.

There have been three epidemiological follow-up studies of children with SLI with very similar findings of high rates of later behaviour problems, social withdrawal and emotional symptoms up to five years after initial referral (Fundudis, Kolvin, & Garside, 1979; Richman, Stevenson, & Graham, 1982; Silva, Williams, & McGee, 1987). These cohorts were between 3–5 years of age at entry and around 8–11 years old at final reassessment. As in the clinical studies, by middle childhood the most prevalent domains of subsequent psychopathology are emotional symptoms and disorders, impaired social relations and attention deficits rather than oppositional, conduct or antisocial behaviours (Rutter & Mawhood, 1991). In the Waltham Forest Study of Stevenson, Richardson and Graham (1985), levels of behaviour difficulty at three years of age were greatest in the children with poor expressive language skills, and these children showed higher levels of emotional symptoms at eight years compared with those with good expressive language at three.

These follow-up studies suggest that some sub-types of early SLI increase the risk for subsequent psychiatric disorders. The risks appear greater for children with comprehension difficulties and perhaps for those with co-existing behaviour problems. By middle childhood there may have been a developmental influence on the expression of the clinical phenotype, with emotional symptoms increasing in prevalence. As many as 10% of children with SLI met criteria for anxiety disorders (Baker & Cantwell, 1987a). Although the majority of children with SLI at any age are boys, it is girls with SLI who appear most at risk for emotional disorders. Challenging behavioural symptoms may be being shaped, perhaps through adverse social experiences and greater cognitive regulation of behaviour, into more internalised negative representations of the self. Girls may be more prone to the development of poor self esteem by adolescence (Block & Robins, 1993) and this might account for the sex difference in the association between SLI and emotional disorder by middle childhood.

Tannock and Schachar (1996) approached the longitudinal relationship between SLI and behaviour disorders via investigations of psychiatric populations. In contrast to those studying behaviour in children with SLI, they noted that in some psychiatric cases, particularly those with attention deficit syndromes, the severity of language-associated behavioural psychopathology increases with age. The degree to which generalisations of language outcome can be made from this study are not clear, as the study population was different from those ascertained by SLI status. There is no evidence, however, that the clinical characteristics of language and behaviour are significantly different between the SLI and psychiatric studies. Rather, the latter may contain cases of greater severity for both language and behaviour and/or greater prevalence rates of SLI with comprehension difficulties and more ADHD disorders in the behaviour group.

It may also be the case that the longitudinal outcome of these complex disorders depends both on the severity of their presenting complaints and how the disorder influences subsequent person–environment interactions. Rather than outcome being evaluated entirely as a function of the language–behaviour profile at one point in time, the more dynamic interrelations between children and their changing environments over time may be important elements in determining the trajectory of early delays and/or disorders.

A striking feature of the studies to date is that comparisons between community, speech clinic and psychiatric clinic cases have not been undertaken. Whether different practitioners are seeing different disorders from distinctive child populations, or those going to psychiatric clinics do so because of the bias in referrers or greater severity of behaviour, is unclear. The current research findings suggest that different populations may indeed be being ascertained from these three domains. The lesson of studies to date is that populations from speech and language and psychiatric clinics, together with community ascertained subjects, should be included in future research. Only by adequate comparisons of the presenting features in different clinical and community settings will a more accurate picture of the phenotype be obtained.

PERSONAL IMPAIRMENT, LANGUAGE AND BEHAVIOUR

For the majority of syndromes in young people it is increasingly recognised that both clinical heterogeneity and level of impairment are important aspects of psychopathology that may indicate independent subtypes of disorder with differing aetiologies and outcomes (Costello et al., 1996a). For example, assessing comorbid disorders in emotional syndromes has resulted in delineating a subgroup of familial panic disorders that are clinically distinct from those associated with major depression (Goldstein et al., 1994). Similarly, in first episode major depression, comorbid obsessive–compulsive disorder at presentation has been noted to specifically predict persistent depression whereas comorbid conduct disorder predicts persistent non-depressive syndromes (Goodyer, Herbert, Secher, & Pearson, 1997). Indeed, in the International Classification of Diseases–10th Version (ICD 10), depressive-conduct disorder is classified as separate syndrome to other depressive presentations. What are the implications of these advances in psychopathological classification for children with SLD, and SLI in particular? First, that classification of language difficulties should consider that some subtypes are less "specific" than previously considered and more emphasis should be given to assessing non-linguistic comorbid characteristics: not only other developmental features, but also behavioural and emotional symptoms. Second, that assessment of the personal impairment of the child should be incorporated to denote a "disorder". Impairment would be present when expected age appropriate behaviours are not present and would include difficulties in personal and social play, and interpersonal impairments with peers and/or family members. It is important to take impairment into account, because emotional and behavioural signs and symptoms are frequent in the community. If we ignore impairment, the prevalence rates of common anxious and conduct disorders (generally considered as those with 12-month period prevalence rates greater than 2%) would be markedly inflated (Costello et al., 1996a). In addition, some children may be impaired in everyday life as a consequence of speech or language difficulties even though they do not meet quantitative criteria for diagnosis. The latter may be equally, or perhaps even more, in need of intervention as those with a diagnosis but with no observable personal or social dysfunction. This group with observable personal and social impairments is likely to contain those with social pragmatic difficulties.

Evaluating the importance of introducing comorbidity and impairment criteria to the classification of children with speech and language difficulties requires large scale epidemiological studies. One such study, the Cambridge Language and Speech Project (CLASP), has recently reported some preliminary findings (Burden, Stott, Forge, & Goodyer, 1996). In this community-based investigation the nature, characteristics of speech, language, behaviour, and social difficulties were evaluated in a representative sample of 3-year-olds, who were reassessed together with their first degree relatives at 8 years of age where cognitive profiles and levels of social impairment in the children were also obtained. A preschool language checklist (PLC) was completed by 1936 parents at 36 months to identify children at risk of language difficulties. Two hundred and seventy-seven children at risk together with 148 controls completed a series of preliminary face-to-face standard language tests to determine expressive, receptive and phonological skills, associated behavioural difficulties and related family and social difficulties. The low concordance with speech therapy involvement at 39–45 months suggested that the overall screening procedure identified a significant proportion (>25%) of children that current surveillance had missed, a finding recently replicated by Tomblin et al. (1997). These preliminary results emphasise the importance of not relying on clinical samples for estimating prevalence. Preliminary findings from the CLASP project suggest, however, that speech therapists are seeing many children for assessment who do not have any significant SLD. This suggests a potential problem in the detection of appropriate children for referral rather than a larger overall prevalence rate. A striking feature of the early

CLASP findings is that more than 50% of the sample have associated significant non-linguistic difficulties with challenging and impulsive behaviour. Ten to twenty percent of parents reported that behaviour problems led to as much functional impairment as the communication difficulties. Since all these children have IQ levels >70 the notion that SLD consists solely of "specific" language disorders in which all other cognitive parameters are within normal limits seems unlikely. IQ within the normal range does not mean that all psychological functions, particularly those associated with attention, impulsivity and behavioural inhibition, are within normal limits.

THE CLINICAL CLASSIFICATION OF SLI AND ASSOCIATED BEHAVIOURS

The classification of language disorders to date has relied in the main on quantitative assessments of specific language skills. The term "specific" indicates that other cognitive functions, including motor and attentional skills, are within normal limits and do not account for the presenting difficulties. The word "specific" is not, however, used in the DSM IV nosology of "communication disorders" which subsume the syndromes of phonological disorder, expressive language disorder and mixed receptive-expressive disorder (American Psychiatric Association, 1994). This classification does indicate that, if the child is assessed as "mentally retarded", then the presenting speech and/or language difficulties must be "in excess" of those expected in such cases. In this classification, little is said about putative underlying causes or natural history. By contrast, the International Classification of Diseases Version 10 (World Health Organisation, 1994) considers that impairments and delays of speech and/or language are likely to be strongly related to maturation of the central nervous system. Children with learning disabilities are excluded. Diagnosis requires very precise quantitative assessments of speech and language skills which are defined in purely statistical terms (generally between one and two standard deviations from the norm). ICD 10 (but not DSM IV) make

it clear that these "disorders of psychological development", which include speech articulation disorder and expressive and receptive language disorder as separate entities, may often be followed by non-linguistic disorders including learning difficulties and emotional and behavioural syndromes. The classifications therefore vary somewhat in their terminology and subtyping of language disorder with neither commenting in any detail on concurrent associated non-linguistic features or level of personal impairment related to language difficulties. This is unique in both of these classifications of mental and behavioural disorders, as psychiatric diagnoses require not only the presence of observable signs and symptoms but also, for the majority of disorders, assigning a level of psychosocial impairment, without which diagnoses should not be made.

A somewhat more inclusive classification for language difficulties is proposed, taking into account the preliminary findings from the CLASP study, and incorporating non-linguistic comorbid features, personal impairments and more complex problems of social discourse. Clearly, this more inclusive framework requires further research to establish whether there is greater phenotypic validity for these putative subtypes than the current classification. Some children who present with externalising behavioural disorders (conduct, oppositional and attention deficit disorders) but with more covert language difficulties would also be classified here rather than in the conduct or motor sections of ICD or DSM. Currently the classification of these conditions does not require an assessment of their language profile (although it is essential to establish that motor symptoms are not occurring as part of a pervasive developmental disorder or emotional syndrome such as generalised anxiety disorder).

Type one: Simple Developmental Disorder

The criteria for classifying children in this group would be the presence of personal and social impairment together with one or more speech, motor or behavioural symptoms. Without impairment these children would not warrant any diagnosis and would be viewed as having an uncomplicated delay in development. These relatively mild conditions will not meet criteria for expressive/receptive language disorders, developmental coordination or attention deficit disorders. The degree of social impairment is likely to be associated with frustration of non-communication but not with social pragmatic deficits. Recovery occurs with maturation over time so that by middle childhood these early delays are no longer overtly apparent, regardless of the pattern of presenting symptoms.

Subtypes: phonology; motor; conduct

Distinguishing between phonology, motor and conduct subtypes at a clinical level would be an aid in determining management priorities. This group of disorders are likely to carry a good prognosis as they are probably dependent on a set of as yet unidentified immature, but not disordered or deficient, neurodevelopmental processes.

Type two: Mixed Developmental Disorder

ICD 10 (but not DSM IV) already has a category of mixed developmental disorder in which there is some admixture of language, motor and literacy disorders. It is suggested that this should only be used when there is a clear overlap between two or more developmental disorders and assumes this to be uncommon. The current literature suggests that, if anything, this may be the most common type of developmental disorder, albeit with varying degrees of severity.

This is a group of disorders with a combination of syndromes across language and motor functions, without pragmatic difficulties but with moderate to marked levels of personal and social impairment as a consequence of the effects of one or more of these syndromes. These cases are likely to have a protracted and adverse developmental trajectory with a worsening prognosis dependent on the number of developmental symptoms at presentation. The known increased risk for further behavioural and literacy difficulties will be related to the combination of developmental syndromes, and not simply to the linguistic profile at presentation. Subtyping for clinical purposes would be based on the predominant presenting syndrome, which may be language (phonology,

expressive/receptive) or motor including ADHD, but not on impairment criteria as all cases will be impaired. Cases may be assigned to moderate or severe categories depending on the level of impairment.

Syndromes may not be stable over time but, even where the original disorder has resolved, residual deficits are likely in developmentally related domains. For example, phonology subtype in early childhood but subsequently "resolved" may correlate with subsequent literacy difficulties. This may occur in the presence or absence of persistent ADHD.

Type three: Complex Developmental Disorder

In some cases mixed comorbid syndromes will also present with significant social communication deficits. Social reciprocity may be impaired with adults as well as children. It seems likely that these children will have a stable and persistent phenotype leading to measurable core deficits of the original presenting syndromes in middle childhood with enduring social difficulties that are amplified by the introduction of school and more complex peer group environments. In some of these cases a differential diagnosis of pervasive developmental syndrome (i.e. a group of disorders characterised by qualitative impairments in reciprocal social interaction, patterns of communication and restricted, stereotyped and repetitive repertoire of interests) may be considered as the boundaries between these, and this group of complex language/behaviour conditions are problematic and may be more artificial than real (Bishop, 1989; chapter 6, this volume). However these cases are unlikely to show overt deficits in symbolic and pretend play or repetitive interests at presentation and can show elements of social reciprocity in familiar social contexts.

Type four: Social Pragmatic Disorder

Members of this group show phonological skills and receptive abilities on formal testing, but possess expressive difficulties and, in particular, poor social communication. Impairment in social abilities is often the characteristic presenting complaint. The clinical criteria for ADHD or Developmental

Coordination Disorder may be absent in many, if not most, cases. Oppositional and defiant behaviour may occur as a result of frustration at their failure to engage in reciprocal conversations and related actions. This group may be the least likely to be noticed in the pre-school years but become more detectable as social environments increase in complexity with age and adults begin to notice and evaluate deficits in interpersonal skills. Individuals may also acquire this disorder if the language environment is impaired in the early years or they are unable to utilise such an environment. The differential diagnosis would be with pervasive developmental disorders, and in particular with Asperger's syndrome in which subjects present with the overarching characteristics of pervasive developmental disorders (see above) but have no history of speech delay.

Whilst there is some preliminary face validity for these descriptions based on clinical phenotype and longitudinal course, the degree of social and personal impairment at presentation is particularly important in this nosology as it is in most other forms of mental illness and behavioural disturbance. Further investigations such as family history studies may also help to produce more homogeneous clinical subsets and aid in further aetiological research, as has been the case in studies of the autism where the assessment of language, social function and affective disorders have contributed to our understanding of the familial and acquired nature and characteristics of these developmental conditions (e.g. Bolton, et al., 1994; Bolton, Pickles, Murphy, & Rutter, 1998).

MECHANISMS AND PROCESSES LINKING LANGUAGE DIFFICULTIES AND BEHAVIOURAL PSYCHOPATHOLOGY

A common neurodevelopmental pathway?

There are two somewhat different neurodevelopmental hypotheses proposed to explain the co-occurrence of language and behavioural symptoms, particularly when the latter involve hyperactivity, attention difficulties and oppositional behaviour. Beitchman and colleagues observed that the risk for behaviour problems increases with the degree

of general language impairment, suggesting that general linguistic impairment is the common underlying cause for both SLI and ADHD (Beitchman et al., 1994, 1996a, 1996b).

By contrast, Tallal and colleagues noted that behavioural problems are not associated with SLI once non-verbal IQ is taken into account, suggesting that the "behaviours" are aspects of developmental immaturity rather than comorbid psychopathologies (Tallal et al., 1989; Tallal, Miller, & Fitch, 1993). In reviewing these hypotheses Stevenson (1996) has noted that even taking out neurodevelopmental features of behaviour there is still an association between behavioural deviancy and SLI. Since SLI is likely to be aetiologically as well as clinically heterogeneous, these two developmental views may be relevant for different types of disorder.

Whether deficits in linguistic and/or attentional processes are highly correlated in infancy and contribute independently to the onset of either SLI and/or ADHD can only be established in a longitudinal prospective study of infants at high risk for SLI alone, ADHD alone and for both disorders.

Connectivity between psychopathologies

A neurodevelopmental model of the co-occurrence of SLD and ADHD assumes that there is a prior cause that increases the risk for both phenotypes. An alternative possibility is that one condition may increase the risk of onset for a second disorder. This connectivity between conditions may be specific within a class of psychopathologies, i.e. measurable deficits in speech and language skills may predict further language difficulties. For example, a significant proportion of children with specific language impairments, particularly expressive/receptive disorders, have deficits in the use of language skills in a social context when conversing with others (Lapadat, 1991). The characteristic features of these difficulties are seen during everyday social discourse. These include failure to appreciate the point of view of the other person, breaking the rules of everyday conversation (e.g. not turn taking, interrupting, talking over a person, deviating from the subject), and not following the agreed behavioural consequences of the conversation. These pragmatic difficulties are hypothesised as increasing the risk for subsequent interpersonal communication failures leading to a heightened sense of frustration with resultant interpersonal social difficulties and emotional and behavioural symptoms (Bryan, Donahue, Pearl, & Herzog, 1984; Donahue & Pearl, 1995). Although there is considerable interest in measuring communication skills and social pragmatic deficits (Bishop, 1998), there have been very few direct tests of this hypothesis. One experimental study examined difficult behaviour in SLI and control children during low and high communication demand tasks and showed that differences between groups were only present during the latter (Caulfield, Fischel, DeBaryshe, & Whitehurst, 1989) providing some support for the hypothesis that frustration leads to socio-emotional problems.

A second type of connectivity is where there is a change over time from one type of psychopathology to another (termed sequential comorbidity in the psychopathology literature, indicating a putative causal process between two phenotypically different syndromes occurring at different points in time). For example, SLD children with comorbid ADHD are less likely to gain from their social language environment because of their non-language symptoms. If so, then a proportion of such children would be expected to show a flat or negative developmental language trajectory, particularly in social communication tasks but perhaps also in those aspects of semantic development related to literacy. Indeed, the higher rates of oppositional behaviour and frank conduct disorder may well be a consequence of such "acquired" pragmatic difficulties, secondary to preceding ADHD.

Thus the presence of pragmatic problems by middle childhood may arise from two distinctive pathways: directly via a language specific route, and indirectly as a consequence of a comorbid non-language disorder that disrupts the social language environment thereby increasing the risk for further language and literacy problems.

As yet there are no longitudinal studies of ADHD where concurrent measurement of language and non-language disorders has been made. Given the high rates of literacy difficulties in children with ADHD, such studies would certainly be worthwhile and may suggest a window of opportunity for intervention in hyperactive children in the pre-school and early school years to improve pragmatic language as well as literacy skills (Tannock & Schachar, 1996).

Behavioural and emotional development and SLD

A similar set of arguments can be advanced for the impact of early impaired social-emotional development on subsequent language abilities. To communicate effectively children must be aware of feelings, intentions and attributions of others. If there are deficits in early emotional development then difficulties in the pragmatics of communication may arise in subsequent social interactions that require such skills. The inappropriate use of language skills may reflect an outgrowth of these early emotional deficiencies but only be apparent at times of high social demand (Crittenden, 1996). As yet, there is little empirical evidence for or against this view.

By middle childhood the most common psychopathological feature of children with a history of early onset SLI is emotional disorder, particularly for girls, implying a longer term negative effect of SLI on social cognitive development (Beitchman et al., 1996a). The dominant psychological theory of emotional disorders across the lifespan proposes that such conditions arise in individuals who possess core latent impairments in self representations which are activated by negative life events. These events carry a negative impact on the self which provoke low mood thereby activating and making available for conscious reflection the latent negative percept of the self (Teasdale & Barnard, 1993). The combination of low mood and negative cognitions leads to clinical disorder with personal impairments in social and physical function as well as mood and negative cognitions. Anxiety and depression are the two broad and complex domains of emotional disorders in childhood. Each has been considered as having somewhat different self-percept components. Whilst both are correlated with an increase in negative judgements about the self, for anxiety disorders the core self percept is "what do others think about me". Individuals vulnerable for anxiety disorders are more likely to reflect that others think badly about them, whereas for depressives the key self percept is "what I think about myself", i.e. depressed individuals are more likely to think they are bad regardless of what others think. Both components may contribute to the complex construct of self esteem, "my overall evaluation of myself as a person".

It may be that children with enduring impairments in speech and language abilities are at increased risk for the development of latent negative self representations, but the evidence to date is somewhat equivocal. Thus, although increased rates of low self esteem have been noted in children with persistent educational failure (i.e. attainment levels lower than expected age norms), there are no reports of SLD in the pre-school period specifically predicting negative self image problems during the school years.

By contrast to the links with emotional disorders, the most common psychopathology associated with literacy difficulties in middle childhood is antisocial behaviour in adolescence (Williams & McGee, 1994). A history of SLI leading to reading disability and conduct disorder may reflect a different sub-group than that of SLI leading to emotional disorder, but the current findings do not allow any firm conclusions to be drawn. In addition, the correlates between reading and conduct disorder are primarily for boys, and, as already noted, those between SLI and emotional disorder for girls. It is well established that in the general adolescent population emotional disorders are more common in girls than boys and conduct disorders more common in boys than girls. This suggests that the gender difference in developmental studies to date is not a function of the type of language or learning syndrome, but reflects the expected pattern of disorder in young people in this age group. This may mean that SLI is a rather non-specific developmental risk for subsequent psychiatric disorder, and not specifically associated with any type of psychopathology in middle childhood or adolescence. There are, however, no longitudinal studies of sufficient methodological sophistication or power to adequately address these complex and differing relationships over time.

AN OVERVIEW OF LANGUAGE AND PSYCHOPATHOLOGY RELATIONSHIPS

Clinical features

In summary, for children in the pre-school years the most salient behavioural correlates of language impairments are over-activity, attentional difficulties, wetting and soiling. Moving into the early school years, emotional and behavioural symptoms and syndromes increase in prevalence but there is also a group with enduring characteristics of ADHD. In early adolescence the association with antisocial behaviour and SLI appears important, but predominantly in those who develop reading disability in middle childhood. Gender differences in the type of associated psychopathology become clearer by the school years but appear to be consistent with the expected differences found in the general population. Late onset language development may compromise the development of pragmatic skills required for social communication and thereby enhance the risk for psychiatric disorders in social contexts where communication between persons is required. This appears more likely by the school age years and may account in part for the increased rate of previously undetected language deficits in children referred to psychiatric clinics.

Origins

In the pre-school years a mutual reinforcement may occur for the overactive toddler whereby parental expectations for language skills are low and optimal stimulation is not provided. These familial risks may account for communication deficits in middle childhood in some children. The origins of low communication skills and a deficient language environment within families may arise from genetic or environmental causes. Determining the relative contribution of genetic and environmental causes to the developmental trajectory of language development requires a longitudinal twin study. There is now strong evidence for early language delay as a distinct disorder with a genetic basis, whereas shared familial environment is more important for general language development (Dale et al., 1998). What exactly it is that is inherited as a risk for subsequent SLI is an important question that requires further research. For example, preliminary findings have noted that variation in performance on Tallal's auditory repetition test (ART) is unlikely to be genetic, whereas deficits on a test of phonological short term memory, the children's non-word repetition test (CNRep) show high group heritability (Bishop et al., 1999). Interestingly, in 7-year-old children CNRep was a better predictor of low language test scores than ART scores but both measures make a significant independent contribution to variance in a test of grammatical understanding, at least in middle childhood.

A longitudinal family study would also contribute to these questions through determining the familiality of linguistic, cognitive and pragmatic factors in relatives of children with SLI only, ADHD only or both. Using family study methods to characterise the phenotypes would then lead to the application of candidate gene or genome wide molecular genetic approaches in more homogeneous subsets of disorders (see Plomin & Dale, chapter 3, this volume for further details regarding the genetics of language difficulties). Family studies are few and somewhat equivocal but current evidence suggests that a family history of SLI may be more associated with deficits in receptive than expressive impairments in offspring (Spitz, Tallal, Flax, & Benasich, 1997; Whitehurst et al., 1991). The Cambridge (CLASP) study has recently reported that the rates of language and literacy difficulties in first degree relatives (FDRs) of children with receptive language disorder were significantly greater than in the FDRs of children with other types of SLI (Bolton, Merricks, Stott, & Goodyer, 1997). Whether this apparently highly familial subtype of SLI is different at the molecular level from other SLI subtypes is currently being investigated. In addition, the possibility that there are phenotypic differences in familiality according to non-linguistic comorbid features of the proband, such as ADHD, is also under investigation.

Increased negative bias in self percept in middle childhood may lead to emotional syndromes in the same developmental period or later during adolescence. Children with SLI may be at increased risk for such biases as they become aware of the resultant functional impairments that arise from their early childhood language syndrome.

By contrast the risks for externalising disorders in middle childhood and adolescence amongst cases of SLI may arise in those with a history of significant phonological deficit in the early years. It is not clear if this is a direct effect of persisting deficits arising from phonological processes or a result of comorbid non-phonological difficulties in attention. It is important to rule out the latter for theoretical and clinical reasons. For example a subset of children in the CLASP project who had delayed onset of speech and language at 45 months were classified into four groups (SLD alone, hyperactivity alone, both sets of symptoms and controls), and were reevaluated at 6 years of age for neuropsychological performance. Deficits in attention and spatial working memory were specifically associated with hyperactivity at 45 months but not any group of SLD symptoms (Williams, 1997). These preliminary findings suggest that impaired behavioural and literacy performance may be due to pre-existing comorbid attentional problems in subjects presenting with SLD in the pre-school years. SLI and ADHD may, however, have different cognitive correlates and the above data is not a sufficiently valid test of the outcome of "pure" and "comorbid phonological subtypes. This will become clearer when the reevaluations of all CLASP subjects carried out at age 8 are reported.

The pathway for externalising problems appears to be via the increased risk for reading disorders in middle childhood and adolescence, giving rise to problems of behaviour, concentration and attention. Pennington, Groisser, and Welsh (1993) noted that reading-disabled children showed phonological processing deficits and children with ADHD alone showed primarily deficits in executive functions (i.e. impairments in attention, short term memory, planning and behavioural inhibition). Children with both disorders showed deficits in phonological processing only. They argued that symptoms of ADHD can arise as a secondary consequence of reading disability, that is, as a phenocopy.

There is no similar study comparing SLI and ADHD directly. However, a recent longitudinal study by Stothard and colleagues followed up 71 adolescents with a pre-school history of speech/language impairment (Stothard et al., 1998). These children were subdivided at four years of age into those with a non-verbal IQ 2 SD below the mean (General Delay Group) and those with normal non-verbal intelligence (the SLI group). Both groups were followed up. The SLI group was further divided at 15 years of age into resolved and persistent SLI. The findings showed if a child's language difficulties are still present at 5/6 years, the prognosis is likely to be poor and the child will be at risk of language, literacy and educational difficulties throughout childhood and adolescence. By contrast, if the child's language difficulties are largely resolved then the outlook for spoken language is better. Although none of the latter group would meet criteria for developmental dyslexia their literacy skills were weak in relation to their peers, possibly as a consequence of their residual phonological processing impairments, including problems of phonological awareness. These longitudinal findings show that non-clinical residual difficulties may continue to carry risks for subsequent literacy problems. Lower educational performance as a result of these persistent difficulties may also influence the liability for psychopathology. These findings also make it clear that the notion of developmental immaturity resolving with a good prognosis may not be taking into account residual latent deficits that leave those children vulnerable for subsequent disorders.

The possibility that there are distinct persistent subtypes of SLI as a result of comorbid psychiatric characteristics in the pre-school years remains unevaluated. It has been proposed, however, that executive dysfunction may be a shared risk factor for comorbid SLI/ADHD cases, which leads to further psychopathology in later years (e.g. Tannock & Schachar, 1996). It has also been suggested by the same group that comorbid ADHD may be an additive burden for subsequent language impairment. These issues can only be resolved by longitudinal studies of pre-school children with SLI alone, ADHD alone and a comorbid presentation.

It may be that gender is also an important general risk factor influencing the form of psychiatric disorder at different points in development. Girls with any residual elements of early SLI may be more likely to experience emotional disorders and boys conduct disorder and ADHD. No studies have yet described gender effects on rates and types of SLI and psychopathology at different ages and stages of development.

Follow-up studies into adulthood are particularly scarce. Rutter and Mawhood (1991) reported a follow-up study of language and behavioural function in a small sample of adults with SLI in childhood. They noted a poor outcome in social education and employment terms for a sub-sample with receptive language difficulties in childhood. This small group of men had significant social impairments, leading solitary lives after living with their parents; three such patients had developed a paranoid psychosis in adult life. The findings clearly require replication and comparison with the outcomes of other types of SLI, taking into account comorbid characteristics in childhood. The implications for children with receptive disorders are worrying. Although they constitute the least frequent group of speech and language presentations in childhood they may carry the worst prognosis.

To summarise, there are already a number of different strands of evidence indicating that non-linguistic abilities, such as attention, working memory and emotional processing, are potentially important processes influencing variation in the aetiology, nature, characteristics and outcome of children with different types of speech and language difficulties. Concurrent measurement of these abilities, more systematic assessments of formal psychiatric disorders, and using more family longitudinal designs will help to delineate distinctive subtypes of these developmental disorders, including the relative genetic and environmental influences on their origins and outcome.

REFERENCES

American Psychiatric Association. (1994). *Diagnostic and Statistical Manual For Mental and Behavioural Disorders. (Vol. IV)*. Washington, DC: American Psychiatric Association.

Baker, L., & Cantwell, D.P. (1987a). Comparison of well, emotionally disordered, and behaviourally disordered children with linguistic problems. *Journal of the American Academy of Child and Adolescent Psychiatry, 26*, 193–196.

Baker, L., & Cantwell, D.P. (1987b). A prospective psychiatric follow-up of children with speech/language disorders. *Journal of the American Academy of Child and Adolescent Psychiatry, 26*, 546–553.

Beitchman, J.H., Brownlie, E.B., Inglis, A., Wild, J., Matthews, R., Schachter, D., Kroll, R., Martin, S., Ferguson, B., & Lancee, W. (1994). Seven-year follow-up of speech/language-impaired and control children: Speech/language stability and outcome. *Journal of the American Academy of Child and Adolescent Psychiatry, 33*, 1322–1330.

Beitchman, J.H., Hood, J., & Inglis, A. (1990). Psychiatric risk in children with speech and language disorders. *Journal of Abnormal Child Psychology, 18*, 283–296.

Beitchman, J.H., Hood, J., Rochon, J., & Peterson, M. (1989a). Empirical classification of speech/language impairment in children II. Behavioural characteristics. *Journal of the American Academy of Child and Adolescent Psychiatry, 28*, 118–123.

Beitchman, J.H., Hood, J., Rochon, J., Peterson, M., Mantini, T., & Majumdar, S. (1989b). Empirical classification of speech/language impairment in children I. Identification of speech/language categories. *Journal of the American Academy of Child and Adolescent Psychiatry, 28*, 112–117.

Beitchman, J.H., Wilson, B., Brownlie, E.B., Walters, H., Inglis, A., & Lancee, W. (1996a). Long-term consistency in speech/language profiles: II Behavioural, emotional and social outcomes. *Journal of the American Academy of Child and Adolescent Psychiatry, 35*, 815–825.

Beitchman, J.H., Wilson, B., Brownlie, E.B., Walters, H., & Lancee, W. (1996b). Long-term consistency in speech/language profiles: 1. Developmental and academic outcomes. *Journal of the American Academy of Child and Adolescent Psychiatry, 35*, 804–814.

Bishop, D.V.M. (1989). Autism, Asperger's syndrome and semantic-pragmatic disorder: Where are the boundaries? *British Journal of Disorders of Communication, 24*, 107–121.

Bishop, D.V.M. (1998). Development of the Children's Communication Checklist (CCC): A method for assessing qualitative aspects of communicative impairment in children. *Journal of Child Psychology and Psychiatry, 39*, 879–891.

Bishop, D.V., Bishop, S.J., Bright, P., James, C., Delaney, T., & Tallal, P. (1999). Different origin of auditory and phonological processing problems in children with language impairment: Evidence from a twin study. *Journal of Speech, Language, and Hearing Research, 42*, 155–168.

Block, J., & Robins, R. (1993). A longitudinal study of consistency and change in self esteem from early adolescence to early adulthood. *Child Development, 64*, 909–923.

Bolton, P., MacDonald, H., Pickles, A., Rios, P., Crowson, M., Bailey, A., & Rutter, M. (1994). A case-control family history study of autism. *Journal of Child Psychology and Psychiatry, 35*, 877–900.

Bolton, P., Merricks, M., Stott, C., & Goodyer, I. (1997). Language impairment: Patterns of familial aggregation. *American Journal of Medical Genetics, 74*, 656–657.

Bolton, P.F., Pickles, A., Murphy, M., & Rutter, M. (1998). Autism, affective and other psychiatric disorders: Patterns of familial aggregation. *Psychological Medicine, 28*, 385–395.

Breton, J.J., Bergeron, L., Valla, J.P., Berthiaume, C., Gaudet, N., Lambert, J., St-Georges, M., Houde, L., & Lepine, S. (1999). Quebec child mental health survey: Prevalence of DSM-III-R mental health disorders. *Journal of Child Psychology and Psychiatry, 40*, 375–384.

Bryan, T., Donahue, M., Pearl, R., & Herzog, A. (1984). Conversational interactions between mothers and learning-disabled or nondisabled children during a problem-solving task. *Journal of Speech and Hearing Disorders, 49*, 64–71.

Burden, V., Stott, C.M., Forge, J., & Goodyer, I. (1996). The Cambridge Language and Speech Project (CLASP). I. Detection of language difficulties at 36 to 39 months. *Developmental Medicine and Child Neurology, 38*, 613–631.

Cantwell, D.P., & Baker, L. (1987). Prevalence and type of psychiatric disorders in three speech and language groups. *Journal of Communication Disorders, 20*, 151–160.

Caulfield, M.B., Fischel, J.E., DeBaryshe, B.D., & Whitehurst, G.J. (1989). Behavioral correlates of developmental expressive language disorder. *Journal of Abnormal Child Psychology, 17*, 187–201.

Cohen, N. (1996). Unsuspected language impairments in psychiatrically disturbed children: Developmental issues and associated conditions. In J. Beitchman, N. Cohen, M. Konstantareas, & R. Tannock (Eds), *Language, learning and behavior disorders* (pp. 105–127). Cambridge: Cambridge University Press.

Cohen, N.J., Davine, M., Horodezky, N., Lipsett, L., & Isaacson, L. (1993). Unsuspected language impairment in psychiatrically disturbed children: Prevalence and behavioural characteristics. *Journal of the American Academy of Child and Adolescent Psychiatry*, *32*, 595–603.

Costello, E.J., Angold, A., Burns, B.J., Erkanli, A., Stangl, D.K., & Tweed, D.L. (1996a). The Great Smokey Mountains Study of Youth: Functional impairment and serious emotional disturbance. *Archives of General Psychiatry*, *53*, 1137–1143.

Costello, E.J., Angold, A., Burns, B.J., Stangl, D.K., Tweed, D.L., Erkanli, A., & Worthman, C.M. (1996b). The Great Smokey Mountains Study: Goals, designs, methods and the prevalence of DSM III-R disorders. *Archives of General Psychiatry*, *53*, 1129–1136.

Crittenden, P. (1996). Language and psychopathology: An attachment perspective. In J. Beitchman, N. Cohen, M. Konstantareas, & R. Tannock (Eds), *Language, learning and behaviour disorders* (pp. 59–77). Cambridge: Cambridge University Press.

Dale, P.S., Simonoff, E., Bishop, D.V., Eley, T.C., Oliver, B., Price, T.S., Purcell, S., Stevenson, J., & Plomin, R. (1998). Genetic influence on language delay in two-year-old children. *Nature Neuroscience*, *1*, 324–328.

Donahue, M.L., & Pearl, R. (1995). Conversational interactions of mothers and their preschool childre who had been born preterm. *Journal of Speech and Hearing Research*, *38*, 1117–1124.

Fundudis, T., Kolvin, I., & Garside, R. (1979). *Speech retarded and deaf children: Their psychological development*. London: Academic Press.

Goldstein, R.B., Weissman, M., Adams, P.B., Horwath, E., Lish, J., Charney, D., Woods, S., Sobin, C., & Wickramartne, P. (1994). Psychiatric disorders in relatives of probands with panic disorder and/or major depression. *Archives of General Psychiatry*, *51*, 383–394.

Goodman, R., Simonoff, E., & Stevenson, J. (1995). The impact of child IQ, parent IQ and sibling IQ on child behavoural deviance scores. *Journal of Child Psychology and Psychiatry*, *36*, 409–425.

Goodyer, I.M., Herbert, J., Secher, S., & Pearson, J. (1997). Short term outcome of major depression: I. Comorbidity and severity at presentation as predictors of persistent disorder. *Journal of the American Academy of Child and Adolescent Psychiatry*, *36*, 179–187.

Haynes, C., & Naidoo, S. (1991). *Children with specific speech and language problems. (Vol. 119)*. Oxford: MacKeith Press/Blackwells Scientific.

Lapadat, J. (1991). Pragmatic language skills of students with language and/or learning disabilities. *Journal of Learning Disabilities*, *24*, 147–158.

Leonard, L.B. (1991). Specific language impairment as a clinical category. *Language, Speech and Hearing Services in Schools*, *22*, 66–68.

Pennington, B.F., Groisser, D., & Welsh, M. (1993). Contrasting cognitive deficits in Attention Deficit Hyperactivity Disorder versus reading disability. *Developmental Psychology*, *29*, 511–523.

Rapin, I. (1996). Praciticner review: Developemntal language disorders: A clinical update. *Journal of Child Psychology and Psychiatry*, *37*, 643–655.

Richman, N., Stevenson, J., & Graham, P. (1982). *Preschool to school*. London: Academic Press.

Rutter, M., & Mawhood, L. (1991). The long term psychosocial sequelae of specific developmental disorders of specch and language. In M. Rutter & P. Caesaer (Eds), *Biological risk factors for psychosocial disorders* (pp. 233–259). Cambridge: Cambridge University Press.

Silva, P.A., Justin, C., McGee, R., & Williams, S.M. (1984). Developmental language delay from three to seven years and its significance for low intelligence and reading difficulties at age eight. *British Journal of Disorders of Communication*, *19*, 149–154.

Silva, P.A., Williams, S., & McGee, R. (1987). A longitudinal study of children with developmental language delay at age three: Later intelligence, reading and behaviour problems. *Developmental Medicine and Child Neurology*, *29*, 630–640.

Spitz, R.V., Tallal, P., Flax, J., & Benasich, A.A. (1997). Look who's talking: A prospective study of familial transmission of language impairments. *Journal of Speech, Language, and Hearing Research*, *40*, 990–1001.

Stevenson, J. (1996). Developmental changes in the mechanisms linking language and behaviour disorders. In J. Beitchman, N. Cohen, M. Konstantareas, & R. Tannock (Eds), *Language, learning and behaviour disorders* (pp. 78–100). Cambridge: Cambridge University Press.

Stevenson, J., Richman, N., & Graham, P. (1985). Behaviour problems and language abilities at three years and behavioural deviance at eight years. *Journal of Child Psychology and Psychiatry*, *26*, 215–230.

Stothard, S.E., Snowling, M.J., Bishop, D.V., Chipchase, B.B., & Kaplan, C.A. (1998). Language-impaired preschoolers: A follow-up into adolescence. *Journal of Speech, Language, and Hearing Research*, *41*, 407–418.

Tallal, P., Dukette, D., & Curtiss, S. (1989). Behavioral/ emotional profiles of preschool language-impaired children. *Development and Psychopathology, 1,* 51–67.

Tallal, P., Miller, S., & Fitch, R.H. (1993). Neurobiological basis of speech: A case for the preeminence of temporal processing. *Annals of the New York Academy of Sciences, 682,* 27–47.

Tannock, R., & Schachar, R. (1996). Executive function as an underlying mechanism of behaviour and language problems in attention deficit hyperactivity disorder. In J. Beitchman, N. Cohen, M. Konstantareas, & R. Tannock (Eds), *Language, learning and behaviour disorders* (pp. 128–155). Cambridge: Cambridge University Press.

Teasdale, J.D., & Barnard, P.J. (1993). *Affect, cognition and change: Remodelling depressive thought.* Hillsdale, NJ: Lawrence Erlbaum Associates Inc.

Tomblin, J.B., Records, N.L., Buckwalter, P., Zhang, X., Smith, E., & O'Brien, M. (1997). Prevalence of specific language impairment in kindergarten children. *Journal of Speech, Language, and Hearing Research, 40,* 1245–1260.

Verhulst, F., & Koot, H. (1995). *The epidemiology of child and adolescent psychopathology.* Oxford: Oxford Medical Publications.

Verhulst, F., van der Ende, J., Ferdinand, R.F., & Kasius, M.C. (1997). The prevalence of DSM-IIIR diagnoses in a national sample of Dutch adolescents. *Archives of General Psychiatry, 54,* 329–336.

Whitehurst, G.J., & Fischel, J.E. (1994). Practitioner review: Early developmental language delay: What, if anything, should the clinician do about it? *Journal of Child Psychology and Psychiatry, 35,* 613–648.

Whitehurst, G.J., Arnold, D.S., Smith, M., Fischel, J.E., Lonigan, C.J., & Valdez-Menchaca, M.C. (1991). Family history in developmental expressive language delay. *Journal of Speech and Hearing Research, 34,* 1150–1157.

Williams, D. (1997) *Cognitive functioning in children with language impairment and/or hyperactivity.* Thesis submitted in part fulfilment of the University of East Anglia Doctorate in Clinical Psychology: UEA, Norwich (UK).

Williams, S., & McGee, R. (1994). Reading attainment and juvenile delinquency. *Journal of Child Psychology and Psychiatry, 35,* 441–459.

World Health Organisation. (1994). *ICD-10 Classification of mental and behavioural disorders.* Geneva: WHO.

14

Language and literacy skills: Who is at risk and why?

Margaret J. Snowling

This chapter discusses the vulnerability of children with spoken language impairments to reading failure, within a connectionist framework (after Seidenberg & McClelland, 1989). Reading development is conceptualised as a highly interactive process with an interplay between phonological and semantic resources. At the basic level, learning to read involves establishing a set of mappings between letter strings (orthography) and speech sounds (phonemes). Children with deficits in phonological awareness (e.g. dyslexia) have problems making these connections. Later in development, particularly for children learning to read English, these mappings have to be supplemented by connections from orthography to phonology via word meanings. Use of this "semantic pathway" is vital for learning to read irregular or exception words and for the development of reading fluency. It is also used to "bootstrap" the learning of children with phonological deficits. Children with semantic impairments have problems with the use of this system. A third source of variance in reading is the ability to use context to activate semantic knowledge. It is suggested that children with grammatical difficulties or pragmatic impairments benefit less from contextual facilitation and that poor reading comprehension is (as it was) a consequence. The role of environmental factors, including the linguistic environment in the home and the teaching the child has received, are also considered.

It is now very well established that learning to read in an alphabetic orthography depends critically upon a child's speech processing or phonological skills (Goswami & Bryant, 1990; Share, 1995). There is indeed a huge body of evidence showing a strong relationship between pre-school phonological processing and later reading and spelling development. Furthermore, dyslexic children have phonological deficits that are considered to be at the core of their reading problems

(Stanovich & Siegel, 1994). Moreover, the phonological deficits associated with dyslexia extend beyond the ability to reflect on the sound structure of words (phonological awareness) and encompass subtle impairments of speech perception and production, limitations of phonological memory, naming deficits and verbal learning difficulties (Snowling, 1998). Indeed, Pennington (1994) proposed that phonological deficits are a key behavioural characteristic of dyslexia, and dyslexia has sometimes been described as a hidden speech disorder (Stackhouse, 1996). Thus it appears, as so aptly put by Mattingly more than 20 years ago, that "reading is parasitic upon speech" (Mattingly, 1972).

But is this the whole story? It is true that learning to read requires the child to establish a set of connections between orthography (the spellings of words) and phonology (the segments of spoken words). However, the view that phonology underpins reading acquisition, on the one hand, a linchpin of our current understanding of reading disability is, on the other hand, a narrow view. Increasingly it is becoming clear that an exclusive focus on the role of phonology in learning to read could lead us astray, particularly in relation to children with spoken language impairments.

Thus, while the majority of follow-up studies of children with speech-language impairments report a high incidence of reading difficulties, the high degree of variability in clinical samples is often masked (Aram, Ekelman, & Nation, 1984; Bird, Bishop, & Freeman, 1995; Dodd, 1995; Felsenfeld, Broen, & McGue, 1992; Magnusson & Naucler, 1990; Stackhouse & Wells, 1997; Stark et al., 1984; Tallal, Allard, Miller, & Curtiss, 1997). This chapter attempts to provide a framework for understanding the observed variation in the literacy skills of language-impaired children.

LANGUAGE SKILLS AND LEARNING TO READ

The strength of the evidence relating phonological skills to learning to read is such that it is hard to

argue against its central role in reading development. However, it is important to be clear of the limitations of the view. The important point is that phonological skills predict reading through decoding ability — specifically, children's ability to process speech sounds is related to their ability to pronounce unfamiliar words by a process that has been likened to letter-sound translation (Share, 1995). But the same decoding skills that allow the child-reader of English to pronounce letter strings such as membership, calculator, sut and trigrup do not yield a correct rendering of exception words like yacht, Leicester, beautiful or biscuit. Furthermore, decoding skills do not allow the accurate reading of ambiguous words such as the word BOW in the sentence "The magician took a *bow*". Neither do they help with the understanding of the pronoun "she" in a sentence such as "Susan gave Jane an apple and she was happy".

Thus, there is more to reading than decoding (Gough & Tunmer, 1986) and therefore more that places a child at risk of reading failure than the ubiquitous phonological deficits seen in dyslexia (Stanovich, 1994). In short, the message of this chapter is that learning to read comprises the development of decoding, word recognition and text comprehension skills. It will be argued that there is an interaction between phonological, semantic and syntactic resources during reading development and the demands of reading change with time. Developmental models of the reading process should guide understanding of who is at risk of literacy failure, and why this is the case.

Learning to read in children with phonological difficulties

A large majority of published studies demonstrating a relationship between phonological skills and reading development have examined how children's performance on tests of phonological awareness predicts their reading skills concurrently or over time. Phonological awareness is a metalinguistic skill that requires children to reflect consciously on the phonological segments of spoken words and to manipulate them in systematic ways. Such tasks tap the phonological substrate of language but also place other cognitive demands on the child. This is well-illustrated by the oddity task (Bradley & Bryant, 1983), in which the child has to decide which is the odd one out in a string of spoken words (e.g. sun, bun, rub, fun). Such a task carries working memory demands. Similarly, the spoonerism task (Perin, 1983) in which the child has to transpose the initial sounds of two spoken words, (e.g. Paddington bear → baddington pear) demands the child to inhibit their usual response which is not a trivial task. It follows that phonological awareness tasks should be considered neither pure tests of processing nor of the child's phonological system. Indeed, scrutiny of the literature on studies of reading skills among children with phonological impairments affecting the speech system indicate that the relationship between spoken phonology and phonological awareness is less than straightforward (see Stackhouse, chapter 5, this volume).

Impairments of expressive phonology

One of the first studies to highlight the differences between expressive phonology and phonological awareness in the prediction of reading was reported by Catts (1993). In principle, children who use speech sounds incorrectly or do not have full use of the normal range of phonemic contrasts might encounter difficulties with processes such as sound blending that are crucial for decoding. However, contrary to this hypothesis, Catts did not find that children with speech-articulation difficulties in kindergarten developed reading difficulties in first grade. Rather, measures of kindergarten phonological awareness and rapid naming were stronger predictors of reading than either receptive or expressive language abilities.

Similarly, the literacy outcomes for 12 children classified as having isolated expressive phonological problems at 4 years by Bishop and Edmundson (1987) were good. Evidence for their poor phonology was taken from a low score on a test eliciting a range of consonants and, importantly, not from an explicit test of phonological awareness. As a group these children did well in reading and spelling tests at 8.5 years, and all but one had normal literacy skills (Bishop & Adams, 1990). More recently, examination of the per-

formance of 10 of these children in adolescence revealed that none had specific reading difficulties and only one had a significant spelling problem (Snowling, Bishop, & Stothard, in press). Interestingly, though word recognition, spelling and reading comprehension skills were within the normal range for these 15-year-olds, they performed less well than controls matched on age and performance IQ on these tests and also on measures of phonological processing (nonword repetition), phonological awareness (spoonerisms) and vocabulary. One might speculate that their weak phonological skills and poor vocabulary accounted for their tendency to show relatively poorer literacy than their peers, but the point is these children could not be classified as dyslexic.

Taken together with reports of normal reading or spelling performance among children with speech impairments associated with structural abnormalities such as cleft palate (Stackhouse, 1982) or neurological conditions, such as dysarthria (Bishop, 1989), these findings suggest that it is necessary to distinguish poor phonological production skills and phonological awareness as predictors of literacy outcome. Children with speech-articulation difficulties do not appear to be at heightened risk of reading problems, but children who have deficits in phonological awareness are unlikely to read well (Lundberg, 1994; Stackhouse & Snowling, 1992).

Children at familial risk of dyslexia

It has been known for many years that reading difficulties run in families and behaviour-genetic studies have shown that there is a substantial genetic influence on reading skills (DeFries, 1991). Moreover, phonological sensitivity, as measured by tests of phonological awareness, shares genetic variance with reading skill, particularly decoding ability (Olson, Datta, Gayan, & DeFries, 1997). It follows that children from families with a history of dyslexia are at increased risk of reading problems. There are currently a number of ongoing studies of children from such high-risk groups. Not surprisingly, many of these have focused on the development of phonological processing skills during the pre-school years.

Lefly and Pennington (1996) followed 73 high-risk and 57 low-risk children from the beginning of kindergarten to just before entry to first grade. High-risk and low-risk groups differed in phonological awareness, letter knowledge and rapid naming in kindergarten. Later, during the second year, the groups differed on phonemic awareness tasks. Byrne, Fielding-Barnsley, Ashley and Larsen (1997) also reported problems of phonological awareness together with limitations of letter knowledge and knowledge of print in high-risk children at 55 months, and Elbro, Borstrom and Petersen (1998), following Danish children at risk of dyslexia, found whether a child became dyslexic or not was predicted by their letter naming and phoneme identification skills in pre-school, together with a measure of the precision of their articulation skills.

However, relatively little is known about the early linguistic profile of dyslexic children and, in particular, how if at all they resemble children with speech-language impairments. Contrary to prevailing opinion that phonological deficits are at the core of dyslexia (Stanovich & Siegel, 1994), the available evidence suggests that children with reading disabilities experience broader language difficulties early in development.

In the first published study of children at genetic risk of dyslexia, Scarborough (1990) compared the early language skills of children who were later classified as dyslexic at 8 years with those of normal readers selected from a control group who had no family history of reading difficulty. She also examined children from high-risk families who were classified as normal readers at 8. These analyses revealed a changing pattern of language difficulties over time for children who later became dyslexic. Importantly for the present argument, language skills outside of the phonological domain were also affected.

At 30 months, children who went on to be dyslexic used as wide a range of vocabulary items in their conversation as the comparison groups, but they used a more restricted range of syntactic devices and made more speech production errors. At 36 and 42 months, vocabulary skills, as assessed by tests of receptive and expressive vocabulary, were less well developed than those of controls and syntactic difficulties persisted. Finally, at 60 months, deficiencies in letter knowledge and phonological awareness emerged and, while naming difficulties persisted, syntactic deficiencies were no longer apparent.

In a UK study along the lines of Scarborough (1990), Gallagher, Frith and Snowling (2000) have been following the acquisition of literacy in 71 children from at-risk families, recruited just before their 4th birthday, compared with controls from families matched in terms of socio-economic circumstances and mother's educational level. At 6 years of age, some 57% of the at-risk group scored more than one standard deviation below the mean on literacy tasks, as defined by the performance of the control sample. By contrast, the incidence of under-achievement among controls was only 12%, which is consistent with what you would find in the general population, assuming a normal distribution of literacy skills.

Once this classification had been done, analyses confirmed that at-risk children who showed delayed literacy development at 6 years did not differ from controls in non-verbal ability at 3 years 9 months. However, they gained lower scores on tests of receptive vocabulary and expressive language and they showed weaknesses in a variety of tasks considered to assess phonological processing, namely, nonword repetition, nursery rhyme knowledge and verbal short-term memory. Importantly, the difficulties of the at-risk literacy-delayed children could not be readily attributed to a lack of linguistic stimulation in dyslexic homes; if this had been the case then it is reasonable to suppose that all children in the at-risk group should have been similarly affected. Furthermore, questionnaire responses supplied by parents suggested that the at-risk children received more assistance with the development of early literacy skills, particularly letter knowledge, than the children from control families with no history of reading difficulties.

Measures of speech and language, together with letter knowledge at 3 years 9 months, were independent predictors of literacy skill at 6, as was performance IQ. Being at genetic risk of dyslexia contributed additional variance to literacy outcome over and above these other factors. However, considering the established role of phonological skills in learning to read, it was noteworthy that speech processing abilities were only marginally stronger predictors of literacy than higher-level semantic and syntactic skills in the group as a whole.

Do these findings change our state of knowledge regarding the precursors of literacy difficulty? On the face of it, they do because it is phonological difficulty that has been considered at the core of literacy failure and here, a wider range of language impairments affected children who went on to have problems.

However on reflection, the incompatibility is not so great because in almost all widely cited prospective studies of reading development, verbal IQ is a strong predictor of reading attainment but its contribution is controlled statistically. Phonology emerges as a unique predictor after variance due to other language skills is taken into account. But this does not mean that the contribution of verbal IQ should be ignored. Notwithstanding the general role of IQ in the prediction of all kinds of educational attainment, it is important to consider its more specific role in relation to the development of reading processes if the sources of literacy failure among children with language impairments are to be understood (see also Catts, Fey, Zhang, & Tomblin, 1999).

Learning to read in children with semantic impairments

Poor comprehenders

The substantial body of evidence concerning the characteristics of children with word level reading or decoding difficulties (dyslexia) contrasts with the paucity of work on children who have specific deficits in reading comprehension. When poor reading comprehension occurs in a child with adequate decoding skills, it means that the problem cannot be traced to a bottle-neck produced by limited decoding ability (Perfetti & Hogaboam, 1975). Recent estimates suggest that about 10% of children experience such difficulties but, because their decoding skills are normal, they often go unnoticed in the classroom (Nation & Snowling, 1997).

The most prevalent view of the causes of children's reading comprehension problems places these outside the reading module in the processes involved in text integration. These children have difficulty making inferences, both elaborative and cohesive, during the course of their reading and they fail to monitor what they comprehend (Yuill & Oakhill, 1991, for a review). However, such children are more generally characterised by poor semantic skills in the face of normal phonology and good non-verbal intelligence (Stothard & Hulme, 1995; Nation, Adams, Bowyer-Crane, & Snowling, 1999). They do less well than controls matched for reading accuracy on tests such as judging whether pairs of words are synonymous, (e.g. ocean–sea), or generating exemplars of semantic categories, such as transport or occupations (Nation & Snowling, 1998a). They also do less well on syntactic awareness tasks.

It is important to consider how these weaknesses in cognitive profile place constraints on the functioning of the reading system. One obvious prediction, given the poor syntactic skills of these children, is that they will be unable to lean as much on sentence context to facilitate decoding when reading as children with grammatical competence. To assess this prediction, Nation and Snowling (1998b) compared poor comprehenders with reading-age matched normal readers and also dyslexic readers in an experiment in which the children were presented with a printed word, either in isolation or in a sentence context. The target word (e.g. aunt) was presented on a computer screen, and in the context condition it was preceded by a spoken sentence frame (e.g. "I went shopping with my mother and my ——"). The speed with which the children read the target words in the two conditions was measured and their accuracy recorded.

There was a significant facilitation effect of context for all children such that their reading was better when the printed words occurred following the sentence context. Importantly, however, the groups performed differently. The poor comprehenders benefited less from context than controls, while the dyslexic readers (who were older but matched in single-word reading skill) reaped the greatest advantage.

The findings of this experiment suggest that the availability of semantic and syntactic information from the sentence frame allowed the children to modify their incomplete or inaccurate pronunciations of target words to bring them in line with context. However, the poor comprehenders benefited less from these linguistic constraints than other groups of children whose word-level reading skills were equivalent. Most likely this was because of limitations in their sensitivity to semantic and grammatical constraints.

A more subtle difficulty that poor comprehenders experience is in their reading of irregular or exception words. Such words as "pint" and "mortgage" do not conform to English spelling-sound consistencies and they take longer for children to learn to read than regular words that can be decoded using phonological strategies (Laxon, Masterson, & Coltheart, 1991). A reasonable assumption is that exception words are learned by creating word-specific connections between their printed and spoken forms, with the support of vocabulary knowledge (Plaut, McClelland, Seidenberg, & Patterson, 1996; Tunmer & Chapman, 1998). Thus, it is possible to modify the pronunciation of an irregular word if its meaning is available, otherwise it is likely to be read as though regular — a process referred to as "regularisation". Examples of regularisation errors are glove → "gloave", ocean → "okeen".

Very few studies have documented the single word reading skills of children with semantic impairments. However, if this conceptualisation of their deficits is correct, then they should have more difficulty reading exception words than normal readers and make more regularisation errors. Nation and Snowling (1998a) tested this hypothesis in an experiment comparing the ability of poor comprehenders and reading age-matched controls when reading different types of word. As expected, the two groups were similar in their ability to read nonwords. They read high-frequency regular and irregular words equally well. However, the poor comprehenders made more errors and took more time to read exception words of low frequency, such as "month" and "dread" than their controls, and the majority of their errors were regularisations.

Arguably, one of the mechanisms that is usually used to "bootstrap" the reading of exception words is semantic knowledge and, since most words appear in context, this source of knowledge is activated during the course of reading. Our findings with poor comprehenders suggest that they may be less able to benefit from top-down resources, possibly because of impoverished vocabulary knowledge. It is reasonable, therefore, to ask what "knock-on" effects such specific comprehension difficulties might have on the development of literacy.

We were able to look at this question in a preliminary way through a follow-up study of a group of children who six years previously had been identified as having specific reading comprehension difficulties. In this study, we assessed the reading skills of 23 children remaining from a sample of 14 poor comprehenders and 14 normal readers originally studied at 7–8 years of age by Stothard and Hulme (1995).

To test the reading accuracy and comprehension of the two groups of children, they were asked to read aloud four difficult prose passages taken from both forms of the *Neale Analysis of Reading Ability — Revised* (Neale, 1989). Following each text, eight comprehension questions were asked. For each child, we recorded the number of words misread and the number of questions answered correctly. To assess word recognition, the *Wechsler Objective Reading Dimensions (WORD)* Basic Reading test of single-word reading was also administered in the same session (Rust, Golombok, & Trickey, 1993).

All but one of the original group of poor comprehenders obtained significantly lower reading comprehension scores than the normal readers, just as they had done previously. Importantly however, they also made more errors in their reading on both the prose and the single-word reading test.

These results need to be interpreted cautiously as the normal readers were approaching ceiling on some of the tests. Nonetheless, they suggest that poor comprehenders experience a relative decline in reading accuracy relative to normally developing children during the later stages of reading development. At follow-up at 14 years, the poor comprehenders were less accurate at reading both text and single words than the children in the normal comparison group to whom they were carefully matched for reading accuracy at 7–8 years. In spite of their promising start, supported by good phonological skills (Stothard & Hulme, 1995), the word recognition skills of these children had not kept pace with development, perhaps because of limitations in their vocabulary and sentence processing skills. More generally, the findings suggest that word-level and sentence-level processing skills interact during the course of learning to read and highlight two sources of difficulty that might be expected to compromise the literacy development of language-impaired children.

Hyperlexia

An extreme form of poor reading comprehension is seen in the case of hyperlexic children. These children often learn to read before they receive any formal instruction, and at a rate much in excess of that to be predicted from their IQ. Hyperlexia often occurs in combination with other developmental disorders, such as autism, and is characterised by a preoccupation with reading to the exclusion of meaning. Indeed, according to Healy (1982), hyperlexic children show excellent oral reading followed by a relative inability to demonstrate comprehension either by retelling or answering questions.

Much of the research on hyperlexia has been at the level of case studies which, although informative about the general features of the syndrome, have not focused in any detail on the reading mechanisms that are involved (Nation, 1999 for a review). Frith and Snowling (1983) reported that a group of autistic children, classified as "hyperlexic" could read words and nonwords as well as reading age-matched controls and that they were sensitive to grammatical distinctions in text. However, they had more difficulty in pronouncing ambiguous words in context, such as "bow" and "lead", and their comprehension of the details of what they read was poorer than that of younger reading age-matched controls. Thus, on the face of it, they appeared like poor comprehenders.

To investigate the nature of the reading comprehension deficit in hyperlexia further, Snowling and Frith (1986) compared autistic readers with two comparison groups, both matched on single-word reading age. One of these groups consisted of developmentally retarded children with mixed aetiologies, the other was of normally developing readers. The best predictor of reading comprehension across the groups taken together was verbal mental age, and the children from the clinical groups whose mental age was above 7 years comprehended what they read as well as reading age-matched controls. It was the children with a lower mental age that showed more "hyperlexic-like" behaviour, namely with advanced decoding skill and very poor reading comprehension.

To explore the nature of these children's comprehension difficulty beyond the single-word level, they were presented with a story to read in which they had to select words to fill "gaps" in the text using a modified cloze procedure. In each case, the child made a choice from three words, all of the same grammatical class but varying in their appropriateness to the context. One alternative fitted both the sentence and the story context (and was designated the story-appropriate choice), the second fitted the local context but not the story as a whole (the sentence-appropriate choice), the third was semantically anomalous. Thus, the story about a beaver contained the sentence *their mother/friends/room led the young beavers to the pond*. The child had to select the story-appropriate choice "mother". If they chose "friends" this was the sentence-level alternative, while "room" was inappropriate.

As already indicated, the higher ability autistic children performed normally on this test, usually choosing the story-appropriate completion. However, the hyperlexic readers performed less well than younger mental age-matched controls; although they could reject the implausible alternatives, they were evidently not following the story as it developed and hence did not show a systematic tendency to choose the story-appropriate alternative. Performance on this test requires the child to go beyond the information given to make inferences across the text as a whole. The results suggest that, like some poor comprehenders, these children have difficulty with the processes that bring about text cohesion (Cain & Oakhill, in press).

The hyperlexic children also had difficulty with text monitoring processes. This was tested by asking them to read through a text, embedded in which were anomalous words, e.g. the *hedgehog could smell the scent of electric flowers*, where *electric* did not fit the sentence context. Compared with younger children of similar mental age, they had more difficulty in detecting the text anomalies, and were just as likely to strike out a plausible as an implausible word.

A number of questions were left unanswered by this study. Although the hyperlexic children were matched in receptive vocabulary to the normally developing children, it is possible that their vocabulary knowledge was not as richly specified. One possibility was that their knowledge of the meanings of single words was sufficient to match the words to pictures but that their knowledge of the varieties and conditions of use of these words was not as extensive. It is important for future research to address the question of whether the deficit these autistic children showed was linked with poor semantic knowledge or if, as seems likely, their difficulty was in bringing to bear the pragmatic knowledge required to judge the appropriacy of single words in the sentences that carried them.

In line with this hypothesis, Happé (1997) extended the work of Frith and Snowling (1983) to show that autistic children showed less of a tendency to modify the pronunciation of written homographs (e.g. tear; lead) according to context than normal readers of the same level of reading skill. They also showed much less tendency to self-correct their reading errors. Moreover, the difficulty that the autistic children had in using context was characteristic of those with near normal levels of verbal ability as well as those who passed second order theory of mind tasks. Happé (1997) interpreted the poor performance of the autistic children as an aspect of "weak central coherence", signalled by a failure to extract meaning from context. She left open the possibility that the problem may not be specific to autism. Indeed, it seems likely that language-impaired chil-

dren who have pragmatic difficulties would display similar difficulties. It follows that they are at risk of failing to develop higher-level text comprehension strategies. While these children may make a good start in reading, it is unlikely that their reading skills will be sufficient to support their educational needs. Moreover, it seems unlikely that they will gain much enjoyment from reading and therefore, as time progresses, lack of reading experience, sometimes called print exposure, will surely stunt the development of their sight vocabulary.

LITERACY OUTCOMES AMONG CHILDREN WITH EARLY SPEECH-LANGUAGE IMPAIRMENTS

The preceding review makes clear that language-impaired children will suffer reading problems for a variety of reasons. As we have seen, the relationship between spoken and written language skills is not straightforward and the linguistic abilities needed to fuel reading change with time. If this is the case, then different children will be at risk of reading failure at different stages of development. We turn now to consider whether studies that have followed the progress of children with speech-language impairments can shed light on our question of who is at risk of literacy difficulties.

One of the most important predictors of literacy development among children with speech-language impairments appears to be the status of their oral language skills at the time when they start to read (Bird, Bishop, & Freeman, 1995). Following a large sample of children with preschool specific language impairments, Bishop and Adams (1990) found that those children whose spoken language difficulties had resolved by 5 years 6 months had a good outcome for reading in its early stages. Such children showed normal reading accuracy, reading comprehension and spelling at 8 years 6 months. They also performed as well as age-matched controls on tests of nonword reading and spelling, indicating that their experience of printed words was generalising normally to the processing of novel items. In contrast, children who had persistent and specific language impairments at 5 years 6 months had widespread reading and spelling difficulties at 8 years 6 months. Interestingly, however, when differences in non-verbal ability were controlled, the persistent SLI group did not differ from controls in terms of reading accuracy but a relatively high proportion of them had poor reading comprehension scores in relation to performance IQ. Overall, the clinical picture in these children bore a closer resemblance to the "poor comprehenders" we have discussed above, rather than to classic dyslexic readers with decoding problems.

Stothard et al. (1998) next saw these children just before leaving school at 15 years. At this time 56 of the original cohort of pre-schoolers with specific language impairment could be traced and agreed to participate. As a group, they performed worse on tests of reading, spelling and reading comprehension than a cross-sectional age-matched control sample, though it is important to note that outcomes were variable and almost half had reading skills within the normal range.

The children whose SLI had resolved by 5 years 6 months continued to be indistinguishable from normal controls in spoken language skills at 15 whereas those who had had a poor outcome showed persistent SLI. However, in spite of the good outcome for spoken language skills, the resolved SLI group were less successful in terms of literacy outcome than controls. Moreover, their difficulties with word decoding, spelling and reading comprehension were accompanied by problems with nonword reading and spelling and associated with deficits in three tasks tapping phonological processing, namely, Spoonerisms (a test of phonological awareness), nonword repetition, and sentence repetition. In short, the literacy profile of the resolved SLI group was similar to that observed in developmental dyslexia, though these children had followed a different developmental course to classically dyslexic children. In particular, they had experienced a good start with reading and their 8-year-old literacy skills had been within the normal range.

The literacy outcome for those with persistent SLI was even worse and they now performed almost as poorly as children who had been classified as having language impairments accompanied by low performance IQ at 5 years 6 months. Examining the SLI group as a whole, the literacy outcomes were particularly poor for those with a performance IQ less than 100 and there had been a substantial drop in reading accuracy, relative to age, between the ages of 8 years 6 months and 15 years (Snowling, Bishop, & Stothard, in press). Whereas the reading difficulties observed earlier in development were primarily characterised by problems of reading comprehension, now word recognition and decoding skills were both affected. Thus, the outcome was similar in some respects to that seen in the follow-up of poor comprehenders described earlier. These results therefore speak to the hypothesis that children who have comprehension difficulties have fewer resources for deciphering unfamiliar words. Consequently, in a language like English that contains many irregular words, the development of their word recognition vocabulary will be compromised. The data also suggested that there had been a relative decline in phonological processing skills. It will be recalled that at 8 years, these children had been able to read and spell nonwords normally which suggests that their phonological skills were intact. Nonetheless at 15, reading problems were accompanied by problems of phonological awareness. These findings support the proposal that learning to read is a highly interactive process. Not only do the mechanisms that support word recognition and reading comprehension influence each other, but also, reading appears to have a reciprocal influence on phonological awareness (Cataldo & Ellis, 1988).

What then are the concurrent predictors of word recognition among adolescents with a history of SLI? As we have seen, performance IQ was a strong predictor of literacy outcome but the specific processes that account for its relationship with reading are not clear. Given the argument we have developed above, vocabulary would be a likely resource to support the reading development of language-impaired individuals who have poor phonological skills. Although it is not clear theoretically why this should be so, it is relevant that, in the SLI sample, performance IQ correlated strongly with vocabulary whereas this was not the case among controls. In line with this conjecture, regression analyses identified two concurrent predictors of word recognition. These were phonological skills, as expected, and vocabulary knowledge; each contributed unique variance to individual differences in reading whereas performance IQ did not. While it is important to be cautious about the causal interpretation of what are essentially correlational data, these findings are consistent with the view that phonological and semantic skills interact to influence reading development. Moreover, semantic resources are likely to be particularly important for bootstrapping the literacy development of children with weak phonological skills.

THE INTERACTION OF PHONOLOGICAL AND SEMANTIC SKILLS IN LEARNING TO READ

In order to consider more formally the mechanisms that place children at risk of reading failure,

we now turn to a framework for the conceptualisation of reading proposed by Seidenberg and McClelland (1989). Within this framework, learning to read can be thought of as a process of setting up mappings between the orthographic forms of printed words and their phonological forms. This process is supported by semantic knowledge and an appreciation of context (see Fig. 14.1).

Seidenberg and McClelland's model is one of a class of models called connectionist or parallel distributed processing (PDP) models. The essential feature of these models is that representations of words are distributed across many simple processing elements. Thus, word forms are not stored as entities, rather the features of words, be they phonological, orthographic or semantic, are represented as patterns of activation that interact during learning to establish connections. The model that Seidenberg and McClelland implemented (SM89) consisted of two types of representational unit: a set of input units coding the letters present in printed words (orthographic units) and a set of output units coding the pronunciation of

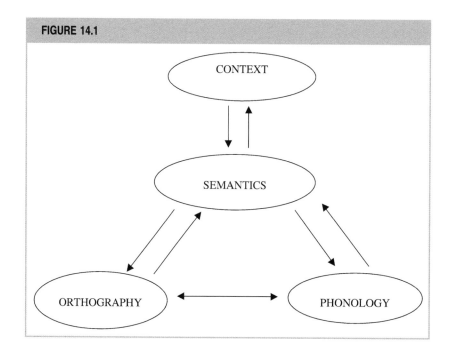

FIGURE 14.1

Schematic drawing of Seidenberg and McClelland's framework of reading.

words (phonological units). The input and output units were connected via a set of intermediate or "hidden" units.

Connectionist models are trained by comparing the desired output for a given input to the output generated by the model. This training process is called supervised learning and can be likened to a child learning how a letter string is pronounced by first reading it wrongly and then being corrected. The model represents knowledge about the words it is trained on in terms of the connection strengths (or weights) between different processing elements. The more well used a connection, the more efficient will be processes that use the same mappings.

One critical feature of SM89, and others like it, is that after training to associate many input patterns (written words) with many output patterns (spoken words), it is able to generalise to words it has not been explicitly taught to read. The knowledge the model embodies after training can be thought of as representing the statistical regularities that exist in English between spelling patterns and the pronunciations of words. This is particularly relevant for the development of the reading system as, in effect, a "self-teaching device" (Share, 1995) is inherent in the architecture of the model.

The model implemented by Seidenberg and McClelland did not deal with meaning, though they did note that a semantic mechanism would need to be implemented in order to fully describe the reading process. More recent models of this type have attempted to implement a system of semantic representation (Hinton & Shallice, 1991). A major innovation has been a model reported by Plaut, McClelland, Seidenberg and Patterson (1996) which contains two pathways by which orthographic information can influence phonological information: a phonological pathway and a semantic pathway. An assumption of this model is that fluent readers use a combination of semantic and phonological information during word recognition. It is this model that is important for considering the ways in which reading may become impaired in children with spoken language difficulties.

In essence, Plaut et al.'s simulation involved training a network in which a semantic pathway provided additional input to the phoneme units, to push them towards their desired outputs. An effect of combining semantic and phonological influences in the model was to increase the rate of learning, particularly of low-frequency exception words. It is these words that we have seen create special difficulty for poor comprehenders. Moreover, in the later stages of training, Plaut et al. (1996) showed that the two pathways become more highly specialised, so that the semantic pathway deals primarily with the pronunciation of exception words while the phonological pathway is left for the pronunciation of words with consistent pronunciations.

Within the connectionist framework, problems in developing either orthography–phonology or orthography–semantic mappings are conceivable. Dyslexic children with phonological difficulties have problems in establishing the orthography–phonology mappings (Snowling, Hulme, & Goulandris, 1994) while it seems that children with language (rather than speech) impairments may have more difficulty creating the orthography–semantic mappings (Nation & Snowling, 1998a).

A second important consequence of learning to read that this class of models has simulated is the reciprocal influence of reading on phonology. Harm and Seidenberg (1999) showed that during the course of training the orthography–phonology connections, feedback to the phonological units could be used to modify the representations themselves. Subsequently, the model's performance on tasks mimicking speech perception improved. In short, models of this type provide a useful metaphor for children's reading development. The framework is also useful for considering children's reading difficulties (e.g. Manis et al., 1996; Seidenberg, 1992). In connectionist terms, a reading disorder such as dyslexia can be modelled by constraining the mappings that are established between orthography and phonology during acquisition. Likewise, the reading problems of children with language impairments that extend beyond phonology can be modelled by reducing the semantic knowledge they can draw upon or by constraining the influence of context, not yet implemented in any of these models.

The role of environmental factors

We have seen that, although phonology is generally viewed as central to the acquisition of reading, its influence is modified by other language skills. In fact, arguments have been made for the role of semantic, syntactic and pragmatic skills in learning to read (cf. Whitehurst & Lonigan, 1998; see also Whitehurst & Fischel, chapter 4, this volume). Discussion of connectionist models reminds us that individual differences between children during the process of learning to read will also depend upon the environments in which they learn. Indeed, one of the most important environmental predictors of reading acquisition is maternal educational level, a factor that is likely to be mediated not only through child-rearing practices but also via the linguistic environment in the home. Moreover, the language of learning is also important.

Languages differ in the inherent difficulty they pose to young readers who are trying to "crack the code". Languages with a regular or transparent orthography, such as German or Italian, are evidently easier to learn than those with opaque writing systems such as English (Frith, Wimmer, & Landerl, 1998). Hence, in spite of their phonological difficulties, dyslexic children can learn to decode in German with relative ease compared to English (Wimmer, 1996). As yet, research has not examined how children with broader language difficulties fare in these regular orthographies and it is reasonable to suppose that reading comprehension difficulties may sometimes be masked in these children by virtue of the ease of decoding that the orthography brings.

Perhaps the most obvious environmental influence on children's reading acquisition is the teaching they receive. There is now considerable evidence showing that children who have reading difficulties benefit early in development from interventions that combine training in phonological awareness with highly structured reading programmes emphasising the links between spellings and sounds (Snowling, 1996, for a review). It is likely that particular forms of speech and language therapy will also play a role in determining the reading strategies a child adopts, though the relevant research to demonstrate this has not yet be done.

Finally, it is important to remember that children's reading development is, at least in part, determined by their own motivation to read and, to an extent, the literacy environment they create for themselves. Most importantly, the development of fluent reading depends upon practice and, in an opaque reading system such as English, this is vital to the acquisition of words that have to be learned "by sight". Stanovich and West (1989) used the term "print exposure" as a proxy for the amount of time an individual spends reading. Measures of print exposure require the recognition of the names of authors or the titles of books and, although the sensitivity of such measures has been questioned, print exposure accounts for variance in reading skills when other critical variables such as IQ and phonological awareness have been controlled. Furthermore, Stanovich and his colleagues have suggested that some children who appear to place over-reliance on word attack skills may suffer only a mild phonological difficulty but also lack print exposure (Stanovich, Siegel, & Gottardo, 1997). Within the connectionist framework, such children can establish basic mappings between orthography and phonology but have not had sufficient experience with different word types (both regular and exception) for the system to function normally.

LITERACY SKILLS: WHO IS AT RISK?

By far the majority of research on children's reading difficulties has focused on the problems experienced by dyslexic children. More generally, studies of normal development have demonstrated that individual differences in phonological processing predict individual differences in reading-decoding skill. However, other language skills are also involved. Dyslexic children exhibit phonological deficits in the face of normal semantic skills; they can use the latter to good effect to promote their reading development. Individual differences in semantic processing predict a separate source of variance in reading skill, namely differences in the use of context and in reading comprehension. Children with impairments of spoken language vary in the extent to which processing is impaired in different language sub-systems and the heterogeneity of their reading disorders need to be understood within this framework.

Thus, while it is widely accepted that good phonological skills are needed to establish a foundation for reading development, children who have selective impairments of expressive phonology are not necessarily reading-disabled. If expressive phonological disorders are accompanied by deficits in phonological awareness, the child is at heightened risk of reading failure (Stackhouse, chapter 5, this volume). Within this same framework, children who have poor vocabulary development will find it difficult to set up word-specific associations and may be forced to rely on phonological decoding strategies; in English, their ability to read exception words is likely to suffer. Beyond the word-level of reading, children with semantic, syntactic and pragmatic difficulties are vulnerable to failure, with knock-on effects at the single-word level. To conclude, it is proposed that children's phonological difficulties place them at risk of literacy failure at the outset of reading and, later, impairments of other language skills compromise development to adult levels of fluency.

ACKNOWLEDGEMENTS

This chapter was prepared with support from Wellcome Trust project 040195/2/93/A. I am grateful to Kate Nation for her helpful comments and Sara Bailey for assistance with the manuscript.

REFERENCES

Aram, D.M., Ekelman, B.L., & Nation, J.E. (1984). Preschoolers with language disorders: 10 years later. *Journal of Speech and Hearing Research, 27*, 232–244.

Bird, J., Bishop, D.V.M., & Freeman, N. (1995). Phonological awareness and literacy development in children with expressive phonological impairments. *Journal of Speech and Hearing Research, 38*, 446–462.

Bishop, D. (1989). Unfixed reference, monocular occlusion, and developmental dyslexia — a critique. *British Journal of Opthalmology, 73*, 209–215.

Bishop, D.V.M., & Adams, C. (1990). A prospective study of the relationship between specific language impairment, phonological disorders and reading retardation. *Journal of Child Psychology and Psychiatry, 31*, 1027–1050.

Bishop, D.V.M., & Edmundson, A. (1987). Language-impaired four-year-olds: Distinguishing transient from persistent impairment. *Journal of Speech and Hearing Disorders, 52*, 156–173.

Bradley, L., & Bryant, P.E. (1983). Categorising sounds and learning to read — causal connection. *Nature, 301*, 419–421.

Byrne, B., Fielding-Barnsley, R., Ashley, L., & Larsen, K. (1997). Assessing the child's and the environment's contribution to reading acquisition: What we know and what we don't know. In B. Blachman (Ed.), *Reading acquisition and dyslexia: Implications for early intervention* (pp. 265–286). Hillsdale, NJ: Lawrence Erlbaum Associates Inc.

Cain, K., & Oakhill, J.V. (in press). Inference making ability and its relation to comprehenson failure in young children. *Reading and Writing.*

Cataldo, S., & Ellis, N. (1988). Interactions in the development of spelling, reading and phonological skills. *Journal of Research in Reading, 11*, 86–109.

Catts, H.W. (1993). The relationship between speech-language impairments and reading disabilities. *Journal of Speech and Hearing Research, 36*, 948–958.

Catts, H.W., Fey, M.E., Zhang, X., & Tomblin, J.B. (1999). Language basis of reading and spelling disabilities. *Scientific Studies of Reading, 3*, 331–362.

DeFries, J.C. (1991). Genetics and dyslexia: An overview. In M. Snowling & M. Thomson (Eds), *Dyslexia: Integrating theory and practice* (pp. 3–20). London: Whurr.

Dodd, B. (1995). *Differential diagnosis and treatment of children with speech disorder*. London: Whurr.

Elbro, C., Borstrom, I., & Petersen, D.K. (1998). Predicting dyslexia from kindergarten: The importance of distinctness of phonological representations of lexical items. *Reading Research Quarterly, 33*, 36–60.

Felsenfeld, S., Broen, P.A., & McGue, M. (1992). A 28-year follow-up of adults with a history of moderate phonological disorder: Linguistic and personality results. *Journal of Speech and Hearing Research, 35*, 1114–1125.

Frith, U., & Snowling, M. (1983). Reading for meaning and reading for sound in autistic and dyslexic children. *British Journal of Developmental Psychology*, *1*, 329–342.

Frith, U., Wimmer, H., & Landerl, K. (1998). Differences in phonological recoding in German- and English-speaking children. *Scientific Studies of Reading*, *2*, 31–54.

Gallagher, A., Frith, U., & Snowling. M. (2000). Precursors of literacy delay among children at genetic risk of dyslexia. *Journal of Child Psychology and Psychiatry*, *41*, 203–213.

Goswami, U., & Bryant, P. (1990). *Phonological skills and learning to read.* Hove, UK: Lawrence Erlbaum Associates Ltd.

Gough, P.B., & Tunmer, W.E. (1986). Decoding, reading, and reading disability. *Remedial and Special Education*, *7*, 6–10.

Happé, F.G.E. (1997). Central coherence and theory of mind in autism: Reading homographs in context. *British Journal of Developmental Psychology*, *15*, 1–12.

Harm, M.W. & Seidenberg, M.S. (1999). Phonology, reading and dyslexia: Insights from connectionist models. *Psychological Review*, *106*, 491–528.

Healy, J.M. (1982). The enigma of hyperlexia. *Reading Research Quarterly*, *7*, 319–318.

Hinton, G., & Shallice, T. (1991). Lesioning an attractor network: Investigations of acquired dyslexia. *Psychological Review*, *98*, 74–95.

Laxon, V., Masterson, J., & Coltheart, V. (1991). Some bodies are easier to read: The effect of consistency and regularity on children's reading. *Quarterly Journal of Experimental Psychology*, *43A*, 793–824.

Lefly, D.L., & Pennington, B.F. (1996). Longitudinal study of children at high family risk for dyslexia: The first two years. In M.L. Rice (Ed.), *Toward a genetics of language* (pp. 49–76). Hillsdale, NJ: Lawrence Erlbaum Associates Inc.

Lundberg, I. (1994). Reading difficulties can be predicted and prevented: A Scandinavian perspective on phonological awareness and reading. In C. Hulme & M.J. Snowling (Eds), *Reading development and dyslexia* (pp. 180–199). London: Whurr.

Magnusson, E., & Naucler, K. (1990). Reading and spelling in language-disordered children — linguistic and metalinguistic prerequisites: Report on a longitudinal study. *Clinical Linguistics and Phonetics*, *4*, 49–61.

Manis, F.R., Seidenberg, M.S., Doi, L.M., McBride-Chang, C., & Petersen, A. (1996). On the bases of two subtypes of developmental dyslexia. *Cognition*, *58*, 157–195.

Mattingly, I.G. (1972). Reading, the linguistic process and linguistic awareness. In J.F. Kavanagh & I.G. Mattingly (Eds), *Language by ear and by eye. The relationships between speech and reading* (pp. 133–148). Cambridge, MA: MIT Press.

Nation, K. (1999). Reading skills in hyperlexia: A developmental perspective. *Psychological Bulletin*, *125*, 338–355.

Nation, K., & Snowling, M. (1997). Assessing reading difficulties: The validity and utility of current measures of reading skill. *British Journal of Educational Psychology*, *67*, 359–370.

Nation, K., & Snowling, M. (1998a). Semantic processing and the development of word recognition skills: Evidence from children with reading comprehension difficulties. *Journal of Memory & Language*, *39*, 85–101.

Nation, K., & Snowling, M. (1998b). Individual differences in contextual facilitation: Evidence from dyslexia and poor reading comprehension. *Child Development*, *69*, 996–1011.

Nation, K., Adams, J.W., Bowyer-Crane, C.A., & Snowling, M.J. (1999). Working memory deficits in poor comprehenders reflect underlying language impairments. *Journal of Experimental Child Psychology*, *73*, 139–158.

Neale, M.D. (1989). *The Neale Analysis of Reading Ability — Revised.* Windsor, UK: NFER.

Olson, R.K., Datta, H., Gayan, J., & DeFries, J.C. (1997). A behavioural genetic analysis of reading disabilities and component processes. In R. Klein & P. McMullen (Eds), *Converging methods for understanding reading and dyslexia.* Cambridge, MA: MIT Press.

Pennington, B.F. (1994). Genetics of learning disabilities. *Journal of Child Neurology*, *10*, 69–76.

Perfetti, C.A., & Hogaboam, T. (1975). Relationship between single word decoding and reading comprehension skill. *Journal of Educational Psychology*, *67*, 461–469.

Perin, D. (1983). Phonemic segmentation and spelling. *British Journal of Psychology*, *74*, 129–144.

Plaut, D., McClelland, J.L., Seidenberg, M.S., & Patterson, K.E. (1996). Understanding normal and impaired reading: Computational principles in quasi-irregular domains. *Psychological Review*, *103*, 56–115.

Rust, J., Golombok, S., & Trickey, G. (1993). *Wechsler Objective Reading Dimensions.* Sidcup, UK: Psychological Corporation.

Scarborough, H.S. (1990). Very early language deficits in dyslexic children. *Child Development*, *61*, 1728–1743.

Seidenberg, M. (1992). Dyslexia in a computational model of word recognition in reading. In P.B. Gough, L. Ehri, & R. Treiman (Eds), *Reading acquisition* (pp. 243–274). Hillsdale, NJ: Lawrence Erlbaum Associates Inc.

Seidenberg, M.S., & McClelland, J. (1989). A distributed, developmental model of word recognition. *Psychological Review, 96*, 523–568.

Share, D.L. (1995). Phonological recoding and self-teaching: The sine qua non of reading acquisition. *Cognition, 55*, 151–218.

Snowling, M.J. (1996). Annotation: Contemporary approaches to the teaching of reading. *Journal of Child Psychology and Psychiatry, 37*, 139–148.

Snowling, M.J. (1998). Reading development and its difficulties. *Educational and Child Psychology, 15*, 44–58.

Snowling, M.J., & Frith, U. (1986). Comprehension in "hyperlexic" readers. *Journal of Experimental Child Psychology, 42*, 392–415.

Snowling, M.J., Hulme, C., & Goulandris, N. (1994). Word recognition in developmental dyslexia: A connectionist interpretation. *Quarterly Journal of Experimental Psychology, 47A*, 985–916.

Snowling, M., Bishop, D.V.M., & Stothard, S.E. (in press). Do language impaired preschoolers turn into dyslexic adolescents? *Journal of Child Psychology and Psychiatry.*

Stackhouse, J. (1982). An investigation of reading and spelling performance in speech disordered children. *British Journal of Disorders of Communicaion, 17*, 53–60.

Stackhouse, J. (1996). Speech, spelling and reading: Who is at risk and why? In M. Snowling & J. Stackhouse (Eds), *Dyslexia, speech and language: A practitioners handbook* (pp. 12–30). London: Whurr.

Stackhouse, J., & Snowling, M. (1992). Barriers to literacy development in two cases of developmental verbal dyspraxia. *Cognitive Neuropsychology, 9*, 273–299.

Stackhouse, J., & Wells, B. (1997). How do speech and language problems affect literacy development? In C. Hulme & M. Snowling (Eds), *Dyslexia: Biology, cognition and intervention* (pp. 182–211). London: Whurr.

Stanovich, K.E. (1994). Annotation: Does dyslexia exist? *Journal of Child Psychology and Psychiatry, 35*, 579–595.

Stanovich, K.E., & Siegel, L.S. (1994). The phenotypic performance profile of reading-disabled children: A regression-based test of the phonological-core variable-difference model. *Journal of Educational Psychology, 86*, 24–53.

Stanovich, K., Seigel, L.S., & Gottardo, A. (1997). Progress in the search for dyslexia subtypes. In C. Hulme & M. Snowling (Eds), *Dyslexia: Biology, cognition and intervention* (pp. 108–130). London: Whurr.

Stanovich, K.E. and West, R.F. (1989). Exposure to print and orthographic processing. *Reading Research Quarterly, 24*, 402–433.

Stark, R.E., Bernstein, L.E., Condino, R., Bender, M., Tallal, P., & Catts, H. (1984). Four-year follow-up study of language impaired children. *Annals of Dyslexia, 34*, 49–68.

Stothard, S.E., & Hulme, C. (1995). A comparison of phonological skills in children with reading comprehension difficulties and children with decoding difficulties. *Journal of Child Psychology and Psychiatry, 36*, 399–408.

Stothard, S.E., Snowling, M.J., Bishop, D.V.M., Chipchase, B.B., & Kaplan, C.A. (1998). Language impaired preschoolers: A follow-up into adolescence. *Journal of Speech, Language, and Hearing Research, 41*, 407–418.

Tallal, P., Allard, L., Miller, S., & Curtiss, S. (1997). Academic outcomes of language impaired children. In C. Hulme & M. Snowling (Eds), *Dyslexia: Biology, cognition and intervention* (pp. 167–181). London: Whurr.

Tunmer, W.E., & Chapman, J.W. (1998). Language prediction skill, phonological recoding ability and beginning reading. In M. Joshi & C. Hulme (Eds), *Reading, and spelling: Development and disorders* (pp. 33–68). Mahwah, NJ: Erlbaum Lawrence Associates Inc.

Whitehurst, G.J., & Lonigan, C.J. (1998). Child development and emergent literacy. *Child Development, 69*, 848–872.

Wimmer, H. (1996). The early manifestation of developmental dyslexia: Evidence from German children. *Reading and Writing, 8*, 171–188.

Yuill, N., & Oakhill, J. (1991). *Children's problems in text comprehension*. Cambridge: Cambridge University Press.

15

Acquired epileptic aphasia (AEA) or Landau-Kleffner syndrome: From childhood to adulthood

Thierry Deonna

Acquired epileptic aphasia (AEA) is a clinical-electroencephalographic (EEG) syndrome occurring exclusively in children. Onset is usually between 3–7 years of age. Onset may be sudden or gradual; in cases of gradual onset, there are often fluctuations in language level. In its most severe form the child appears to become aphasic, although in many cases the disorder is more accurately described as an auditory agnosia. The onset is followed by loss of verbal production together with paroxysmal bilateral "epileptic" EEG discharges in the temporal lobes. Diagnosis depends on the EEG because affected children do not always have recognised epileptic seizures. It is now accepted that the language loss is a direct consequence of the focal epileptic disorder, which in most cases is not caused by any underlying brain damage. AEA is increasingly considered to be an exceptionally severe form of a common inherited epileptic syndrome, "benign partial epilepsy with rolandic spikes". However, it is possible that some cases are related to a focal pathology, e.g. areas of misplaced cells (dysplasia) or other brain lesions. Some cases may result from a combination of genetic factors and brain damage. AEA provides a unique opportunity to study the effects of a focal epileptic dysfunction during development, for example, how a prolonged disruption of the activity of auditory cortex during a critical period of language development can permanently impair some components of auditory functioning.

INTRODUCTION

Imagine a bright 5-year-old who, over a period of a few weeks, ceases to respond to everyday questions, without giving any explanation why, and who gradually stops speaking. He does not appear unwell, though he is very ill-tempered and sleeps poorly. The first thing one would think is that he has become deaf, and, if this is excluded, that he has become mute or has some psychiatric disease. All too often, the diagnosis of acquired epileptic aphasia (AEA) (Table 15.1) is not considered, especially when the child has not had any recognised clinical seizure. The diagnosis is even more difficult to suspect when the onset of AEA is very gradual, the symptoms are transient or mild, and when there is spontaneous recovery.

The symptoms described above are due to an acquired auditory agnosia, i.e. a failure of the brain to decode sounds. This is the consequence of epileptic activity in one, or more often both, cortical auditory areas in the temporal lobe (Fig. 15.1), which renders these areas non-functional. Epilepsy is a disorder of the electrical activity of the brain consisting of the sudden temporary abnormal hypersynchronous firing of a group of brain cells (neurons). During this period the part(s) of the brain involved cannot perform their normal function. This epileptic activity can be seen on the EEG in cases of AEA (Fig. 15.2). Until recently there were no other demonstrable laboratory signs of brain disease. Complex new methods of functional brain imaging can now show metabolic derangements in the brain areas involved, but these are not routinely done for clinical purposes (Deonna, 1991).

Soon after the child loses the ability to understand language, speech begins to deteriorate. The quality of speech sound production (output phonology) will be affected if one cannot monitor the auditory results of speaking, but how fast this occurs and how independently such input and output processes can function has not previously been studied in AEA.

Our group studied one 6.5-year-old child, (G), at a time when he was losing most of his comprehension (1 to 2 months after onset). Output phonology and syntax, though abnormal, were still relatively intact, whereas morphology was more impaired. It was concluded that early impairment of production occurs as a result of the decoding deficit (for instance, he repeated "pama" for "dame" and "ivan" for "livre"). Impaired production may be even more apparent in the domain of grammatical morphology, because applying appropriate function words and inflectional endings requires "on-line" computation (Zesiger et al., 1999).

TABLE 15.1

Characteristics of acquired epileptic aphasia (Landau-Kleffner syndrome)

Acute or insidious onset of aphasia in a child, with typical age at onset of 3 to 7 yr (although younger and older can be observed)

Paroxysmal EEG abnormality, usually bitemporal with or without continuous spike waves during sleep (CSWS)

Normal brain imaging

Severe persistent aphasia (auditory agnosia) with variable recovery

Close relationship between aphasia and abnormal EEG activity

Little response to anti-epileptic medication in many cases

FIGURE 15.1

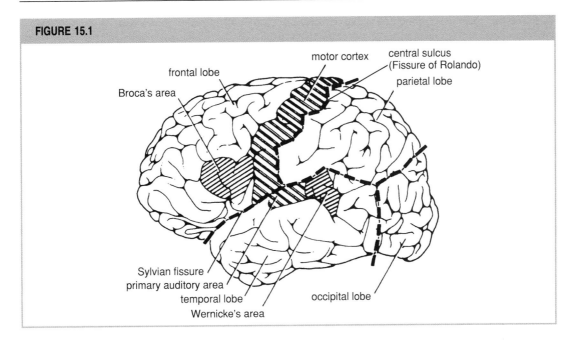

The lower part of the motor cortex above the Sylvian fissure is involved in movements of the articulators (lips, tongue, palate, pharynx). It is typically involved in so-called "benign partial epilepsy with rolandic spikes". Just in front of it is Broca's area, involved in speech programming. The area below the Sylvian fissure corresponds to the cortical auditory area. The "perisylvian region" corresponds grossly to the area around the Sylvian fissure. From Bishop, 1988b. Reprinted with permission from Churchill Livingstone.

FIGURE 15.2

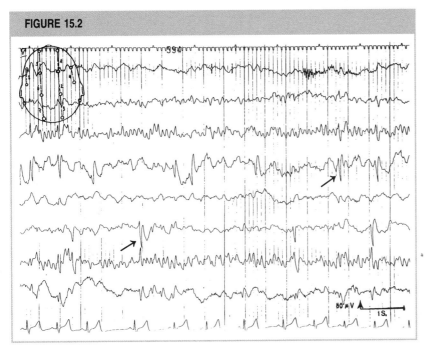

This figure shows an electroencephalographic recording over the scalp of a boy aged 6 years 6 months with acquired epileptic aphasia (Landau-Kleffner syndrome). There are paroxysmal epileptic discharges (spike-waves: arrows) occurring independently over the right and left hemispheres in the centrotemporal regions (perisylvian).

In some cases speech output, rather than verbal understanding, is first and predominantly affected because the epileptic activity involves mainly the anterior perisylvian area including the motor speech cortex, (Marien et al., 1993) but the clinical course and EEG findings are otherwise similar to AEA. In some children, the deficit predominantly or exclusively affects "non-linguistic" oromotor functions (anterior operculum syndrome) (Deonna, 1993).

Acquired epileptic aphasia: Additional impairments

It is important to realise that children with AEA, especially the more severe forms, often have associated major behaviour problems, such as hyperactivity, attention deficits or aggressiveness, and may have more general cognitive impairments in addition to the basic verbal communication problem. These are often attributed to the child's reaction to his language deprivation, but there are recent data indicating that extension of the epileptic discharges to frontal and other brain regions also plays an important role.

In some cases, the behaviour disturbance and/or cognitive problems are so severe that a specific impairment in the area of verbal language is not readily apparent. In younger children, some of the behavioural characteristics can suggest an autistic disorder. However, I am not aware of a detailed and convincing published case of typical autism as the manifestation of AEA.

SITE OF INVOLVEMENT WITHIN THE AUDITORY/LANGUAGE SYSTEM

There are no definite data at the present time on the specific level of processing that is involved, and it is not clear that this is the same in all cases. Initially, it was thought that the problem was at the level of the decoding of phonemes (i.e. a verbal auditory agnosia or a phonological agnosia; Korkman, Granström, Appelqvist, & Liukkonen, 1998), because children with AEA are often able to decode many non-speech (i.e. envir-

onmental) sounds. However, this is not always the case. In severe cases or early after onset, most significant sounds are not recognised. Environmental sounds are much simpler acoustically than speech sounds, and this may explain why mild cases or cases who are recovering can recognise them.

There are at the present time no conclusive electrophysiological data to resolve this issue (Boyd et al., 1996). It seems likely, however, that the involvement is very early in the auditory cortex where the processing of the incoming flow of the auditory information takes place.

A virtually unexplored area is the understanding of speech melody (prosody) in AEA. Prosody conveys emotional information (e.g. whether the speaker is angry, neutral, anxious, etc.). It also conveys propositional information, such as which word is the focus of attention: e.g. "do *you* want to go in the car?" vs. "do you want to go in the *car*?". In a recent study, two severely affected children with auditory agnosia were able to derive some meaning from prosodic contours of heard utterances and had oral productions with some recognisable and appropriate prosodic cues (Doherty et al., 1999). One of our cases who has recovered completely has normal tested comprehension of both emotional and propositional prosody. Furthermore, his expressive prosody allows one to recognise his local accent, although there has been a subtle change recognised by his close relatives and peers. He is poor at recognising melodies and singing. This was not good before the disease, but there was a definite change. In fact, there are no systematic studies on musical abilities in AEA, which, from various comments in case reports, often seem to be affected. This is important, because we know that music and verbal language are processed by different cortical networks, as shown from the study of brain-damaged patients.

NEUROPATHOLOGY OF AEA

AEA appears to be unique in childhood neuropathology and psychopathology for several reasons. Unlike acquired focal brain lesions, which destroy specialised brain circuits or systems at a given time in development, in AEA there is prolonged recurrent dysfunction with possible intervals of normal functions in between. We know that some kind of permanent damage can result from persistent abnormal epileptic discharges, especially if they occur at the time of major development and stabilisation of the networks involved in a given function. This is totally different from pathology resulting from an acute destruction of the same area. So both the nature of the injury and the duration of its impact over time are unlike any traditional brain pathology. Notions such as plasticity and reorganisation of functions have to be thought of differently in these special circumstances. It follows that unique consequences must also be expected on the clinical side.

Comparison between other childhood aphasias and AEA

Brain plasticity is evident in the fact that young children, unlike adults, show a capacity for rapid and complete language recovery after a lesion in the language zones. AEA is different because the language disturbance is often prolonged, and recovery most often incomplete. This observation, and the predominant impairment of language comprehension, has led to the conclusion that the pathology in this condition is fundamentally different and is not the result of a "simple" focal brain lesion in language areas (Deonna, 1996).

Two possibilities may be considered. First, relocation of language functions may be prevented because the pathology is bilateral. Second, the pathology could be unilateral but progressive, preventing either local reorganisation in the same hemisphere or a switch to the contralateral hemisphere.

Bishop (1985) noted that the cases with an early age at onset had a worse prognosis than those with later onset. She proposed that loss of verbal comprehension in AEA leads to a gradual loss of productive language, just as is seen in acquired deafness. This may well be a part but not the whole explanation. The sequelae are prob-

ably mainly due to the prolonged effects on brain function of this particular focal epilepsy whose age at onset, severity, extent and duration are extremely variable.

Evidence for a direct role of epilepsy in AEA

For a long time, it was believed that both the language problems and the epilepsy were the consequences of the same unknown underlying brain disease. In the last few years, there has been a shift to the idea that the language problem is the direct consequence of a special form of epilepsy without any newly-acquired disease. An acute onset, a fluctuating course, a frequent correlation of language symptoms with the epileptic activity on the EEG, and the sometimes rapid recovery with antiepileptic drugs, are strong arguments implicating a functional inhibition of the areas involved in the epileptic process. More recently, results of functional imaging and electrocorticography in cases of AEA submitted to surgery (multiple subpial transection; Morrell et al., 1995) have clearly shown the role of the epilepsy in causing the language and other problems. It is still disputed whether this focal epilepsy belongs to the family of "non-lesional" genetic epilepsy (partial epilepsy with rolandic spikes or benign partial epilepsy, BPE) or if developmental or early acquired epileptogenic lesions in the same location(s) can sometimes account for the disorder (Roulet et al.,1998).

Medical treatment of AEA

There is now a consensus that suppression of the abnormal brain epileptic activity is of utmost importance to allow the involved cortical areas to be functional again. Antiepileptic treatment is fraught with many problems that are beyond the scope of the present review. Most of the classic antiepileptic drugs are ineffective or only temporarily effective in AEA. One often needs a systematic trial of different drugs (which may include unconventional ones such as steroids or even immunoglobulins), alone or in combination, and repeated EEGs are necessary to monitor the therapeutic effect. There is no simple one-to-one relationship between the EEG and the clinical improvement, especially in cases with an already long-standing language deficit. EEG improvement may precede clinical improvement; the opposite is rare. In resistant cases, surgical treatment, namely subpial transection (that is, the severing of horizontal fibres which propagate the abnormal electrical activity from the original epileptic focus) has been advocated with good results, but this is extremely difficult to evaluate (Morrell et al., 1995).

MANAGEMENT OF LANGUAGE AND EDUCATION IN CHILDREN WITH AEA

Management depends on the type and severity of the language impairment and associated cognitive and behavioural disturbances. When there is a complete loss of comprehension of oral language and when there is no realistic hope that the situation will change in a short time (which is the case when the disorder has been present for more then a few weeks or months and when medical therapy has not brought any significant improvement), an alternative mode of communication is crucial, both to keep the child out of his tragic isolation and for educational purposes.

Sign language must be considered but, as is the case for deaf children of hearing parents, its implementation is often fraught with resistance or other practical difficulties. As the disorder improves or if the child is willing to pay attention to sounds and is not clearly avoiding this source, systematic and gradual "retraining" in this modality can be proposed. This should start at the most basic affected level (i.e. attention to presence of sounds), moving on to listening for contrasts between simple words which are meaningful to the child and can be pictured (see Vance, 1991). One of the problems is that the child must consciously realise the purpose of such exercises. This may not be obvious to a young child who may have lost most memories of sounds or all belief that sounds can have a meaning! It is not known how far improvement is due to the functional recovery of the underlying circuits and what role is played

by conscious training in the defective modality. What is known, however, is that treatment is crucial: untreated and unstimulated children with severe AEA may have permanent total auditory agnosias (Deonna, Peter, & Ziegler, 1989).

Management of children with AEA has to take into account the possibility of recurrences, so that educational programmes and school choices must adapt to the variable performances of these children. This is very demanding, stressful and discouraging to both child and teachers. Often, no school is really adequate for these children. It is a long but worthwhile battle, because there are increasing examples of significant recoveries of severely affected children who continue to progress after adolescence (Deonna & Roulet, 1995).

NATURAL HISTORY AND PROGNOSIS OF AEA

Considering the wide range of severity of the syndrome and modalities of treatment, it is not surprising that no generalisation can be made about outcome. Table 15.2 illustrates this situation.

Prognosis depends also on many factors, including age at onset of the disorder, and its intensity (persistent or intermittent epileptic activity), and duration (weeks, months or years). An important factor is the local extent of the abnormal epileptic activity, and how far it spreads (both within the same hemisphere and to the contralateral one), and whether it affects areas involved with other cognitive functions, such as the frontal lobes. Outcome may also depend on individual variations in brain organisation. Last but not least, prompt and effective suppression of the abnormal epileptic activity is probably a crucial factor. Consequently, older cases who had delayed diagnosis and therapy cannot be taken as the reference. The final outcome in educational and social terms will be decisively influenced by psychological factors. The fundamental issue is to maintain communication at all costs, as discussed above, and to realise the anxiety, feeling of isolation and the frustrations these children suffer.

To summarise, some children have only a brief period of aphasia and recover fully, whereas

TABLE 15.2

Follow-up of 2 children with AEA

	Gregory	*David*
Age follow-up	10 yr	15 yr
Age at onset	6;3 yr	3;6 yr
Delay to diagnosis	2 months	3 years, 6 months
Maximum deficit	partial auditory agnosia preserved speech	total auditory agnosia mutism
Medical therapy (efficacy)	excellent	± mixed
Alternative means of communication	not necessary	sign language
Recovery	total (2 months)	partial (over years)

others may have a permanent auditory agnosia with residual mutism for the rest of their life. All intermediate situations can be encountered.

Some recent cases, followed prospectively and who are now reaching adulthood, show surprising continuing progress beyond adolescence, even though they remain impaired (Deonna & Roulet, 1995). One of the boys, who was 19 years old at the time of our follow-up study (Deonna et al., 1989), was seen again 7 years later. His fluency, length of sentences and overall conversational abilities had markedly improved during this period. Also, there are children who had no verbal comprehension whatsoever for several years and who gradually recover a significant amount of competence in this modality (Zardini et al., 1995).

AEA AS THE TIP OF THE ICEBERG

Link with frequent and usually "benign" forms of partial childhood epilepsy

There is a strong suspicion that some of the learning disabilities and school difficulties frequently encountered in children with otherwise "benign" childhood partial epilepsies with rolandic

spikes (BPERS) and variants could be part of the spectrum of AEA (Deonna, 1999). There are several arguments for this conclusion which have been reviewed in detail elsewhere (Deonna, 1993; Deonna et al., 1993; Prats, Garaizar, Garcia-Nieto, & Madoz, 1998). From this perspective, AEA is the exceptionally severe and protracted course of this syndrome in which most cases have either no or only mild and transitory cognitive disturbances. Indeed, transitory cognitive problems can pass either unnoticed or are attributed to causes other than the epilepsy. They are very difficult to study because there are many reasons for variations in test performances, the more so if these are not major and are still within the normal range. This is even more so for school results.

Language is only one of the modalities that can be affected, presumably because the main dysfunctional "epileptic" cortical area (or areas), though usually around the perisylvian region, are not always in exactly the same location and may spread variably to the same or the contralateral hemisphere. There are also other possible reasons, including individual variations in cerebral organisation.

Knowing that some children with AEA never had recognised clinical seizures, one wonders if and how often one might miss mild cases who could have, for example, "auditory inattention" as the main symptom of a mild and fluctuating auditory agnosia. There is only anecdotal evidence that such cases do indeed exist.[1] Speech and language therapists and psychologists should now be aware that an unexplained drop in school performance, fluctuating attention, and acquired language problems (oral and written) could be epileptic in origin, even if the child does not have a known epilepsy. This statement could lead one to conclude that most school children should have an EEG, which would be both unrealistic and unwise! For an EEG to be considered, the problem should be persisting for some time or be significant or be clearly recurrent. Children with BPERS, even when the epilepsy is very active, do not behave like those suffering from attention deficit disorder with hyperactivity (ADD-H) (Deonna, 1999). Behaviours suggestive of underlying epilepsy are when children regularly complain of not understanding what parents tell them, and when the quality of their speech and written language fluctuates. In the final analysis, indication for an EEG, which should include a sleep record, must remain the decision of a specialist.

Specific language impairment (SLI) and pervasive developmental disorder (PDD) as early forms of AEA?

When AEA became better known, it was realised that some of these children had abnormal language development before the onset of the disorder and also that AEA could actually start quite early (between 2–3 years). The question naturally arose of whether AEA could be acquired so early that it actually presented as SLI.

Now, 30 years later and after EEGs have been done with this question in mind in thousands of children with SLI, the answer to this question is probably "no" in the vast majority of children with SLI (see Table 15.3). Of particular interest are cases who present with major receptive difficulties (auditory agnosia) and who usually have associated non-verbal communication and behavioural problems. It is difficult to sort out whether a specific problem in decoding language is present in these children with general communication

---

TABLE 15.3

Situations when epilepsy may be suspected of playing a role in causing language impairment

Predominance of receptive language disturbance
Presence of clinical epilepsy with EEG abnormality
Stagnation in language development
Loss of previously acquired words followed by lack of progress
Regression after good progress in a child with SLI
Presence of a sibling with an unusual kind of SLI

---

problems, who are usually referred as having pervasive developmental disorder (PDD). In most children diagnosed as PDD however, AEA is not the cause.

Bishop (1997) has made the point that children with alleged SLI and severe comprehension problems do not seem to be the more severe cases along a continuum, but a special group, as far as etiology is concerned. Some could be early cases of AEA in whom a regression has not been documented or looked for or for whom indeed there was never a period of normal early language development.

Temple (1997) has reported identical twins, one with autistic regression and the other with SLI and epilepsy, as examples of Landau-Kleffner syndrome. I am aware of several unpublished affected sibling pairs with severe SLI and/or PDD where one or both siblings have regression and paroxysmal EEG abnormalities (with or without continuous spike-waves during sleep). These familial cases are important for several reasons. They cannot be dismissed simply as cases of genetic encephalopathy with symptomatic epilepsy (or with an abnormal paroxysmal EEG as a marker). The documented regression, the fluctuations of the deficit, the improvement with therapy, which in some instances coincide with decrease of the epileptic activity, all argue for a direct role of the epilepsy. The clinical (and EEG) similarity between these cases and some of the more typical AEA is also suggestive. One puzzling feature is the clinical dissimilarity observed in these affected sibling or twin pairs (different deficits or absence of regression in one of them). Considering all the individual factors (genetic and non-genetic even in identical twins) which will influence brain development and organisation, it should not be surprising that the actual manifestation, age at onset and severity of the epilepsy and its consequences can be different.

There are conflicting views on the indication for an EEG in the basic work-up of children diagnosed with SLI (for a review see Deonna & Roulet, 1995) or other specific developmental learning disabilities and also in the children discussed above, often diagnosed as PDD. There are no definite guidelines but Table 15.3 shows the situations in which epilepsy could be suspected as playing a role and in which an EEG is justified. This is not a small decision, because EEGs are not easy to perform in these children and because a sleep EEG is mandatory. (Abnormalities tend to be more marked and sometimes can be seen only during sleep.) The use of anti-epileptic medication in those without clinical epilepsy (where only abnormal EEG discharges are found) must be considered. However, it must be borne in mind that the presence of abnormal EEG discharges (of which there are different types) does not prove their causal role in the clinical problem.

Other acquired disorders of cognitive development of epileptic origin in relation to AEA

It is now increasingly suspected that AEA is only one possible manifestation of a spectrum of acquired neuropsychological disturbances which are epileptic symptoms of some age-related epilepsies. AEA has been the first recognised, probably because loss of verbal communication is such an immediately perceived catastrophic event.

Focal epileptic discharges outside the perisylvian region in areas which support other developing cognitive functions can probably cause a whole range of other acquired neuropsychological disturbances beside language impairment. What is still disputed is whether the epilepsy in typical cases of AEA has a different pathophysiology from

that of the known focal epilepsies caused by brain damage.

Effects of prolonged auditory agnosia on language development: Evidence from long-term follow-up

Phonological representations. Defective auditory recognition will lead the child to acquire imprecise or erroneous phonological representations at different but crucial periods of language development. How will these affect lexical, grammatical, semantic capacities and production phonology as well as written language acquisition (Metz-Lutz et al., 1996)?

Children with AEA have had to construct their language representations on the basis of an incomplete and distorted input. This has consequences at several different levels of oral language, the most obvious being phonology with mistakes in production matching those in comprehension. These distorted phonological representations are probably variable from child to child, depending on their stability at the time the disease started. This will probably be a function more of the child's level of language development rather than chronological age, and may also be influenced by the extent to which articulatory feedback and written language can be used to stabilise phonological representations. Some of these representations are probably idiosyncratic, depending on the opportunities and situations when they were constructed, with a mixture of semantic and phonological elements in the same word (Peter & Assal, 1992; Vance, 1997).

Interestingly, some children can correctly repeat phonemes which are regularly distorted in their spontaneous speech, indicating a sparing of the motor programming for these same phonemes when not initiated from their own representations (Vance, 1997).

Development of grammar. Baynes and colleagues (1998) showed persistent problems in grammar and syntax in an adult woman with partially recovered AEA. They interpret this as meaning that adequate phonology is crucial at the time grammatical development is taking place. They conclude that AEA offers an opportunity to study if and how phonology and grammar are interdependent in development, and they make a plea that new cases should be evaluated with these questions in mind.

Learning language in another modality: Sign language in children with AEA

Roulet et al. (1999) had the opportunity to study a boy, (DR), with severe and early AEA (onset at 3 years 6 months), who learned natural sign language of the deaf in a residential school from the age of 6 years. He made excellent school progress, gradually recovered efficient (although still incomplete) abilities in verbal language with specific training, being educated however primarily in sign language. Sign language in this case made a dramatic change in his social life, personality development and education. It also shows that it did not prevent, and may even have facilitated, the return of oral language.

At 14 years, DR was compared to a congenitally deaf child who was a natural signer, and matched on age and IQ in classic tests of both receptive and expressive language "translated" into sign language. He performed well on all tasks and no significant difference was found between the two children. In particular, the quality of signing in DR (equivalent to expressive phonology) was excellent. So, his most severe AEA with almost no receptive and expressive language for about 6 years was compatible with the acquisition of a normal formal visual language. This finding has important theoretical implications. It suggests that AEA does not involve those cortical networks which mediate language as such, and it supports the idea of a limited but crucial interference with auditory input at a peripheral cortical level in AEA.

An allegedly "fully recovered" case of AEA: Implications for SLI

Gregory had AEA at 6 years 6 months. Within 2 months, he became unable to understand most words and his production became poorly intelligible. He recovered rapidly under corticosteroid treatment. Now at the age of 10 years, he scores normally on formal language tests including measures of phonology, the lexicon, grammar, and syntax and has learned to read and spell normally and rapidly.

He is one of the best students in his class. He still complains of difficulty when there is considerable background noise, and his teacher thinks that he is inattentive, because when told long stories in class with test questions at the end he fails, much to his despair. The most likely explanation is that he must decode language input on-line at a rate which exceeds his system's speed (Bishop, 1997). This is probably what happens with some children who have SLI.

Gregory's situation begs the following question: could a subtle form of AEA manifest simply as "auditory inattention" and intermittent school failure in language areas, without there being any indication of AEA on formal tests or clinical history? Could evidence of such a condition be obtained by asking an insightful child about problems with rapid processing or distracting noises? These are entirely open questions.

LESSONS FROM AEA FOR CHILD PSYCHIATRY, CHILD NEUROLOGY, AND DEVELOPMENTAL NEUROPSYCHOLOGY

The history of AEA is fascinating because it allows a journey through many conceptual developments of this century in child psychiatry and neurology, epileptology, psychology, and communication sciences. It serves as a source of study and potential answers to several questions in these domains. It should be realised that the present concept of AEA, even though still far from being completely understood, has come a long way. What is now obvious has not always been so. It involved many steps:

1. The recognition that loss of language in a child is not necessarily a sign of global mental deterioration (dementia). There are older papers in the literature reported as

childhood dementia which were clearly instances of acquired aphasia.

2. The recognition that an isolated language loss in a child can be a neurological rather than a psychological manifestation. A case in point is a famous story reported as a case of sexual abuse perpetrated on a 4-year-old child, which was finally diagnosed as AEA (Koupernik, Masciangelo, & Balestra-Beretta, 1969).

3. Recognition that language could be lost as a consequence of a localised brain dysfunction without other signs of brain disease.

4. The gradual realisation that some epilepsies can manifest as a progressive loss of cognitive function without recognised clinical seizures.

5. As an extension to point 4, the idea has emerged that early epilepsy can lead to non-development or stagnation of emerging cognitive or communicative functions, without signs of loss of acquired competence (Deonna, 1993).

NOTE

1. Hirsch, E. (personal communication, 1998).

REFERENCES

Baynes, K., Kegel, J.A., Brentari, D., Kussmaul, C., & Poizner, H. (1998). Chronic auditory agnosia following Landau-Kleffner Syndrome: A 23 year outcome study. *Brain and Language*, *63*, 381–425.

Bishop, D.V.M. (1985). Age of onset and outcome in "acquired aphasia with convulsive disorder" (Landau-Kleffner syndrome). *Developmental Medicine and Child Neurology*, *27*, 705–712.

Bishop, D.V.M. (1988b). Language development after focal brain damage. In D.V.M. Bishop & K. Mogford (Eds.), *Language development in exceptional circumstances*. Edinburgh: Churchill Livingstone.

Bishop, D.V.M. (1997). *Uncommon understanding: Development and disorders of language comprehension in children* (pp. 76–77). Hove, UK: Psychology Press.

Boyd, S.G., Rivera-Gaxiola, M., Towel, A.D., Harkness, W., & Neville, B.G.R. (1996). Discrimination of speech sounds in a boy with Landau-Kleffner syndrome: An intraoperative event-related potential study. *Neuropediatrics*, *27*, 211–215.

Deonna, T.W. (1991). Acquired epileptiform aphasia in children (Landau-Kleffner syndrome). *Journal of Clinical Neurophysiology*, *8*, 288–298.

Deonna, T. (1993). Annotation: Cognitive and behavioural correlates of epileptic activity in children. *Journal of Child Psychology and Psychiatry*, *34*, 611–620.

Deonna, T. (1996). Troubles du langage et épilepsie chez l'enfant. In C. Chevrie-Muller & J. Narbona (Eds) *Le langage de l'enfant. Aspects normaux et pathologiques* (pp. 386–398). Paris: Masson Publishers.

Deonna, T., Peter, C., & Ziegler, A.L. (1989). Adult follow-up of the acquired aphasia-epilepsy syndrome in childhood. Report of 7 cases. *Neuropediatrics*, *20*, 132–138.

Deonna, T., & Roulet, E. (1995). Acquired epileptic aphasia (AEA): Definition of the syndrome and current problems. In A. Beaumanoir, M. Bureau, T. Deonna, L. Mira & C.A. Tassinari (Eds), *Continuous spikes and waves during slow sleep* (pp. 37–45). Paris: John Libbey Publishers.

Deonna, T., Roulet, E., Fontan, D., & Marcoz, J.P. (1993). Prolonged speech and oromotor deficits of epileptic origin in benign partial epilepsy with rolandic spikes: Relationship to acquired epileptic aphasia. *Neuropediatrics*, *24*, 83–87.

Deonna, T., Zesiger, P., Davidoff, V., Maeder, M., Mayor, C., & Roulet, E. (1999). Idiopathic benign partial epilepsy of childhood and associated cognitive impairment. A longitudinal neuropsychological study. *Developmental Medicine and Child Neurology*. Manuscript under review.

Doherty, C.P., Fitzsimons, M., Asenbauer, B., McMackin, D., Bradley, R., King, M., & Staunton, H. (1999). Prosody preservation in Landau-Kleffner syndrome (LKS): A case report. *European Journal of Neurology*, *6*, 227–234.

Korkman, M., Granström, M.L., Appelqvist, K., & Liukkonen, E. (1998). Neuropsychological characteristics of five children with the Landau-Kleffner syndrome: Dissociation of auditory and phonological discrimination. *Journal of the International Neuropsychology Society*, *4*, 566–575.

Koupernik, C., Masciangelo, P.M., & Balestra-Beretta, S. (1969). Conséquences d'un attentat sexuel commis sur une fillette de 4 ans. *La Psychiatrie de l'Enfant*, *12*, 267–298.

Marien, P., Saerens, J., Verslegers, W., Borggreve, F., & De Deyn, P.P. (1993). Some controversies about type and nature of aphasic symptomatology in Landau-Kleffner syndrome: A case study. *Acta Neurologica Belgica*, *93*, 183–203.

Metz-Lutz, M.N., de Saint Martin, A., Hirsch, E., Maquet, P., & Marescaux, C. (1996). Auditory verbal processing following Landau and Kleffner syndrome. *Brain and Language*, *55*, 147–150.

Morrell, F., Whisler, W.W., Smith, M.C., Hoeppner, T.J., de Toledo-Morrell, L., Pierre-Louis, S.J.C., Kanner, A.M., Buelow, J.M., Ristanovic, R., Bergen, D., Chez, M., & Hasegawa, H. (1995). Landau-Kleffner syndrome: Treatment with subpial intracortical transection. *Brain*, *118*, 1529–1546.

Peter, C., & Assal, G. (1992). Comportement verbal atypique après trente ans d'évolution d'un syndrome d'aphasie-épilepsie acquise. *La Psychiatrie de l'Enfant*, *35*, 109–125.

Prats, J.M., Garaizar, C., Garcia-Nieto, M.L., & Madoz, P. (1998). Antiepileptic drugs and atypical evolution of idiopathic partial epilepsy. *Pediatric Neurology*, *18*, 402–406.

Roulet, E., Seeck, M., Mayer, E., Despland, P.-A., De Tribolet, N., & Deonna, T. (1998). Childhood epilepsy with neuropsychological regression and continuous spike-waves during sleep: Epilepsy surgery in a young adult. *European Journal of Paediatric Neurology*, *2*, 303–311.

Roulet, E., Davidoff, V., Prélaz, A.-C., Morel, B., Rickli, F., Metz-Lutz, M.-N., Boyes Braem, P., & Deonna, T. (1999). *Analysis of sign language in a child with acquired epileptic aphasia (Landau-Kleffner)*. Poster presented at the 3rd Afasic Symposium, York, March 1999.

Temple, C.M. (1997). *Developmental cognitive neuropsychology* (pp. 41–49). Hove, UK: Psychology Press.

Vance, M. (1991). Educational and therapeutic approaches used with a child presenting with acquired aphasia and convulsive disorder (Landau-Kleffner syndrome). *Child: Language Teaching and Therapy*, *7*, 41–59.

Vance, M. (1997). Christopher Lumpship: Developing phonological representations in a child with auditory processing deficit. In S. Chiat, J. Law, & J. Marshall (Eds), *Language disorders in children and adults: Psycholinguistic approaches to therapy* (pp. 17–41). London: Whurr Publishers.

Zardini, G., Molteni, B., Nardocci, N., Sarti, D., Avanzini, G., & Granata, T. (1995). Linguistic development in a patient with Landau Kleffner syndrome: A nine year follow-up. *Neuropediatrics*, *26*, 19–25.

Zesiger, P., Le Normand, M.-T., Davidoff, V., Gubser-Mercati, D., Sester Gerber, M., & Deonna, T. (1999). *A longitudinal study of a child with acquired epileptic aphasia*. Poster presented at the 3rd Afasic Symposium, York, March 1999.

16

Research into practice:
Future prospects

Michael Rutter

The interconnections between research, policy and practice are considered in relation to five somewhat different types of research: 1) descriptive studies that provide information about either language disorders or patterns of services for children with such problems; 2) studies to test competing hypotheses about causal mechanisms; 3) investigations of risk processes; 4) evaluations of interventions; and 5) basic research into some aspect of neural functioning. Attention is drawn to the needs for adequacy of measurement, representativeness of sampling, and the use of appropriate comparisons. The various ways in which descriptive studies may be useful are discussed — including understanding of patterns of dysfunction, of outcome, of associated problems, of prognostic factors, and of correlates that provide leads on possible causal influences. Studies of services provide findings in the clientele served and on patterns of service provision. Causal research requires attention to a range of alternative explanations (including artefacts of sampling or measurement, "third variable" effects, and direction of influences). Strategies to test causal hypotheses require a means to "pull apart" variables that ordinarily go together (as through twin and adoptee designs and a variety of natural experiments), the use of longitudinal data, multiple measures, and a means of pitting one causal hypothesis against others. Similar needs apply to the study of risk processes. Prevention/intervention research requires operationalised specification of the treatment, randomised controlled comparisons, adequate sample size, "blind" measurement, assessment across settings and over time, determination of whether there are "dose-response" relationships, the relating of changes in the postulated mediating mechanism feature to changes in the outcome variable, and measurement of the size of effects. Basic research involves similar considerations; it includes studies of normal language development, of neural processes, of psychopharmacology and of the different aspects of brain functioning. Note is made of the criteria to be considered in research reporting and the features discussed are pulled together to consider briefly the ways in which research matters to practitioners, clinical practice matters for research, and some of the prospects for the future.

In considering the interconnections between research, policy and practice, it is necessary to start with an appreciation that there are several rather different kinds of research. They may be conveniently summarised under five main headings. First, there are descriptive studies that provide information about either language disorders or patterns of services for children with such problems. Second, there are studies that seek to test hypotheses about causal mechanisms. These differ from the first group of studies in their aim to go beyond patterns of associations or correlations to inferences about causal processes. There are a variety of critical requirements for research that aspires to take that step. Third, there is research that is designed to investigate risk processes. Like the second group of studies into causal mechanisms, this aims to test causal inferences. The difference, however, is that the starting point is defined by biological or psychosocial or other risk factors, rather than defined clinical groups with language disorders. Accordingly, although many of the same research needs are present, there is the particular requirement to examine a range of outcomes that extends well beyond language disorders. Thus, it is important in this sort of research to determine the extent to which any consequences in relation to language disorder are specific to the risk factor or, rather, are shared with a variety of other adverse outcomes of one kind or another.

Fourth, there are studies that are involved with the evaluation of interventions that are designed either to prevent language disorders or to alleviate their effects. Again, such research has particular rules of its own and it is important for practitioners to appreciate the differences between rigorous research that truly can test the efficacy of interventions and weaker studies that provide only plausible leads or suggestions.

Finally, there is basic research into some aspect of neural functioning. The aims here are different in that they are concerned with an understanding of how brain mechanisms "work" and how brain processes influence the functioning of the mind (including, of course, those associated with receptive and expressive language) and with their associated behaviours.

DESCRIPTIVE RESEARCH

The three key issues with respect to the quality of descriptive research are those that apply to all studies: the adequacy of measurement, the representativeness of sampling, and the use of appropriate comparisons. The type of measures used will necessarily depend on the questions being examined and, for different purposes, psychometric methods, observational approaches, interviews and questionnaires all have a place. Nevertheless, multiple methods of assessment need to be used (Horton, Laird & Zahner, 1999; Rutter & Pickles, 1990). The point is that the interest does not lie in the results with respect to a particular measure but, rather, with the implications for the function which that measure is supposed to index. It is usual to find that the intercorrelations among measures that are supposed to tap the same function are only moderate. For example, this has been shown to be the case with respect to phonemic awareness (Yopp, 1988). This arises partly because, as is usually the case, the reliability of individual tests is not very high, and partly because each test taps a slightly different facet of the function being considered. Both the reliability and predictive validity of test composites are substantially better than those for any single test on its own.

Accordingly, much greater reliance should be placed on studies that use multiple measures and employ appropriate statistical approaches either to combine the measures or to use the pattern of intercorrelations among them to derive an inferred value for the latent construct that the measures are meant to reflect.

There is no one sort of sample that is ideal for all purposes; again, it all depends on the question being studied. Sometimes, it may be crucial to have a sample that is representative of the general population and, in other cases, the need is to have one that is representative of children receiving a particular form of treatment or being dealt with by a particular kind of service. In evaluating the quality of research, the reader needs to think what sort of sample would be appropriate for the questions being tackled and then ask whether the sample actually used measured up to what was ideally required. Particular attention needs to be paid to whether or not a high participation rate has been obtained and whether the investigator has determined the nature of possible biases associated with the participants who are not included in the study (because they could not be located or because they declined to take part). It is a general rule that participants who are missed for one reason or another tend to be systematically different from those who take part. This was shown in early epidemiologic studies (Cox, Rutter, Yule, & Quinton, 1977) and it applies equally to recent studies dealing with language delay (Dale et al., 1998). Readers should be wary of statements that the sample is representative of the census population (or other general comparisons of that kind). That is because the census data are rarely in a form that ensures adequate comparability with the study sample (with respect, for example, to age or phase of family formation) and because the variables available will rarely include the relevant risk factors. The only pertinent statistic concerns the extent to which non-participants differ from those taking part in the study. That is because this is the only sure means of knowing whether the study sample is biased with respect to key risk factors.

A further critical research design issue for descriptive studies is the need for comparisons of one kind or another. These are always implicit and it is much better that they be made explicit. Thus, if research shows that language disorders are characterised by a particular pattern or by some particular set of correlates, these findings are only meaningful if they differ from what would be found with respect to children without disorder, or to children with other types of disorder. Accordingly, in evaluating descriptive studies, the reader needs to ask what sort of comparisons were made and whether they were with appropriate groups. A necessary accompanying question is whether the groups that were compared were selected in similar ways and whether steps were taken to ensure that there were no biases in group selection that might lead to artefactual differences between the groups. There is a particular problem in that connection when controls are volunteers of some kind, especially when they are obtained through advertisement. It is scarcely likely that such volunteers will be representative of the normal general population. It is well established, for example, that twins who volunteer are disproportionately likely to be identical (monozygotic) rather than fraternal (dizygotic).

Whenever comparisons between groups are being made, it is necessary to go on to ask two other questions. First, could these differences have arisen by chance? This may be assessed by taking into account features such as the degree of spread or variation within each of the groups being compared, and the size of the samples being studied. Typically, statistical tests are employed to determine the likelihood that the differences found were not due to chance (Dunn & Everitt, 1995; Everitt & Hay, 1992). Second, in addition to statistical significance, it is important to know how far the findings may be applied to individuals. Ordinarily, this may be provided by statistics dealing with "confidence limits" (meaning the range of scores that is found for the great majority of individuals in the sample — confidence limits can be set for different proportions of the population), or "effect sizes" (dealing with the size of the difference as compared with the spread). For example, Bishop et al. (1999) found a difference on an auditory repetition test between language-impaired and normal-language children that was highly statistically significant ($p = .004$) but the effect size was only moderate (.55), being equivalent to a difference of some 8 IQ points. This meant that most of the language-impaired children had scores well within the normal range. Conversely, the score on the auditory repetition test was a very weak predictor of the children's language level. The difference, therefore, was highly significant in statistical terms but only weakly significant in clinical terms. Readers of research need to be alert to whether or not the research reports provide information of this kind that enables the practical implications of the research findings to be understood.

Descriptive studies of disorder

Descriptive studies of disorders may be highly informative in providing findings on a range of different features. For example, they may delineate the patterns of dysfunction associated with language disorder — the extent to which impairments in, say, syntax are associated with those in semantic features or pragmatics or phonology (Bishop, 1997; Conti-Ramsden & Botting, 1999). With respect to language disorders, it has been particularly important that research has shown the extent to which these disorders are accompanied by a broader range of cognitive impairments (Bishop, 1992). The traditional notion that developmental language disorders constituted "pure" cases of dysfunction involving a skill, namely language, that was quite distinct from other aspects of cognition, has had to be rejected, or at least very considerably modified. Also, there are reasons for supposing that these associated cognitive deficits may be involved in the causal processes underlying the language disorder (see Tallal, chapter 8, this volume). There are good theoretical reasons why researchers may sometimes be interested in the existence of pure cases of a language deficit (see van der Lely, Rosen & McClelland, 1998), however atypical they may be. Nevertheless, it is important that practitioners appreciate that they do not represent the general run of cases of specific language impairment seen in clinics or in general population studies.

Descriptive studies have also been very helpful in the findings provided on the outcome of language disorders (see Snowling, chapter 14, this volume). Thus, it was important to learn that the great majority of children who show substantial language delay at age 2 years later go on to have normal functioning with respect to both language and other features (Whitehurst & Fischel, 1994). Even with children who show marked delays in language at four years of age, nearly half had caught up in their language functioning by their first year in school (Bishop & Edmundson, 1987 a, b). Nevertheless, it has been equally important to know from the findings of follow-ups at a later age that some of these children who seemed to have caught up in language have, nevertheless, continued to show subtle, but important, indications of minor impairments in aspects of literacy and phonological processing (Stothard et al., 1998). However, by no means all children with language delay go on to have problems in scholastic achievement (see Paul, chapter 11, this volume) and, conversely, many children with severe reading or spelling difficulties in middle or later childhood have not been substantially delayed in their acquisition of language (see Snowling, chapter 14, this volume).

Numerous studies of both epidemiological and clinical samples have also shown the relatively high frequency with which language delay is associated with abnormalities in social, emotional and/or behavioural functioning (Howlin & Rutter, 1987; Beitchman, Cohen, Konstantareas, & Tannock, 1996; see also Goodyer, chapter 13, this volume). It might be supposed that these associated problems are simply the consequence of the inevitable difficulties experienced by children whose language disorder has made it difficult for them to communicate with, or understand, other people. It is likely that this is a part of the explanation but, at least with respect to severe developmental disorders of receptive language, substantial social impairments often continue into adult life (Rutter, Mawhood, & Howlin, 1992; Howlin, Mawhood, & Rutter, in press; Mawhood Howlin, & Rutter, in press). The implication is that the social deficits may constitute a more intrinsic part of the language disorder, and not simply a secondary consequence. It is worth noting that the social impairments found in these long-term follow-ups do not take the form of any of the traditional psychiatric diagnostic categories. It is an important characteristic of good descriptive research that it should be conducted in such a way that unexpected findings can be detected. This means that it is usually a mistake to tie measures too closely to the prevailing concepts and it is also important that the form of data gathering, whether it be observational or interview, should include detailed descriptions of functioning and not just yes/no answers to predetermined closed questions. It is also clear that findings are likely to be more informative if experienced clinical investigators have participated in the data gathering and have not solely relied on scores and ratings provided by inexperienced research assistants.

In relation to outcome, descriptive studies have also been crucial in the information they have provided on the features that are associated with good or bad prognoses. Thus, it has been found that the outlook is best when the disorders involve a relatively "pure" phonological problem and are least good when they involve a serious impairment in receptive language (see Stackhouse, chapter 5, this volume; Snowling, chapter 14, this volume).

Descriptive research is important, too, in the information that it can provide on the correlates of language disorder. Thus, it has been helpful to know that, on the whole, severe developmental language disorders are not particularly associated with psychosocial disadvantage but are associated with a much increased familial loading for speech and language disorders (see Rice, chapter 2, this volume). These findings were the ones that first alerted people to the likelihood that genetic factors might play a significant role.

Data on correlates with physical abnormalities are also potentially important. Thus, it has been found that otitis media with effusion (OME) (i.e. the transient, but sometimes severe, conductive hearing impairment associated with the adhesive secretions following successive middle ear infections) may be associated with some minor impairments of language functioning but that it is much less often associated with serious language disorders (Haggard, Birkin, & Pringle, 1990; Bennett & Haggard, 1999).

It is evident from the above that there are many ways in which descriptive studies can be very important with respect to their policy and practice implications. Thus, the findings have obvious practical clinical implications with respect to prognosis (and, most crucially, with respect to the features associated with variations in outcome); to the planning and organisation of services (particularly with respect to the types of disorder where interventions are most needed because of the relatively lower likelihood of spontaneous remission and recovery); and with respect to questions regarding classification and diagnosis. For example, descriptive studies have been crucial in indicating the need to take account of disorders where the most prominent dysfunction involves pragmatics (see Bishop, chapter 6, this volume). The question as to whether pragmatic problems are best dealt with in terms of dimensional or categorical distinctions remains a matter of disagreement, but what is clear is that the traditional tripartite subdivision into phonological disorders, disorders of language expression and disorders that involve mixtures of receptive and expressive problems is no longer adequate.

Descriptive studies also frequently have important theoretical implications, as already indicated. They have raised crucially important questions about the nature of developmental language disorders and about whether these are best conceptualised in terms of modular language functions or, rather, possible underlying specific cognitive deficits.

The findings on correlates are particularly important in providing the basis of hypotheses about causal mechanisms. Thus, this was noted with respect to the implication from the finding of the familial loading from language disorders that genetic factors might be important. On the other hand, descriptive studies, on their own, are not appropriate for the testing of hypotheses about causal mechanisms. That requires a rather different type of research, discussed later in this chapter.

Descriptive research on services

Considerations already discussed with respect to descriptive research on disorders apply in very comparable fashion to descriptive research on services. Thus, descriptive studies may provide invaluable information on:

1. the types of disorders catered for by services;
2. the differences between those language disorders that lead children into special education and those that allow children to remain in mainstream schooling;
3. the differences in the clientele catered for by different services;
4. the extent to which children receiving special education in primary school continue in special education at secondary level (see Conti-Ramsden & Botting, chapter 12, this volume);
5. the extent to which access to services is influenced by family characteristics as distinct from features of children's language disorder; and
6. the degree to which children receiving treatment for language disorders also have associated problems.

In other words, the information provided is on the clientele of services, on the patterns of service provision, and the differences among the variety of services for children with language disorders. For obvious reasons, such information is crucially important in understanding how services work and in planning for services in the future. In addition, descriptive research on services may be very helpful in pointing to the major disparities that can exist between geographical areas or local authorities in their patterns of service provision.

REQUIREMENTS FOR CAUSAL RESEARCH

Sometimes it is assumed that causal questions can be posed in a simple fashion such as, "do genetic factors play a role in the causation of developmental language disorders?" However, this is not sufficient for a whole variety of reasons. First, it is important to define the disorder being investigated with respect to causal processes. Is the focus on delays in language at age 2, or on language disorders that are still present after the children have entered school? Is the focus on phonological dysfunction or on impairment of receptive language? Is the causal question contrasting the causal mechanisms involved in one sort of language disorder with those involved in some other? Or, is the focus on the causative factors in relation to language disorder as contrasted with those that apply to variations in language development within the normal range (see Plomin & Dale, chapter 3, this volume)? Alternatively, causal questions can be focused, not on the causes of disorder as such, but rather on the explanation for why individuals differ in their susceptibility to some proven risk process.

It is important, too, to appreciate that each cause cannot be reduced to just one question, even for a highly defined outcome variable (Rutter, 1994; Rutter & Smith, 1995). Thus, for example, is the focus on why one child has a language disorder but another does not, or is the focus on why the overall rate of language disorders is higher in one group than another, such as in males as compared with females? Causal processes involved in these two sorts of questions are by no means the same. Alternatively, the focus may be on why the language disorder in one child resolves by the time the child starts school, whereas the disorder in another child persists into adult life. With all these causal questions, it also cannot be assumed that the answer can be reduced to one feature. That is because, so frequently, not only are multiple susceptibility factors involved, but also many of the causal processes involve indirect chain reactions that operate over time.

Having sorted out the causal question to be examined, the next need is for an articulated theory on the alternative explanations that may be proffered to account for the observations to be explained. It is rare for there to be only one plausible possibility. The need is to pit one possible hypothesis against another. In so doing, it is crucial for the investigator to consider the strategies and tactics needed to do this. In particular, it is help-ful to consider what findings would *disprove* each hypothesis.

Range of alternative explanations

At least four different sorts of alternative expla-nations always need to be considered.

First, are the correlations or associations an artefact of sampling? For example, is the finding of an increased familial loading for language delay a function of the particular way in which the sample was obtained? Were parents who had other children with language delay, or who were themselves delayed in speech acquisition in child-hood, more likely to be included in the sample?

Second, there is the possibility of an artefact of reporting or measurement. Thus, taking the same feature of familial loading, could the raised rate be due to a bias in terms of the parents of children with a language disorder being more likely to know about such disorders in other mem-bers of the family? Perhaps parents who have a child with a disorder are more likely to enquire of relatives whether they too have had children with such problems. Also, particular care needs to be taken when the information on some risk factor is given by the same person who provides informa-tion on the language disorder. Could the associa-tions be due to the fact, for example, that both sets of data derive from the parent? This sort of consideration, as already noted, is one of the rea-sons why it is always important to have multiple sources of information.

A further set of explanations concern what have come to be called "third variable" effects. In other words, this reflects a recognition that meas-ures may function as risk indicators because they happen to be associated with the true causal pro-cesses but are not themselves involved in the risk mechanisms. For example, does an increased fam-ilial loading reflect genetic mediation stemming from the fact that parents pass on their genes to their children? Or, does it arise from those who themselves have language impairment providing a disadvantaging communicative environment for their children? Alternatively, is the familial load-ing important, not in its own right but simply

because it reflects some other environmental fea-ture such as social disadvantage? Yet another pos-sibility is that the associations derive from another aspect of the children's functioning. Thus, could the increased familial loading be a consequence of language disorders being associated with social deficits or psychiatric problems or specific cognit-ive difficulties? Obviously, the plausibility of these various third variable explanations will not be the same with each causal question or with each pos-tulated causal process. Nevertheless, the essential point is that it is always necessary to consider what third variable effects might be operating and to consider how they may be examined and excluded, or confirmed.

The fourth sort of alternative explanation con-cerns the direction of effects. Does the association derive from the child's effect on the environment or the environment's effect on the child? For ex-ample, suppose that the starting point is an asso-ciation between the communicative environment provided by parents and the presence of language disorder in the child. Given such an observation, it would be essential to consider whether the parents are talking to their child in the way that they are because the child has a language dis-order or whether the child is delayed in language because of the ways in which the parents speak to him or her. Of course, frequently the causal processes will be bi-directional but it is neces-sary to consider the relative importance of each. There is considerable evidence that children's characteristics do influence how other people respond to them, interact with them, and talk with them (Bell & Chapman, 1986; Rutter et al., 1997). Despite Bell's (1968) seminal paper rais-ing important questions about direction of effects and socialisation research, far too many studies continue to ignore the possibility that the find-ings are a consequence of child effects on the environment.

Strategies to test causal hypotheses

There are four key requirements in selecting or designing strategies to test causal hypotheses (Rutter, Pickles, Murray, & Eaves, submitted). First, it is necessary to find a means to "pull apart" the variables that ordinarily go together. For instance, because parents both pass on genes to their children and also shape the rearing environments provided for them, it is ordinarily very difficult to decide whether parent–child associations are due to genetic mediation or environmental mediation.

Twin and adoptee designs, with their several variants, constitute a means of separating genetic and environmental effects (Rutter et al., 1990; Rutter, Silberg, O'Connor, & Simonoff, 1999; see also Plomin & Dale, chapter 3, this volume). Adoptee designs achieve this by virtue of the fact that the biological parents who pass on their genes are not the parents who rear the children and, conversely, the adoptive parents who rear the children do not provide the genes. Twin designs provide the separation because monozygotic ("identical") twins share all their segregating[1] genes whereas, on average, dizygotic ("fraternal") twins share only half. Though these are by far and away the best-known experiments to pull apart variables, there are many other varieties of "natural experiment" that offer a similar purpose (Rutter et al., 1997; Rutter et al., submitted). Second, longitudinal data are almost always required in order to determine the direction of effects. Thus, in one way or another, it is important to find out whether the risk factor at Time 1 predicts the language outcome at Time 2 (after taking account of confounding variables and the like). The possible role of child effects can, of course, be determined by looking at whether the child feature at Time 1 predicts the environmental feature at Time 2.

For the reasons already given, the third requirement is the availability and use of multiple measures. The fourth requirement is the employment of appropriate measures, research strategies and statistical techniques for two purposes:

1. measurement of the latent construct that is being considered, with respect to both the risk process and to the language disorder outcome (as discussed above in the section dealing with descriptive studies); and
2. to test alternative mechanisms by pitting one hypothesis against another.

Thus, as already noted, twin methods may be used, if the appropriate statistics are applied, to determine whether, when two children in the same family both show a language disorder, this is because they share the same genes or the same environment (see Plomin & Dale, chapter 3, this volume). In the same way, twin studies can be used to determine whether the associations between a specific phonological processing feature and language impairment derive from the same underlying genetic liability or some aspect of the shared environment (Bishop et al., 1999). However, there are many other ways in which competing hypotheses can be compared. Some of these have come to be called "natural experiments".

"Natural experiments"

There are many different sorts of "natural experiments", but their characteristics may be exemplified by considering three somewhat different types.

First, the starting point may be an unusual difference in the frequency or level of the language feature being considered. The most striking example of that is provided by the evidence from numerous studies that, on average, twins lag behind singletons in their language developments to the extent of about a 3-month difference at the age of 3 years (Rutter & Redshaw, 1991). This provides a "natural experiment" because, although genetic factors will play a role in individual differences within groups of singletons and within groups of twins, there is no reason to suppose that genetic vulnerabilities found in twins differ from those found in singletons. Also, because the social background of twins is closely comparable to that of singletons, there is no reason to suppose that the difference derives from social disadvantage. Accordingly, it is possible to contrast, and examine, two main alternative explanations. First, the difference could derive from the substantially higher rate of obstetric complications associated with twinning. Alternatively, it could derive from the rather different patterns of family interaction associated with having two children of the same developmental level at the same time

(Rutter & Redshaw, 1991). The one attempt so far to use this "natural experiment" has shown that the explanation probably lies in the features of the post-natal environment rather than in any aspect of obstetrical complications (Rutter, Thorpe, & Golding, 2000).

A quite different strategy is provided by circumstances in which there is a radical change in rearing conditions. Thus, for example, the effects of severe psychological privation on cognitive development (including language development) was examined in children from Romanian orphanages who were adopted into UK families (Rutter et al., 1998; O'Connor et al., in press). Prior to adoption, the children experienced quite extraordinarily extreme and pervasive psychological deprivation. Following adoption, by sharp contrast, they experienced rearing that was somewhat above average in quality (as is usual in adopting families). The causal hypothesis in relation to the suggestion that psychological deprivation led to language delay or cognitive deficit as a result of environmental mediation could be tested in two ways. Provided certain assumptions were met (and that needed to be determined) the inference that the initial deficit was due to the prior psychological deprivation could be tested by whether or not the children caught up or recovered following the radical change of environment. The second test was provided by the extent to which continuing deficits could be associated with dose-response relationship with aspects of deprivation (such as its duration or severity). In this case, the findings showed that from both the tests, the psychological deprivation did indeed cause cognitive deficit. This included language delay but, so far as it could be tested, it did not appear to involve language any more than non-verbal aspects of development.

The third approach is provided by the examination of naturalistic within-individual change over time in relation to some defined and measured risk variable or process. For example, with regard to language functioning, this strategy is relevant with respect to the experience of OME (Bennett & Haggard, 1999; Haggard et al., 1990) and also to the effects of maternal depression (Cooper & Murray, 1997).

Requirements for "natural experiments"

With all "natural experiments" five key requirements must be met. First, as is implicit in the terminology, the strategy must involve a clear separation of risk variables, pulling them apart in ways that do not arise in ordinary circumstances. Second, there must be an explicit specification of the assumptions on which that particular form of "natural experiment" is based. Thus, for example, the adoption design requires the assumption that there has been no selective placement in which the characteristics of the biological family are matched with the characteristics of the adoptive family. Similarly, the twin design requires the equal environments assumption, which specifies that, with respect to the key environmental risk mechanisms as they affect the outcome being studied, the environments within monozygotic pairs are not more similar than those within dizygotic pairs. The radical change in rearing conditions design requires the assumption that children who experience such a radical change do not differ systematically from those who did not experience such a change, at least with respect to features that are relevant to risk processes. Similarly, the within-individual change over time naturalistic design (as exemplified by the study of children adopted from poor-quality Romanian orphanages) requires the assumption that the children who experience particular risk conditions do not differ from those who did not experience risk, or that the effects remaining after such prior differences have been taken into account statistically. It has to be said that many research reports are not as explicit as they should be on the assumptions being made and on the testing of whether such assumptions are actually met within the study. Readers of research need to be alert to the necessity of querying such assumptions.

The next four requirements are ones that apply much more generally, that is:

- there must be high quality measurement of relevant risk variables;
- the sampling must include the key comparisons;
- there must be assessment of within-individual change over time; and

- there must be appropriate and rigorous use of statistical methods.

For example, a study of a highly-selected clinic sample led to claims that autism might be caused by the combined measles-mumps-rubella (MMR) vaccine (Wakefield et al., 1998). The chief reason for inferring causation was that autism first became manifest shortly after MMR was given. The main problem in this line of argument was that the second year of life is the time when it is usual for the first indications of autism to be apparent. Because this is also the time when MMR is given, the two were bound often to occur together by chance alone. The causal hypothesis needed to be tested by determining if children given MMR were more likely than other children to develop autism, or by determining if the rate of autism went up after MMR was introduced on a massive scale. The evidence so far from research of this kind has cast doubt on the causal hypothesis (Taylor et al., 1999).

STUDIES OF RISK PROCESSES

There are numerous examples of studies of risk processes. What they have in common is that they start with a defined risk variable in the representative sample with a prospective longitudinal follow-up to determine the outcomes associated with the risk variable (Kraemer et al., 1997). For obvious reasons, that requires a comparison with a random sample of the population who did not experience the risk variable being examined. The issues that apply to the testing of causal hypotheses all apply equally here (indeed some of the examples given concerned the study of risk processes). The difference is simply that the focus of the study is on the range of outcomes associated with the risk experience, rather than the causes of a narrowly defined disorder. Key features of this research, then, concern a proper assessment of the range of possible adverse (and positive) outcomes, together with appropriate sampling and appropriate measurement of the risk variable.

The risk processes may involve categorical features such as chromosome anomalies (Ratcliffe, 1994), or specific medical conditions such as Williams syndrome (Metcalfe, 1999), or they may involve risks where it is crucial to assess both severity and specificity of pattern — as would be the case, for example, with acquired brain injury (Rutter, Chadwick, & Shaffer, 1983) or situations in which it is particularly important to assess associated features.

Similar considerations apply to psychosocial risks as already indicated in the discussion of the natural experiments of children adopted to UK families from Romanian orphanages, and the use of twin–singleton comparisons.

Physical environmental hazards involve comparable issues. In relation to the consequences of obstetric complications, it is necessary to determine whether the effects on language can be correlated with the effects of obstetric complications on brain structure and function (as indexed by brain imaging studies). With many such risks, the key question concerns the nature of a mediating mechanism. OME constitutes a comparable example. In other words, do the effects on language derive from the degree or duration of conductive hearing impairment associated with OME, or are they a consequence of some entirely different feature? For example, are they a consequence of the fact that poor living conditions predispose to ear infections, or that socially disadvantaged families are less likely to obtain effective early treatment for such infections?

PREVENTION/INTERVENTION RESEARCH

As with other types of research, questions involved with prevention/intervention research are multiple. Thus, the investigator may wish to determine whether the treatment has been effective, but it is also crucial to go on to ask for whom it has been effective? At least as crucially, it is necessary to know why or how the intervention has been effective; that is, why and how the effects have been brought about. The answer to that last question raises the further issue of the implications for the understanding of the mechanisms and pro-cesses. Finally, it is essential to ask whether the treatment methods that have been shown to be effective in highly-controlled circumstances, when delivered by experts, can also be applied on a community-wide basis.

Requirements for prevention/intervention research

In addition to the more general considerations already discussed, there are several special require-ments for top quality prevention/intervention research. It is crucial to have a specification and measurement of the "treatment". Unless there is further specification, it is no more useful to find out that "speech therapy is effective" than it is to obtain a similar answer for "psychotherapy" or "medication". Practitioners cannot apply the findings unless much more is known about the treatment involved. With respect to psychological treatments, there has been a movement towards "manualisation" (Carroll, 1998). What this means is that it has been possible to create a manual that specifies the "rules" and "procedures" to be followed in the treatment that is being studied. Without doubt, there are many advantages in "manualisation" (despite the ugly nature of the word!), but there are worries that undue rigidity in creating treatment manuals may actually destroy or distort the essential therapeutic elements in the treatment (Klein, 1998). The somewhat similar consideration concerns the question as to whether the treatment has been "operationalised". In other words, has it been possible to translate the con-cept or notion of what the treatment is meant to provide into measurable behaviours? The point of the question is that it is highly desirable for any treatment study to include a systematic, quanti-fied assessment of the extent to which the treat-ment as planned has actually been delivered.

In addition, it is often helpful to break down treatment approaches into highly specific interven-tions focussed on just one feature, in order to deter-mine just which feature brings about the desired change. Thus, treatment methods may be devised to focus on one particular facet of linguistic pro-cessing (see Ellis Weismer, chapter 9, this volume).

The second crucial requirement is for a random-ised controlled trial (RCT). The design require-ments for these, as well as the arguments in favour of their use, were put forward by the statistician Bradford Hill many years ago (Hill, 1962; Hill & Hill, 1991). It would be misleading to suppose that RCTs are easy to undertake. They are not. Never-theless, they provide much the best means of test-ing the efficacy of treatment. That is because, unless there is random allocation, it is highly likely that those who receive a particular treatment will differ systematically from those who do not receive it. Random allocation is the only really satisfactory way of dealing with this particular problem.

The third requirement is that the sample size be adequate to provide appropriate statistical power. It is commonly supposed that, if positive findings derive from small samples, they must be more significant, and more meaningful, than if they derive from large samples. In fact, although at first it seems counter-intuitive, the opposite is the case (Pocock, 1983). Chance positive findings are equally likely in small and large samples. That means, for example, that regardless of sample size one in twenty differences that have arisen by chance will be statistically significant at the 5% level. However, in large samples the findings are more stable and have a smaller range of error. Consequently, the proportion of all positive results that are false positives is much higher in small samples. Accordingly, the readers of research must beware of findings based on small samples. The problem is compounded when, as is usually the case, there are far more small than large studies.

The fourth requirement is for "blind" meas-urement of effects. In other words, it is important that those who are assessing the outcome, or effects, of the intervention should not know whether the child received the experimental inter-vention or whatever it was being compared with. The point, of course, is to avoid biased assess-ments that derive from knowing the treatment that has been received.

The fifth requirement is of measurement across settings. The importance of this consideration is that it is necessary to differentiate between benefits that are confined to the situation in which the intervention has been delivered and effects that are pervasive across different situations and different social circumstances.

A somewhat similar requirement is for measurement over time. The issue in this case is whether such benefits as are gained from treatment are confined to the time period during treatment, or immediately after it, or whether they persist after treatment stops.

Seventh, it needs to be determined whether or not there are "dose-response" relationships between the treatment and the change in the outcome variable. The rationale here is entirely straightforward; namely, that if the treatment truly is bringing about benefits it should follow that the greater the intervention effect, the greater the change in the outcome variable, in this case, language functioning. Inevitably, although there may be threshold effects, there must be some doubt if there is a difference between treatment and no treatment, but no variation according to the length, intensity or successful implementation of the treatment. If a threshold effect is thought to be present, it is, of course, essential to test for it and not simply to assume it.

Eighth, and in some respects the most crucial of all, there is the need to determine whether there is a within-treatment association between changes in the postulated mechanism feature and changes in the outcome variable. It is only in this way that treatment studies can be used to test a postulated causal mechanism (Bishop, 1997). The fact that a treatment is based on a causal hypothesis is no indication that the treatment efficacy is actually due to a change in the postulated causal mechanism. In order to make that jump, it is essential to go on to determine whether changes in the postulated mediating mechanism are systematically related, in a dose-response way, to the treatment benefits. It needs to be appreciated that very few treatment studies have undertaken this test and, because of this, there must be considerable caution in accepting their claims.

Finally, it is necessary to use and report statistical tests of treatment effects that determine the size of the effect, and not just whether the effects were statistically significant. As discussed in relation to descriptive studies, effect sizes are often the most meaningful statistic. In other words, the question is not just whether the intervention made a difference but how much difference it brought about and, therefore, whether this was of a magnitude to be clinically useful for an individual child.

"BASIC" RESEARCH

The research considered thus far has all focused relatively specifically on issues that are fairly close to questions concerning language disorder. It is important to appreciate, however, that as with medicine and biology as a whole, there is a need for research that is "basic" in the sense that it is concerned with the study of processes that have no immediate connection with disorder but in which an understanding of those processes may, in the course of time, be informative with respect to the causes or course of disorder. Such research is sometimes termed "blue skies", with the implication that it has no obvious focused goal. Actually, that is a rather misleading way of thinking about "basic" research. Of course, almost by definition, it will be driven by the curiosity of the scientists concerned. On the other hand, high-quality basic research is focused on testing specific hypotheses and not simply on gathering facts in a "suck it and see" approach in the hope that if enough facts are accumulated something of use and interest will come out of them. The "rules" and "principles" of basic research are not that different from those that concern applied research. It is just that the goals focus on questions that are much further removed from the clinical issues that concern practitioners. On the other hand, it is clear from the lessons of medical history that such basic research is often crucially important in leading to advances in prevention and treatment (Dollery, 1978). One difference in the clinical research considered up to now is that the ways in which "basic" research will lead to advances in practice are not usually evident at the time the research is undertaken. There are many examples of different sorts of "basic" research. This is not the place to review them in detail; nevertheless, the range may be illustrated by noting several rather different sorts of examples.

As reflected in several chapters in this volume, studies of normal language development may be very important. Ideally, these should involve a combination of naturalistic and experimental approaches (see Tomasello, chapter 1, this volume). It cannot be assumed that the processes involved in normal language development are the same as those involved in the genesis of language disorders but, nevertheless, understanding of normal development is likely to be extremely helpful in guiding research into abnormalities of that development. It may also be informative to determine the extent to which patterns of language acquisition are similar across languages (see Leonard, chapter 7, this volume). In recent years, functional brain imaging has become an important way of investigating the ways in which brain functioning is associated with functional performance (Posner & Raichle, 1994; Rugg, 1997). Sometimes, this is thought of as "seeing the brain in action" but that is a misleadingly over-dramatic way of describing what is involved. What such studies can do, however, is indicate which parts of the brain are activated when particular tasks (such as those involved in language or memory) are involved. It is not that, in itself, it is necessarily helpful to know which part of the brain underlies a particular form of mind functioning. Rather, it provides a means of determining whether the mental processes used by individuals with disorder to solve particular problems, or to undertake particular cognitive tasks, are the same as those that apply in the general population. There are numerous technical requirements that are essential for the proper use of functional brain imaging in this way (see e.g. Fletcher et al., 1995) but there is no doubt that such methods are going to be increasingly useful in studying cognitive processes. A note of caution is necessary, however, on the practical and ethical issues involved in using imaging methods with young children, and on the problem in interpretation when studying brain function over a period of growth when major changes are taking place.

On the face of it, one might think that studies of psychopharmacology are not likely to be particularly important in relation to language disorders because, at the present time, drugs play no substantial role in the treatment of language disorders. On the other hand, it has to be presumed that disorders of language functioning are going to have a substrate in variations or anomalies in brain functioning. A better understanding of how drugs affect those processes may, therefore, in the long run be helpful to language disorders, as with other forms of problem.

Much the same applies to "basic" research into studies of brain development, of gene action, and of brain chemistry and the functioning of neurotransmitters. At the present moment, all of that seems light years away from the clinical issues involved in the diagnosis and treatment of developmental language disorders but, given the importance of brain–mind relationships, it must be supposed that such research will ultimately have clinical benefits, even though it is not obvious at the moment quite what those might be.

RESEARCH REPORTING

In evaluating all forms of research, attention should be paid to *how* it is reported, as well as to what findings are claimed. Thus, in general, there should be considerable caution before accepting what is said either in papers published in journals that do not use rigorous peer review or in those published only as chapters. Because it is unusual for the latter to be peer-reviewed, it is much easier to "spin-doctor" the findings by failing to note serious biases in sampling, or by ignoring methodical limitations or negative results. Readers should also routinely note whether the research has commercial implications (either through its source of funding or the products it is championing). As already noted, they should expect independent replication and validation (as shown in refereed scientific papers and not just in general reports by others that the intervention "works" or that their findings are similar). All of these caveats may seem ultracautious but it is prudent to remember the American saying: "It ain't ignorance that does the harm; it's knowing so many things that ain't so!"

"TAKE-HOME" MESSAGES WITH RESPECT TO RESEARCH

As is implicit in the discussion of research so far, six "take-home" messages may be identified.

- First, it is essential to be alert to the good ideas. Research is involved with creative, innovative thinking as much as with experimental testing. Even with research that is flawed with respect to some of its characteristics, there may be good ideas that we need to take note of.
- Nevertheless, the second point is that it is also important that we be very sceptical about the claims of the evangelists. The field of language disorders is no different from any other in having its fair share of researchers, as well as practitioners, who beat the drum, in uncritical fashion, to champion their own particular ideas.
- Whilst being aware that, however outrageously expressed, their ideas may be correct, we need to look carefully at the evidence: the third point is that this means looking carefully at the details of the research methodology with respect to strategy, assumptions, sampling, measurement and testing of alternative explanations.
- In that connection, the fourth key take-home message is that readers of research need to ask whether the inferences underlying the research design have been specified and justified empirically.
- The fifth essential point is to ask whether the findings have been independently replicated. However good the quality of a single study, there should be little confidence in its findings until they have been replicated by an independent group of researchers on a separate sample. That is a basic rule of science and one that is far more important than the level of statistical significance within any one study.
- Finally, the sixth take-home message is that it is necessary to ask whether the findings

are likely to apply to one's own clinical population. In other words, can we take the findings as relevant for the particular clinical groups with which we work?

DOES RESEARCH MATTER TO PRACTITIONERS?

It should be obvious from what has been said already that research very definitely does matter to practitioners. It does so because it provides a means of audit in relation to the planning of services, in the provision of individual treatment programmes, and in strategies of prevention. It is absolutely essential, too, because research findings can disconfirm one's opinions. It is important to appreciate that research is not just common sense (Wolpert, 1992). The findings may or may not confirm common sense assumptions but the power of science lies in its ability to show that what seems obvious and reasonable is in fact mistaken. Research is also important because it is a source of good ideas. Also, as emphasised, both "applied" and "basic" research are crucially important because they may lead to totally new ways of prevention or intervention.

DOES PRACTICE MATTER TO RESEARCH?

The answer to this question is equally positive. As illustrated by the story of the interface between research and practice in relation to autism (Rutter, 1999), it is a two-way traffic in which clinical experience and findings lead on to research; research findings modify clinical practice; and the application of research findings in practice serves to indicate the extent to which the findings apply, as well as modifying some of the more extreme research claims or inferences. In other words, clinical practice is crucial to research because it provides ideas and hypotheses that require systematic investigation; because it raises queries on the validity and meaning of such findings; and because close integration between research and clinical practice is likely to lead to better research.

PROSPECTS FOR THE FUTURE

In seeking to use this review of the interface between research and clinical practice as the basis for considering where we should go from here, it is clear that there are several rather different sorts of needs. First, it is going to be very important that the field capitalises on the potential of new basic science methodologies such as those provided by molecular genetics (Plomin & Rutter, 1998; Rutter & Plomin, 1997; Rutter et al., 1999) and functional brain imaging (Posner & Raichle, 1994; Rugg, 1997). Major advances in the prevention and treatment of developmental language disorders are likely to be fostered by research into the neural mechanisms underlying such disorders. It is not enough, however, that such basic research proceeds. It is also important that there is a good collaborative working together between clinical researchers and laboratory researchers. The mere application of new technologies will not in itself be adequate. There is a special need for researchers who can bridge clinical and laboratory approaches.

As discussed above, it is equally important that investigators capitalise on the range of strategies that are available to test causal hypotheses with respect to environmental risk factors, both physical and psychosocial. It will also be crucial to use treatment research in ways that can allow the testing of hypotheses on causal mechanisms.

The third need is to capitalise on the potential of improved intervention and prevention research methodologies. Many of the evaluations of treatment that are being undertaken do not make use of the most powerful research strategies and data analytic techniques and it is important that they do so in the future.

Fourth, there is a need to retain an awareness of the importance of innovative clinical observations. Chapter 15 by Deonna (this volume) gives examples in the medical arena and the appreciation of the importance of pragmatic difficulties (see Bishop, chapter 6, this volume) does so in relation to language features. We need to be aware that future research is likely to show that the concepts that prevail today are either inadequate or seriously mistaken in some key respects. The point about the connections between diagnostic concepts and the problems seen in everyday clinical practice was well exemplified by the title of the provocative essay by Kanner (1969) three decades ago: "The children haven't read those books: Reflections on differential diagnosis". Kanner's (1943) own identification of the syndrome of autism provides a splendid example of the power and importance of observations by astute clinicians who note patterns that have escaped the attention of all their colleagues. The identification of Rett syndrome (see Rett Syndrome Diagnostic Criteria Group, 1988, for the English language version) and its further exploration by Hagberg, Aicardi, Dias and Ranos (1983), provides a more recent example, again in the field of developmental disorders involving impairment of language. Each of these examples, however, serves to make the final point; namely, the need to ensure an effective two-way partnership between practice and research (Rutter, 1999).

NOTE

1. Segregating genes means those genes that differ among individuals. Thus, some people have genes associated with black hair, whereas others have those associated with blond hair. There are also genes that, over the course of evolution, do *not* differ among individuals. Thus, *all* people have genes that lead to having the potential for some form of symbolic communication. That is a general characteristic of being human and is a result of the genes possessed by all humans but not by mice. Nevertheless, the *degree* of skill in language may be associated with genes that do differ among individuals.

REFERENCES

Beitchman, J.H., Cohen, N.J., Konstantareas, M.M., & Tannock, R. (Eds) (1996). *Language, learning and behavior disorders: Developmental, biological and clinical perspectives.* Cambridge/New York: Cambridge University Press.

Bell, R.Q. (1968). A reinterpretation of the direction of effects in studies of socialization. *Psychological Review, 75,* 81–95.

Bell, R.Q., & Chapman, M. (1986). Child effects in studies using experimental or brief longitudinal approaches to socialization. *Developmental Psychology, 22,* 595–603.

Bennett, K.E., & Haggard, M.P. (1999). Behaviour and cognitive outcomes from middle ear disease. *Archives of Disease in Childhood, 80,* 28–35.

Bishop, D.V.M. (1992). The underlying nature of specific language impairment. *Journal of Child Psychology and Psychiatry, 33,* 3–66.

Bishop, D.V.M. (1997). *Uncommon understanding: Development and disorders of language comprehension in children.* Hove, UK: Psychology Press.

Bishop, D.V.M., Bishop, S.J., Bright, P., James, C., Delaney, T., & Tallal, P. (1999). Different origin of auditory and phonological processing problems in children with language impairment: Evidence from a twin study. *Journal of Speech, Language, and Hearing Research, 42,* 155–168.

Bishop, D., & Edmundson, A. (1987a). Specific language impairment as a maturational lag: Evidence from longitudinal data on language and motor development. *Developmental Medicine and Child Neurology, 29,* 442–459.

Bishop, D., & Edmundson, A. (1987b). Language-impaired 4-year olds: Distinguishing transient from persistent impairment. *Journal of Speech and Hearing Disorders, 52,* 156–173.

Carroll, K.M. (1998). Manual-guided psychosocial treatment: A new virtual requirement for pharmacotherapy trials? *Archives of General Psychiatry, 54,* 923–928.

Conti-Ramsden, G., & Botting, N. (1999). Classification of children with specific language impairment. *Journal of Speech, Language and Hearing Research, 42,* 1195–1204.

Cooper, P.J., & Murray, L. (1997). The impact of psychological treatments of postpartum depression on maternal mood and infant development. In L. Murray & P.J. Cooper (Eds), *Postpartum depression and child development* (pp. 201–220). New York: Guilford Press.

Cox, A., Rutter, M., Yule, B., & Quinton, D. (1977). Bias resulting from missing information: Some epidemiological findings. *British Journal of Preventive and Social Medicine, 31,* 131–136.

Dale, P.S., Simonoff, E., Bishop, D.V.M., Eley, T.C., Oliver, B., Price, T.S., Purcell, S., Stevenson, J., & Plomin, R. (1998). Genetic influence on language delay in two-year-old children. *Nature Neuroscience, 1,* 324–328.

Dollery, C. (1978). *The end of an age of optimism: Medical science in retrospect and prospect.* Rock Carling Fellowship: London, Nuffield Provincial Hospitals Trust.

Dunn, G., & Everitt, B. (1995). *Clinical biostatistics: An introduction to evidence-based medicine.* London: Edward Arnold.

Everitt, B., & Hay, D. (1992). *Talking about statistics: A psychologist's guide to data analysis.* London: Edward Arnold.

Fletcher, P.C., Happé, F., Frith, U., Baker, S.C., Dolan, R.J., Frackowiak, R.S.J., & Frith, C.D. (1995). Other minds in the brain: A functional imaging study of "theory of mind" in story comprehension. *Cognition, 57,* 109–128.

Hagberg, B., Aicardi, J., Dias, K., & Ramos, O. (1983). A progressive syndrome of autism, dementia, ataxia and loss of purposeful hand use in girls: Rett's syndrome: report of 35 cases. *Annals of Neurology, 14,* 471–479.

Haggard, M.P., Birkin, J.A., & Pringle, D.P. (1990). Consequences of otitis media for speech and language. In B. McCormick (Ed.), *Practical aspects of audiology: pediatric audiology 0–5 years* (2nd ed.). London: Whurr.

Hill, A.B. (1962). *Statistical methods in clinical and preventive medicine.* Edinburgh: Livingstone.

Hill, A.B., & Hill, I.D. (1991). *Bradford Hill's principles of medical statistics* (*Twelfth edition*). London: Edward Arnold.

Horton, N.J., Laird, N.M., & Zahner, G.E.P. (1999). The use of multiple informant data as a predictor in psychiatric epidemiology. *International Journal of Methods in Psychiatric Research, 8,* 6–18.

Howlin, P., & Rutter, M. (1987). The consequences of language delay for other aspects of development. In W. Yule & M. Rutter (Eds). *Language development and disorders.* Clinics in Developmental Medicine Nos 101/102. London: MacKeith Press/Blackwell Scientific.

Howlin, P., Mawhood, L., Rutter, M. (in press). Autism and developmental receptive language disorder — a follow-up comparison is early adult life: II. Social, behavioural and psychiatric outcomes. *Journal of Child Psychology and Psychiatry.*

Kanner, L. (1943). Autistic disturbances of affective contact. *Nervous Child, 2,* 217–250.

Kanner, L. (1969). The children haven't read those books: Reflections on differential diagnosis. *Acta Paedopsychiatrica, 36,* 2–11.

Klein, D.F. (1998). A psychotherapeutic context for clinical trials is promising, but manualization is not. *Archives of General Psychiatry*, *54*, 929–930.

Kraemer, H.C., Kazdin, A.E., Offord, D.R., Kessler, R.C., Jensen, P.S., & Kupfer, D.J. (1997). Coming to terms with the terms of risk. *Archives of General Psychiatry*, *54*, 337–343.

Mawhood, L., Howlin, P., & Rutter, M. (in press). Autism and developmental receptive language disorder — a follow-up comparison in early adult life. I. Cognitive and language outcomes. *Journal of Child Psychology and Psychiatry*.

Metcalfe, K. (1999). Williams syndrome: An update on clinical and molecular aspects. *Archives of Disease in Childhood*, *81*, 198–200.

O'Connor, T., Rutter, M., Beckett, C., Keaveney, L., Kreppner, J., and the ERA study team (in press). The effects of global severe privation on cognitive competence: Extension and longitudinal follow-up. *Child Development*.

Plomin, R., & Rutter, M. (1998). Child development, molecular genetics, and what to do with genes once they are found. *Child Development*, *69*, 1223–1242.

Pocock, S.J. (1983). *Clinical trials: A practical approach*. Chichester: John Wiley & Sons Ltd.

Posner, M., & Raichle, M. (1994). *Images of mind*. New York: Scientific American Library.

Ratcliffe, S.G. (1994). The psychosocial and psychiatric consequences of sex abnormalities in children based on population studies. In F. Poutska (Ed.), *Basic approaches to genetic and molecular biological developmental psychiatry* (pp. 99–122). Berlin: Quintessatz Verlags.

Rett Sydrome Diagnostic Criteria Working Group (1988). Diagnostic criteria for Rett Syndrome. *Annals of Neurology*, *23*, 425–428.

Rugg, M.D. (Ed.) (1997). *Cognitive neuroscience*. Hove, UK: Psychology Press.

Rutter, M. (1994). Beyond longitudinal data: Causes, consequences, changes and continuity. *Journal of Consulting and Clinical Psychology*, *62*, 928–940.

Rutter, M. (1999). Autism: Two-way interplay between research and clinical work. [The Emanuel Miller Memorial Lecture 1998]. *Journal of Child Psychology and Psychiatry*, *40*, 169–188.

Rutter, M., Bolton, P., Harrington, R., Le Couteur, A., Macdonald, H., Simonoff, E. (1990). Genetic factors in child psychiatric disorders: I. A review of research Strategies. *Journal of Child Psychology and Psychiatry*, *31*, 3–37.

Rutter, M., Chadwick, O., & Shaffer, D. (1983). Head injury. In M. Rutter (Ed.) *Developmental Neuropsychiatry* (pp. 83–111). New York: Guilford Press.

Rutter, M., Dunn, J., Plomin, R., Simonoff, E., Pickles, A., Maughan, B., Ormel, J., Meyer, J., & Eaves, L. (1997). Integrating nature and nurture: Implications of person-environment correlations and interactions for developmental psychopathology. *Development and Psychopathology*, *9*, 335–364.

Rutter, M., and the English & Romanian Adoptees Study Team (1998). Developmental catch-up, and deficit, following adoption after severe global early privation. *Journal of Child Psychology and Psychiatry*, *39*, 465–476.

Rutter, M., Mawhood, L., & Howlin, P. (1992). Language delay and social development. In P. Fletcher & D. Hall (Eds). *Specific speech and language disorders in children* (pp. 63–78). London: Whurr.

Rutter, M., & Pickles, A. (1990). Improving the quality of psychiatric data: Classification, cause and course. In D. Magnusson & L.R. Bergman, (Eds), *Data quality in longitudinal research*, (pp. 32–47). Cambridge: Cambridge University Press.

Rutter, M., Pickles, A., Murray, R., & Eaves, L. (submitted) Testing hypotheses on specific environmental risk mechanisms for psychopathology.

Rutter, M., & Plomin, R. (1997). Opportunities for psychiatry from genetic findings. *British Journal of Psychiatry*, *171*, 209–219.

Rutter, M., & Redshaw, J. (1991). Growing up as a twin: Twin-singleton differences in psychological development. *Journal of Child Psychology and Psychiatry*, *32*, 885–896.

Rutter, M., Silberg, J., O'Connnor, T., & Simonoff, E. (1999). Genetics and child psychiatry I: Advances in quantitative and molecular genetics. *Journal of Child Psychology and Psychiatry*, *40*, 3–18.

Rutter, M., & Smith, D.J. (Eds) (1995). *Psychosocial disorders in young people: Time trends and their causes* (pp. 7–34). Chichester: John Wiley & Sons Ltd.

Rutter, M., Thorpe, K., & Golding, J. (2000) *Report to Mental Health Foundation*.

Stothard, S.E., Snowling, M.J., Bishop, D.V.M., Chipchase, B.B., & Kaplan, C.A. (1998). Language-impaired pre-schoolers: A follow-up into adolescence. *Journal of Speech, Language, and Hearing Research*, *41*, 407–418.

Taylor, B., Miller, E., Farrington, C.P., Petropoulos, M.C., Favot Mayaud, I., Li, J., & Waight, P.A. (1999). Autism and measles, mumps, and rubella vaccine: No epidemiological evidence for a causal association. *Lancet*, *353*, 2026–2029.

van der Lely, H.K.J., Rosen, S., & McClelland, A. (1998). Evidence for a grammar-specific deficit in children. *Current Biology, 8,* 1253–1258.

Wakefield, A.J., Murch, S.H., Anthony, A., Linnell, J., Casson, D.M., Malik, M., Berelowitz, M., Dhillon, A.P., Thomson, M.A., Harvey, P., Valentine, A., Davies, S.E., Walker-Smith, J.A. (1998). Ileal-lymphoid-nodular hyperplasia, non-specific colitis, and pervasive developmental disorder in children. *Lancet, 351,* 637–641.

Whitehurst, G.J., & Fischel, J.E. (1994). Practitioner review: Early developmental language delay: What, if anything, should the clinician do about it? *Journal of Child Psychology and Psychiatry, 35,* 613–648.

Wolpert, L. (1992). *The unnatural nature of science.* London: Faber & Faber.

Yopp, H.K. (1988). The validity and reliability of phonemic awareness tests. *Reading Research Quarterly, 23,* 159–177.

Author Index

Subject Index